ALANA FAIRCHILD

CRYSTAL MASTERS
333

INITIATION WITH THE DIVINE POWER
OF HEAVEN AND EARTH

BLUE ANGEL®
PUBLISHING

CRYSTAL MASTERS 333
Initiation with the Divine Power of Heaven & Earth

This printing 2020
Copyright © 2014 Alana Fairchild

Published by Blue Angel Publishing®
80 Glen Tower Drive, Glen Waverley
Victoria, Australia 3150
Email: info@blueangelonline.com
Website: www.blueangelonline.com

Edited by Tanya Graham
Artwork by Jane Marin

Blue Angel is a registered trademark of Blue Angel Gallery Pty. Ltd.

ISBN: 978-1-922161-18-5

DEDICATION

Dedicated to the beautiful humans who work tirelessly on their path to bring about genuine healing change for the benefit of all beings.

ACKNOWLEDGEMENTS

Special thanks to Toni, for honouring me with support and the freedom to create without restraint, even when it thwarts convention.
Sincere appreciation to Tanya and Michael at Blue Angel Publishing for their talent and assistance, and for Lydia, my lovely admin angel, and Richard, my manager who manages to stay calm in the face of my constant stream of new ideas and makes me laugh at least once during every meeting. And of course, to those not-so-invisible helpers, the Ascended Masters. May this book touch the hearts of those who read it, just as you have touched my heart.

CONTENTS

INTRODUCTION

WHY AM I ATTRACTED TO THIS BOOK?

There is an old expression that when the student is ready, the teacher appears. This is just as true with spiritual work on the inner planes as it is on the physical plane. The Ascended Masters are the teachers who work on the inner planes and you are drawn to this book because at some level, you are connecting with the Masters more deeply for your own spiritual evolution.

We can connect with the inner planes through dreams, meditations and energy work. This inner work opens our perception beyond ordinary day-to-day awareness. We become capable of perceiving subtler worlds of energy. These worlds lie within and also beyond the physical world. They are limitless and can be very beautiful. The higher spiritual intelligence that exists on the inner planes, which includes the Ascended Masters, is very aware of you and is keen to support and encourage your spiritual growth. You are drawn to this book because the Masters on the inner planes wish to help you grow.

The Ascended Masters connect with us for healing, spiritual growth and initiation (the most advanced type of spiritual growth for humans) when we are ready to work with their energy. Whether you think of yourself as a beginner, or recognise that you are more advanced on the spiritual path, the Masters will only connect with you when they can constructively assist you. It would be of little benefit for you to connect with the Masters if you were not able to constructively receive their vibration. If their energy is of too high a vibration to be noticeable or effective in transforming your own energy, then you will simply not be interested in them. As your own energy transforms through spiritual growth, interest in high vibrational beings naturally tends to increase.

Once you have journeyed far enough along the spiritual path, over many, many lifetimes, the energy of the Masters will eventually become accessible and helpful for you. You will be able to grow in your ability to consciously perceive or sense their guidance because your heart is more open and receptive to the high vibrational energy of love that they radiate. When we are cloaked in fear, it is hard to really feel divine love. But there comes a point when our hearts become capable of registering divine presence, despite our human fears, and consciously receiving divine assistance. As we realise that we are worthy of help, we find it easier to allow the Divine to help us.

This is when our interest in the Masters, and other beings of light such as Angels and Goddesses, Star Beings and even crystals, deepens. Every time we grow, we will feel a deepening connection to divine beings of unconditional love. This book, and the others in this crystal spirituality series including *Crystal Angels 444*, is written to help you surrender into the loving help of all the wonderful light beings that want to assist you to live your full divine potential. You are drawn to this information now which means this process has already begun for you.

The Ascended Masters serve our soul development and seek us out when we are ready to work with them. This means that you are now ready to take the next step, to ascend to a new, higher vibrational reality. This may translate as changes that need to come into place in your work, your lifestyle, your relationships with others, with Spirit, with yourself. 'High vibrational reality' might sound very floaty and vague but it is a shift in consciousness which has very real, practical effects. It changes lives, working from the inside, out. No matter what the changes look like for you, they will at least involve a shedding of fear-based beliefs and behaviours, and an opening up to discover, believe in and live more of your divine beauty in the world. When you do so, it is like a beautiful instrument – your own soul – sounding its heavenly note throughout this world and beyond, into the inner planes.

It has been my experience that the Ascended Masters introduce themselves, when the initiate is ready, according to the soul learning and needs of the initiate. The initiate, dear reader, is you. Initiates are advanced souls that come to Earth school for a lifetime (or a series of lifetimes) of conscious and accelerated spiritual growth. These are souls that are compelled to work on themselves and who want to bring healing to the world around them. Their hearts are on fire with a powerful inner urge to grow and serve. They might not always know exactly how and so they yearn and strive to find their purpose, their passion, their divine mission or special talent, and then to live it as much as they possibly can. Initiates are the ones who see and live this life as a transformational journey, with a heart full of fire for the Divine. They will not always know where their path is leading them, but they do know that they are learning to trust and surrender and to cultivate the bold courage of faith in themselves too. They know their life is somehow helpful to others, even just through their willingness to work on themselves. And they make a difference in this world. That is an initiate, and that, dear soul, is you.

I will share a funny moment with you. When I received the first copy of *Crystal Angels 444*, the first book in this series, my partner at the time held it in his hand and was astonished at the sheer size of it. "Where does all this information come from?" he wondered aloud, looking at my head, as though somehow there was an entire library hidden in there. I laughed as I thought back over the process of writing that book, and this one too. I had no idea what I was going to write before I sat down and started. I rarely do. There is a creative process for writing that happens every time I am going to write a book or an oracle deck. For a moment, I baulk and wonder how the blank page in front of me is going to turn into a book! Then I drop out of my mind and into my heart and the words just flow. My partner's astonishment about the workings of this inner 'writing machine' in me, as he put it, confirmed to me that actually, these books just want to be written. Yes, I do work hard to write them and the wisdom within them comes from years of practical experience, but there is a magic that takes place, an ease, which I accredit to the divine grace inherent in something that is meant to be. I can see that I have been prepared over the years to write them, through my experiences and learning, so that others can be helped and supported by the work. The light beings that I have been blessed to connect with throughout my life want just as much to be in conscious connection with you, to guide you, to assist you, just as they have done for me. As you begin the journey of this book, I suggest that you ask for this connection if you are open to it, especially if you have not yet consciously felt the Ascended Masters reaching for you. Then, trust in whatever unfolds and when.

This book can be seen as a spiritual training course for those old souls, called initiates, for some of the important lessons on Earth school at this time of spiritual transition on our planet. So, while you are drawn to the book because you are an initiate, you also have a role as an Earth healer or planetary server and this book will offer you great assistance for the path you are on. That assistance will come in the 'a-ha' moments when you read a sentence and it flicks on an inner switch for you; or something will suddenly make sense to you that didn't make sense before. Old souls often feel that they are remembering or having some inner knowing confirmed when they encounter truth. Even if at one level they feel they are learning something new here, at another level they are somehow aware that they already knew it. This is the ancient wisdom of the heart and the loving guidance that light beings, such as the Ascended Masters, offer to us. It is the same ancient wisdom that we all have access to, via the heart, when we take the journey within.

WHAT IS INITIATION? WHO ARE INITIATES AND AM I ONE?

Every human being on this planet is on a course of spiritual growth. Sometimes the human is conscious of this and spiritual growth is made a high priority, perhaps even the highest priority, in life. Others however are not at all interested. This doesn't mean that they aren't growing spiritually! Rather it just means that for the moment at least, spiritual study is perhaps not going to serve them on their path. That may change this lifetime or not until later lifetimes. Each soul is unique and has its own spiritual star of destiny to follow.

For advanced souls, whether they are consciously interested in spiritual study or not, a more challenging spiritual path is offered. In the same way that you wouldn't expect a high school student to study at a primary school level, the universe wants you to have the spiritual training and education that will serve your level of ability.

As I mentioned above, initiation is a path for advanced souls. It is an accelerated path of spiritual growth. Often it is taken by those with conscious spiritual inclination and understanding, such as those who practice healing or are very passionate about growth and awakening, but it can also be taken by those with a natural spirituality who don't study and perhaps have never ventured into a metaphysical bookstore in their life. The difference between those that are closed off from spiritual growth and the rarer souls that are initiates without any obvious spiritual interests is that the latter are living a spiritually aware life – they may just have a different way of doing so. These unusual people may not consciously study spiritual matters but they will demonstrate love, wisdom, kindness and interest in others, and often have a soothing or healing presence, or an inspiring, uplifting energy, which benefits those around them.

I remember when I was a little girl, I was introduced to a friend of my grandmother, whom I loved instantly. She was charming, interested in people, kind and friendly. When

I heard that she didn't believe in God, I was so shocked! I thought about the many people that I had met that had more religious beliefs than she did, but lacked the same quality of heart. I realised, even at the tender age of 7, that religious beliefs did not necessarily equate with spiritual maturity.

Initiates come from all walks of life. They are old souls with an ability to serve something greater than their own personal agenda, and to do so with a heavier workload than younger souls would tolerate. Initiation is not for the faint-hearted, that's for sure. To put it in somewhat dramatic perspective, there is a story of Jesus, one of the great initiates who became an Ascended Master (another term for an awakened son or daughter of God, if you come from a Christian tradition) to help humanity grow spiritually.

The story takes us to the ending of the life of a great prophet called Elijah. The prophet had a devoted disciple, Elisha, who loved him greatly. As death drew close for Elijah, he asked his beloved and faithful student if there was anything that he could offer to him. Elisha replied, somewhat boldly, that he would like to be bestowed with 'double Elijah's spirit' (showing not a small amount of spiritual ambition!). Elijah knew that he could not pass on what he didn't have and so he made a decision to honour the request by leaving it up to God. He said to his student that if he could bear witness to his death, then God may bestow upon him the gift of twice his spirit. Well, Elisha did not leave Elijah's side for a moment! He was present at his passing and the story goes that Elisha was reborn as Jesus, presumably with twice the soul power of his former teacher Elijah. Elijah was said to have been reborn as Jesus' initiator and teacher early on in his life, John the Baptist.

Now we all know how that ended! The power that the soul had requested (perhaps proving that God is all things, including flesh and ambition) led to an extraordinary life, of great bliss and divine union, but with deep suffering on all levels in order to eventually access that bliss. Anyone who is genuinely on the spiritual path will tell you that living in closeness with the Divine can be a lot to bear – there can be great sorrow and tremendous joy. This doesn't mean that all great spiritual initiates have to suffer to the same extent in order to grow, but the spiritual path of awakening does require that for the light we experience on Earth, we must experience equal darkness. Learning to work with that darkness constructively for healing is one of the major themes of this book and indeed this series of books (especially *Crystal Goddesses 888* which is the next book in the series). There is always divinity to be found in the darkness, but this is not, by any means, an easy task.

For initiates, the challenges in life are often great. However because of their ability to heal and transform and to bring something constructive to the world, even out of the ashes of their struggles, the challenges are recognised as a path to greater connection with divine presence. Initiates have tremendous reserves of inner strength and resolve, and even when faced with circumstances that may seem to break the spirit, somehow, they eventually emerge from it with deeper faith, spiritual ability and more love for the Divine than ever before. It may take a while, but their 'resurrection' always happens eventually.

If you are dedicated to a spiritual path consciously and you struggled, sometimes apparently more than those around you who don't do the same amount of spiritual work that you do, then you are more than likely realising that you are capable of holding greater light – and greater darkness – and still allowing the divine light to shine through. You see, you are an initiate, undertaking an advanced spiritual training program (dare I say Master's degree?) along with the basic undergraduate program that everyone else is studying. You are perhaps an ambitious soul, but certainly you are one who is here to serve the growth of spiritual consciousness on Earth through your own personal path that naturally serves the greater good.

WHO ARE THE ASCENDED MASTERS?

The Ascended Masters are those whom have already taken the path of initiation and are no longer subject to the karmic law of rebirth. They are karmically clear and able to walk upon the Earth at will, in service to the greater good. Sometimes they work through the souls of other teachers and very often through the souls of workers in various fields of politics, health, education and the arts to help support human evolution. They are all operating with the same objective in view, which is the spiritual liberation of humanity, they just approach it according to their own unique talents and abilities.

Ascended Masters are graduates from various spiritual schools. The ones we focus on in this book, with the exception of Ascended Master Helios, have all been through the human school of development and therefore offer a particularly useful gift to humans. I don't know about you, but I know for me personally, if someone is going to show me how to do something, I want to know that they have already mastered it themselves, at least more than I have.

Helios, or the soul of our Sun, is included in this book because I very strongly felt to include him – and who am I to gainsay the life source of our solar system?! His intimacy with the Earth makes his wisdom, though transpersonal, useful and relevant to us humans.

The Ascended Masters are dedicated and devoted to you and yet not possessive. They won't fight over you but they will all fight for your spiritual growth. Connecting with one Ascended Master helps you connect with a level of guidance that is very inviting of love, assistance, support and divine presence into your life.

WHY AND HOW CAN I WORK WITH THEM?

You will work with the Ascended Masters because when they connect with you, you naturally feel drawn to do so. It's like a beautiful smile from a friendly, loving person that just makes you want to move closer and connect somehow. There is no more 'good' reason that this.

That being said, underneath the feeling that you are interested in working with them will be a strong impulse from your own higher self. The Ascended Masters are soulstrengtheners. Their presence builds the conscious connection that we have with our higher self or soul, and through that, our direct connection with the divine source – be that the Universe, or God, or the Goddess, depending on your spiritual or religious beliefs. We'll talk about this more particularly in chapter 9.

To work with the Ascended Masters is an agreement to embark upon a phase of more intense spiritual growth because they only work directly with initiates. If you aren't an initiate, you won't be interested in the Master vibration, it will just be too high for you to even register at an intuitive level.

I remember doing a spiritual training course with advanced students of Raym, one of my crystal teachers from Byron Bay in New South Wales, Australia. In this course we had to learn how to travel swiftly in and out of altered states of consciousness. I already had some experience in this – I had been doing it in my spiritual channelling and healing work, so that I could have a 'conversation' with the person sitting before me and their higher spiritual guidance simultaneously during a soul therapy session. In the workshop with Raym, we were instructed to work in pairs, to go into an altered state and meet each other at a soul level, then meet the other person's spiritual team of guidance, and then together, complete a particular healing task.

The person I was partnered with for this exercise was a healer and teacher too and was regularly exposed to spiritual energy, being a devotee of a local spiritual community where I knew there was a guru present. I figured we'd get through the exercise together fine.

What happened surprised me and taught me something valuable.

As we connected, we were to meet each other's guidance. I would energetically 'wave hello' to her guidance and wait for her to do the same with mine. However it seemed that this healer could never see my guidance! I knew that they were there and not playing hide and seek with her, so in my mind, I asked my higher guidance to "please alter your vibration so that you are perceptible to my partner in this exercise." On cue, a few moments later my partner for the exercise said, "Oh, now I see them!" Interesting!

We completed the exercise and then gave feedback and prepared to do the next step. We connected and again my partner said that she was having trouble perceiving my guidance. Again I spoke my request, this time aloud, and a moment after she said, "Ah yes, I can see them now."

What I learned from this experience was high vibrational beings may vibrate at a level that is beyond consciousness for many, even if they are themselves already somewhat spiritually-attuned. The higher up the vibrational spectrum that we go, the more subtle the vibration becomes. It's sort of like escalating pitch to a point that humans can no longer hear but dogs can! As you work through this book, developing your capacity to consciously connect with Ascended Masters, you will come to know that their presence can be very subtle.

Of course subtle doesn't mean weak. I have had a number of clients contacting me saying that they felt Kuan Yin not so gently pushing them to work with me. "Oh, I know she is gentle," they will say, "but I keep getting the same card repeating in the *Kuan Yin Oracle* deck and I really feel she is pushing me to work with you!" The number of times

I have heard this makes me realise that no matter how gentle a being is, and Kuan Yin is pure gentleness, higher beings will still give you a shove when needed. The difference is that it comes from love and in no way causes harm, but instead, promotes growth.

This is how I started working more consciously with the Ascended Masters, which led to my spiritual training with them, and eventually, to being able to write this book. At first, they arrived in meditations, which I dismissed as imagination on my part, believing that I was not yet ready to work with such highly evolved beings. Suffering from self-doubt and denigrating my own ability, I pushed my intuitions aside. Some time later, they started 'hovering' over the heads of many of my clients. It became a bit too repetitive to ignore! Over and over again I would sense their presence, the energies of certain colours and even sometimes names. Eventually, around three years after my first connection with Master energy in meditation, I allowed myself the benefit of the doubt, instead of just doubt, and decided to attempt to receive their instruction and realised that they were indeed seeking connection with me.

They provided information for teachings through meditations, dreams and channelling sessions which I shared in spiritual circles that I started at the time and through a series of meditations which are now available on CD and as digital downloads, published by Blue Angel. Those original three CDs are available now and published as *Radiance, For Love and Light on Earth* and *Mystical Healing*.

The teachings became the draft of an unpublished manuscript, which has interestingly been used in some places in this book. Before I began writing I was told to use what I had already created in that text. I had completely forgotten about that manuscript and then all of a sudden, I realised (in meditation one morning) that the time had come to utilise the work that I had done so many years earlier, now incorporating some of the teachings into the current work. On more than one occasion when writing this book, after writing a paragraph that seemed significant, I would feel strongly to go back to my old unpublished manuscript to see if there was any further information that I had left out and ought to be included in this book. Even though it was many years since I had re-visited that original manuscript, I was stunned to see that a number of times, I had written, word for word, exactly what I had written with the help of the Ascended Masters over ten years ago. They are certainly consistent in their message!

Even just reading this book will get your vibration humming at a frequency that is more aligned with the Ascended Masters, but you can also start working more consciously with Ascended Master energy simply calling them in prayer.

I recommend starting with St. Germain and Lady Nada, but you will find your own favourites on this journey. The Ascended Masters are a package deal, so to speak, in that when you access one, you get access to them all, because they share a group consciousness. So you can 'shop around' at the Ascended Masters mall when you get there, and find the best fitting, most suitable Master energy for you. If you love music and are an emotionally driven person, you'll tend to attract Masters who have a similar flavour. If you are more intellectually oriented and perhaps also love science and deductive reasoning, then you'll attract Masters who radiate a similar style of consciousness. The most resonant energy will tend to seek you out, truth be told, you just have to practice recognising and receiving it. Don't worry if you don't receive a name straight away – or even ever! Some light beings don't have much use for names. As long as you can recognise that their energy is unconditionally loving (without a trace of fear or judgment) then you'll be connecting with a light being who can help you grow. If you do receive a name, whether it is included in this work or not, take your time and be open to getting to know that being and how they like to work with you – through dreams, meditations, visions, impulses to create or write, thoughts that flow through your mind and bring you peace, feelings in the heart, or sensations in the body that indicate their loving presence, and so on.

Before you sleep, you can request that the Masters work with you during your dreams. You may request that work be done on your etheric or physical body, that you be supported in emotional or mental healing, that supportive work for your current soul initiation is undertaken. Or you can even request that you journey to their ashram or temple, active on the inner planes, for healing and instruction. It's a big old world out there (and I mean 'out there'!) so there are many ways that you can connect and receive with these loving beings. If you are not sure what way is best, that's just fine. They will reach for you in the best ways, so don't worry.

WHEN YOU WORK WITH THE MASTERS, THEY WORK WITH YOU

Writing this book involved working with the Ascended Masters in concentrated ways, channelling their energy for hours at a time whilst I wrote usually a chapter a day, with a few breaks here and there. It took exactly four weeks, to the day, to write the first draft. That might seem quick but it is a long time to do such intensive spiritual channelling for consecutive days, for hours at a time. Usually I like to have longer rest periods when I am channelling because it can deplete vital energies. For me personally, channelling is a bit like spiritual weight lifting. It does make you energetically stronger but you need time to heal through rest in order to grow, too.

During that intense month, my own growth became very focused and I found that I was experiencing some spiritual highs and lots of personal challenge, as old energy arose for me to deal with. I have always considered this 'Alana-body' to be something of a crucible in a great experiment of spiritual growth. So much nicer than saying I am my own guinea pig, don't you think? It is this body for which I am grateful that allows me to create an offering based on these experiences to share with the souls that I love and want to see prosper spiritually – and that includes you. But that willing body goes through the rigours of spiritual growth every time I create and writing this book was no exception. It reminded me that I needed to include this section in the introduction.

When working with high-level beings, change occurs. It is not always hearts and flowers, either. Sometimes it is challenging and doesn't feel so great. Healing is happening however and while we can always recognise the growth and feel better for it when it comes to resolution, when you are in the mess of a healing crisis, those benefits can seem a world away.

So it is up to us to remember that spiritual energy is alchemical in nature and sometimes we need a break. Let yourself read only as much of this material as feels right for you at any one time. Do the healing processes when they feel right for you. Take care of yourself. This stuff works. I regularly receive feedback from people who work with my channelled processes about how it has shifted things for them, sometimes powerfully so and in an extraordinary way. It might seem like subtle work, but it digs deep and moves things around. So be patient and integrate, integrate, integrate! One of my favourite sayings is an old Sufi proverb which goes something like this – 'To eat is human, to digest, divine.' Give yourself time to take in what is happening and allow your own healing process to work its magic.

KEEPING THE WORK PURE AND HELPFUL

When I first started channelling I received some positive feedback from a new client who then proceeded to share an experience she had gone through that was not so pleasing to her. It was the first time I heard such a story, and sadly, not the last.

She said that she had been to see a woman who claimed to channel John the Baptist. Now from the Elijah story above, we can assume that John the Baptist has a fairly refined soul energy. What was delivered as channelling in her healing session however was not highly refined at all. The information was tainted with judgment and fear. The client was genuinely upset and never returned. Now this woman may well have been channelling a spirit that referred to itself as John the Baptist but it may not have been the 'real' John the Baptist at all! I can call myself 'Madonna' but that doesn't mean I am a pop star!

Through this entire series we will learn about the different levels of spiritual consciousness that exist on the inner planes, from the most blissful and loving levels of consciousness to the fear-based energy fields that weigh the human heart down in fear-based realities of racism or poverty-consciousness, for example. Put simply, it is unwise to trust that all information that comes from the inner planes is pure love. Many spiritual worlds are loving and beautiful, but there are spiritual worlds that are fear-based too. It's just part of life. It can take a while to learn to sense the difference between the two, and how to work with them so that you can step out of the energetic influence of fear-based realities and into the uplifting helpful love-based realities of the inner planes, but through this book you will gain valuable guidance to help you do so.

If something like this has happened to you, perhaps you went for spiritual healing or a reading and ended up fearful rather than feeling loved, then know that this is not uncommon. It doesn't matter how educated, intelligent or discerning you are, if you have opened up to someone, and they do their best but perhaps are not as up-to-par as they thought they were, it can be a painful or frightening experience. Don't feel badly about it.

Chalk it up to an experience, congratulate yourself on being brave enough to explore the other realms through channelling and pray to the Ascended Masters to help you choose a being who is of a higher vibration for any future forays into channelling or readings that you may choose to take. Also know that connection with genuine guidance, even if a challenging message is being delivered, does not fill you with fear, but with love and a sense of hope.

Some years later, I heard another story on this topic from one of my teachers, crystal master and shaman, Raym. He had trained another teacher that I had studied with for a short period of time who undoubtedly had a lot of spiritual talent and a charismatic personality. There were times when studying with her however, that I questioned whether what was 'coming through' was from a very high source. Sometimes I knew her actions were pure but at other times, her words didn't quite ring true as higher guidance. There was nothing wrong with what she was saying perhaps, but the energy behind it didn't resonate. Whilst she is an accomplished teacher with a lot of knowledge and ability, and has no doubt helped many people, she is, like the rest of us, human with particular quirks and flaws.

Early in her training with Raym, she was trance channelling an Ascended Master, or so she thought. After she came out of her trance, noticing somewhat shocked expressions (and Raym's undoubtedly bemused expression, given his sense of humour), she was told that she had channelled a lot of dirty jokes! Entertaining perhaps, but not exactly the work of a genuine Ascended Master. Even the most talented channellers can make mistakes sometimes.

This doesn't mean that channelling cannot be helpful or isn't worth pursuing. It is channelling that has created most of this book and so obviously I hold it in high esteem. The important thing is that we seek always to find the heart of what is being said, no matter how impressive a source may seem for any information or guidance, and always ask ourselves, 'Is this coming from genuine love?'. Guidance who loves you unconditionally is never, ever going to try to win you over, manipulate you or make you agree with them. It just isn't in their nature. They are just going to speak truth in a way that is constructive and empowering to you, and loving towards you. The material that they communicate to you will be helpful. It will speak to you genuinely. It won't sound impressive but confusing. It will feel loving to you. If anything else is going on then either the channel is having an effect on the material coming through and distorting it, or the source that is claimed to be of a high, unconditionally loving vibration, such as an Ascended Master, is not actually that at all. If we become aware of this, then the weight that we place on the words will be proportionate to their actual worth. And the worth of any guidance is completely determined by its ability to help us on our path, and in our lives.

To sort the wheat from the chaff at the beginning of all our healing processes in this book, in every invocation or prayer we say, "I call upon the true Ascended Master who loves me unconditionally." If you are ever calling on a spirit and receiving guidance that doesn't quite feel as though it is helping you, always, always challenge that source and declare that you are only interested in beings helping you if they love you unconditionally.

No exceptions to this rule! Ever!

If you are still in doubt about what you are receiving in any spiritual context, whether in a healing with another, or from a book, or from a meditation or vision or channelling, that is okay. Use your discernment and ask yourself if it feels like a truth based in love. If it is, go for it. If it feels a bit dubious, then use some common sense and caution. There is a lot of love in the higher spiritual worlds of Angels and Masters. There is also a lot of horseplay in the lower spiritual planes of deceased relatives and the like. It might be entertaining, or the guidance that you long to hear (or are terrified to hear) but that isn't necessarily going to be the most helpful information. Even if lower vibrational beings are trying to help you, if they are not loving you unconditionally, then they aren't going to serve you by attempting to guide you because they will have their own agenda and will be creating karma for all concerned, so best to leave that sort of job to the professionals!

If this all seems a bit difficult to grasp, don't worry at all. Throughout this entire series we will be exploring and learning together. Through the healing exercises you'll come to know in your heart what I am explaining to your mind in this section. Have patience and do the healing processes.

WHAT IS 333?

Numbers hold vibrations and messages. The number three is the result of the union of the spirit of the number one with the feminine relationship energy of the number two, resulting in the birth of a new energy, the three. This is divine creation. The number 333 is the energy of divine creation, the bringing together of masculine and feminine, and the result of that at the highest level of spiritual graduation for us earthlings, is ascension. So working with the number 33 or 333 is like dialling up the vibration of the Ascended Masters and the divinity that they seek to awaken and stimulate within us. The vibration of 333 resonates throughout this entire work. It is in the exercises and behind all the writing. I received an email recently from a man in the United States who said that he was just holding the *Kuan Yin Oracle* and could feel the high vibration of it emanating out of the physical package. Words and intention are energy and this book is filled with the energy of 333. Just sitting with this book, even before you read any more of it, brings you into that vibration. May you feel it, know it and enjoy receiving it.

HOW DO I WORK WITH THE CRYSTALS?

With the exception of Citrine, which doesn't actually need cleansing, it's a good idea to regularly cleanse your crystals.

You can cleanse all crystals by visualising a vibrant violet light, flecked with white. Imagine it sparkling and crackling above the crown of your head, flowing down through your head and into your mouth, then blowing it out on the breath.

Don't just breathe on the crystal though! Gently and intently blow the violet energy out of your mouth, straight into and through the crystal with the intention of cleansing it of all negativity. Do this until it feels clean or for at least seven breaths. When you get very focused you'll be able to clear a crystal with one short sharp breath, but that may take a little practice before you feel confident with it. You can also play beautiful music in your home (a CD with chant or the OM mantra are good options) and burn incense to clear the space and your crystals all at once.

Cleanse before and after use in healing if the crystal has touched your body. If it is just in your environment and doesn't get handled then cleansing every few months, or every few days or weeks if there is a lot of emotional energy or stress in your home, will be fine. Trust your sense of whether the stone is clear or not. The energy will feel vibrant and clear when the crystal is clean. When it is dirty, it will feel like sunlight trying to get through a dirty window – you'll know there is good energy there but it's a bit muddy and hard to really feel it. This means your crystal has been working hard and clearing energy, absorbing a lot and it needs some clearing so that it can continue to do its wonderful work (which it wants to do).

You can never over-cleanse a crystal and you will never clear its good energy away. Cleansing removes that which isn't pure in the crystal – it's a bit like giving it a spiritual shower. It is safe to do and will not harm you or the stone. Just don't expose crystals to water or sunlight as for some, this can cause fading or dissolving. For most it's not a problem, but better to be safe than sorry in this case.

If you are wondering where the negative energy goes when you cleanse a crystal, know that when you use the violet light breath technique, the energy gets transmuted, from one form into another (which is one of the healing properties of the violet light and St. Germain, whom we will meet in this book).

If you are unsure about the breath technique, then you can also hold the crystal in one hand, raise the other one and quite simply say aloud (if possible, or silently in your mind if you prefer), "I call upon the beings of unconditional love who can assist with cleansing my crystal and transmuting negativity energy into unconditional love. Through my own free will, so be it!" Then either leave it at that or go about burning your incense and/or playing your music.

Crystals that you wear will need cleansing more often than crystals in your environment, usually. Trust your intuition. I remember once feeling the urge to cleanse all the crystals in my healing room in one go. It took hours and the room felt incredible afterwards! There is a lot of spiritual light in that space, yet the stones still benefitted from a good cleanse.

WHAT ARE THE ANGELS OF A CRYSTAL?
WHAT IS A CRYSTAL ANGEL?

Every crystal has its own angel. It is sometimes also called a nature spirit, oversoul or deva (which translates loosely from Sanskrit into English as a 'Shining One'). These crystal angels are the spirit, consciousness, wisdom and vibration of the entire crystal 'species'. These are the beings we call upon in our healing processes.

So if you were holding a piece of aquamarine, for example, which might have a lovely blue-green hue to it, you would be working with the energy of that individual crystal, plus the entire consciousness of all of aquamarine everywhere, discovered or undiscovered! That means every piece of aquamarine that has ever been created, from the bluest blue to the greenest green blue, is energetically linked to every other piece of aquamarine through the consciousness of the crystal angel of aquamarine. It is divine, holographic unity that we are tapping into through our intention! Although your particular piece will have its own unique energy, particular to its unique colour, shape and size, the greater consciousness of aquamarine more generally will be emanating through that stone too. This is why even a small piece of crystal can be very powerful. It is a holographic intelligence, whereby even the smallest part contains within it the power and wisdom of the whole.

Calling on the crystal angel helps you tap into the greater power, healing properties and energetic potency of that particular crystal type as a whole, as well as the special personality of the individual piece you are working with. This is why we can work with a particular crystal, through calling on the crystal angel of the crystal we need, even if we don't have it available physically at the time. Through connecting with the angel we can call on the healing energy of the crystal anyway.

I have worked with this technique for years. If someone is struggling and a crystal intuitively comes to mind, I simply call upon the angel of the crystal and ask for its consciousness to channel into the body and soul of my client through unconditional love. It works! And it doesn't interrupt the client as they are in the middle of their experience, whilst I rummage around in my crystal cupboard looking to see if I have the exact stone that holds the vibration they need in that moment!

Working with the crystals physically is fun and beautiful, and can make the experience feel more tangible and real to us as we are learning to sense energy, yet it is good to know that it is not the only way to tap into the healing intelligence of crystals, especially if we are very drawn to a crystal and know instinctively that it can help us, but we just don't have it on hand at that precise moment. We can simply close our eyes for a moment and silently or aloud say, "Through unconditional love, I call upon the Crystal Angel for Malachite (or whatever crystal it is that we need) and I ask for you to bring your healing power to my body, mind and soul now, with compassionate grace. Through my own free will, so be it." Breathe in and out slowly, with your awareness in your heart, and an intention to receive. Done!

HOW DO I WORK WITH THE MANDALAS?

In this book, as in the first in the series, *Crystal Angels 444*, we work with mandalas as possible replacements for the physical stone.

Use them in the healing processes and use them as you would regular stones – in your healing room, under your pillow at night for healing, to look at, to meditate upon ... whatever speaks to your heart.

I have received such wonderful stories from people about how powerful it is to work with the mandalas. I am happy to say that we are going to continue to use them in the future books of this series and also in a special *Crystal Mandala Oracle* deck, soon to be published by Blue Angel and based on the first three books in this series – *Crystal Angels 444*, this book, and *Crystal Goddesses 888*, which is the next book in the series.

HOW DO I READ THE HEALING PROCESS AND DO THEM?

The healing processes go deep and you can either read them as you go or record them before hand, perhaps on your mobile phone or computer, and then play them back. If you do this, remember to pause a lot between speaking and speak slowly! You'll find if you speak at a normal pace when you record the processes, it will seem far too quick when in meditation.

I have included one healing process for each chapter as I found the healing of body, mind and soul came together easily in one process in this book, even though in *Crystal Angels 444* there were three different processes included. The Masters are unique light beings, just like the Angels are, and they work in their own way. If you need more healing in body, or in emotions or mind, or soul, that is where the energy of the healing process will flow. As with all divine energy, we are given what we are most in need of, so don't worry. Just do your work and trust in the process.

Finally, please do mention to your doctor or therapist that you are doing energy work, especially if you are on a mental health program or medication. Whether your health care provider believes in energy work or not, they need to know how to work with you and keeping them informed is one way to ensure as good a working relationship as possible. If that working relationship isn't good when you inform them of your spiritual work, you may want to consider changing health care providers for someone who is more interested in you doing whatever works for you rather than you agreeing with their belief system! One of my Reiki teachers used to drum this advice into all her students – energy changes consciousness. Your medication may need to be altered as you heal. I have seen this happen. If this situation is relevant to you, then it you may find it best to be in consultation with an open-minded health care provider as you do this work. You deserve such care.

1.

ASCENDED MASTER SERAPIS BEY (Karmic Grace)
CLEAR CALCITE (Detoxification)

INITIATION OF DIVINE ALIGNMENT

Stillness awakens within. Then from all directions a clear light emanates, alive with divine intelligence. It shimmers with spaciousness and presence. Old energy releases. There is light where there once was darkness. The light gathers and flows powerfully, directly towards the goal, without obstruction. Divine alignment assures successful progress.

Divine alignment means coming into healthy relationship with the divine plan that your soul or higher self has agreed to honour this lifetime. Your part in the divine plan includes a commitment to master certain lessons, heal particular relationships and express your various skills and talents, perhaps also developing new ones. This is your karma for your lifetime. I have never thought of karma as punishment, despite this popular use of the term. Karma is our set of life lessons and gifts.

The soul is assisted by divine alignment, which helps it stay on course and true to its unique purpose, rather than getting seduced, dazzled or distracted by the paths of others throughout its experience of a human life. Being in divine alignment is a bit like having very regular spiritual-coaching sessions with the Universe. The soul is helped to align with the divine plan by its team of higher spiritual guidance that love and serve unconditionally. Ascended Masters, Angels, spiritual guides and goddesses help each soul to fulfil its spiritual destiny. Provided we remember to ask for help from those guides that love us unconditionally each day, they are able to be present in our lives and help us live up to our divine potential. This is one expression of divine grace. It is the energy given in love that helps us to lighten our load – enough that we can continue moving and not be weighed down, but not so much that we don't fulfil our karma and learn whatever it is that our soul needs to master this lifetime so that it can progress spiritually.

Even with support from your team of higher spiritual guidance in aligning with divine will, you still have free will and choices to make in your life. Free will is our ability to choose if we wish to go one way or another, respond typically to a situation or try something different. Even if you receive a clear message from your guidance and are lucky enough to understand it consciously too, you don't have to follow that guidance. It is always your choice. Sometimes we only come to know the value of our own intuitive sense of guidance after we ignore it a few times and end up in a bit of a mess! Or is that just me? Then we might try listening for a change, and realise that it is worth our attention. Mistakes, which I like to call learning experiences, can teach us that listening to our inner guidance is very useful.

Because your guidance loves you unconditionally, they will never judge you and never become exasperated with you. Even if you constantly ignore their suggestions and still want their help! I cannot tell you how often I have encountered the unlimited love and patience of higher guidance and felt blown away by how incredible it is that we receive so much from Spirit. Especially in those moments when, in my more human self, I feel impatience or frustration that myself or another keeps making particular mistakes and just doesn't seem to be learning a lesson. Feeling the love of higher guidance helps me remember that we are all learning and growing in our own way and that everything serves the unfoldment of the Universe. We are all learning through choice and free will, even if sometimes it really doesn't feel like it.

Part of becoming a spiritual adult is learning to take responsibility for the consequences of our choices. We are not asked to take on responsibility for aspects that we cannot foresee or control, including those choices of another human being, but we are asked to become aware of our intentions and motivations, and the quality of what we put out into the world.

Sometimes this demands that we enter into a challenging dilemma. We might feel that we have no choice but to work in a job that drains us or remain in a relationship that abuses us, but we always have a choice. Our choice in that situation would be to confront the fear of moving on, if we wish to leave. There may be fear that we are not worthy of something different or that we deserve this suffering in some way. Our choice will be to challenge and then heal this so that we can be free. We may then change, and perhaps the relationship will be able to change with us, or perhaps not, but we will have met the challenge and found our power of choice more readily available. It isn't necessarily easy. We may wonder if it is easier to remain in the suffering rather than do the work to outgrow it. Either way, however, it is our choice.

Through our power of free will, we can make choices about whether or not we wish to proceed in a particular way. When we make mistakes, we can choose compassion and to learn something constructive and do things a little differently next time, rather than judge.

We can also choose what sort of person we wish to become, and do our best to act accordingly. At first this may be a moral decision, perhaps not to lie or cheat or steal, not to be mean to others and to learn how to have empathy and tolerance for others, and ourselves. Then we may progress to choices at a higher level, perhaps seeking to make a positive contribution to the world according to our own talents and abilities. Eventually we will grow into the spiritual level of an initiate on planet earth and our expression of our free will becomes to progressively surrender into the will of the Divine no matter what it asks of us, doing our best to come from a compassionate heart and let go of expectations of how the Divine should operate through us. We surrender. Usually many times over!

No matter where we are on the spiritual evolutionary scale, we can always choose to come back to our hearts as our grounding in the world, a place from which to move and be and make choices in our lives. We can choose to honour that which will give our heart a voice. In living in this way, our talents gradually unfold. You may know what your talents are, or you may wonder if you have any talent within you at all! But we all do have something within us that wants to be born, and to be born specifically through us. If you stay with your heart and release expectations of what your talents should look like, then they will show themselves to you in time.

Our talent is where the Divine is most concentrated in us. It is where we can come back to when we have wondered away from our own path, perhaps dazzled temporarily by another. We can then choose to forget about competition or if we are as good as so-and-so, and focus on growing our own light instead, to work through the talents that reveal themselves to us when the time is right, gently and step by step as we learn to believe in ourselves. We then have a great choice we can make that earns lots of lovely positive karmic brownie points for us and others – which is to serve the greater good, if we choose to express our talent with that motivation.

Our talents may seem to affect others (like an ability to run a thriving company) or may seem to be more personal (like an ability to find the humour in our various life situations). No matter how important they seem to be, or how small, our talents are the light within that can help us remain consciously connected to the Divine, especially if we are going through a phase of darkness or struggle. The light of your talent may be visible for others around you too, lending them support during their struggles. We can use our talents to strive for ego glory or we can surrender them in devotion and service to the awakening of spiritual love within our heart, and perhaps the hearts of all beings. That choice is always ours to make.

Whether your talent is a powerful singing voice or the precious ability to really listen to another, it will serve divine purpose. No matter how subtle or how dramatic your gifts or talents appear to be, the Divine is in them. Sometimes a talent might seem to be so ordinary, that we don't even consider it a talent. We can miss an opportunity to participate consciously in this great Universe by honouring our divine talents if we fail to recognise what we have going for us.

My most cherished example of an apparently ordinary talent (that is anything but ordinary) is the ability to listen. To be capable of listening is to be capable of receiving another completely. My soul therapy sessions all begin with deep listening – I can hear the person's soul, their feelings, their energy, really take them in – and then from that place, I speak, or sing, or channel or whatever is meant to happen in that moment.

To hear without analysis, without formulating response, without doing anything other than being present and receiving is a rare and wonderful talent. To be heard in such a way is a gift that can change the life of another in a moment. When I am in the presence of someone who really hears me, I feel understood, connected, loved, present and alive. That is not a small offering by any means! Many times during my private consultations, I will be listening intently and a client shares that they are only 'just now having this realisation' about something important to them. Being listened to creates space for our own wisdom to emerge.

If you want to know more of what your talents may be, don't be afraid to ask the beings that love you unconditionally, including Ascended Master Serapis Bey who loves you unconditionally to show you. We will also be exploring spiritual talents in later chapters of this book.

We are initiated into divine alignment repeatedly through our lifetimes. Our free will is always honoured and yet there are times when we are assisted by higher guidance, upon our request, to get out of a mess of our own making. Spirit can help lift us out of patterns that we have created for ourselves through our choices that are becoming too difficult for us to rise above on our own. We might have unintentionally made our own path more difficult than it needed to be. We had the right to do so and to learn, but we are not punished for it. We will have to learn the lesson of it, but we can also be helped in cleaning up our mess. Fortunately for us!

An example of this is a belief system that I had to learn to outgrow as I sought to have my work published. I was fed a lot of stories about how difficult it was to be published and how I had to go through so much struggle to fight the 'slush pile'. To this end I was told that I had to endure endless (boring!) writing workshops and compile tedious book proposals to editors and agents, none of whom would really read or reply to them, but I had to keep going anyway, and I would never get anywhere unless I experienced lots and lots of failure at first. The thought of it, let alone trying to live that reality, was utterly exhausting!

Now that belief system may be part of our journey, but also, it may not be. That belief system may become so entrenched that we stop seeing other possibilities for our work finding its way to where it is meant to be. We may unconsciously be preventing ourselves from receiving assistance from our guidance, as they try to inspire us through our intuition to make a telephone call or speak to a certain person, which would lead to our meeting with our future publisher in a far more organic, natural way. To be capable of aligning with that divine plan, we would need to be free from the heaviness of our own expectations (and the negative stories of others) so that we could feel enough hope and openness to accept the inspiration, act on our intuition and let the situation unfold with divine assistance.

Fortunately enough for me, I quickly rejected the heavy and depressing publishing process that I had tried to break into using typical means. I gave up on making cold calls, writing proposals, emailing editors, attending workshops and entering competitions. I felt like I wasn't learning anything from those experiences except how depressingly unattainable the path to publishing seemed to be! So my choice was to focus instead on working with what I had available to me, and learning to detach and let go.

As it turns out, I just had to wait a while. It was quite a while really, it was nearly ten years that I had to wait. And then eventually, a series of events conspired and I was lucky enough to meet my future publisher, quite unexpectedly. It happened through the intervention of a lovely 'unofficial mentor' for me, a woman named Sue who runs a gorgeous metaphysical bookstore called Phoenix Rising Books in. At the time, my publisher didn't even know that I could write, he was just interested in some meditation CDs that I had self-published and that Sue was selling through her store. It was still a couple of years later, after the publication of the successful *Kuan Yin Oracle* and *Isis Oracle* card decks, before my publisher and I would discuss writing books. This crystal spirituality series was born soon after.

In this case, I had to shed some heavy belief systems and be open to divine timing. My alignment was not out of touch with my purpose – to write books and be published was part of my spiritual life plan, but learning patience and that the Divine was more powerful than all the 'rules about publishing' was also part of it. My alignment meant that I had to let go of trying to make it happen and learning to allow it to happen according to the timing seen to be right by the Divine.

My guidance certainly helped me have faith and let go with trust through their loving reassurance that I was on my way. You can see that specifically in the story that I tell of my encounter with Mother Mary's grace which I'll share with you later on in this book. When our guidance steps in, through divine grace and love, they help lift us up and help us clean up our thinking, our beliefs, and get out of our own way. They are helping us through the gift of divine alignment. We may have gone off on a tangent as we have lived our life, perhaps wandered down a dark path, or got in a strop because we think something isn't happening fast enough, or at all. That is our right, of course. It is all learning. But we may have unintentionally gone 'out of tempo' with the spiritual rhythm of our life and we are given some grace to help us get in time again.

Rather than being too slow and heavy and perhaps needing help to be sure that we are ready for an opportunity coming our way, we could have also tended towards racing ahead and through a stupendous amount of inner healing work, being so far ahead of where we were meant to be, we have to wait for some time for those that are karmically destined to assist us to catch up! It took me a while to realise that I could rush to the finish line, but if there was no one there to receive what was offering, then I wouldn't have exactly done myself any favours. Instead I am encouraged by guidance to trust and allow life to happen, with my growth and blossoming an integral part of that process.

So even if we may feel as though we are waiting at a spiritual bus stop for our ride to come along, divine alignment can help us use that waiting period as a rich time for spiritual growth instead. We might develop patience, trust, endurance and inner peace. Guidance can help keep us aligned with the divine plan by inspiring us to master these lessons as best we can, realising that there isn't actually any waiting at all – there is just growth happening. Without that divine assistance, we might slip into believing that not only are we waiting, but it means something negative – that we will not be given what we want, that we are not going to succeed, that we are in the wrong place or pursuing the wrong path, for example. This may well take us out of divine alignment in the other direction again – becoming too energetically heavy for the life we want to co-create with Spirit.

I have been in both of these situations – energetically too heavy and energetically too fast – at different times in my life and I had to learn to allow the world to turn as it will, whilst relying on the support of my divine team to help align me with my own divine plan. As I did so, I discovered more talents to utilise and found that, of course, everything turned out perfectly when I just prayed, did my own personal spiritual practice, let life happen and didn't worry so much. Easier said than done, at times, no doubt.

There can be a real panic that emerges from us sometimes, an urgency to get the job done, so to speak. We have to remember that whilst a jolt can give us the needed impetus and energy to get on with a task, there is always enough time for us to complete our spiritual work. It's built into the divine plan. Do you think the Divine would give you a task and no time to finish it? That would be rather poor organisation and this Universe is exceptionally well-organised (whether we are privy to the divine design behind the apparent chaos and randomness, or not, it is a highly efficient system nonetheless). When we are in divine alignment, it's easier to trust in how our life is unfolding, because we feel held from within, that we are in step with the flow of our life and we can recognise that all is happening as it should.

For us to be initiated into divine alignment, we need several components to be in place. We need to be in a trusting relationship with our higher guidance. We need to know what our talents are - or be willing to discover them and accept them if we are as yet unaware of our spiritual gifts. We need to be willing to surrender into a force greater than our own personal will, ambition or desire, which is the force of the universal plan. The universal plan is a spiritual blueprint for the evolution of all of creation. You could imagine a supreme being, like a cosmic architect, drafting that blueprint perfectly so that all beings would ultimately become happy and free. We will attend to these essential needs for divine alignment to occur in the healing process for this chapter.

ASCENDED MASTER SERAPIS BEY – KARMIC GRACE

I experience Serapis Bey as a masculine presence that is subtle, powerful and technically adept at working with energy. He is associated with Ancient Egypt, and in particular, the deity of wisdom, knowledge and divine judgment from that culture, the Ibis-headed god known as Thoth. Serapis Bey is acknowledged as having an ability for healing the soul at a karmic level. This is a profound ability which changes the types of experiences we need to have on earth for our spiritual growth. Healing the soul at a karmic level shifts our life experience rapidly. We can begin to feel so much change taking place that it is almost like we are living two of three lifetimes in quick succession, instead of just one! If you have ever thought back to your past and found it to be so different to how you are living now, almost like you were a different person then, or living a whole other life back then, you'll know what I mean.

I began working with Serapis Bey many years ago when I started teaching spiritual healing circles in Sydney. I was intrigued by his unusual name and his connection to ancient Egypt, a place that I had been fascinated with, especially as a little girl. Not long after I began channelling his healing energy, I also felt inspired to channel a healing meditation using his energies for karmic healing and grace. It is available on my meditation CD, *Radiance* through Blue Angel Publishing.

One of the most vivid encounters I had with Serapis Bey occurred several years after beginning to work with him, around the time that I created my first series of meditation CDs. It was a time when I was taking a leap of faith and making my work more publicly visible. I felt an urge to do so, and yet I had my concerns about it too.

Around that time I had a vivid and very short dream. I was standing opposite of Serapis Bey in a natural setting. It was a low-key environment, very quiet and peaceful. We seemed to be enacting some sort of spiritual marriage ceremony by placing a gold ring on each other's crown chakra, loosely connected by a soft white ribbon. It was a very special experience and most unexpected. I awoke from the dream feeling gently connected to his healing presence.

This dream was given to me at a time in my life when my work was about to grow in a very strong way and I would need a lot of energetic support to do what I felt was asked of me, especially in the months following. At that time I was working ten or more hours a day with clients one-on-one and teaching two large spiritual groups each week and writing for magazines as well as travelling for workshops. It was an exceptionally busy time for me where I was able to be of service to more people than I had been previously able to reach, and I learned a lot and grew a lot in the process.

It was a very intense time for me, spiritually speaking, as I learned to live in the light. Quite a few years after that phase, my inner journey took me to some much darker places, from which I have also learned much and which were essential for me to have a balanced consciousness. Yet whenever I feel Serapis Bey strongly in my life, or around the aura of another, I know that there is a lot of light present and that learning will happen at this time, at least, through the presence of spiritual light. It can be an exhilarating time when you may feel like you can just fly, you are filled with so much light. The soul always seeks balance eventually, but this part of the process can be very enjoyable and uplifting. It can also be a bit frightening if you fear where that light is taking you, or haven't yet established a strong spiritual connection with the light that you trust. If you feel that way and also feel some resonance with Serapis Bey, then it is likely that he is teaching you how to trust in the light. If you are in need of the qualities of light and feeling uplifted, perhaps having endured plenty of darkness and struggle in your life already, then Serapis Bey is likely to be the Master you will most benefit from calling upon.

The clients I have that work with Serapis Bey are beings of light themselves. They are radiant and natural channels for a higher conscious of light. Though down-to-earth and practical, they have refined crown chakras that allow them to channel high-level consciousness. It just feels lovely to be in their presence and people instinctively sense that they are spiritually-inclined even if they don't say a word about it.

Many people who are channels at this level are instinctively drawn to others who hold the same vibration (even if a spiritual word has never been exchanged between the two of you as you go about your daily business). This is because they subconsciously recognise the vibration of their soul tribe. It is like travelling in a foreign land and then meeting someone from your hometown. The recognition and familiarity can help you remember who you are and where you come from, and you feel more comfortable, even whilst you continue your adventures, and interact with the locals.

Whilst Serapis Bey radiates high-level spiritual light, he is an extremely practical guide interested in getting things done at the physical level, through working intelligently with light. I credit him with the conception of the Ascended Master meditations that I recorded, and with the technique of Invocative Meditation which was developed through my work. I coined this term to explain the techniques behind the meditations that I channel – which is to call upon and draw beings of higher consciousness in (invocation) so that the spiritual light can enter the body (rather than leaving the body to join the light) through meditation for healing and spiritual growth.

Serapis likes to see light being utilised through technical methods that can be taught and then shared with others because the techniques can be replicated. He would agree with the notion that if you give a man a fish, you feed him for one meal, but if you teach a man to fish, you feed him for a lifetime. To that end, he is quite methodical and clear, which for someone like me, who tends to meander into this, that and the other, somehow all at once, can be very refreshing and structured.

If he is connecting to you in guidance, you'll feel that clarity, simplicity and practical wisdom in his messages to you. It is a bit like 'talking to a man', and if you are woman, you'll know what I mean. I conducted a session recently with a gorgeous yoga teacher. She was struggling with the studio in which she taught. The administration team seemed all shiny on the surface of things but it didn't take long to reveal the studio managers were a rather toxic bunch that seemed intent on breaking her beautiful spirit. We talked for a while about what was best for her in that situation and after several minutes of this I suddenly felt inspired to say, "Your boyfriend has something to say about this, what was his opinion?" "They're rotten. Leave," she said. Nothing like a masculine viewpoint to cut right to the chase.

The Ascended Master Serapis Bey creates advanced healing technologies that are, as yet, relatively unknown upon our planet, but are being revealed to healers as the need for more sophisticated and refined ascension techniques grows. He is very interested in efficiency and economy in the sense of 'the most bang for one's spiritual buck,' so the techniques that he develops and shares with us are often very simple and effective. This is so because humans are growing more capable of working with the divine grace of instantaneous healing, as we learn to accept that all matter is energy.

I have personally found it helpful and responsible to have myself as the guinea pig with spiritual work and concepts before sharing them with others. It really is essential to 'walk our talk,' and you wouldn't be reading this book if you weren't interested in living and applying your spirituality to your life. Serapis Bey encourages us to live our own inner wisdom and spiritual knowing as best we can, to put faith in our spiritual principles (like trust, for example) and to live according to our higher beliefs. He really is a cheerleader in our corner and encourages us to try things out for ourselves, which has always appealed to me. Someone else can describe the taste of an apple to me, but I want to bite into it and experience it for myself.

Serapis Bey also helps you make your inner light more visible in the physical world. The Master Serapis can assist you in clearing old karmic patterns around being comfortable with your own light and feeling safe and secure enough to 'come out of the spiritual closet' and let others know what you are about. This helps you be able to truly share your loving vision with others. He is that guide beckoning you to the edge of your own comfort, to leap beyond your current limitations, knowing all along that you would soar.

This Master is also adept at assisting with the relief of mutational symptoms (such as sharp pains in the head and heart regions and nausea) that can be temporarily experienced as chakras open and clear as we grow. When this happens, old pain is releasing. Sometimes we feel it emotionally and sometimes physically. We'll explore this further on in the book in more depth. It is sensible to refer to health care practitioners and not assume that pain is just energy, but there will be many times when energy is all that it is. I have personally experienced energetic release of pain so physically powerful that I felt as though someone was repeatedly slamming into my chest with their elbow! With tremendous force! The physical pain associated with the emotional release shocked me at the time. It is not always so dramatic, but when I was dealing with some unresolved issues from my childhood, for me at least, it was intense physically as well as emotionally.

Those are the times when your doctor may look at you like you are nuts and tell you that there is absolutely nothing wrong with you. Yet the pain you are feeling is real – it is just energetic and contemporary medicine does not have the capacity to monitor such energy. At least not yet. I have had situations where the doctor has thought I was delusional, and within five seconds of an acupuncture session, the therapist has accurately diagnosed my symptoms without me saying a word. The difference is that I feel energetic imbalance as a physical phenomenon. Acupuncture and other forms of energetic healing (also the terrain of Serapis Bey) can also work at that level, whereas what we currently consider to be modern medicine is unlikely to be able to register that which is energetic. It tends more towards healing that which has become concretised as disease. That will undoubtedly change in time.

If this situation seems relevant to you, know that your vibration is elevated through the release of fear-based density, which is what is happening. So you are growing and it's good. You'll feel better for it in the long run and for now, call upon Serapis Bey for help and trust your intuition to find some good energetic healers if more prosaic medical techniques don't seem to be working. This Master energy is excellent for clearing negative energy and sealing the aura as the clear flame (a symbol of Serapis Bey) is a powerful tool for purification and cleansing. We'll explore it together in the healing process for this chapter.

Serapis Bey is truly a Master Healer, and he works particularly well with Isis (whom we'll meet in *Crystal Goddesses 888* and in the bestselling *Isis Oracle*). So if you have a question or issue to do with healing of any kind, pray to him (and perhaps also her) for assistance and trust that you will be helped.

This Master can also be invoked regularly for the dispensation of divine grace and karmic absolution – his particularly special healing talent. What this means is that you are praying for divine healing of karma through love and his particular talent for karmic soul healing. This is a sort of accelerated healing jolt, a realisation of truth within yourself that takes you from the constant repetitive struggles of karma and seems to lift you into a higher vibrational way to be. You either become more capable of dealing with your situation or the situation may even fall away altogether with something better in its place. This is the effect of being lifted by grace into divine alignment, which we discussed at the beginning of this chapter, and we are certainly entitled to request it.

CLEAR CALCITE – DETOXIFICATION

Clear calcite is commonly available in large and small pieces. It is also available cut into squarish or rhomboidal shapes. If you look at clear calcite, especially in its rhomboidal form, you will see striations in the rock in various directions. The crystal is mostly clear but with some opaque lines that hint at its capacity to move energy. It can often have a slightly waxy appearance, though there is one type of clear calcite that is absolutely clear. It is called Iceland Spar or Optical Calcite and it's nature's magnifying glass. You can hold it over things and they will be magnified. This hints at the particular purpose of that type of clear calcite – to make situations more clear and visible to us. In this section we are essentially dealing with regular clear calcite, but if you have Iceland Spar already in your crystal collection, or are drawn to use it here, it will work also.

Calcite clears and amplifies energy, not unlike Clear Quartz, but with a gentler and more persistent action. Simply having a piece of clear calcite around you will work over a long time period to remove blockages and strengthen your energy field. It is gradual alignment over time that allows us to adjust and hold new vibrations. You wouldn't go from one extreme in consciousness to another and expect to be as stable and competent as you would be if you took it one step at a time, unfolding and mastering the journey with each step. So too with clear calcite. It understands the value of a process and gets you to where you need to go without excessive haste that might undermine and destabilise your overall progress.

Different coloured calcites work on different issues and chakras in particular – blue for the throat, pink or green calcite for the heart and orange for the sacral and navel chakras, for example, but clear calcite is an excellent general healer working through all the chakras, especially the crown.

The crown has to be open and clear for us to receive the divine grace that Serapis Bey wants to bring to us. If our crown chakra is blocked, the energy of grace can feel like a big leap to allow, a leap that we don't feel capable of taking. I often say that it is not what is on offer to us from the Divine that is in question, it is rather our ability to receive it. It isn't that grace won't reach us – grace by its nature can cut through anything – but our ability to be open and willing to receive it, to recognise it and allow it, can be hampered by our own fears and holding back. It's like trying to receive a hug with your arms crossed over your chest. The hug might still be given but your ability to be affected by it might increase if you open your arms and let yourself surrender into being held. But we have to have trust to do this, and in the case of divine grace, it is spiritual trust that is required, and that means the crown chakra must be at least starting to open up.

An example of this happened in one of the earlier spiritual circles I was running when I first started working with the Ascended Masters with my students. A woman was sharing with the group that she wanted to be open to abundance to receive money to attend a spiritual workshop that really appealed to her. Instantly another group member and friend sitting next to her said, "Oh, I'd be happy to give you the money to attend!" Instant grace!

Unfortunately the first woman didn't recognise that and responded, "Oh no, I couldn't possibly accept that." The grace was presented to her, but her energy field was such that she couldn't receive it yet. We might hear this story and think, "Oh, I would have accepted it," but sometimes when grace is offered to us, we react without realising that it is actually grace. We sometimes have to remember that the Divine acts through people as well as circumstance. We might have to remember to let the Divine help us, even through everyday people and situations.

Grace manifests in various guises, sometimes even in a closed door that forces us to go in a different direction; one that is ultimately going to be more appropriate for us. If we accept and receive this willingly, then we are open. If we have struggles and resist or fight to get things accomplished according to our own view of how it should happen, then we might need to soften and become more receptive.

Holding a similar vibration to the clear flame of Serapis Bey, clear calcite moves density from the energy body and particularly the crown chakra, which allows for higher vibrations to enter your chakras and become established there. What this means on a practical, everyday level, is that you become capable of holding more loving belief systems, less anchored in negative or fearful expectations. This naturally renders us more receptive to karmic grace and healing.

Lower density vibrations can be quite sticky. They can be difficult to release, tending to build upon themselves and attracting other similar vibrations easily. It is a negative experience of like attracting like. It reminds me of that expression, 'misery loves company'. We need the subtle, persistent and graceful energies of stones like clear calcite to help support us in releasing sticky, lower vibrational thoughts and beliefs so that we can begin to lighten up, resonating at a more loving vibration, more consistently.

The more established the higher vibration, the shorter and less compelling any slipping out of loving consciousness is for us. We may dip in and out of that loving place within from time to time, but we will be able to come back to it more easily and more swiftly. It has happened to me on occasions, where my ego has kicked in, or that of another person has, and the interaction feels so empty, like we are just going through some motion or other. The vibration is so low that it seems fake – like really bad acting! The urge to shift back into genuineness, into love, feels so inviting by comparison.

This is one way that clear calcite helps us let go of density – we start to recognise when our ego-based behaviours are creating a silly soap opera and they are no longer so compelling to us anymore. This might sound like a small shift, but it is a really important one. Losing attachment to emotional drama is a key step in our personal healing process. Even unpleasant emotional states – like anger or sadness – can become addictive, repetitive patterns of reaction. To learn to let them go, to be capable of receiving the healing grace for that to happen, is a significant sign of spiritual growth. When we are in that phase, we actually want to let go and we become ready to do so. Then we open up to more refined alternatives in thought, feeling and behaviour. It just has become more natural to do so. Clear calcite supports us in attaining this.

As this process happens through working with clear calcite, our inner world changes and eventually this is reflected in outer world changes too. The sorts of people and relationship situations that have been in our life start to change – sometimes very dramatically. If you are going through dramatic changes where you seem to be 'shedding' friendships or other connections faster than you are making new ones, don't panic. More than likely you are just growing fast.

Sometimes enduring loneliness as we let go of dysfunctional friendships or other relationships, that were perhaps based in pain, judgment or fear, is an important gift. It helps us deepen our connection with ourselves and with the Divine. From that deeper inner connection, there is less desperation to avoid loneliness, and so we can choose more wisely, with more discernment, whom we invite into intimacy in our lives. We can choose friendships that feel uplifting and nurturing, though these may be more rare. It has been my experience that waiting for friendships that are truly nourishing makes any kind of letting go – even if a time of loneliness follows it – absolutely worthwhile.

Clear calcite supports this process and helps you shed old relationship patterns, doubts and fears. It helps you gently release fears that you will be alone if you do not accept things as they are, if you ask for more loving, supportive relationships aligned with your life purpose.

If you want to believe that life could be different but never really seem to experience that difference, clear calcite can help. Perhaps you believe it is possible that you could have better health or easier financial situations or more love and friendship. It is! You'll find that clear calcite will help you realign your inner world, clearing out what you don't need, so you have space to generate and receive what you do need to live a higher-vibrational life. The stone will help you have patience as you do the hard work that is sometimes required to heal. As 'airy-fairy' as this may sound, a shift to higher-vibrational energy through the inner work outlined in this book, does bring practical changes into our lives. It is not a question of whether or not it will happen, it is just a question of when. If we are still 'waiting', that is nothing more than an indication from the Divine to continue with our inner work.

HEALING WITH SERAPIS BEY AND CLEAR CALCITE

You will need a quiet place to rest and be in as much silence (or free from external distraction such as telephone calls, and wireless technology) as possible.

With either a piece of clear calcite or the mandala for clear calcite in front of you, close your eyes and focus on your breath.

When you have counted seven slow breaths in and out, say the following invocation (or divine prayer), "I call upon those beings who love me unconditionally including my own higher self and my spiritual team. I call upon the true Ascended Master Serapis Bey who loves me unconditionally and his clear flame. I call upon the Angel of Clear Calcite. I ask for healing, purification and perfect alignment with the highest expression of my divine plan now. Through my own free will, and merciful divine grace, so be it."

Close your eyes and perceive, sense or intend to be open to a beautiful crystal angel created of clear light. She rises up from the earth now. This is the Angel of Clear Calcite. Allow this angel to create a grid of light around you. Sense that there are clear but perceivable lines of energy criss-crossing underneath you until you are held in a soft but powerful netting of light.

Imagine that you can lay back and relax into that netting and let it hold you.

The edges of your being and the edges of the netting begin to energetically fuse until you realise that you can draw in healing light naturally by breathing in whilst you lay in this netting. Take a few breaths and enjoy this feeling of drawing in pure healing energy and light of clear calcite.

You also sense that you are able to expel energy naturally into the netting, allowing it to be drawn away from you and released into the earth for transmutation as you exhale. Notice this for a few breaths now as you exhale more fully, letting go, sensing the release of negative energy.

Allow this drawing in of healing light and energy and release of old energy to happen as you breathe in and out for around 33 breaths.

When you have completed this, say aloud, "I give thanks to the Angel of Clear Calcite for your unconditionally loving assistance."

Close your eyes again and perceive that the netting is falling away and your own boundaries are strong again, distinct and clear. If you can, sense how your energy is clearer now too, stronger and lighter, but also more grounded.

Then perceive a clear flame descending in through the crown of your head, spreading through you like cool fire, cleansing and purifying you from the inside. Let the clear flame grow until it radiates around you in all directions, until you feel completely enveloped in the flame.

If any energy, emotion, pain or mental distraction arises during this part of the process, you can choose to let the flame burn through it, evaporating it into mist or ash, and letting it disintegrate completely.

Say, "I release into the karmic grace of Serapis Bey all density from my physical body, emotional body and energy body, that no longer supports my spiritual growth and personal healing at the most refined level possible now. Through my own free will and divine grace, so be it."

Then breathe in and out slowly for around 33 breaths, allowing the flame of Serapis Bey to do its work. You may shake or spontaneously shudder, or feel very peaceful. Trust your body and let it express itself.

When you are ready, say the following declaration aloud, "I now choose of my own free will to release all past experiences of distrust, perceived betrayal or abandonment that are preventing me from trusting my higher spiritual guidance this lifetime. I ask for divine grace to help me release the beliefs or energetic memories that are preventing me from being fully open to receive divine grace and karmic healing. Through merciful grace and divine love, so be it."

Then breathe in and out slowly for around another 33 breaths, imagining that you can breathe in and out through the crown chakra in particular, and any other part of your body that captures your attention. Try not to think or analyse, rather, if you can, just surrender into allowing the work to occur at a subtle level and focus on your breath.

When you are ready, say the following declaration aloud, "I now choose, of my own free will, to discover and develop the talents and gifts that I have agreed to experience and share as part of my spiritual mission this lifetime. I ask for divine grace to help me release beliefs that I am unworthy, incompetent, incapable, or superior or inferior, or any other belief or energetic memory that would prevent me from taking the journey of personal development and spiritual growth necessary for me to fully activate my soul talents in this lifetime. Through loving divine grace, so be it."

Then breathe in and out for a final round of 33 breaths, either focusing on the crown chakra at the top of your head, or just intending that your whole body breathes in and out. You can visualise, if you wish, being stirred up by the inhalation, and that which is dislodged by the breath is released on the exhalation. On each exhalation, you are a little more empty within, free from old blockages. On each inhalation, you are brighter, light has more room to naturally grow and be within you. You are becoming more radiant.

When you are ready, say the following declaration aloud, "I now choose, of my own free will, to be supported by my spiritual guidance in surrendering to the extent that serves my spiritual growth, into the genius of the divine plan. I give permission that all aspects of my life be rearranged through unconditional love in service to the plan. May I be open to the grace of divine realignment, with kindness, mercy and compassion, and under the care of Ascended Master Serapis Bey and the Angel of Clear Calcite. So be it."

Become aware again of the clear flame all around you and imagine a beautiful clear light pouring into your energy field from above your crown chakra, filling the flame and stabilising it, making it even more powerful.

Sense the flame expanding until it completely covers all parts of your being, and floods into your life experiences including all aspects of your outer world such as your work, your relationships, family and friendships, your finances and your health, your living arrangements and anything else that occurs to you. Sense that clear flame gently growing to encompass all aspects of you, including your physical and emotional life.

Breathe in deeply and then breathe out slowly. Place your hands in prayer at your heart chakra in the centre of your chest and say, "So be it."

When you are ready, just open your eyes.

Be prepared for emotions and thoughts to arise after this process. This may happen randomly with insights or emotional upheavals or crises that are a sign you are clearing over the next few days or weeks. Your dreams may become more vivid too. You may find comfort in observing that these are a part of your clearing process and a sign that you are letting go to allow more goodness in.

Keep the piece of calcite or the mandala by your bedside table and ask for healing each night before you sleep if you have having difficulty handling the amount of emotional release or purging of thoughts that are happening for you following this exercise. It will not always be so intense, but if it happens quickly for you, it is because there is something far better calling you forward and you just can't take that old psychological baggage with you.

Changes *will* occur after this exercise, to the extent that you are ready to handle them. If a lot of change happens, and you are not sure if you can handle it (you can of course, otherwise it wouldn't be happening, but sometimes this is hard to trust) then do the St. Germain and Amethyst healing process, after repeating the healing process above, for extra support.

2.

ASCENDED MASTER EL MORYA (Higher Will)
BLUE STAR SAPPHIRE (Focus)

INITIATION OF YOUR PATH

A deep blue light pulls energy from all directions into a single point. All that was hazy and disorganised is now drawn into singular focus. No distractions exist. The singular point of light grows more intense. It pulls more and more energy into its centre until it reaches critical mass, unable to contain any more without changing form. The energy contained in the point of light is unleashed into a forceful laser-beam, piercing through confusion, cutting through doubt. One-pointedness and focus. It easily and swiftly reaches its target.

Your path is you. Sometimes we worry that if we don't make a particular choice, or take a particular action, we will not be able to walk our divine path. There is a belief that prevails in spiritual circles that the path is before us, and we have to work hard to find it, to not take the wrong direction. Many of us fear that we won't find our life purpose or mission, that somehow we can miss out on living our path. Recently I read an article in an online blog about the top five regrets of the dying. One of them was that they allowed others' expectations to rule them rather than living their own life. It expressed a genuine fear that we might not live our own life, or meet our divine destiny.

Yet the guidance of the Masters on the topic of our life path does not support this belief system. What I have been taught by the Masters, and what I seek to live and share with others is that we cannot actually miss our path. You may wonder how this can be stated with such certainty. Surely someone might easily make a wrong turn and end up under the influence of another who does not have their best interests at heart? That person may rather use them to serve their own personal agenda, rather than encourage them to find their own soul truths! Surely another might make a mistake or become fearful, hiding from their own talents and settling for a half-lived life!

We can taunt ourselves with fear that we won't make the most of our life, that we won't find what we are meant to be doing. If you are one such person, one who fears that they are not living their path or that something that is meant to be happening on their path is not yet happening, and you are fearful about that, then this message is particularly relevant for you. You cannot miss your path because your path is you. Your path is you, in the world. Your path is you, when you are withdrawn into yourself and in reflection or meditation. Your path is you when you realise that you are a timeless divine soul and not only a human body with a mind and emotions attached to it. Your path is you when you forget your divinity and end up in a mess because for a while you trusted more in the illusion of physical security than in the security that comes from trusting in your divine connection. Whether up or down, black or white, or everything in between, you are you and you are your path. You cannot miss it. You are living it right now.

So then, what is the initiation into your path all about?

Imagine travelling to a new country and visiting a city that you always dreamed of visiting. On your first trip, you may see as many of the sights as possible. On your second trip, you might begin to delve a little deeper, exploring one or two areas with more attention. Instead of breadth of experience you begin to look for depth. And perhaps you are lucky enough to have an opportunity to return to your beloved city again. Then you might choose to stay in one place and really connect with it, play with what it would feel like to live there as a citizen perhaps, get to know the people of that place and make some meaningful connections with that city. You become more focused. You move your energy into singularity rather than diversity. You are visiting the same city, but each time you choose to go deeper, you have a different experience of what it is to be in that place. Your life there takes on new meaning. Perhaps you become an even more valuable contributing member of the local community in some way. You engage. You relate. You share yourself.

It is similar with our life path. There are deeper levels of experience and expression that call to us when the time is right. There will be times in our lives when diversity, exploration and breadth of focus are important and helpful. It is like casting a wide net out into life and then sifting through what comes back, exploring, experimenting and getting a taste for life from different view points. Then there will be times when that no longer serves us, when we have connected with what is real for us, and we need to focus.

This can be a dilemma in the modern world. We often have so many choices available to us that the discipline of commitment, of saying 'no' to something in order to say 'yes' to something else with all of our being, can be hard to accept. Sometimes it will be the child within us that demands to remain open to all possibilities. Sometimes it will be the fearful adult that believes it is selfish to pull one's energy into focus on our own spiritual or creative path, believing that we should be looking after everyone else instead.

Yet you will know, deep within, that to walk a spiritual path of personal healing and evolution of consciousness takes a lot of energy and requires a deep commitment and discipline. At first it can be a lot of fun – exploring new possibilities and ideas, and being able to sense a new kind of personal freedom and power that could come from your inner work. It can be intoxicating and exciting. Later on, when there is eventually some degree of mastery of the teachings, it can be a lot of fun too, living the realities you once only dared to dream about. Rather than dreaming, there is then demonstration of one's power and ability – hopefully in service to others – which can feel really good, like using all your muscles at their full capacity.

Yet there is a whole gamut of experience in the middle of discovery and mastery that may not be quite so much fun and in fact at times can be very challenging. If we are growing, we will go back to that place of challenge time and time again. That's how we learn and grow stronger. If we were to try to face that challenge with a half-commitment, with our energy and focus scattered about on a million different projects or ideas, we would find progress more difficult and the challenge greater. As mentioned earlier, there is a time to be open and multi-faceted in our approach to life, but there are also times to pull in focus and get a job done, so to speak.

When initiation into your path is happening, you will feel stressed if you have too many pots on the stove. You'll feel a certain inner compulsion to cut off the dead wood in your life. It might be in the form of setting stronger boundaries with people who take you for granted, do not treat you with respect or simply drain your energy. You may need courage to shelve some projects for a while and simply work on one. You may feel the need to become as honest with yourself as possible about what really has meaning for you, what you value and how you organise your life to meet those values.

There is a workshop exercise that I have used in the past – I ask people to list their top five values, what means most to them, and then I ask them to list how much time and energy goes into those top five values. Realising the disparity is often all it takes to jolt someone into taking their own values more seriously. It's difficult to know what to focus on, if we don't even know what really matters to us, or believe that what matters to us really matters at all.

I have often found that living a creative, spiritually-aware life requires a balance of the flow outwards and the flow inwards, of learning to be open to new ideas and learning when to put your focus into something and work in a one-pointed way until it is accomplished. For us to be able to sense these energetic rhythms in our own souls, we often need help from the Divine. This heavenly assistance can help us get out of our own beliefs and opinions about how our life should or should not be, and allow the divine energy of our own soul to flow through us. For creative people, in particular those that have many, many ideas, assistance in discerning which ideas to follow and which to leave alone (for now at least) can be so very helpful.

When you are being more deeply initiated into your path, you can be pretty sure that some things are going to fall away and focus will become more intense for you, usually on one or two areas of your life that really demand your attention because they need to be 'moved forward' for your spiritual growth to continue to unfold and manifest as your highest possible life expression.

The soul is naturally discerning. Once you learn to connect more with your own divine essence, the inner pull to focus becomes more obvious. What is of particular interest to your soul will call your attention naturally, it will be where your focus goes, whether you think it should be heading in that direction or not. What is of interest to your soul may be very alive spiritually and yet not particularly active or dynamic on the physical level. At least for a while. Often when the soul is guiding us, rather than our own ego opinions, we are asked to place our energy and attention in that which is still growing.

It can be hard to trust in this sometimes. Especially if what is growing is really still in energetic form and hasn't become physically established as yet. For many, many years I prayed for help with my work. I went through fear and frustration, sadness and doubt, disappointment and anger in cycles. I also had a stubborn streak and realised that all of those difficult feelings would be far worse for me if I tried to walk away from my spiritual calling. No matter how difficult things became, or how frustrated I felt that I wasn't in the position that I wanted to be in yet, I just couldn't bring myself to stop putting my energy and passion, my love and focus into spiritual work. It was because that was who I was, even despite my frustrations and doubts at times. My soul urged me, despite many obstacles and even mis-guidance from others at times (well meaning as it may have been) to stay present and be patient.

After a over a decade of hard work, without me seeing the results I had hoped for, I certainly had some moments where I questioned if I was just deluding myself. How long was I supposed to follow my inner sense of knowing in the absence of external validation? I wanted some proof, some confirmation in a physical sense, that where I was heading, what I was putting my energy into, was in fact the correct path. When I needed a sign, it always came to me, and although it was comforting in that moment, my path was still difficult for me to bear at times and I required a lot of personal healing and spiritual growth to keep going.

I had to learn to focus on what was helpful and not allow my powerful mind to scatter my energy into unwanted directions. I know when I am going through a 'spiritual growth spurt' because this lesson will often arise again, and my curious mind will go off on mental adventures – what if this could happen, or that? As I have inspired new ideas popping into my mind at least once a day, sometimes more than once an hour, I had to learn how to focus if I was going to actually get anything finished! As I learn to handle more energy and consciousness and not crack under the weight of it, falling back into old patterns, I find that I am tested to be open to inspiration yes, but also to focus on what needs to be completed now with hard work and discipline. I find that the joy in completing the task – such as writing a book or recording a healing CD – makes the hard work more enjoyable (even though I do so love to spend time dreaming of inspiring bold ideas and new adventures).

It is focus, however, which naturally comes as the soul grows stronger in us, that helps us through. Focus is a bit like meditation in some ways – it is the stepping aside of the drama to deal with the present moment requirements. So even if we feel lost in a violent sea of emotions, doubts and fears, our soul becomes the searchlight, which reveals a rope thrown to us from spirit. If we can focus our attention on that helpful rope, we can grab it, and be pulled to safety.

For some of us, we may also find that what we thought was really important begins to change quite dramatically as our soul connection increases and our focus shifts significantly. This doesn't mean that what we once focused on was wrong, but rather that as we change, so too do our needs. What served the baby for entertainment and education might be somewhat underwhelming for an adult! As we progress spiritually our needs and desires naturally change. Even if you have one thing that you just know you want to do this lifetime – to heal or teach, for example, the way that happens may shift and change in unexpected ways over the course of your spiritual development. For example, I always loved singing and teaching, that was no surprise, but the way that those talents have evolved has been most unexpected. I never really imagined that they would connect with each other, but somehow, organically, they have naturally done so. I had to focus on areas of learning that often didn't seem to have so much to do with the development of those talents, yet actually helped me greatly. I had to trust and follow the movement of my own soul and focus where I was directed inwardly to focus. It wasn't always easy, but it always eventually proved essential to my growth into the next stage.

As you are reading this chapter, if you feel some 'light bulb' moments happening for you, or you feel as though there is something in this topic that is relevant for you somehow, then the following paragraph of guidance, dictated by spirit, is especially for you:

You are going through a shift in your spiritual self, an important phase of growth, and because of this, your focus is shifting too. This shift in focus is not something to be afraid of, but something to embrace. Beloved, do not hold fear about what you may be leaving behind, instead focus on what feels relevant now. If something is meant to be, it will surface again like a second wind in your life when the time is right. If it falls away naturally, then it has served its purpose and will benefit you no more. You do not have to attach to anything out of fear of loss. Trust. Let your awareness dwell where it naturally wants to go. If you are not sure where that is, ask yourself this question, "What would I naturally dream about or focus upon if I had no fear in my heart at all?" The answer to that question is where your soul is directing your attention and focus, so that your initiation into your path may deepen now.

ASCENDED MASTER EL MORYA – HIGHER WILL

My first conscious connection with El Morya this lifetime was when I was in my early twenties, having only recently moved out of home. It was an exciting and challenging time for me. I was growing up in an emotional and psychological sense, as well as in a physical way, and spiritually, it was a good time for me to step into more of my power as well. I had started in my work as a spiritual guide doing psychic readings. I was really right at the beginning of my spiritual career this lifetime (if we don't include that phase I went through, about age 9, giving advice to my primary-school class-mates in the school yard, before I had the lucid thought that I needed more life experience to do this job properly!).

So I was sitting on my second-hand lounge, donated by a friend, in my first apartment, meditating, when I sensed a deep indigo blue smudge of light hovering above my crown, slightly to my right side. I sensed a masculine presence and the name "El Morya" popped into my mind along with the visual of a man with dark hair and a turban wrapped around his head, with a sort of veil behind it.

Unlike my other connections with angelic names in meditation, where I had no idea who Michael or Raphael actually were at first (see *Crystal Angels 444* for those stories), I actually did know who El Morya was to some degree. I knew he was an Ascended Master. Unfortunately for me, that knowledge actually hindered rather than helped me at the time. I instantly doubted what I sensed and believed my conscious mind had somehow conjured the whole experience as one big delusion.

Even to this day, I much prefer not knowing something consciously, connecting intuitively and then only later confirming what I have sensed in some way. One of my favourite moments of this was after I had written a class for my spiritual circle in Sydney which I had channelled relatively quickly one afternoon. Some months later I travelled to Adelaide, South Australia, where I discovered a haven of a metaphysical bookstore. I was delighted to find an entire section devoted to material about the Ascended Masters. I picked up one book written by Alice Bailey, a woman who had written the channelled teachings of the Masters some decades earlier. I randomly opened up to a page in the middle. Lo and behold, of course, there was my channelled teaching!

It was written in a more formal and old-fashioned style, but it was, in essence, the exact same teaching. I felt several emotions pass through me at once. Happiness and confirmation. Crankiness and a feeling of being pipped at the post, so to speak, with someone getting in there before me. Perhaps most strongly I felt even more trust in my own abilities and divine connection.

After some more lounge room meditations, I eventually worked through my doubt about El Morya's presence in the first place, which was connected to a sense of unworthiness and inadequacy. I couldn't really imagine why such an evolved spiritual being would be so interested in someone as flawed as myself.

His persistent appearances eventually prompted me to get over my issue and just accept his presence, not make it mean anything about me personally and instead just work with him to help others if I could. He kept popping up in my psychic readings, above people's heads, just a hovering face in a blue smudge of light. When this happened I found that the messages for those people were very strong and clear and that they were usually very old souls at an important phase in their spiritual journey. I became grateful rather than doubting of his presence and it wasn't long after that when the other masters began making their appearances in my life.

El Morya's energy is straight-shooting. He doesn't soften things but instead is clear, direct and to the point in how he communicates his truth. What I felt from this Master was a sort of honesty and love that wasn't particularly interested in self-doubt or fear, but just wanted to get on with the job. He is like a boss that knows what you are capable of and is not interested in hearing excuses. This can make him seem a bit scary at first. If that is the case for you, you may find that perhaps the softer loving energies of Lady Nada or the Christ work for you, but El Morya is a loving presence nonetheless. He just expresses his love in a less emotionally-driven way.

One of the greatest gifts that I received from this Master was the realisation that if I didn't believe in myself and dispense with unnecessary self-doubt, I would never allow myself to progress in my work and my life. I learned that genuine humility and self-doubt are not the same thing! I could have a positive and realistic estimation of my spiritual abilities and still choose to be humble.

As a guide, El Morya helps us connect with our inner spiritual warrior (instead of spiritual worrier!), finding the courage needed to commit to the path and feel empowered, and capable of manifesting our spiritual light on Earth, in whatever way is most true to us. This is a quality that makes El Morya a wonderful guide to call upon when you need to summon clarity, courage and strength to walk your path. He will help you confront the doubts within you that would sabotage you if left in your subconscious. His presence helps mobilise us out of paralysing fear and self-doubt, into purpose-driven action, like a nice 'kick in the behind' from the spiritual world. If we are feeling insecure and need some strong encouragement in the right direction, if it is time for us to step up into another level of our divine expression (or in other words, be initiated into our path at a deeper level), El Morya helps us.

Apart from being a powerful motivator, the Master El Morya teaches us how to work more consciously with destructive or death energy. This can seem dark or negative at first, but destructive or death energy is essential on the path. We cannot let go and outgrow old habits or consciousness without it. It is one and the same with the life and creative energy. They are just different sides of the same life force.

We cannot grow without this energy. It is simply the winter season of the soul, and it always precedes the rebirth of the spring. It helps us let go of that which would hold us back. This is the healing wisdom that El Morya shares with those that are open to him. He helps us actualise an 'out with the old, in with the new' philosophy, which rather than being something scary, to be avoided at all costs, can actually bring us greater peace and happiness.

Many spiritual people are afraid of the violence of destruction, or eschew it at least. Yet if we don't try to own this energy and make it conscious, it will just keep expressing itself as unconscious violence against ourselves and our planet. If you are a soul with a lot of power, and even if you are a gentle soul you can still have a lot of spiritual power, then your dark side might manifest unconscious violence. This could look like constant self-criticism or inhuman demands for perfection, or hatred or judgment of others, for example, or as gossiping about others.

These forms of violence actually weaken us because they are not constructive uses of our destructive energy – as odd as that may sound. To consciously work, creatively even, with destructive energy means that we use it in service to life. For that to happen we need to claim our shadow violence – rather than leaving it hidden in violent dreams or nasty tendencies in our behaviour. Even if we don't intend to be nasty, we may find it seems to happen anyway – this is just our shadow trying to break out of hiding and be integrated into our consciousness. Acknowledging that we have a destructive side means that we can start to catch it before it lashes out at us or another in criticism and instead we can use it in more helpful ways.

So instead of claiming to only be gentle beings, sometimes we need to own our anger and stamp our feet (perhaps even dramatically) and say, 'No!'. It might be 'no' to depression, 'no' to an abusive friendship or 'no' to beating ourselves up. These are helpful uses of our strength. We might have to summon a lot of anger to say no in a healthy way. That is an example of a constructive, creative and healing use of destructive energy. This is El Morya's specialty.

If we are unconscious about our own natural destructive impulses and don't try to make this part of us conscious and integrated, we actually project it outside of us, making it available to those that may seek to use it in a manipulative fashion for their own selfish gain. We can unintentionally empower the very forces that we are using our light to overcome. It isn't something to worry about or become fearful of, more just a tendency that we can avoid through gaining awareness.

Terrorism can be expressed in the form of the political suicide bomber or the wounded tyrant of a boss generating a culture of fear and misery in your workplace. No matter how it is expressed, it thrives on the unconscious and denied aggression of those it seeks to manipulate and harm. The more we choose not to integrate our own (sometimes hidden) fear and violence, the more we can unintentionally energise and enable expressions of terrorism. I mention this so that we can see how much power there is in taking our individual inner journey to help heal the world.

The real war on terrorism is not a political catch-phrase used to justify various wars and growing armaments, it is a battle that we are waging within ourselves. This inner battle is best waged by learning to accept and work consciously with our own destructive capacity, rather than pushing it away and allowing it to grow into unruly monsters of our own unconscious creation. We cannot afford to lose our power through fear. We need to own our devil, so to speak, and to put him or her to good use, rather than pretending he doesn't exist and unwittingly doing ourselves more harm than good. When we know that we are innately divine, we don't worry so much about having to 'be good'. Instead we might aim for kindness and mercy, but most of all, for becoming more conscious so we can serve the divine plan for healing the world. So saying 'no' to the local bully, for example, can require some natural gumption and anger to rally ourselves into rejecting what they are dishing up. It is perhaps one of the most spiritually-advanced choices we could make for ourselves and the greater good. Rage and anger, when properly channelled, can be tools of the Divine. We explore this much further in our work with the dark goddess in *Crystal Goddesses 888*.

To get our heads around this concept, we must first establish where destructive energy is operating within us. In the Hindu tradition, the Divine is a trinity comprised of a creative expression, a preserving expression, and a destructive expression. We have all those aspects of the Divine within us too, because we are fundamentally divine beings. Once we can admit that, then it's just a matter of searching for the signs of our disowned destructiveness. This can come out in self-harming addictions, constant self-doubt or feeling not good enough, or in more extreme examples, such as people acting out in murderous rages or lighting bush fires, and generally harming our environment. You can quickly see why it is worth becoming conscious of it.

Benevolent destruction is that which allows for the old, unhealthy and dense ways of being to be obliterated, creating space into which the soul can manifest and create higher and more loving ways of being. This is the other gift that El Morya can bless us with as he instils within us the ability to surrender doubt. We can let go of the lies we have told ourselves about who we should be and more freely accept who we actually are. Then when we are being ourselves, allowing our false beliefs about ourselves to die, our path naturally opens up with greater clarity. We realise that we are our path and the obstacles to our spiritual success become less and less. As one of my yoga teachers once put it, "If you want rebirth, you have to go in for the kill."

The invocation to bring forth the powerful energies of this Master and his consciousness of positive uses for destructive energy is: "From death comes new life." Say it, breathe in and out and let go, allowing the light within you to emerge stronger, freed from the dark weight that falls away and no longer suppresses it. This is the dying that creates greater life.

For some of you, this material will resonate deeply. Every soul has its own unique flavour and purpose and healing comes in many channels and forms. However you who resonate with the dark truths of divinity are quite special and particularly important at this time of spiritual transition. I would refer to your soul tribe as the shadow healers. You are the ones who have come to find the divine light hiding in darkness, and liberate it, so that we can truly know and live the truth that everything is love and everything, including the darkness, ultimately serves the light. Although your initiation into this journey will have included living some truly dark times in your life. Learning that they were just experiences rather than any 'truth of who you are' will have been challenging. Yet from that place you have gained a wisdom that can benefit the world and I thank you for your courage, love and divine service to the greater good of all beings on this planet.

I have created a powerful meditation featuring the vibration of El Morya on my *Mystical Healing* meditation CD, released by Blue Angel Publishing and also available on iTunes. I find this meditation particularly helpful for those of us seeking clarity on the next step of our spiritual journey or life path, and for those of us that want to heal our relationship to the Divine Masculine (perhaps through healing old father issues of abandonment or distrust). The encounter with this Divine Masculine being in this meditation can trigger healing of our relationship to masculine energy as men and women, allowing for greater feelings of protection, safety and acknowledgement in our experience of the world. You can also connect with the energy of El Morya through the healing process at the end of this chapter.

BLUE STAR SAPPHIRE – FOCUS

Sapphire can be gem-quality as we find in jewellery or less often found in raw formation, or only slightly polished, but still stunning and perfect for use in healing work. While Sapphire is probably most commonly thought of as blue, it also comes in other colours including yellow, orange, black, pink and white.

What makes a Sapphire somewhat unusual is the rutile crystal formation in the stone, creating the visual impression of a star reflecting back at you, as you gaze at the stone. Star Sapphires are rare and as such I was given guidance to mention that the use of the mandala or any Blue Sapphire (even raw, rather than gem quality) will support you in the healing process below.

If you are blessed with a connection in the physical world to a Blue Sapphire or even a Blue Star Sapphire, you will find that it resonates very strongly to El Morya's energy, however it is not essential for working with the healing properties of the stone. That is why we have Crystal Angels! One of the most effective ways to work with healing crystal energy is to call on the spirit or angel of the crystal, which we do in our healing process outlined below. If you are sensitive to energy, you will feel this method as being powerful, perhaps even as much as having the physical stone with you. If you like the presence of a physical stone to remind you, then ask the Universe to provide you with what you need for your growth and trust.

The first time I encountered a blue Sapphire was when I was a very young girl. My jewellery-loving mother decided it was time for me to have my first gold ring. Thus began an enduring love affair with jewellery and precious crystals. Eventually I chose a tiny yellow gold band with two miniscule diamonds, one on each side of a very small square cut dark blue Sapphire in the centre. Looking back, I believe this was a gift not only from my mother but also from spirit. I believe that ring helped strengthen my soul presence in my little child body at a time when I needed it, because I started my initiations at a very young age this lifetime.

Many of you may be able to relate to this too, in your own journey, or in the journey of your children. If you also started your spiritual growth process intensively in your youth, or have a child that seems to be struggling from an early age with their own growth process, finding it somewhat more intensive and challenging perhaps than others their age, then it is likely that you – and that child – are initiates who are very old souls.

Actually you wouldn't be drawn to this book if you weren't a relatively old soul with a lot of spiritual awareness and a great desire for spiritual growth this lifetime, no matter whether you believe this about yourself or not. The older your soul, the more significant your 'personal spiritual growth' will be for others around you and the planet as a whole, as we explored in the discussion about terrorism earlier.

Working with Sapphire, especially blue Sapphire and the more intense version of this, Blue Star Sapphire, helps us not only connect with El Morya, but also with our spiritual truths, inner knowing and soul purpose. It helps us calm down, strengthen ourselves from within, and find peace amongst the chaos of change. It helps us trust in the reassuring voice within that tells us that indeed, everything is going to be alright, even if we cannot quite see how that is possible from a more human perspective.

Blue Sapphire is associated with the planet Saturn and even if you are not very much into astrology, this planet will have an effect on you and your life experience. Wearing blue Sapphire can help ameliorate difficult Saturn transitions. This means that if you are in a phase of your life where you are encountering an abundance of hard life experiences, tough love or really difficult lessons, then you may well be getting some cosmic pressure from the planet Saturn! If you feel your whole life is like that (!) then you probably have come to Earth to learn to master the Saturn teachings of power and responsibility, and that can mean a lot of hard work, at least at first. Later on, Saturn delivers the gift of the hard work, which is recognition and genuine authority.

Every human being will go through a Saturn cycle in their lives, usually at least two or even three times, with each cycle lasting around 28 years or so. In each cycle we eventually gain mastery of our life lessons in Earth school, which are a little different for each of us. What Saturn brings out in all of us that is the same, no matter what our individual flavour might be. Saturn's gift of sometimes tough lessons teaches us how to deal with fear and how to best express discipline in our lives – not too much and not too little. Saturn teaches us how to live well on the Earth.

From a spiritual perspective, Saturn leads us to mastery, and is known as the planet of initiation itself – so it is a blessing to be connecting with Saturnian energy, but the path can be tough. If you can relate to this, and if it intuitively feels right for you to do so, you may wish to not only work with blue Sapphire in the healing process of this chapter, but to also wear a blue Sapphire on your person for a time. It won't stop the effect of Saturn and the progress of your initiation, but it will help you soften some of the rough edges. The energy of Mother Earth can support you through the crystal angel in the stone and the sympathetic vibration of El Morya supports you through the energetic qualities of the stone. Combined, these energies can help you through the harder lessons of Earth school.

Like El Morya, who is said to have had past lives in the East as royalty, Sapphire is known as a stone of royalty, and of dignity and protection. The Star Sapphire in particular boosts hope, faith and trust. Looking at the star in the Blue Star Sapphire actually helps us see what the pull of focus into a single point of energy looks like – all forms returning to the one central point. It is a visual metaphor for our enlightenment and as such a powerful spiritual stone to connect us to remembrance of our connection to Source.

In particular Blue Star Sapphire works on opening the channel, and the third eye, to receiving impressions from the higher planes. The energy of the higher spiritual planes is very refined. I often liken trying to connect with the higher planes (for us humans anyway) as being like listening for the tiny 'ping' of an angelic-sounding triangle through the chaotic thrashing about of a rock music concert in full crescendo! The rock concert is our thoughts, emotions, and repetitive patterns of energetic habit – feeling this, doing that, reacting in this way or judging in that way. They can be very hard to outgrow! Despite our best intentions we can find ourselves slipping back into those ways again and again.

Put simply we need help to grow. That is why the healing processes in this book and any sort of regular prayer and meditation practice are so helpful if you want to advance spiritually. Otherwise you are only ever going to be rearranging what you already have, rather than going somewhere further in your consciousness, or if you do, it will only be to a certain point. Asking for divine help and learning to receive it more intelligently or consciously will support you in outgrowing that which is holding you back. It's not always a smooth ride – often it's downright hair-raising – but it's more satisfyingly alive than being stuck in a rut.

Clearing and opening the third eye to receive is what Blue Star Sapphire does so well. Even just looking at a picture of this stone can send me off into an altered state where the light of the Divine begins to throb at my third eye, pulsing in waves of light and non-thought. It is a very powerful stone.

Sometimes people wonder, especially when they are just starting their psychic awakening, how can they know if something is real or made up? A figment of their imagination? We know what we are perceiving is real when the third eye is clear. It is a bit like how one knows when one is in love. If you are in love, you know it. If you are not, you'll question it. When a vision is gifted to you from spirit, given to you when your third eye is clear and free enough from fear to receive the vision, you'll know its real and not a figment of your imagination. You know it absolutely. Without doubt. It may last for less than a second, but it will speak volumes to you, instantly affecting your physical and emotional body, causing perhaps quite a reaction within and even around you. That might sound very dramatic, but it is actually an incredibly subtle experience – just with powerful effect.

I psychically see things often but I wouldn't classify them as divine visions. I see impressions, energy fields, past lives, thoughts and feelings, even health issues of those around me – sometimes more than I care to see. Often I automatically switch it off when I am not working but even then, impressions can still seep through. If you have already done some work on awakening your psychic abilities or are sensitive enough to be what I would refer to as a 'natural psychic', then you may have similar experiences.

Or perhaps that sounds like a bizarre and wonderful – or terrifying – world to live in, if your experiences of what your third eye can perceive have been limited up until this point in your life. If that is the case, by the way, it doesn't mean you are a less powerful soul, it just means psychic awakening wouldn't have served your growth too much before now, or your psychic talents are awakening but tend towards non-visual lines, such as through feeling or inner knowing. Your path is perfect and serves the needs of your soul growth, and El Morya and Blue Star Sapphire will work with you in a way that meets your spiritual needs, whether they exactly fall into the descriptions of this chapter or not.

Apart from helping to clear and purifying the third eye so that we can see at a psychic level, Sapphire also assists us to perceive the higher planes and see at a spiritual level – to see the Divine as it reveals itself to us.

Psychic and spiritual vision are very different. Psychic vision is not necessarily unconditionally loving, while spiritual vision is. Psychic vision is not necessarily healing or helpful; spiritual vision is. Psychic vision may create karmic energy, especially if we are judging what we see or sticking our psychic nose where it doesn't belong, whereas spiritual vision helps heal and uplift karmic weight. Psychic vision can be sought out and even sometimes forced, spiritual vision is only ever bestowed as an act of divine grace. Psychic abilities usually operate on the emotional level but can operate on the mental level as well – we emotionally sense or intelligently understand an insight, for example. Spiritual vision operates at the soul level. We can receive a divine or spiritual vision, and be completely moved and energetically changed by it, and yet not necessarily able to explain it in words or even understand it. We may feel emotional in response to it but not understand why we are responding in that way.

These differences exist because of the difference in the vibration. Higher vibrations of the soul are always unconditionally loving and move us at a deep inner level. Psychic abilities are a gift of the mind and emotions and can be used in service to the soul (without judgment and with unconditional love) or for personal agendas (such as manipulating others to gain the best business deals!). A cut-throat business person may naturally be very tuned in to the emotional and intellectual responses of those around him, and use those perceptions to his fiscal advantage. It is possible that a gift can be distorted at this lower level of vibration. It is a choice then how we use it. There is nothing wrong with psychic gifts, but we have to choose how we will use them and realise that just because we perceive something – even if we know it is accurate – doesn't always mean it is in anyone's best interest to share it.

I have included a short discussion about psychic awakening here for those of you who are psychic or interested in awakening more at that level, and for those of you who have ever visited a psychic or are planning to do so! There isn't a lot of good information that I have found about 'psychic etiquette', so I hope to provide a little here. It seems appropriate given that working with Blue Star Sapphire will stimulate the third eye and open up those abilities within us to whatever extent is meant to be this lifetime. We often open up psychically before we open up to receive spiritual visions, so some boundaries and etiquette for how to deal with psychic impressions can be useful.

There is a good tip that I like to rely upon when having a 'psychic moment'. I ask myself if the information being perceived needs to be shared and if it seems so, how can that happen from love and for the greatest good.

Sometimes even though information about other people, very intimate details, is available abundantly, it just isn't right to share it, especially if it is about someone other than the person sitting in the chair opposite you in a psychic reading session, for example. I had this situation arise many times early on in my career with parents wanting to know information about their children. Being a parent doesn't necessarily give you the right to access all information about your child. If you are in this situation, you have to trust in higher guidance and your own discernment. If you are a parent and worried about your child, it is very appropriate to call on your child's higher self and team of unconditionally loving spiritual guidance and ask that you be told or shown anything that will help you do your best job in being a parent for your child. If you are a psychic and you are unsure how to deal with a demanding client (be it a parent or lover or business colleague who wants information about someone else for example), you can ask that you only be shown what is helpful to share, otherwise you don't want to see it. Your guides will then help monitor the information that comes to you.

I remember being asked early on in my career as a psychic to stick my nose into all sorts of business deals, personal lives of others and so forth. That wouldn't have been very respectful. It was one of the reasons that I moved away from working as a psychic, I felt that I wasn't helping the greatest spiritual potential of people, although that being said, a lot of genuine psychics do really good work and bring a lot of comfort through their work. That can be so helpful to people going through difficult times. I know from personal experience about some of the challenges in working as a psychic and I have a lot of admiration and love for those that bravely do their work, with integrity in their hearts.

However there are some spiritual no-no's with psychic awakening of the third eye too.

Some years back, a spiritually-inclined friend and I ventured into a new age bookstore in Sydney's inner west. We loved to browse through the sweet-smelling shop packed with incense, gazing at crystals, books and witchy things like wands and pentacles. Whilst the store owner rang up our purchases, the woman standing behind her at the desk, one of the psychics who worked in the store, latched on to me energetically and tried to read me. Not because I asked her too, we hadn't exchanged so much as a greeting, but because she sensed something about me and wanted to know more. I was shocked as I realised what was happening, mostly because it seemed so obvious and I thought it would have been much more subtle. I quickly blocked her energetically from accessing my energy field with a clear intention that she was not welcome and to stay out! I felt the cord that she had tried to use to gather information about me just fall away, as though it was slipping off Teflon. We still had not exchanged a word or even a direct glance.

Afterwards my naturally psychic friend and I walked down the stairs from the store and out on to the street. My friend, in her typical dramatic, suffer-no-fools way, huffed, "What was with that psychic woman? It was like she was right up in your face!" I told her what I had sensed and she affirmed that she had felt that was what was happening also.

That was a good experience for me to have had – it taught me not to be a nosey psychic because I didn't like it when someone was like that with me. I consider the lesson to be this – treat others as you wish to be treated. When it comes to looking for and sharing psychic information, ask yourself how you would feel if someone would do likewise to you. That guidance will keep you out of unnecessary dramas as you open up psychically. And the other basic rule: always, always ask permission before tuning in to someone else's energy field. Even if your intention is to offer healing.

So what about spiritual visions through the third eye? They are not something that we can create with intention. They are divine happenings. They are given when needed, through divine grace, and we need to be open to receive them. That is all we can do – be receptive and refine our vibration enough, so that it comes less from fear and more from love, and we are an attractive vessel. For psychic information, we can go looking for it, with spiritual visions, we can only be ready for it.

Through the third eye chakra I have been blessed to receive visions that were so real, so shocking and so tangible that the world I lived in faded away and my personal experience of the universe became much, much larger and more beautiful. In such times I often cry and for a moment can be completely speechless, so caught up in the simple grace and beauty of what is being shown. These visions are precious gems on the path, helping me grow. They have cost me a lot of work though – stripping away my fear and my sense of self over and over again to be capable of receiving them. May we all be gifted, mercifully, with such vision as serves our own spiritual growth.

Blue Sapphire helps to calm the body, strengthen and pacify the nervous system and purify our energy of fear, particularly around the third eye and throat. This is what makes it so useful for learning to open up to higher vibrations and becoming receptive to spiritual vision, as well as becoming stronger in our psychic abilities. The clearer we are, the less we have a constant rock band playing in our heads and the more we can discern and perceive the loving presence of higher guidance helping us through various moments of our lives. Blue Sapphire helps cut through distractions of unnecessary noise within, clearing it out and allowing us some room to breathe and greater ability to focus.

The stone also supports us in not being swayed by popular opinion and helps protect us from the influence of others. It clears our eyes and ears, and helps us let go of conditioning and begin to trust our own perceptions and truths more. It helps to free us from our own mental prison, erroneously believing that things have to be as they appear to be now and instead opening us up to new perceptions that can help us go deeper into who we are and live our path with more relish.

HEALING WITH EL MORYA AND BLUE STAR SAPPHIRE

You will need a quiet place to rest and be in as much silence (or free from external distraction from family and electronic gadgets) as possible.

Having either a piece of blue Sapphire, Blue Star Sapphire or the mandala for Blue Star Sapphire in front of you, close your eyes and focus on your breath.

When you have counted seven slow breaths in and out, say the following invocation (or divine prayer): "I call upon those beings who love me unconditionally including my own higher self and my spiritual team. I call upon the true Ascended Master El Morya who loves me unconditionally and his blue flame of truth. I call upon the Angel of Blue Star Sapphire. I ask for healing, and through divine grace and mercy, to receive the deeper initiation into my path now. For my highest good and through my own free will, so be it."

Close your eyes and focus on your breath.

As you breathe in, you sense a bubble of blue light forming around you, built by your intention. Don't focus too hard, just be gently aware of a blue light creating a perfect bubble around you – over the top of your head, reaching down through the earth underneath you and rising up on all sides of you. Feel the shades of blue that seem right for you at this time – dark, light or a combination of different layers of blue. Then let the inside of your bubble be lined with pure white light.

Imagine that you can look directly ahead of you but with your eyes closed, seeing from your inner eye, your third eye. Don't try to force anything. If this feels comfortable, fine, if not, just relax and be with whatever happens for you.

Perceive a soft point of pure white light. Then notice blue light expanding out from that soft point of pure white light.

To help you focus on the light, and to stop your mind from wandering, you may like to repeat a simple mantra as you gaze at the light from within. You may softly say in your own mind or gently out loud, "I receive the light now" or "I see divine light."

Don't worry if you cannot visualise consciously – that just means that you are perhaps more of a 'feeler' than a 'seer', so to speak, even though that may change later on, and that is just fine. Instead of attempting to visualise the light, just intend to feel it either through your third eye or your heart if you prefer. You may prefer to say a simple mantra such as "I receive the light of God (or the Goddess) now" or, "I feel the divine light."

As you visualise or feel this light, allow it to grow higher and wider, noticing that the light is most concentrated in the core, and fans out with rays, like a sun or petals of a flower, but maintains its centre. Imagine that you can lose yourself in the centre of this light and repeat the mantra if you like, for around 33 breaths.

When you feel you are ready to move on, say this invocation and prayer, "I gratefully receive the loving blessing of El Morya (sounds like ELLE-MORE-YA). I now open my heart and mind to your guidance for my spiritual success and growth. Please help me live my path as fully as possible, with grace, abundance, peace and healing, as appropriate for this lifetime. I am now willing to be guided to trust in my own wisdom, to connect with higher guidance, to let go of my need for the approval of others in order for me to pursue a course of action. I am willing to trust more in the Divine than I do in my fears, to trust in the divine order that is always present, even if the appearance in my life is sometimes hidden. I know that I am loved and safe and that all happens according to divine will at the perfect time and in the perfect way. I choose to release the fear that I will not find my way through confusion and instead I now open up to trust in the Divine in you and within me. Through divine grace and my own free will, this is now so!"

Close your eyes and perceive or feel the presence of a masculine being of great strength, power and dignity. Feel his presence emanating from the core of light within the centre of the energetic Star Sapphire that you have connected with already.

If you are prone to epilepsy or seizures of any kind, or are prone to any mental illness other than depression, it is recommended that you do NOT do the following part of the visualisation where you pull light directly into your head centres. Simply skip the next two paragraphs and proceed straight to the invocation and continue on from there.

Feel a rich blue light radiating from El Morya right into your third eye, swirling around into the deep recesses of your head. Sense that light reaching into your mind and your physical body and know that you can receive this spiritual gift. You are capable, you are deserving.

Notice any thoughts or feelings, distractions or fears, or even peacefulness and calm that arise for you as this occurs. Imagine the light washing through your third eye, flowing in and out like waves of the ocean, removing debris and old thoughts and creating an opening for new impressions. Breathe in and out for around 33 breaths as this takes place.

The Invocation

You may like to repeat this simple mantra to help keep you focused: "I open my mind to God" (or Goddess or the Divine – whatever you prefer). If you feel light-headed or dizzy, be patient and wiggle your toes to help you stay present. Letting go of your mind to any degree can be an interesting experience, giving rise to all sorts of physical symptoms as energy releases, including nausea and dizziness, and even panic. Just take your time, wiggle your toes, breathe. If it becomes too much for you, gently open your eyes and focus your attention on those wiggling toes! If for some reason you cannot open your eyes or wiggle your toes, focus on the weight of your bottom on the chair instead. It will ground you again.

When you are ready and have completed your breaths, say the following aloud if possible, "I now declare that I am ready to mercifully receive the next download of information, energy, consciousness and help from my higher guidance so that I may successfully navigate my Earth school challenges at this time, including those challenges that are soon to arise for me. I open to receive this with perfect trust. So be it!"

Imagine a big stamp, like an old style ink stamp, with deep indigo ink and a beautiful pure design which you may or may not consciously perceive, descending from El Morya and stamping the inside of your mind. After a moment the imprint gets absorbed into your energy field, travelling from the third eye into the centre of the brain and then funnelling down into the nervous system, along the spinal column and fanning out to all the nerves, expanding out from the energetic channels of the spine, nourishing your entire energetic being with loving guidance and support, wisdom and divine assistance.

When you feel this has happened, or you have taken several slow breaths in and out, simply place your hands at your heart centre and say, "Thank you to those that have assisted me today and continue to assist me on my path always. Those that love me unconditionally have my complete permission to continue with that assistance. So be it."

When you are ready, open your eyes, take your time in standing up and then jump lightly up and down, rocking on the balls of your feet and allowing the blood and energy to distribute more evenly through your body. You may like to roll your wrists around, and lightly tug at each of your fingers and toes to help ground yourself after such an energetically focused session.

There will be shifts and changes after this session. Keep grounded using the technique above, plus plenty of wiggling of toes. If you find that there is a lot of mental processing happening for you in your sleep or just during your day – or even when you are trying to find stillness in meditation, do more grounding. If you sense inner agitation occurring, do not be concerned, it's just mental clearing taking place and it will settle down. If you are still struggling even with the grounding technique, you may enjoy lying with your head face down on the ground and imagining any excess energy draining out into the earth. And perhaps you will also enjoy an ocean swim or salt bath which will help you energetically cleanse and refresh yourself whilst you are going through your clearing.

It is important to note down thoughts and impressions which occur to you in the days, weeks and months following this exercise. Divine guidance has a habit of seeming so obvious when it occurs to us and yet if we don't make a note of it, it can sometimes slip away in even just an hour or two and we can be left wondering what that thing was that made us feel good and made so much sense some time earlier! Don't let this happen to you. If a thought occurs, even if you are not sure if it is guidance, jot it down. Over time you'll see patterns emerging and the communications of your guidance will begin to stand out quite clearly. Then the steps for you to take will become clear.

Remember too that we are shown what we need to know, when we need to know it. I have thrown many a tantrum in my time about wanting to know something more about some life situation or other, yet when the full story unveiled itself I realised that the timing was perfect. It would have been easier to just trust, and as I realised this time and time again, my ability to trust really grew.

3.

ASCENDED MASTER LADY NADA (Sensitivity)
RHODOCHROSITE (Emotional Healing)

INITIATION OF THE CHILD WITHIN

Caressing waves of pink and white light move toward you now. The heart relaxes, enchanted by the gentleness. Light, pink and white, creates patterns, bands and swirls of healing energy. Peace, kindness, safety. Old pain releases, transformed into an opportunity for growth, there is healing now. The child within is finally granted peace.

The child within lives in each one of us, even if we are now in adult bodies. The child within is not a physical child as such, but an energetic part of us which is important to our spiritual success and material wellbeing. It is this part of us that feels and experiences the magic in life. It is this part of us that is open to ideas and inspiration, to learning and is naturally very curious and adventurous. It is also often the part of us that was taught to fear, to hold back and dampen down our individuality, boldness and uniqueness.

Prior to societal conditioning, some of which is helpful and plenty of which is not, our child nature is naturally fearless and growth-oriented. I vividly remember learning to fear as a child, suffering high levels of near constant anxiety in a household with much emotional intensity and minimal emotional boundaries. My anxiety was my constant companion for over two decades of my life, mostly as a result of being emotionally overloaded, with insufficient constructive outlet for my feelings and a need to learn how to build emotional boundaries. It was so familiar to me, that I didn't realise I was carrying it until one day, after learning in therapy about how to express my emotions, I began to feel some intermittent relief. I started to learn the difference between natural, healthy fear as a self-protective mechanism (for example, to stop one from walking into an oncoming truck!) and unhealthy fear that would block me from living a full life. Several years after this, anxiety was no longer my constant companion and my child within began to reveal herself as being so much more than a fearful creature.

For a long time, however I believed that I needed to nurture, protect, comfort and soothe the child within and that her role was to be held by this inner nurturing state and that was about it. Then one day I heard a casual remark that changed my view of the child within, hinting at her power rather than her need for protection. The comment was something along the lines of trusting the child within to lead me.

I started to remember myself before I really learned to fear, in those precious moments of raw being before I encountered the full forces of social conditioning that came with schooling. I had memories of the child within me as being curious, a wild gypsy soul with a passionate love for nature and a gentle, sensitive heart drenched in compassion. She hated to see suffering and she had a fierce sense of natural justice and morality. She didn't judge but she knew when someone was coming from fear rather than love. She had a rich inner world and loved to play, to feel free, to let her imagination soar and to feel the Divine alive in the trees and the wind that rustled their leaves. She could feel eternity speaking to her through the endless waves of the ocean and the soft sunlight filtering through the foliage of her beloved trees. She would lie on the ground and be transfixed by the endlessness of the sky and the mystery of the moon. She was bold and open, and introspective and sensitive. She found it easy to accurately read people as soon as she met them. Though she was shocked and saddened by the darkness in people's actions at times, she maintained her curiosity and openness to others.

I realised that this child within offered me so much more than a chance to develop self-parenting techniques to heal her fear. She was my original self in human expression. I loved her and I wanted not only to heal her past pain, but to honour her in the present moment too. Whilst I realised that yes, I needed to care for her and offer her the protection of sensible boundaries and support in following her dreams, I could also trust her passion for life and let her wild playfulness and curiosity about people and places guide me into rich experiences of life. I needed her as much as she needed me. In fact, I was her and she was me. Suddenly inner child work wasn't about healing the past, it was about being able to really be myself and live fully in the present.

To gain access to our uniqueness and passion for adventure, and to shed our conditioning of fear and doubt almost always requires healing of the child within. Even if we have done work on this already, I have personally found that there can be deeper layers to be released so that we can really be as a child to life – open, receptive, curious and eager to explore the vast possibilities for spiritual growth available to those of us living within this planetary energy field.

Although healing the child within can be emotionally intense and challenging, as we learn to stay present to our emotions without getting completely caught up and swept away by them, we will also gain psychological strength and emotional maturity that are essential if we want to lead a genuinely fulfilling life. It is not only learning how to respond as a loving and wise parent to the child within that improves our quality of life. Being able to healthily express the child within makes life much more fun for us too. We will feel more in touch with our creativity, feel inspired and able to play, have fun and feel real joy without needing a particular reason to do so. If we are finding that we are lacking in fun or play, or that our emotional lives seem to lack stability and we don't feel very safe and secure within ourselves, we can be sure that the child within needs some healing.

It has been my experience of inner child healing and in working with Lady Nada and Rhodochrosite, that much of the healing of the child within has to do with letting go of the false selves that we had to take on to cope with the world and earn love and approval. For healing of the child within to happen so that our approach to life can dramatically change, we have to become present to what we felt as children, even if we don't understand it logically. Being present means accepting whatever arises and responding with compassion rather than judgment, especially when we feel something without understanding why or having a story to explain or justify our feelings.

We are learning in this process of being present without judgment to become capable of hearing our own stories, truly receiving our experiences and listening to ourselves. Our story might be a trauma that left an impact. Or it might be a number of challenging feelings that don't seem to belong to any incident in particular and our challenge is to be present to the absence of a clear reason behind our feelings, without dismissing our feelings.

It is only with genuine compassionate presence that we are able to truly feel and consequently release our feelings, and any stories attached to them. As this happens, we can finally move on to create and attract new experiences for ourselves. This feels more alive and empowered than getting caught up in history seeming to repeat itself (such as when we see our father in our employer or our mother in our lover, for example, or hearing our parents' words coming out of our own mouths when trying to parent our own children, despite our best efforts to do things more consciously).

To embark upon healing the child within takes a lot of courage. I have seen people who are quite fearless in some areas of their lives buckle at the thought of doing inner child healing. When a childhood wound is hidden deeply in the unconscious and the only evidence of its existence is a persistent painful pattern in one's life experience, or a persistent disease in the body, it can be hard to accept that there is a problem within us, rather than something external to us or unrelated to the past.

Subconscious fear of meeting what it is within us that is in so much pain can give rise to avoidance tactics and excuses that sound so convincing, we believe in them instead of the truth hiding underneath our feelings. So inner work might be rejected as being self-indulgent or victim-oriented, or just plain silly, for example. One common excuse is that the past is the past and our parents did the best they could and what's the point of going back and reliving something that's over? The point is however, that healing the child within is not about blaming your parents for being human, but about living what is not over and is still haunting your current life experience.

Eventually, the emotional experiences of the past that are not allowed to come out of your body as emotional energy that is recognised, held and accepted, and consequently released, will have nowhere else to go but back in to the body, where it will be concretised. Eventually this concretised energy will show up as somatic symptoms (such as panic attacks, rashes, sleep disturbance and chronic illnesses). If left long enough, the unconscious wounding has no choice but to eventually express itself as disease. Then energy has to be spent on healing the disease, which may be resistant to healing because it is like trying to heal a wound without getting to the real cause of the wound – such as the splinter that is causing an abscess. The emotional healing, often through tears or other emotional release, is the cleansing that then allows the wound to heal.

Disease is not something to be ashamed of though, as it can be a powerful catalyst for spiritual growth. Sometimes disease is a karmic requirement for a lifetime, for reasons that we may not understand intellectually, and no matter how much inner work that we do, we may experience it anyway because it will help our soul grow in some way that could not be achieved by other experiences.

However there are also times when disease could have been avoided by more conscious inner work. Sometimes we just won't know if disease could have been prevented or not and judging and shaming ourselves (or another) isn't very constructive. It will always be helpful however to work with disease from an emotional perspective to help cleanse the underlying wound and encourage healing. Healing may result in eradicating the disease or it may manifest at an emotional level alone. Either way, once the emotional work is completed, our experience of life will improve dramatically and limits to our next stage of spiritual growth fall away. We will be able to step into the next level of divine empowerment and express that empowerment in our lives.

Our subjective experience of our family of origin may be completely different to that of our siblings and parents. Getting clear about our own experience and discovering the truth of our feelings about our childhood experiences, is a powerful step towards healing. Giving that subjective experience and associated feelings some expression (preferably through journaling and writing letters that you do not send, but use for your own therapeutic emotional expression) is an effective way to connect with and heal the child within. It is a way to get to the truth of our experiences and let them go. It is a way to be heard by our own hearts and to feel empowered that we survived our pain and can move on. It will hurt but it is also the way to end the repeated suffering.

To do this we have to be brave and to trust ourselves. It is common for people who have been conditioned heavily by various family members or members of their community groups to believe that their mother is a saint, or their father is a devil, or that they were the bad child, and their sister the good child, and so on, to have a really hard time in finding their own truths. They may feel, as they begin to challenge the previously accepted assumptions about their family life, that they are making things up, lying or going a bit crazy.

This is a normal part of the process of waking up and finding one's own truth. Maybe to that child, the mother was not a saint but passive-aggressive, controlling and emotionally punitive – in some ways loving and yet also withdrawn, unavailable and cold. This could be very confusing to a child. Maybe to that child the father was not a devil but a lost child himself that couldn't offer the child any emotional protection from the cold rage of the mother. Maybe that child felt like they were very bad and a great disappointment to the family, and subconsciously acted that out through various types of rebellion or even trying to be the hero and achieve endlessly instead, but underneath it all felt very lonely, rejected, weird and afraid.

Being willing to experience our genuine feelings, even when they conflict with what other people seemed to think the truth was, is so important. You don't have to convince anyone of anything, nor do you have to convince yourself of anything. The only mystery you are trying to solve here is the mystery of your own feelings. If you felt something, there was a reason for it, regardless of whether that reason is utterly invisible to you and everyone else. It doesn't matter if you can see or know the reason or not. What is important is to listen to your feelings and give them expression – preferably in a journal or letters that you do not send, or in the healing process below.

I rarely, if ever, advocate that you take this healing back into your family of origin by trying to get your family to understand your reality, unless you have a very strong emotional support system outside of the family, and perhaps somewhere also within the family, and you feel that even if you are shot down in flames of rejection and criticism for what you are speaking of, you would still feel better for voicing it to various family members anyway.

The reason I mention this is that whether or not there is any objective truth to the reality you experienced as a child is unimportant. For example, your siblings might have experienced their childhood reality very differently to yours, even if you were raised in the same family, with the same parents. This in no way should make you question your own experience. What IS important to your own healing process is to discover, express and accept how you felt at the time. Whether or not you would have actually lost your parents' love if you did something that you wanted to do, but stopped yourself from doing out of fear of abandonment, is not important. It is the fear that you felt about possibly losing that love that is significant to the choices you made and that is the reality you experienced. Perhaps that is the reality that gave rise to various emotions that even now may be holding you back from pursuing your dreams out of fear of losing love and being abandoned by your husband, for example.

You don't need the approval, validation or agreement of anyone to justify your feeling experiences from childhood. They just were what they were. What is important in this work is that you create an inviting, accepting space to listen to the child within and do not criticise or reject what is expressed, even if it is different to what another says happened or if you are chided not to think or feel a certain way because it makes you seem ungrateful, for example.

Just think of a child terrified by a nightmare. Telling her that 'it isn't real' and dismissing her fear or feeling rejected by her because she doesn't trust you to protect her teaches her that she won't be really heard and that she ought to try and repress her fear. This is likely to create even greater underlying anxiety as one passes through life as an adult – a sort of baseline terror that surges up from time to time, without the poor adult really understanding what it is that they are fearing.

A more constructive option is for the adult to say to that terrorised child something along these lines, "I am here for you. I can see and feel that you are very frightened now. I know that probably doesn't feel very good at all. I am sorry that you are suffering but I am here with you. I am listening to you and I am with you. It's okay to feel afraid. I am here to protect you but it's okay to feel what you are feeling too and it will pass eventually." With that attitude and not coming from fear of your child's fear, allowing the child to be with their fear and find their own way through it, with you right there with them, creates some exceptionally beneficial emotional coping mechanisms that will serve that child throughout life.

That child learns that fear is a feeling and it can be received, it can be handled, and it can be alright even to feel afraid sometimes. She is no longer a little girl left to fend with an overwhelming terror that is dismissed as nonsense while feels very real to her. She doesn't have to feel that fear is terrifying to her because she was not taught to contain it and respond to it effectively. Instead she can be a sensitive child who learns that even big feelings are nothing to be frightened of and can be held within a loving and safe container as they are felt and then eventually released naturally. She learns not to fear her fear and deep within, she learns to feel secure within herself.

This is the sort of difference we want to give to ourselves through healing the child within. What we are healing is actually the relationship between ourselves in the here and now, the adult within us, which may need to learn some new parenting skills, and the child within that wasn't able to be parented in the way she needed as a child. That may have had nothing to do with whether or not she was loved, by the way. She perhaps just had needs that the parents had not been equipped to deal with. Inadequate parenting can come from a lack of love but more often it just comes from a lack of skill. Anyone who thinks parenting is easy quite possibly is not doing a great job at it! Fortunately we can learn new skills about how to parent our child within as adults and transform a once-frightening and lonely inner landscape into something that is warm, nourishing and secure.

As your child within becomes aware that she can trust you to be there for her, without judging, invalidating or hiding from her emotions, then that child within will feel increasingly safe in fully expressing and releasing those emotions. The weight you'll release, energetically and perhaps even physically, and the habits that will lose their grip on you, may astound you.

Spending time fostering your relationship with your inner child opens you to greater authenticity and a sense of being yourself, which can feel really good, especially if you have tried to be someone else for a long time. It also gives your adult self permission to have fun, be curious and connected with life, live in the moment, feel comfortable in your body and be more playful and creative. These qualities feel very enriching and add a sense of joy and awe to our lives. Your adult self will feel more empowered to make responsible, creative and psychologically safe decisions in your life because it is less hampered by unconscious distrust and fear, anger, guilt, shame and such, which would have made clear decision-making more challenging. From a place of connection to a healthier child within, those decisions will include choices that are more heartfelt and personally rewarding too. You'll just want to live a life that supports your wellbeing in all ways, and you'll be more capable of doing so.

You might be relate to some of this discussion, feeling that it is relevant to issues in your life now, in which case the healing process at the end of this chapter will be especially pertinent for you. If that's the case, then you are obviously at a time of growing personal power where you are ready to tackle a past wound. Or perhaps you have moved through these issues to some extent already and this chapter may be an encouraging reminder of how far you have come on your personal healing journey.

LADY NADA – SENSITIVITY

Lady Nada is often sensed as a cloud of soft pink and golden light. She is a very special guide. She embodies the strength of gentleness, which makes her a perfect companion for any work with children, including any child within. She is powerful enough to be gentle and this makes her non-confronting for those that have experienced abuse and become either broken or overly aggressive as a result. Her absence of fear and her genuine sweetness has a capacity to soothe, calm and melt the troubled heart.

She is a spiritual guide that works especially with those who are sensitive or needing to develop their sensitivity to perceive spiritual communication more consciously. She teaches us to manage our sensitivity constructively, without having to withdraw from the world to avoid feeling overwhelmed by it.

For those that are naturally very sensitive, high-feeling level personalities, this can be essential learning. We need sensitivity to be open to subtle spiritual worlds and to experience them as being real. Cultivating this level of exquisite awareness becomes a sacred task of holding light in a darkened world. Then we have to learn how to manage that sensitivity so that we are able to be involved in the world that needs our subtle perceptions, our realisation of the light, and our trust in it, without feeling overwhelmed and having to withdraw from it altogether to cope.

Lady Nada's energy supports us in learning that we can be empowered through our spiritual awareness translated into action. It can be all too easy to feel victimised, insulted, attacked, despairing, confused, frightened or grief-stricken about the state of the world or various circumstances in our lives at times. Lady Nada supports us in feeling the divine love that lies within all things, even if it is sometimes well disguised. From this place, we can stay connected to that divine presence and allow it to be the healing force that it is, flowing through us and transforming the world, one heart at a time. Starting of course, with our own.

Our world is in tumultuous transition. This is the nature of birth. If you have ever given birth, or heard it happening, then you'll know it's a gutsy, raw and wild happening. At a spiritual level it is just as raw and wild, perhaps even more so because it is happening at an even grander scale.

Many of us sense that what we most need is trust, yet fear can be easily fuelled by uncertainty. Fear-based advertising and media-manipulation tries, and often succeeds, in seducing us to believe that we need to buy certain things, or appear in a particular way, in order to be safe, secure and successful. This cultivates a spiritual immaturity that is dangerously distracting, especially for those of us who are so consciously on the divine path and meant to be helping the human race find its way forward. I count you in on this because otherwise you wouldn't be reading this book. It is so important that you and I treat our own consciousness as the precious resource of light for the greater human evolutionary process that it is.

Spiritual immaturity, amplified by media-induced insecurities, makes trusting ourselves and the workings of the Divine through us and our lives much more difficult. It puffs up the appeal of an ego apparently in control and makes our addiction to symbols of power – stuff, money, status, appearances of success and beauty and so forth - even harder to give up because there doesn't seem to be a genuine alternative available to us. Spiritual immaturity breeds blindness to subtle light. So the more we descend into trusting in only what we can physically see, touch, taste and hear, the more the utterly stunning and gorgeous light of divine love is veiled, becoming almost completely dimmed and unseen. With our inner vision, our true vision, cloaked by a love of the glittering and shiny, whether it is genuine gold or not, we are more easily seduced into lies of advertising, which can waste our precious energy. The blinding and garish false-light of all that media razzle-dazzle then seems to be so much more than it is. It's a bit like mistaking the heavenly light for the lights of Las Vegas. Dazzling they may be, but divine illumination they are not.

The humans who have enough insight and heart-vision to be able to consciously recognise what is going on will encounter a deep divine rage. However this is often followed by a sense of helplessness at how to deal with a system that is so deranged and unworthy of the great spiritual light that wants to manifest through the awakened human heart. The system needs to heal, and it is being forced to do so by breaking down, but humanity needs to heal too if a new culture is going to prevail.

With Lady Nada we are supported in remaining connected to a greater truth which gives us energy to deal with the immediate situation in the ways that we can – one step, one choice, one day at a time, without becoming so enraged at ignorance and folly that we lose our compassion. That greater truth is that divine love and presence is always there. It is the only thing that is eternal. Our job is to let it come through us, to move us into the action that is appropriate for each one of us, to surrender to it. Lady Nada helps us keep our sensitivity open so that we can feel and sense the direction that divine love gives us, and still be in the world without becoming depressed and losing our way, imagining that the problem is too big to be solved and collapsing under the weight of it all.

In times when the pain of the world does seem too much, when our outrage at some injustice or other is so raw, we need the love of Lady Nada, her gentle balm and tenderness. It is not to push away the pain that we feel but rather to support us to access the strength and reassurance we need to continue on with our work, to use that pain as a motivation to work hard and commit to our spiritual healing work, charity work, and service in whatever way we are best equipped to offer.

My small piece of this puzzle, as I understand it at this time, is to help the light-bearers, such as yourself, to strengthen yourselves, to connect with Higher Beings that are here to help, and to become even more empowered to do their sacred work, your part in this awakening. You may have a similar task which you carry out in a different way. I rely upon the divine light to help me complete my tasks, not to numb me or offer an escape into an otherworldly realm of perfection, but to inspire me to channel my heart energy and my focus into constructive channels in the here and now where love, light and power in service of love are so needed.

Lady Nada has taught me to treasure my sensitivity and to use any pain that I feel within me in response to something happening in my life, or in the greater world around me, to give me energy and motivation to do my spiritual work and personal spiritual practices. This motivation is a gift because there are times when the work of claiming divine consciousness in a human body is not only hard, but seems impossibly daunting, to put it mildly. In those moments, we might need some help in accessing the great divine love, so instead we can use any pain that we feel to remind us why we are doing all this work; tackling the obstacles to becoming conscious and living it as much as we can and even then, still reaching for more.

If you are sensitive, aware and brave enough to bear conscious witness to the pain on the planet and are motivated to heal yourself, the rest of humanity and the planet (including her animals and plants), then you are a sacred gift on this earth right now. As one of those on the path helping the human race forward in our own unique, humble and important ways, we need to recognise the mess and find the power of our own rage, our own willingness to be completely unreasonable, stamp our feet and become pig-headedly stubborn about doing our work with integrity and our spiritual practices with commitment, no matter what another may feel about the subject. Only then will we have enough feistiness to bear the sensitivity that gives us access to the pain of the world, and also to the tremendous spiritual radiance that lies hiding within the darkness. It is the guidance of Lady Nada to stay awake to our feelings, to honour our sensitivity and the divine connection that this allows us to make conscious, and then to trust unconditionally in the Divine happening through us. Only then can we safeguard ourselves against becoming lost in the haze of confusion going on around us.

There are those who can connect with the heart and the presence therein of the Divine, to be able to feel trust and serenity in the unfolding dance of the divine presence on Earth at this time of great rebirth (and associated change and upheaval). These are the light-houses, the light-bearers that can say to their fellow human beings – I am in this mad divine dance of change too, and I am going through upheaval, just like you, but I know a secret that can help – this is divine transformation! The more you trust, the more you come to know that the pain is the pain of birth, with hope and a precious gift being delivered at its end, the more inner peace you will feel.

There are many more who are working for the light from a place of service that is deep in the darkness itself – they struggle at times to stay conscious of that divine connection, of the light in their own heart, and not become swallowed up by fear, doubt, confusion or even just the sheer extent of ego suffering happening around them. These are the healers who need healing too. We all do at times. It's important to ask for it and give yourself permission to receive it.

Then there are those who don't feel the certainty of divine connection at all, who are quite simply terrified of the upheaval and struggle that they are experiencing as their lives appear to be falling apart around them, even whilst they try everything they can think of to keep change at bay – perhaps addiction, perhaps dissociation, perhaps blaming another or perhaps falling into the most prevalent attempt at defence against divine happening – denial. And so there are those who deny change at all, who keep trying to do things as they always have, who are madly stepping over whomever they can to gain the next foothold on a ladder that doesn't lead anywhere, yet supposedly promises worldly success and security, or whatever else the ego in question finds most attractive.

All of us are in this together, and no matter where we tend to vibrate in this stream of consciousness, higher beings like Lady Nada can help us come more into the heart where we can be most effectively restored and then stimulated into the right actions on our various paths to live our light which in turn helps everyone else move along the path of consciousness.

As we walk that path of truth, we are regularly empowered by divine presence. Fear becomes less compelling and divinely inspired action and continued discipline becomes more possible. We can see things through and bring our inner visions to life in the world. This is about fulfilment of our need to contribute to the world and we can become more generous in what we want to give to the world, how we want to allow the Divine to flow through us, even if that means sacrificing personal plans and preferences about how we thought we would most be happy. As we do let this happen, we open up to a joyfulness of spiritual fulfilment that we perhaps once thought would only happen if our vision unfolded exactly as we thought it should. The divine intelligence often has a far more outstanding vision held for us than we would ever even dare to dream of for ourselves.

As the fear leaves us, we become capable in ways that previously were unavailable to us. That is because we are more one with the Divine than before, more allowing and more surrendered, and more able to sustain divine vibration. Our capacity for sensitivity and receptivity renders us more powerful over time. It allows us to act powerfully without coming from a position of dominance. The divine loves a paradox! It is often that which seems most gentle which can be where the real action is taking place. One only has to think of the actions of Mahatma Gandhi's revolution of non-violent civil disobedience or Mother Teresa's lifetime of passionate service to the poor, even when that meant she had to defy certain mandates of the religious path to which she was devoted, to get the gist of how much power can exist within a gentle heart dedicated to divine love and truth, and how this can move the ways of the world.

What these wise human beings had in common, and what Lady Nada helps us realise, is that with trust in the Divine and a release of fear, we become capable of moving in the world with less force and more effectiveness. We use our will in alignment with divine prompting and things that could be impossible otherwise, become accessible to us. The inner child healing work is our place to start. To clear fear and learn trust is essential for our spiritual growth to approach the levels demonstrated by human beings like Mother Teresa. We have this potential within us. Our job is to create a fertile inner environment where that potential can grow and develop and eventually flower into consciousness and divinely-inspired action.

I remember watching a television program that unexpectedly illustrated the wisdom of Lady Nada. Oddly enough it was a program on shark handlers. Sharks are considered by many to be a most fearsome creature, yet there are those that seek to protect these animals because they are a part of the ecosystem that balances and maintains the health of the oceans.

The program documented live in-the-field testing of a shark repellent that could be applied to fishing nets to deter sharks from getting caught and harmed in the nets. This would help fishermen secure a more abundant catch and minimise unnecessary harm to local shark populations.

To test the efficacy of the shark repellent, the shark handlers had to get close enough to touch the shark so they could spray some repellent near its nose to see how the shark would respond. Initially, to avoid the danger of being attacked as they got close to the animal, the handlers were practicing a technique of inducing the shark into a natural catatonic response. This is an altered state, not unlike what a human would experience through fainting, where the shark is healthy and alive but semi-conscious. In such a state, the shark is able to react to the repellent (proving that the repellent works) without being able to attack the handler (making the testing procedure safer). The problem was how to best get the shark into that trance-like state.

A group of shark handlers were working with a scientific approach. By having a group of men around a smaller shark, they could each tie a fin and together, flip the shark over on to its back. In this unnatural position, the shark's nervous system slows down as a reaction against the shift in gravity which would normally support its internal functioning. It then temporarily enters into a catatonic or stupefied state.

This procedure worked on smaller sharks that could be physically flipped by human beings. The inability of human beings to physically flip larger sharks on to their backs meant a new method of testing was needed.

This led the group to meet a shark handler who worked with large reef sharks. Instead of inducing them into catatonic response, this handler's approach was an invitation to the animal to connect. She would calm herself into a meditative state where she was free from fear of the sharks. Diving deep, she would descend into the shark's environment, focusing on being, feeling centred, calm and present. This allowed her brain waves to slow down. It was a form of active meditation, consciously entering into a peaceful altered state. She then released a small appetising meal of sardines around her, which attracted the reef sharks towards her.

Throughout the years, she had developed her technique of presence and connection. She had it so refined that she knew how the sharks would respond to her energy. She noted that if she was nervous, they would become aggressive and test her with physical pushing and other aggressive behaviour. Yet when she was calm, the sharks became calm too and, astonishingly enough, eventually they would start nuzzling close to her belly, nudging each other out of the way so that she could stroke their noses which was very soothing to the shark and would eventually send it into a tonic trance.

This gently induced trance, willingly entered into by the sharks, was not as deep as the reactive catatonic state that scientists thought they needed to be able to get close to these animals. It turns out that the more aggressive physical disabling wasn't necessary at all. A voluntary relaxed state, evoked from a place of calm, would render these fearsome creatures docile enough even for the woman to be able remove fishing hooks that had got lodged in the sharks' mouths.

There was no need to attempt to aggressively induce a deep catatonic state, because the sharks actively sought the more peaceful experience with this capable handler. Throughout the process, other sharks in the group would nudge each other away from the woman so that they could have their noses stroked too, until eventually the woman was surrounded by blissed-out sharks seeking her loving attention. To watch this on film was utterly breathtaking.

The female handler taught these scientists that they could commune with the sharks through an invitation rather than try to overpower them through aggressive (though well intentioned) interference. The lesson the scientists learned from this handler is one of the same lessons that Lady Nada seeks to teach us – we can achieve more through power that comes from wisdom than in head-to-head confrontation. My grandmother captured the same principle with her oft-used expression, "You get more flies with honey than vinegar."

I had a far more mundane experience of this recently with my cat, whom I adopted from the local Cat Protection Society some years ago. After several years of apartment living, we finally moved into a house with a garden where he could climb trees and have feline stand-offs with the local cat population (who all seemed inexplicably drawn to try and claim our home as their territory, thus prompting me to call our home the Greenwich Chapter of the Temple of Bast, after the cat-headed Egyptian goddess). My cat was in feline heaven. Unfortunately, so were the rampant fleas that thrived in the garden and on the other local cats.

I often laughed ironically at TV commercials where the cat calmly sits as the owner applies some anti-flea liquid or other to the back of the cat's neck, the cat peaceful and somehow grateful for the owner's intervention for its wellbeing.

The scene in my house was somewhat different. Leo, my cat, would rise up with the fury of hell urging him on, as though he had been scorched by devil fire whenever I attempted to gently squeeze the smelly anti-flea liquid on the scruff of his neck, no matter how much soothing and patting I could summon up, before snatching my hands away from his vicious swiping claws. I endured this for a while but then the liquid didn't seem to work anymore anyway. After trying a recommended essential oil blend to counteract fleas on him, in a bath (an experience that neither he, nor I, wish to ever repeat), I consulted the local vet for some further suggestions.

He recommended a tablet to arrest the persistent flea problem. The other problem, however, was getting the tablet into the cat. After some thwarted attempts, my partner and I eventually developed a technique whereby one of us would hold his legs in placewhile the other would quickly put the tablet in Leo's mouth and stroke his nose to make him swallow it. It was somewhat bloody – Leo may look like Garfield; large, fluffy and orange, but he can move like a Ninja when so inclined. Nonetheless, this approach got the end result accomplished. We came to dread the monthly de-flea treatments. Possibly even more than the cat.

Then one day, Leo was sitting on my desk as I was writing on my laptop. He was in a zen, peaceful state, perhaps hypnotised by the repetitive sound of keys being struck, or more likely, just because he felt like chilling out at that moment. I quietly asked my partner if he would bring the anti-flea tablet so we could try to administer it whilst the cat was so peaceful. With a somewhat resigned expression, my partner brought the tablet over, then paused, put it on his fingers and held it under the cat's nose. Under our truly astonished gazes, Leo promptly ate it.

The following month, with a mixture of hope and trepidation, I attempted to re-enact this wondrous miracle. The tablet accidentally slipped from my fingers onto the carpet. Leo promptly ate it, and then proceeded to go and eat some cat biscuits from his bowl before laying down for a snooze.

Silly as this example may seem (unless you are a cat-owner in which case, you'll probably have been there yourself), I couldn't help but feel that somehow Lady Nada had descended in through the crown chakra of my partner, prompting him to invite rather than demand that the cat eat the tablet. What was most astonishing to me was not so much that Leo ate the tablet (because now that I think about it, he'll try to eat the most random things sometimes) but that I had managed to make something that ended up so easy into something so challenging, for so long, simply because I thought that it had to be that way.

This is another example of Lady Nada's wisdom – that loving grace can be more effective in creating a desired outcome than trying to force it to be a certain way.

One of the first lessons that I learned in working with the Masters, and Lady Nada in particular, was that approaching force with force was not necessary or even particularly productive. Far from being weak, to be present without judgment allows for new consciousness to emerge and real change to occur, rather than a destructive battle of wills where someone has to win and another must lose. In such cases there is no real winner at all. The presence of Lady Nada can dissolve so much hatred, anger and aggression, not by pummelling it or zapping it with divine vengeance, but with the gentle pervasiveness of love.

She can help us to learn a way other than reacting to anger or fear with more anger and fear. She can help us remain present and centred in the heart, to remain aware even in the face of another's rage, and make spiritually-intelligent choices about how we wish to respond. Sometimes we won't respond at all, except in the sense of feeling compassion for that person's suffering.

Our lack of reactivity might help destabilise the painful patterns running wild in that person's psyche, slowing the momentum of that which is causing them pain. The person may challenge us as being selfish or uncaring because we are not responding in the way that their ego wishes we would, so that the drama or story would continue, but with gentleness in our heart, we can be strong, present and accept the person's right to be in the drama without having to jump on into it with them. Even her name, Nada, which can translate as "nothing", can remind us that so much of our fight is just hot air and requires nothing to heal it because it is not actually as real as we think it is at the time. She is the embodiment of the ultimate paradox of love – that it is the kindest, gentlest force in our Universe, and the most powerful.

Nada is associated with the colour of golden pink and with two special symbols. The first being a cross within a heart representing spiritual love and Christ Consciousness (which we will explore more in Chapter 5) manifest on the Earth. Her second symbol is the Pink Rose of Compassion and Grace. This rose represents Nada's compassion especially for those that appeal to her for help in healing patterns of karmic-based behaviour that no longer serve soul development. She will often work with Serapis Bey (see Chapter 1) to help heal such patterns.

Along with Serapis Bey, Lady Nada is a member of the Karmic Board, a group of guides and angels that assist us in understanding our soul lessons for this lifetime and from other lifetimes. It is helpful to know that we can appeal to the Karmic Board through prayer, asking for assistance and grace in sorting through lessons with which we may be struggling.

Lady Nada is particularly helpful for those of us seeking to accelerate karmic clearing, really outgrowing our old issues, and shifting into a more gentle way of being in the world, a way of divine grace. This doesn't mean we become floppy and without a backbone! When we need to act in the world, and healers are called to really engage with the world, not shy away from it, then her gentleness helps us stay connected to our hearts. To act, even with great fire and passion, from a place of love, gentleness and devotion, is going to give you spiritual stamina and boldness, especially when compared to acting from a place of fear. To act from a place of love, even if you are acting in sacred rage against an injustice, fired up to take practical steps to make a change in the world, attracts all manner of divine support to your cause.

This is especially relevant when we are in a challenging phase of our lives, perhaps even through spiritual crisis where the qualities of endurance, trust and faith in the higher workings of the Universe are required because we cannot sense the divine purpose or meaning behind what appears to be happening to us at the time. During such times we can be more vulnerable to those that – with good intention or not – believe that they hold our answers for us and perhaps want us to follow the path that they think we should follow. Lady Nada is particularly helpful for those who would tend to look outside of themselves for meaning, direction and purpose, rather than seeking answers within, trusting that their own divinity is enough, and its timing is perfection. She encourages devotion to the soul and the ability to find and trust in one's own path.

I have a gentle healing meditation with the Lady Nada on my meditation CD, *Radiance* (released by Blue Angel Publishing) focusing on healing the heart centre and the inner child, balancing energies and evoking feelings of bliss and nurturing. The healing process at the end of this chapter will assist you in personal healing through Nada's grace too.

RHODOCHROSITE – EMOTIONAL HEALING

Rhodochrosite is coloured with various shades of pink, usually more of a candy pink, than rose pink. It features white bands swirling into patterns. Often available as a in tumbled stone, it is also commonly used in jewellery which is a wonderful way to work with this stone when you are going through a healing process. Just remember to cleanse your stone regularly. There is information in the introduction about how and when to do this.

This stone is a bestower of peace, heart healing and emotional release. It helps us remain positive without shutting off from negative feelings through denial and even helps us access feelings that have been stored unconsciously in the body, manifesting as physical symptoms. It helps us to unearth them, to become more conscious of the emotion that was 'hidden' in the symptom, to become more able to express it and therefore release it.

You must trust your emotional process when working with this stone as there will be times when you may well be surprised at what arises – in both positive or more challenging ways. Often when there is a challenging emotion arising, there is something extremely valuable that has been repressed underneath it, and it wants to come to life. That might be a beautiful singing voice, the ability to have a healthy, fit body, some fierce fashion sense or a strong natural psychic or healing ability, for example. It might be your inner power and clear sense of your truths. It might be spiritual leadership ability. It might be a talent for a form of art or music. You may have no conscious clue that this ability was within you, until you release the emotion and its surrounding story of pain and suffering, honouring it and then letting it go. Then all of a sudden you find yourself writing poetry and singing, or filled with energy and joining a group that does healing inner dance or wild group drumming. Once shy, you may find a more extroverted side and become more social. If more extroverted naturally, you may find a deepening of your inner world as your connection to inner guidance becomes stronger, or more rich, visual and lush, without old pain obscuring the inner vision. The possibilities here are endless.

Rhodochrosite also encourages natural and free emotional expression, which can be very exhilarating and different if you have lived a life where you had to control or repress certain emotions in order to feel accepted. That would include many of us. Your loved ones might not know quite how to respond to the new and more expressive you at first. Rhodochrosite will help you stay present and confident through any such changes or challenges, remaining true to yourself and not falling into the trap that you should go back to how you were to make others more comfortable (which doesn't serve your growth, or theirs).

This stone helps heal the emotions and the emotional centres in the body, especially the solar plexus chakra (and issues around eating, shame and self-worth) and the heart (and issues of feeling blocked, stuck or drained, physical effects of asthma or depletion of the lung energy through constant analysis and over-thinking as a response to anxiety or fear of not being in control).

If you have a dislike of this stone, which can arise as a revulsion or a sense that you really don't need it, or any other quite negative reaction (despite its pretty and harmless appearance) then you can be sure that it is already working with you to dislodge something that your mind is resisting in an effort to avoid the pain. Congratulate yourself on being so instinctively intuitive and give yourself permission to stay with the process and not run from it.

I have a saying when it comes to releasing emotional toxins – better out than in! So whilst it isn't fun to release the pain because you feel it on the way out, you'll feel so much better for it once it's out of your system and no longer affecting you. If you can relate to this experience with Rhodochrosite, don't give up. Perhaps work with St. Germain and Amethyst in Chapter 9 or Serapis Bey and Clear Calcite in Chapter 1 and then come back to this chapter and complete the healing process if you feel you cannot continue with Rhodochrosite at the moment. Despite its gentle nature, it is a powerful healer and healing can be painful for a time.

Rhodochrosite helps restore an ability to play, to be creative, sexually comfortable and energetically more at home with your body. You will feel more at peace with yourself, clearer and also more emotionally aware of your talents and your darker side too. You'll have a sense that you can accept yourself more fully, without having to be perfect, which can be the greatest gift of peace to a soul who encountered a troubled childhood and once believed that they had to somehow be different, better or more worthy before deserving love and acceptance.

HEALING WITH LADY NADA AND RHODOCROSITE

The purpose of this healing is to clear and refine the substance of the emotional body so that it can be receptive to love, acceptance and impressions from your own higher guidance, who can communicate to you through your heart. It will help you release deeper layers of fear so that you can become more empowered to act on your divinely inspired ideas. This healing will also help you to attract the assistance that you need to succeed in your divine mission this lifetime.

If you ever struggle to know what you feel, it is probably that you were a sensitive and open child and have a backlog of unprocessed emotional material to clear out. Sometimes we think we feel nothing, but we are numbing out because we have been feeling too much and cannot process it all. Much of that backlog may be your own feelings, and a fair portion may also be the unexpressed feelings of others that you subconsciously picked up and took on from the emotional environment around you.

If you have a tendency still to feel the unfelt feelings of another, perhaps with certain people or in certain situations in particular, then this healing will help you with that too. It is then advised that you practice a daily checking in with your emotions by just asking yourself how you feel at various times of your day and being patient as you sit with yourself. You'll develop the ability to recognise your feelings by giving the feeling part of you some regular attention. You'll also become better at identifying when something you are feeling actually isn't about you, but is someone else's emotional energy that has seeped into your energy field. This can be tricky to identify sometimes, especially if you are naturally a psychic person, with a tendency to merge and blend with others emotionally. With awareness and practice you will improve in your ability to discern your own emotions and become more aware when you are feeling something that is the emotion of another person. That awareness is usually enough to release it immediately. If it does not release easily, the healing process below will help you cleanse your emotional body.

As you do this inner healing work, your emotional body will lighten up and you can become more present-time based, responding to what is actually happening now, rather than being triggered by an over-loaded emotional body into painful reactions. If you have repeatedly painful encounters in life that leave you wondering, "Why do I keep attracting the same relationship patterns? Why do men leave me? Why is every woman I date like my controlling mother? Why do I always end up working for a bully? Why do I keep having the same problems with money?" then a thorough cleanse of your emotional body to dislodge old patterns will be most helpful. This healing will help with that and can be repeated over several weeks or months to heal any stubborn patterns.

Please note that in the healing process below, I have used "she" to refer to the child within, instead of "he or she." This is so that the instructions stay as simple as possible only. If you feel your inner child is a male, then work with that. Usually the child within is the same gender as the adult, but not always. Sometimes you are working with wounded masculine or feminine instincts, which we all have within us, men and women both. You may find that sometimes the child within is male and then changes at other times to be female. Trust in what your inner process is presenting to you and don't worry if you don't understand it. There is a wisdom in the inner healing process that always works, whether it appears to be logical or not.

Let's begin.

Start by having a piece of Rhodochrosite or the mandala with you and make sure that you are in a private place where you will not be disturbed.

When you are ready, say the following invocation out loud, "I call upon the true Ascended Master Lady Nada who loves me unconditionally and the Angel of Rhodochrosite. I ask for your compassionate grace and emotional healing now. Please help me receive the karmic grace that I need to release old emotional patterning from my body and from my mind, and from my energetic field. I now accept that I am worthy, I am strong and I am capable of connecting with my child within, to offer her protection, comfort, unconditional love and acceptance which is what she deserves. I ask for help in completing this task now. For my highest good, so be it."

Close your eyes and become aware of the breath. Imagine that all around you is a soft pink light and as you breathe in and out, that soft pink light becomes deeper and deeper in colour and thickness until you realise you are encased in the velvet petals of a large pink rose.

Let your heart soften and relax into these petals, sensing their softness, perhaps even the exquisite perfume, of this sacred encounter.

When you are ready to progress deeper, perceive that within the rose there is a swirling of white, pink and golden light. The light within the rose creates patterns all around you whether you sense them with your inner vision or just intend that they be around you now.

Breathe in and out slowly for around 33 breaths, just being present in the rose of light.

Imagine resting on one of the petals as you become aware of a soft sound, somehow feeling it emerging from your heart. You may sense or feel the presence of a loving feminine being in a pink robe with golden light around her. She gestures towards her own glowing heart, radiant and visible in her energy field. She looks at you lovingly, sending light from this glowing heart chakra to your own heart now.

Perceive the glowing light of the heart flooding all around you and moving through you. Golden pink, soft and cleansing.

As this happens, repeat this invocation aloud, "I now invite my child within to enter into the safety, peace, acceptance, love and emotional healing grace of myself and beloved Lady Nada. I now accept anything and everything that my child within wants to say or express and everything that she feels. I accept all sadness, shame, anger and doubt, fear, rage, confusion and violence so that I may release it and be free. I accept all grief and despair, guilt and torment so that I may come to release it, and be free. All of this is accepted in this pure heart of love. I accept all, holding on for as long as I need to hold on so that when I let go, I can do so completely and of my own free will. I accept however long this takes me to process. I accept that it can be processed quickly. I accept the need of my child within to be loved, received, heard and valued and I love, receive, listen to and value my child within now. Through my own free will, this is so."

Then close your eyes and imagine that you are in a sacred place, let that place be a temple in nature or anywhere that feels good for you. Know that Lady Nada is there with you, either obviously or discreetly in the background, whatever feels best for you. Know that there is an abundance of natural Rhodochrosite in this sacred space either visible or hidden in the earth, depending on what feels right.

Then be aware of a child that lives within you becoming visible to you in that space. You may sense, feel or simply intend that she be there with you now.

Allow that child to have as much space or closeness with you as they like. Offer her the energy of Lady Nada and Rhodochrosite and let her know that you love her, are so proud of her and want to tell her how special, unique and precious they are to you. Apologise for taking so long to get to her and let that child know that you are there with her now and that you want to get to know her better and to find a way for her to feel safe all the time by knowing that you really love and accept her without condition.

Spend at least 33 breaths with that child in that sacred space. You may sit, explore, swim or just be, imagining that you are holding that child, her head resting on your chest as you relax in that beautiful natural setting.

When you are ready, say, "I now ask for divine blessings that I may heal and release emotional pain of the past, outgrow past conditioning and make a healing and unshakeable connection with my precious child within. I ask for divine support and grace in living my own truths, in honouring my own experiences without judgment, now and always. So be it."

Take your time and imagine bringing that child into your heart. Creating a safe and beautiful space for them to be, with all their favourite things, favourite colours and even perhaps intending that there be pets and animals that they love in your heart too. Let it be a child's paradise. Feel the safety of it in your heart as you relax into the healing visualisation.

No matter what adult concerns may come up from time to time, that your adult self is most capable of dealing with – even if that means getting help from others at times – your child self can always come into the sacred place in your heart and feel secure within you.

You can imagine gazing into that child's eyes and letting her know this. Let her know that she doesn't need to worry about love, or money, or being successful or liked or anything else. She just needs to know that you love her absolutely and she is safe in your heart, that she doesn't have to take care of you or anyone else, that you will take care of her now, and always, instead.

If you would like to, you can complete this healing with a visualisation of Lady Nada, wrapping you in her heart, in a warm and healing vibration, and you then wrapping your child self in your heart within that sacred embrace. You are held by Lady Nada as you hold and love the child within. You are empowered and safe, and you recognise and allow genuine unconditional love to bubble up within you.

When you are ready, follow your breath and draw your awareness back to the present moment, feeling your body in the room, the air on your skin.

Visualise or intend to surround yourself from head to toe in a bubble of whatever colour feels good for you. Use layers of different colours if you wish, perhaps allowing the child within to choose some colours too, and make sure that you are covered from over the top of your head, to underneath your feet, deep in the earth.

Allow yourself to wiggle your hands and feet and when you are ready, open your eyes. When you are finished grounding, place your hands at your chest in prayer position, say 'thank you' to yourself, and to higher guidance.

Notice your dreams and be prepared to write them down if need be – that is a way that your inner healing process can find its way to completion through your conscious participation in its story or symbols. If you feel emotional following this exercise, that is good. It is all a way of releasing energy. You may have aches or pains too. Take a salt bath, do yoga or dance or walk in nature. Be gentle. Let yourself release in your own time. You may like to record your thoughts or feelings in a journal as a way of valuing your process and honouring yourself too.

The more you access this gentleness for yourself, the more capable you will be of owning your strength and boldness, when they are required, too. In fact, in the ancient spiritual teachings, it is said that only the strongest and most powerful are capable of true gentleness. Remember this, eschew any teaching that tells you it is weakness, and embrace the loving softness that your sensitive child within needs.

4.

ASCENDED MASTER HILARION (Higher Mind)
GREEN CHRYSOPRASE (Renewal)

INITIATION OF DISCERNMENT

An apple-green light expands outwards from a single point. It breathes. Breathing in, it retracts slightly, becoming brighter and more intense. Breathing out, it rapidly expands in all directions. The process repeats. Slight contraction, rapid expansion. The light grows stronger. It refreshes all that encounter it. Minds are soothed, cleansed of mental chatter, and uplifted into openness and peacefulness. That which was hidden is now revealed, clouds of confusion are cleared away and truth is perceived.

In my late teens, I ventured into my first formal spiritual class as a student. My teacher was beautiful and enigmatic. Her teachings were so much more exciting than the ones I had been exposed to at university lectures, which by comparison seemed so dreary and dull.

My relationship with my teacher was neither simple nor easy though. I struggled in being her student because I was headstrong and always wanted to know and test things for myself. She referred to this as me having reluctance to submit to the authority of another. Undoubtedly this was at least partially true. The rebel in me saw this as a useful trait to have, given that those in authority do not necessarily also have wisdom and integrity. However my teacher believed it would block me from learning from her. She believed that I didn't want to be shown a different way to be, that I wanted to stick to what I knew. I actually didn't agree with that estimation. I was hungry for new ways of being in the world and the spiritual knowledge that she taught felt very natural and acceptable to me. What I didn't want was to be told what to believe. I wanted to sense for myself if something felt like truth or not. I imagine I may have been a challenging student.

So when my teacher said one day that we should never judge, I piped up with a question: "How can we navigate life if we cannot choose if something will work for us or not?" I asked. I wasn't being a smarty-pants. I took her teachings seriously and I wondered how I could live my life and make choices if I wasn't supposed to judge anything. My teacher responded that judgment would slow down spiritual growth and I had to let it go. I found this answer inadequate but attempted to follow her guidance nonetheless.

Unfortunately this caused me confusion as I began to distrust my own instincts about people and situations, labelling those thoughts as judgmental and therefore best avoided if I wanted to progress spiritually. I ended up tolerating situations and circumstances that I could have avoided, and this caused me pain and further confusion.

Some time later my teacher confided in me that I had asked an important question at the time. She said that the answer was in fact that I needed to use discernment rather than judgment. She explained that she didn't want to say that in class at the time because everyone would have just claimed to have been discerning when they were judging and the value of her lesson would have been lost. By that time I had worked out the answer for myself and wasn't particularly enamoured with her approach, though I understood the cleverness of it.

Discernment and judgment are very different. The simplest way I can describe the difference is that discernment is compassionate and judgment is not. Compassion removes any possibility of judgment, and judgment precludes genuine discernment. Judgment pulls us into the energy of what we are judging – even as we might be trying to resist it. It is emotionally-driven by old wounding, usually based on unresolved fears. Often we are not conscious of the wounding and if this is the case, the judgments can feel very vicious and absolute. We might be absolutely sure that someone is evil to the core! Yet this is only one side of the story. As the saying goes, there are three sides to every situation – yours, mine and the truth. Discernment, on the other hand, is intuitively obtained. It requires detachment and neutrality from a more spacious, peaceful emotional body, in order to see clearly.

As we move through the emotional healing offered by Lady Nada in the previous chapter, we become increasingly less likely to be emotionally triggered, or when we are, we can work through it with awareness more quickly. With less emotional pain driving us, our judgments naturally lessen. This is a preferable way to move into less judgment. If we want to become non-judgmental, it is best to ask why we are judging when we do find ourselves behaving in that way. Then we will heal our way out of it, which is, in my sense of it, the only organic way to gradually release judgment from our lives, becoming freer and wiser in the process. If we try to force our way out of judging, as I once did, we can end up in a bit of a mess because we may not have developed enough discernment – and trust in our own discerning instincts – to be able to make life choices that serve us well.

Discernment comes from the soul. It is insight and understanding of vibration and resonance. For example, if you have a number of choices and you feel attracted to one choice over the others, because that particular choice has a sense of joy or openness about it (even if you cannot logically explain why that may be the case) then you are using your discerning faculty. You are sensing the frequency or vibration in a person, place or thing. If a particular choice has a frequency that is compatible with your own, it will feel like a comfortable choice to make. If the frequency is lower than your own frequency, making that choice will evoke a sense of anxiety, fear, depression, doubt or uncertainty within you. If it is higher than your current frequency, which can mean it will help you to grow, it will feel exciting. The more your soul is present, the more you will find that people, places or things that do not vibrate at a harmonious frequency to your own will simply fall out of your life. I have experienced this many times with relationships, with groups of people that I was working with and even with the location of my living and day-to-day activities. When the Divine wants you to move, you'll move! Sometimes literally!

Discernment gives us the ability to make choices that feel harmonious with our own vibration and allow others to do the same for their own vibration, which may be very different to ours. This isn't just a sneaky way to stick with what we know or what we feel comfortable with either. It is often quite the opposite. As we are more in touch with the child within and less emotionally reactive, our spiritual vibration increases and we naturally seek out growth, like a plant seeking the sun or reaching deep for water. We naturally seek out what nourishes us, which means a higher vibrational field. Discernment and saying no can help us say yes to what really matters to us – spiritual growth.

We become even more able to surrender judgment in favour of discernment in this way as we grow. We start to realise that there is no wrong or right, there is just experience. I remember when a dear client of mine shared her realisation of this with me during a mentoring session. It was a special and emotional moment, a moment where she claimed her spiritual freedom, her willingness to let go of having to judge to feel safe and ordered in the world, and instead chose to trust in the divine experiment of life. We were both a bit teary! It is this realisation that takes us to a place where there is nothing else in existence other than the Divine growing as a soul and having the experiences that it needs to reach enlightenment.

When you realise that everything around you and in you, all of life in fact, is divine, it can put your mind into a tailspin. That is why we often float in and out of this awareness, having judgments popping up and then realising the error and moving to a more compassionate place. This is how we grow. We take a step forward, and a half step back, and on we go. Yet there will be a point in our lives when we feel that something has shifted somewhat more permanently within us. In initiation, the intense spiritual growth process of the soul, there are times when certain lessons are mastered just enough to proceed to the next set of lessons. We may not have absolutely mastered those lessons to perfection, but we have enough mastery to be able to withstand further growth. At some level, we finally 'get it' and rather than being awkward behaviour that we have to become conscious of – perhaps replacing our judgments, when we catch them, with more compassionate realisations – we start to reside in that new state of being more naturally.

Initiates at this level of spiritual integration seem to radiate a sense of positive expectation and wellbeing, as if they know something that most others do not. They do! They know that everything is working out perfectly in their lives, just as it is throughout the Universe. Because they recognise the perfection of divinity unfolding, no matter what appearances may be, they are somewhat more relaxed about things that can drive others to distraction.

This knowledge doesn't make them sit back and observe the struggles of the world with disinterest however. Genuine initiates work hard to help the healing growth of the human race because they would like to see the human race survive and flourish. They play their part in the game of life with passion and commitment, all whilst trusting implicitly in the divine process unfolding. They will undoubtedly have moments where their feathers are ruffled – life is nothing if not unpredictable and even shocking at times – and yet they will understand that this is part of the divine game of life and it is as it should be. Fight for what your heart feels is worthy, whilst trusting that all is unfolding as it should. That is the somewhat paradoxic mantra of the genuine initiate.

You'll sense this level of spiritual growth in another when you know that they genuinely care about you, that they love you and want you to grow and yet they don't seek to rescue you, to live your life for you, or tell you what to do. They are very safe people to learn about power from; because they have conscious access to their own, and so they don't need to lay claim to the power of another.

There is a strengthening light that begins to emanate from the initiate at this level of spiritual integration, which can be perceived using spiritual sight and can be sensed and felt, even when it is not consciously perceived. At this level we are light bearers for humanity and our presence has an effect – even if we are just standing around in a group of people chatting at a party or in some fairly ordinary everyday exchange with another.

The radiance of divine light through an initiate can be subtle and yet as our discernment grows, our ability to sense the divine presence in ourselves and others can become very acute. We may not consciously register that it is spiritual light that is strong in another and that is what is drawing us to them, but we might have a general sense that there is 'something about' that person that is appealing, or magnetic, or even perhaps a bit confronting or powerful. If you are familiar with energy and fairly conscious of it, which more and more people are these days, then you may be aware that you are drawn to the light in another, for example. In initiates, the presence, the light, is stronger than what one may usually encounter, so it is even more palpable to our inner senses, and when it is very strong, we are more likely to be conscious of what we are sensing.

I had an experience of an energetic encounter in an ordinary scenario recently when I met a shop assistant in a home-audio store. I was in the role of detached observer as my partner discussed HDMI cables and the like. We were about to leave after a brief discussion between my partner and the store assistant.

For some reason, I did something that I very rarely do, unless I am working with someone in session. I intentionally sought to perceive the auric field of another person. Discreetly gazing at the store assistant's aura, I noticed something flash through his energy field, a sort of light transmission. He seemed to change his mind about ending the interaction with my partner, instead opening up further discussion for another minute or so. I sensed some subtle exchange of energy between him and my partner. I also had the sense that the store assistant was quite possibly conscious of this energy exchange. A moment later he then he bid my partner and I goodbye for a second time. I smiled my goodbye and my appreciation for his good works, and he gazed at me with a knowing look. I had the distinct impression that we were both wondering how much each of us knew about the subtle energy healing that had just taken place! I noticed a general feeling of enhanced wellbeing and happiness within my partner and in the energy around us as we peacefully left the store. I wondered if the undercover healing was part of what kept that business afloat for so many years, even in tenuous economic times.

Being able to discern the inner light within us and others is a pleasing symptom of spiritual growth. It happens naturally when we have let go of enough of our emotional pain that we can be present to others with compassion rather than expectation. Then we become capable of perceiving divine inner radiance. This is the real light within, the presence of the Divine that can only be perceived through an awakened heart that is at least somewhat cleansed of fear.

It has been my experience that all sorts of people feel safe and at ease in the presence of such an awakened person, even if they come from very different backgrounds or would not normally feel socially comfortable with such a person. However love, and spirit, even with the presence of compassion, is not all hearts and flowers. There are times when people can become quite confronted and angry in the presence of compassion and genuine spiritual power. Judgment might have us blaming the other person, whereas discernment would have us seeking insights into our own behaviour.

Love is a powerful force and although our human minds equate it as 'good' and 'positive', the presence of it can trigger a great deal of rage from the wounded inner infant hiding in an adult body. That inner child may feel deprived and abandoned and may wish to enforce that suffering on others, begrudging them good feelings about life and themselves, believing that all should be denied. The most adverse reactions to your growing light, especially when you reach certain levels of spiritual power, will come from those that are for some reason wounded and disenfranchised from their light. They can often be the beings who are most hungry for love and illumination, and most fearful that it will be withheld from them. If you can keep this understanding in mind, it will help you remain compassionate and respond appropriately in the face of a verbal or any other kind of attack. Remember that it is very likely not about you so much as the attacker's own wounding.

It is important however that we keep in mind that compassion isn't about you denying your need for healthy boundaries, just as judgment is not about dispensing with discernment. There have been times when I have made silly mistakes in allowing myself to ignore my own discernment about working with someone, for example, because I 'didn't want to judge'. What happened was that I got stung in an unsurprising and yet very unpleasant way and I learned that my discernment should be listened to, and that compassion applied just as much to me as it did to others.

Compassion teaches that you do not condemn the choice of another, whilst discernment teaches that nor do you accept that which is fundamentally contrary to your nature. Would the Dalai Lama approve of violent actions against Tibet? No. Would he condemn those that act in such ways? No. He seeks not to inflame, but to educate and heal. Most of us understand the concept to 'live by the sword, die by the sword.' The hallmark of a compassionate being is that they have no interest in vengeance, only in healing. The Dalai Lama sits in several hours of meditation daily. I can imagine that part of the reason for this is to stay in contact with his compassionate essence. Compassion takes work, all the more so when you are 'in the trenches' with fearful, angry people who are disconnected from their own inner divine essence.

Compassion takes us out of judgment and allows discernment to come into play. It is our discernment that gives us the power of choice – to respond in ways that will enlarge or deplete our spirit. When a choice arises and you are unsure, ask yourself, Will this enhance or degrade my soul?" and let the response come not from analysis but from an impression from the higher mind, which is a knowing rather than a logic, and can often be felt as a sensation of 'yes' or 'no' in the heart. The healing process at the end of the chapter will help clear and strengthen your connection to your own higher mind so that you can discern your guidance more clearly.

As you become more powerful with your discerning ability, your capacity to sense what feels resonant for you and what does not will grow. You'll find that you'll be relying on your sense of self-worth and self-esteem to practically implement the decisions that arise for you. We actually need a lot of self-confidence and self-esteem to walk the spiritual path. It can be a surprising realisation, especially if our focus is on how we can contribute positively to the lives of others through our spiritual path. Yet if you are going to honour your own insights, trust in your own discernment and say yes to some things and no to others, then you will need a lot of personal courage and you'll need to not only trust in the flow of life, but also in yourself. You will also need self-belief and a willingness to have a go at trusting your own divine connection, even if that means falling flat on your face (I have done this many times, if that is any help to you!), dusting yourself off, getting up and trying again and again, refining your conscious connection with your own divinity each time.

Can you see why you would have needed to do plenty of emotional self-healing on issues of trust, abandonment, self-worth and so on with in the Lady Nada chapter before progressing onto working with the Ascended Master Hilarion and these next stages of spiritual development? Falling flat on your face and saying, "Oh well, I could have listened more closely to what I sensed – I'll pay more attention next time," is one response, but if old emotional triggers are fired up when something doesn't seem to be working out, we might make falling flat on our face the most traumatic indication that the Divine doesn't love us and has no interest in us growing or succeeding. Same situation, two different responses. One response is calm and constructive, the other is inflamed and destructive. If we fall into the latter, we might end up in a deep depression for months or years! All because we just needed to spend a little more time with Lady Nada before moving on to

Master Hilarion.

I mention this so that at any time on your path when you need to go back and work with the child within, you'll allow yourself to do it. If there is something in my life that I cannot perceive, where I can only judge and not discern or find compassion, no matter how hard I try, then back I go to Lady Nada and the child within, to heal my way out of blindness caused by old emotional wounding so I can eventually find my discernment and compassion from a clear heart again.

As our capacity for discernment increases and the divine communicates with us directly through our own higher mind, there will often be some impulse to get honest with oneself about the relationships we have and how they impact upon our spiritual growth in a constructive or destructive sense. If you feel that you are outgrowing family relationships, friendships, work relationship dynamics or even a partnership or marriage, this can be intimidating guidance. It might ask you to put faith in an unknown future, rather than the 'devil you know,' as the saying goes. It might also be internal guidance that brings huge relief that you no longer need to play at being the proverbial square peg trying to fit into a round hole.

What will support you through such guidance, from being brave enough to honestly accept it, right through to having the courage and trust to act on it, is a belief that your own spiritual growth is of the utmost importance. It can also be helpful to remember that anything that you sacrifice on the altar of your spiritual growth will be received by the Divine and returned to you in far superior form eventually. Any step you take in genuine intention to grow spiritually will be supported by countless loving higher beings with very real power and capacity to assist you.

I have surrendered numerous relationships because of receiving such inner guidance. It has been extremely hard at the time, and even harder afterwards as I dealt with my own doubts and second-guessing about my decision, and sometimes coping with the anger and hurt of the person I no longer chose to have in my life. I always believed however that Spirit does not serve one over the other. I have no doubt that the people I left behind are living their own lives in harmony with their own vibration and better off without my different vibration causing disharmony in their lives. We all must be what we are! So in time I came to not only accept that I acted from genuine need but also had a lot of gratitude for my own courage because where I had gone in the absence of that relationship was somewhere I could not have gone with it. And that has always ended up being a more powerful and happy place. But I must say, it always took some time to get there and it was often a heart-breaking journey. I needed time to grow into my new future. So it wasn't easy but it was more than worthwhile, eventually.

Pouring energy into an attempt to salvage a dysfunctional relationship is sometimes an unwise choice. Perhaps that energy could be better used to fuel your inner journey, nourish other healthier relationships and contribute to global healing. If you are a person, like myself, who is on a highly transformational path this lifetime, then you will be changing a lot because you will be growing a lot. You may find that the company that you keep changes as you grow. When you are coming from discernment rather than judgment, you'll be able to let people go whilst wishing them well and from a place of understanding and compassion for them and for yourself.

This doesn't mean that you cannot have long-term relationships. What it does mean is that your long-term relationships will need to be able to keep up with your changing vibration or that you will need to keep up with theirs. Sometimes our relationships will have longevity and sometimes it is best to cut our losses and have compassion for the entire situation, whilst moving on. As the saying goes, sometimes we have to lose the battle to win the war. In spiritual growth there will be occasional casualties and unhealthy relationships can top the list of that which won't survive the growth process.

Thankfully there will also be times that there will be enough love and respect in a relationship that it will withstand great rigours of growth, a lot of stress and tension and actually be improved rather than ended through that intense spiritual growth process. I have had experiences of this in personal and professional relationships. It is a rare gift, to find a connection with so much devotion and genuine love that both parties are willing to go the distance, bear discomfort and difficulty and rather than blame each other, seek to grow through the pain, and become a better version of themselves, for themselves, and for each other. It is a triumph of human love when this happens.

You'll know which kind of relationship you are in because your discernment will tell you. You'll feel it from within. You'll sense if you are meant to stay or go, and if you are unsure, you'll know that when you need the guidance, it will come. In the meantime you'll do your best to be conscious and to stay committed to your spiritual path.

If you need extra help – and we all do at times – the healing process at the end of this chapter will support you in accessing the higher mind, and your discerning faculty, to be able to sense your own higher truths about any relationship or other situation that you are perhaps struggling with at present, wondering if you should release it for good or for now, or keep carrying on.

THE ASCENDED MASTER HILARION – HIGHER MIND

One of the gifts that I received in meditation when in connection with the Master Hilarion was a green flame of mental cleansing. I used it soon after in one of my meditation gatherings and how everyone fell in love with it! It is a light, bright green, and feels slightly astringent and cooling. It can be used along with the Violet Flame (which we will explore in Chapter 9 along with St. Germain) for environmental cleansing too. One of my students at the time, who is now a teacher and healer in her own right, shared with us that she would zap pollution whilst driving using the green and Violet Flame with great enthusiasm! I am certain that her part of the world was all the cleaner and happier for it.

Hilarion teaches us the power of new beginnings at a mental level. He is a master of the mind and knows that clearing and refreshing our mental faculties can help us have a fresh take on situations. He teaches the wisdom of changing one's mindset, of stepping outside of what we think will happen or has to happen, or how, to open up to divine solutions and extraordinary happenings. When we are willing to get out of our own way, life can open up for us and we can be far more effective and empowered divine initiates on this earth as a result.

When we connect with Hilarion, we are entering into a learning process about how to access the higher mind. This is a completely different way of 'thinking'. It is not really thinking at all, actually. It is a receptive rather than analytic process.

To encounter the higher mind consciously is to experience yourself being impressed upon by the higher spiritual worlds. The higher mind is much more like the heart than the more typical Western definition of mind as being intellect, reason and logic. Where the intellectual mind may be called the monkey mind, in that it loves to continually move about (and make plenty of mischief!), the higher mind is more spacious, simpler and yet able to grasp the most complex and sophisticated concepts in an instant. It is a truly wondrous faculty which connects us consciously to a level of gracious and loving higher guidance. I have had many encounters with such high level guidance, through my higher mind, where a simple, singular vision is given to me, and it completely dissembles me, pulverising all my concerns in a moment and opening me up to a more beautiful reality.

The higher mind receives high vibrational spiritual information that cuts through the endless machinations of the intellectual mind with its ability to argue this way and that. Instead the higher mind presents truth. A vision that comes from the higher mind, or even a sense of knowing or a feeling, can undermine the most persistent and enduring mental despair, in a moment, with a mere second of divine intervention. The sheer grace and power of an encounter with divinity through the higher mind always floors me. It is not that I forget how incredible it is, it is just that so much genius is distilled in the simplest of ways, so efficiently, so perfectly relevant to what is needed. It just breaks my heart open, again, in the best possible way.

The higher mind is a receiving unit for the divine gifts of truth and grace. It is not something we can order about and send on missions, like our intellect which we might use to research a topic, for example, or to construct an argument. The higher mind is a receiving dish for the divine transmission. So in terms of building the higher mind function, we can learn how to align to the divine presence, how to clear ourselves to be as receptive and sensitive to it as possible, and the rest is up to the workings of the Divine itself.

Hilarion helps us build a more conscious connection to our higher mind and to learn to receive its language – which is abstract and symbolic. It will often communicate in images and universal languages such as colour and numbers. This is why when you see number patterns a part of you clicks, and believes that there is a message held within that number pattern. Your higher mind has opened and behind the apparently everyday occurrence of seeing numbers, you have the sense that there is a divine communication taking place. When you feel that way, there is. You are connecting to your higher mind, and the divine communication that can flow through it.

Hilarion also teaches that the higher mind, like the heart, is receptive, responsive to light and subtle impression of energy more than concrete ideas or reasoning. You can argue with your heart about how a person that you love isn't right for you, but you won't get very far because the heart is not informed by logic. So no matter how good your argument, it won't matter to the heart. Likewise for the higher mind – it knows what it knows and no amount of wishing or arguing changes the truth. To go back to the numbers example, someone may scoff and say that it doesn't mean anything, but when you keep seeing 444 or 333 or 11:11 you just know that the Divine is nudging you. Well, your higher mind knows and you are open to its wisdom.

One way that we can begin to tap into the incredible function of the higher mind is through meditation. Hilarion can help us with this practice if we ask. He can act as an amplifier for the higher mind, helping its frequencies reach our consciousness more powerfully than we can do on our own, not unlike spiritual training wheels.

Contrary to popular belief, meditation doesn't mean that we have to sit still necessarily, in fact physical activity that becomes meditation through focus on the breath, that transports our awareness, such as yoga, or for some perhaps even running, can help us reach that place of absence of thinking, allowing us to enter into an active meditation. For a friend of mine, dance is her meditation. Sometimes activity in the body actually helps redirect energy from thought patterns, into fuelling physical movement and this allows us to enter more readily into mental stillness. The practice of kirtan, or singing sacred mantras, as a spiritual practice can evoke deep inner stillness underneath the activity as well.

In hatha yoga practice (where a series of physical postures are performed along with a focus on the flow of the breath), we use our eyes to help us enter such a meditative state. This visual practice is called drishti, which we would translate from Sanskrit as insight, focus, and perhaps even 'place of mind'. In yoga this is utilised to still eye movement. It is hard to balance on one leg and engage many different muscles of the body to let energy flow in clear channels if one's eyes are busy darting about to the person next to you or observing your own pedicure. When the eyes are still and gently focused, the mind soon follows.

The idea behind this practice is to draw scattered focus into a singular place. So we choose a point of focus where the physical eyes are gazing at one spot – perhaps the tip of a finger or a toe, so focused on it with gentle but persistent gaze, that eventually our awareness naturally bounces back inside of our mind. Our physical eyes see without really seeing anymore and our inner sight is ignited. We become present to a reality beyond physical reality that is nameless, formless, without words, beyond the mind, even if just for a moment. It's a bit like what would happen if you were listening to what someone was really saying, rather than the form of the words that they were using. You are eventually getting to a deeper truth. And in the case of drishti, your outer sight is redirected inwards, becoming insight.

Placing mental focus with a gentle, pervasive and yet focused gaze whilst performing meditative physical activity such as yoga or tai chi can be a wonderful way to open to experience your own higher mind. Eventually you will be able to choose to take yourself to that space simply through focusing attention on a single point, externally or internally, and experiencing a type of inner switch flicking on. This is a tricky task to master and it takes time and patience. You'll most likely have practice sessions where it is harder than others, and sometimes it will feel easier and more natural to focus.

You may already experience this if you already work with spiritual energy, feeling that shift in your consciousness as you move beyond the personal and into an expanded sense of self, until eventually you will move beyond self altogether, feeling wordlessness and primordial peace. That place exists within each and every one of us already, whether we have glimpsed it already or feel like we are just taking our first steps towards connection with inner peace. Some who seem to access this state more easily than others will have spent lifetimes in pursuit of the goal. We are all making our way back home, spiritually speaking, we just need to trust that we will find our own way there, and at the right time too.

Perception beyond the physical is how the higher mind 'sees'. This is in essence what our higher mind is for – to allow us to see beyond the physical into the essential, to see past appearances and into reality. From that place we can know the direction of our path and highest potential this lifetime in any given moment – well at least as much as we need to know at any given moment. Spirit usually doesn't startle us with more than we can handle. What will seem like a natural progression to you over six months might freak you out completely, triggering much anxiety if it was asked of you right now, before you had the chance to grow through some important life experiences over the next few months. We receive from the Divine, via the higher mind only as much as is constructive at any given time.

It is the higher mind which provides access to that part of you that knows you need to leave your job, that there's something better for you on the horizon. Your heart may leap because the job is killing your spirit and destroying your peace of mind, draining your enjoyment of life. Your higher guidance – from your own soul and the angels and Ascended Masters – communicating through your higher mind transmits an energy to you that soothes you, lets you know that you are not crazy, and that this impulse to move on is in fact sensible and true. It may come to you as continual inner impressions of sun rises, or doors being closed and new doors opening, for example, symbols of new starts. Or it may come to you as a symbol of a beautiful healthy baby being born, which you perceive in a meditation, or through healing dreams gifted to you from your higher guidance to help you find your way forward, or from a sense of inexplicable trust that emerges from within. It may come through feeling inspired because you randomly see a poster that calls you to feel the fear and take the leap anyway, and so forth. You might get inspired by a Nike ad with its catch phrase – "just do it" – which seems to be speaking directly to your heart somehow, or you keep seeing 11:11 and you just know something new is starting for you. There is no limit to how higher guidance can speak to us, and it is our discernment that allows us to sense behind the ordinariness of something and to realise that the Divine is actually speaking through it, directly to us, and to trust it.

Your intellect may resist this, especially if you still have some personal healing work with Lady Nada to complete, perhaps in this case relating to trust and safety. So your intellectual response to the higher mind might be to put up a fight, saying, "No, we are not going to take the risk of never finding another job," and creating an inner battle within you. It might reject the guidance you sense, believing it to be whimsy or imagination only. Or perhaps your higher mind will win through and your intellect will accept the guidance and contemplate a course of action to carry it out.

Hilarion helps heal the relationship between the higher mind and the intellect so that the intellectual mind can relate to the guidance that comes through and do its part, which is to put the insights into action in the world, planning or researching if need be. By cleansing our intellectual mind with his green flame, we actually open up to connection with the higher mind and all that it offers. Then you can discern when you are resisting genuine guidance, instead giving yourself a chance to let go and allow your life to be guided by divine wisdom instead of old fears. We'll explore this in our healing process together at the end of this chapter.

GREEN CHRYSOPRASE – RENEWAL

I ended up with a piece of Green Chrysoprase before I knew what it was. I was drawn to a large pendant measuring several inches long, so heavy it leaves an imprint on my skin when I wear it. Debate raged amongst friends, storeowner and myself. Eventually, quite without thought, I received a clear intuition that it was Chrysoprase. Not that it mattered, as I loved it anyway, but it was nice to satisfy my curiosity about it.

Green Chrysoprase is vibrant, bright and has an apple-green tone to it, rather than an emerald or forest green. It has a yellow-ish undertone, rather than blue-green. It works on the solar plexus and heart chakras, removing blocks between the two and helping energy to flow.

Holding the consciousness of the green healing ray, Chrysoprase cleanses, renews and refreshes our energy, not unlike the green flame of Hilarion, just at a more physical level.

Resonating with the same qualities of the higher mind including dissolution of fear or confusion in favour of honesty and truth, Chrysoprase is very helpful for those of us who have suffered under a weight of disinformation in our lives – which would pretty much be most of us! We hear lies for many reasons in our lives, especially as children. It may be because the speaker thinks those lies are true, such as in the case of those teaching us that we need to be fearful. We may hear lies that the speaker knows are not true, but they want to manipulate us because they themselves are fearful and wounded. We have all been fed the lies of mass culture, whereby an entire collective believes certain things because others seem to believe them. Even if those things are not true at all.

Our minds can be filled with so many opinions and the problem with opinions is that they are partial. They are just opinions, and they are not, no matter what anyone may say, absolute. To claim that they are is a lie. If you grew up with authority figures demanding absolute obedience and acceptance of their rules – whether it be a parent or a church – and if there was no room for individual reflection and coming to your own truths even if they differed from the norm, then you would have been obstructed by those imposed conditions in your quest to access your own higher mind. Considering that you are reading this book, there is more than likely quite a powerful spiritually rebellious side to your character and you want to know truth irrespective of what others have to say about it, so you weren't completely conditioned out of knowing your spirit! Nonetheless, I have learned that cultural conditioning goes deep, and is not avoided by education which can actually enforce that conditioning rather than shatter it. It is only our spiritual journey that can take us beyond opinion and conditioned responses into reality and truth.

Chrysoprase helps heal this situation, clearing and strengthening the energy channels of our own being, and shifting out of a pattern of believing simply because someone else said so, or you read it in a book or so forth. Chrysoprase helps heal and build the self-esteem needed to challenge what you are told – even if that challenge is done internally only – to find your own truth. You may wish to shout that truth from the mountain tops, or you may not have any need to be so public with your truths, but with Chrysoprase you'll eventually know what your own truths are, and that is a powerful state to enter into.

This stone also helps work through relationship issues – so that they can be released and you can move on with a greater understanding of what 'went wrong' so to speak, and with more self-awareness and an ability to learn from the situation and perhaps choose to do things differently next time. Chrysoprase helps you gain a higher perspective, to no longer judge yourself or the other but to have compassion and be able to discern the motivations that you and the other had – perhaps how you used each other, where you loved well and where you or the other were driven by fear. Armed with that understanding you can do some inner healing work on yourself (perhaps going back to Lady Nada in Chapter 3) to let go of any old programming that would contribute to a repeat performance of those wounds with another in future.

In fact you can work well with Lady Nada and her pink ray and Hilarion and his green ray, and the associated stones of Rhodochrosite and Chrysoprase together. Combined, these stones are powerful heart healers and the loving energy of the Masters in conjunction with each other is quite beautiful. They are very different but support each other's work.

The green ray in Chrysoprase doesn't just reveal, it also heals. Hence its gift of renewal. It helps regenerate and repair our nervous system after the detoxification of emotional healing. As it strengthens the nervous system, it supports opening to the higher mind on a physical level because as we open up to receive more spiritual energy into our system, we are essentially running more divine electricity through our energy field and our physical body. We'll learn more about that in Chapter 16 when we meet the dynamic combination of the Ascended Master Merlin and the powerful (and buzzing!) stone of Mystic Merlinite. For now however it is enough to know that Chrysoprase supports our nervous system and is a very helpful healing stone for any time we are opening up to higher levels of spiritual consciousness.

If you are new to working with the Ascended Masters, or haven't worked with them for a time and want to reconnect, Chrysoprase will support your body as you do so. It is a changing experience working with the Masters. They have a highly refined energy and I have to mention that when I first started working with them, I had what I can only call stinking great headaches as old energy released and my head energetically and physically opened up to be able to receive their presence. It was not pleasant and although I loved their presence and was so grateful, the symptoms of connection were challenging. We'll look at that in more depth in Merlin's Chapter 16 too. Before you get to that chapter however, trust that Chrysoprase will prepare you for your physical symptoms of spiritual growth so that they are at least somewhat less challenging.

HEALING WITH HILARION AND CHRYSOPRASE

You will need either a piece of Chrysoprase or the mandala in this book, or both.

The purpose of this healing is to clear and refine the substance of the mental body or intellectual mind so that it can be receptive to impressions from your own higher guidance and divine soul through your own higher mind.

Sit down in a private place where you will not be disturbed. If possible, have a fresh green apple, or other green food with a reasonably high water content (such as celery, green beans, snow peas or slices of cucumber) as part of your offering for this ritual healing. Make sure it is washed and ready to eat, on a simple plate, and is something that you know you can eat and that it will agree with your stomach. This is not a time to eat something that you can't usually digest. It is not essential to include the food offering part of the practice, but it can add some healing energy to your process if you choose to include it.

When you are ready, say the following invocation out loud, "I call upon the true Ascended Master Hilarion who loves me unconditionally and the Angel of Chrysoprase. I ask for your healing, cleansing, refreshment and renewal, for your discerning wisdom and insight. Please help me receive all that I need to release opinion and mental conditioning or other psychological and emotional patterning from my mind, my body and energetic field. I accept that I am worthy of this process and that it is in service to my own growth and the highest good of all. Through divine grace, so be it."

Close your eyes and become aware of the breath. Imagine that all around you is a bright green light and as you breathe in and out, that bright green light grows until it is all around you, and eventually it moves through you.

As you feel the light move through you, it is hard to know where you stop and start and where the light stops and starts. Let yourself just dissolve somewhat into this light. Breathe in and out slowly for around 33 breaths.

Repeat the mantra, "I let go," as many times as you need before you feel energy beginning to shift within you. This may be a dramatic sense or a subtle one. If you cannot feel anything consciously do not worry, it just means your healing is happening at a subconscious level. Your healing is still taking place. The Divine always responds to our prayers whether we are conscious of it or not!

Then become aware of a brilliant white light flecked with luminous apple-green tones pouring into the top of your head and radiating out through your head, your physical brain and your mind, saturating you in rich white and green light.

As this happens, repeat this invocation aloud, "I now invite the true Ascended Master Hilarion to assist me in connecting with my higher mind, with the Divine. So be it."

Perceive or intend to allow a beam of light to form a bridge between the top of your head and a beautiful star above your crown. Sense Master Hilarion sending love and light and power from his hands and heart, his beautiful green and white light, to that bridge, making it stronger so that more and more light from the beautiful star above your crown can flow into your body. Be aware of a channel of pure white light now flowing along that bridge between your crown and the star above you. Let that channel flow and be supported by Hilarion.

Just breathe for 33 breaths or however long feels right for you. Maintain your gentle awareness on the channel of light above your head and allow yourself to exhale and release anything that arises out of your head. It is like you can breathe the light in through your head now and exhale old energies that are no longer needed out of your head. You may be aware of the top, back, front and sides of the head, breathing and releasing.

When you are ready, the channel of light extends down to the heart and the solar plexus chakras at the centre of your chest and the abdominal area respectively.

Imagine breathing the light in to those centres either together, or if you prefer, one at a time. Perceive yourself breathing in beautiful green and white light on the inhalation and breathing out old energy from those centres on your exhalation. Whatever you think or feel as this is happening is fine, just keep breathing slowly and steadily, with your awareness on the light that is flowing from the star above you, in through the top of your head, down into your heart and solar plexus. Do this for around 33 breaths.

When you are ready, allow yourself to focus again on the star above the crown of your head. This is the light of your own higher mind. Can you sense the quality of that light? You may not have words for it. You are tuning into your higher mind and so it will feel different to 'regular thinking'. You may feel your thoughts scramble a little as you try to articulate what you sense, or you may feel slightly disoriented or unsettled. That is happening because you are adjusting to its high vibration. Breathe calmly for around another 33 breaths.

The Master Hilarion then appears before you, with his hands in prayer at his chest and he smiles, before reaching over and gently touching your third eye, between your eyebrows. He sends pure white light in through the third eye. Relax, breathe and receive.

He then lightly touches the centre of your forehead slightly above your third eye and sends white light again. Relax, breathe and receive.

He repeats this, touching your hairline at the top of your forehead. Relax, breathe and receive.

Finally, if you have a piece of food as an offering, he places his hands lightly over the piece of food, and you can place your hands over it too. Perceive that Hilarion's hands are resting lightly over yours, sending light through his hands, and yours, into the food. It is blessed with healing energy. Focus on receiving light into that food with gratitude.

If you don't have food for an offering, place your hand at your heart and sense his hands over yours, at your heart, and receive the final blessing there instead.

After several breaths, with your hands in prayer position at your heart, simply say, "Thank you, I give you permission to continue this healing for the next three to seven days, as serves my highest good, so be it."

When you are ready, imagine a warm nourishing red light glowing around you as your awareness returns to your body in the room. Imagine your hands and feet are glowing with soft red energy and when you are ready, just open your eyes.

You can finish your ritual here, or complete it by eating your offering which will help you 'digest' the energy. Enjoy!

5.

ASCENDED MASTER JESUS (Christ Consciousness) ROSOPHIA (Love of the Mother)

INITIATION OF SACRIFICIAL LOVE

Rich blood red and deep rose coloured light swirl in your heart, then flow like honey, slowly spreading through your entire being. From your heart, this rich energy rises up to the crown of your head and moves down to the soles of your feet simultaneously. Feeling expanded and grounded, open and powerful, you are one with the Christ Love of the Divine Mother.

The idea of sacrificial love used to make me very uncomfortable. Some of my earliest memories this lifetime included feeling like I was energetically submerged in the emotions of those around me, for better or worse. With my natural receptivity and emotional sensitivity, I seemed to have no choice but to feel the feelings of others and even think their thoughts sometimes. This led to me feeling like I didn't really exist, except as a repository for the psychic content of others.

It wasn't until I was a teen that I began to question this as my lot in life. A compassionate woman who worked as a naturopath was the first person who gave a voice to the wisdom that I needed. In the midst of a conversation about a health issue, I mentioned how much guilt I felt around a certain situation in my life, because a person was making a lot of sacrifices for me. The naturopath looked at me and said, "But you didn't ask for any of those sacrifices to be made for you." Her simple statement flicked a switch inside of me. It was the start of my development of emotional boundaries.

At that moment, I chose to do something about this seemingly unavoidable enmeshment in the emotional worlds of those around me. Rather than feel condemned to swim in a sea of the suffering of others, and consequently my own suffering, I realised that I did have a choice. I could learn to find myself amongst all the emotions and thoughts of those around me, beginning to extricate myself from the psychic confusion I had felt.

It was a long and exceptionally difficult journey. Those that had been used to me behaving in a certain way found it hard to accept the changes in my behaviour. There were times when it was difficult to bear the experience of those that I loved feeling betrayed and abandoned as I set boundaries. Yet I wanted and needed to learn who I was and how I felt and thought in response to life. There were many around me who thought that this was a truly selfish and ungrateful choice and were deeply disappointed in me as a result. This caused further emotional pain for all involved, yet I couldn't sacrifice myself on the altar of others' suffering anymore. I had to find a way to breathe and live for myself. Deep within I also knew this was part of my spiritual path. I realised as a teenager, perhaps with more wisdom than my years would warrant, that I was going to have to be strong enough to honour myself even if that meant disappointing others whose positive opinion and love had once meant so much to me.

As I began exploring the experience of myself as an individual being with rights to my own thoughts and feelings, I also wrestled with my own conditioning which told me that I was obligated to carry the pain of others for them. I believe that this was a distortion of my soul desire to serve and heal, that had somehow become tangled up in unresolved emotional wounds. To heal this pain required an inner battle that spanned more than a decade of inner work and gave rise to a lot of anger, deep sadness and at times, a crushing sense of despair.

During this time my spiritual notions of Jesus and sacrificial love, were cast to one side. To me, his dying for the sins of others (as I was taught in my early school days) felt so much like the way I felt I had unconsciously martyred myself to others. I didn't want to explore that at all! I was ready for a different experience, to feel that I existed, that I had a right to be happy and free!

This process of liberating myself happened in stages, over many years. I learned to confront the external demands of others that I somehow 'save' them, carry their pain and be what they needed me to be to feel secure within themselves. Some of you might know this pattern yourselves, if you are learning not to be the rescuer in the lives of others, or not to demand that others rescue you. I learned to become more aware and responsive to the part of me that attracted such situations, and let them continue, sometimes for far too long.

Sacrificial love had become something that was painful for me to contemplate and I wasn't much for it. However I couldn't avoid my fundamental nature. What I came to realise next was that although the way I was expressing my natural tendency towards sacrifice in my earliest years was emotionally immature, the spiritual impulse behind it was a genuine expression of my inner nature. I really wanted to help ease the suffering of creatures on earth. I couldn't help but feel that way. I was never a person who delighted in the suffering of another – even if I didn't really like that other person, it never occurred to me to wish unhappiness upon them. I was honestly baffled as a young child as to why someone would take pleasure in hurting another.

Eventually I worked out that such behaviour is an expression of unresolved pain and a misguided attempt at securing power. Before that understanding, however, I was utterly puzzled by the behaviour of some of the schoolyard bullies and even some of my teachers. I was bullied several times through my primary and high school years and though I always fought back, I only did so to protect myself and my heart was never in the battle.

What I experienced, particularly as I entered into pre-school, was a childhood world of suffering and pain, anger and power games. What I wanted in my heart was a world where beings could feel safe, free, happy and loved.

I realise now that this heart desire was the Divine Mother expressing herself through me. One of the more advanced clients who works with me from time to time, who is in conscious connection with the spiritual worlds and the Ascended Masters herself, once She is an Earth Mother, she will nurture many on to their path." Not being in the habit of chatting with the Ascended Masters about myself, it was an unexpected pleasure to hear their estimation of my abilities. It was a confirmation of my inner nature.

I realised that my expression of sacrificial love didn't have to be about unconscious martyrdom, although it would include my willingness to endure certain experiences through my life in order to know the Divine and be able to offer myself as a vehicle for the beautiful healing presence. It is a humbling honour to walk that path, yet there is paradoxically a sacrifice of the self over and over again, on the altar of the divine presence, that is arduous. There is exquisite divine beauty that reveals itself, often through the core of the suffering, but this doesn't mean that the pain is 'taken away'. It just becomes part of the divine journey. Somehow that pain is easier to bear when it is not a result of self-defeating behaviour and instead is a symptom of healthy spiritual growth.

I had to learn how to let go of the toxic and self-defeating ways of expressing sacrificial love, to stop making it about denying myself freedom in life, in order to carry the burdens of others. I had to accept that my spirit had come to a planet that I loved deeply even whilst not always understanding the interplay of darkness and light that unfolded in her midst, like a most spectacular spiritual theatre. My love didn't guarantee an easy path. It would often ask me to endure great suffering, as it does of all of us on the path to greater consciousness. Yet it did guarantee that I would also experience much bliss, divine assistance on my path and a deepening of the love that prompted my essence to incarnate within this planetary field in the first place, an enriching and multiplying of an original spiritual investment, so to speak.

I learned what sacrificial love could be if it was healthy, spiritually inspired and emotionally functional. It could be the vehicle through which the soul found the Divine again, but instead of only in heaven, this time also upon the earth, through human experience. It could be the awakening of heaven on earth. To me that is the realisation not only of the transcendent light of the Divine Masculine, but the imminent radiance of the Divine Feminine, experienced as one divinity, occupying the same space, always in heavenly embrace, whilst appearing on the surface to be distinct lovers, mother/earth and father/heaven.

If there is something in this chapter that you relate to, then I believe that this is your soul path too. Most healers who have incarnated at this time will have sacrificial love in the core of their hearts. They will be here in a body, out of love, and they will be growing from a place of love upon the earth. They will be enduring challenge because they choose to grow and that is from a place of love – even though sometimes it won't feel like that so much.

When this is our soul path, sacrificial love isn't actually about sacrificing ourselves, our happiness or freedom, in order to carry the pain of others. It is about being spiritually empowered to the point where we can be lighthouses in the storms of others. We become strong enough to become the light that we are and in doing so we become a light for others too, realising that they might need it to see the way. We do this by surrender, by sacrifice, by devotion, into the divine presence. It is not something we do once and then we're done. Rather, it's a way of living.

Those of us on this path realise at a soul level that human consciousness on this planet was struggling with darkness and was in potential danger of losing its clear, lighted path home to divine love awakened. We recognise that the more the energy on this planet seems different to our own innate spiritual nature, the more it was in need of our light. So we came here. We came here to explore the dark divinity in its dance with the light, and to become able to perceive the radiant divine light that is within all of existence, including the darkness. Who else but you, a soul that loves the Divine, that has hunger for it and the courage to walk the path, could help show the light in darkness? Who else but you could help those that are unable to taste the light let alone realise it is calling them home? Those who can, must. The Christ Consciousness is about the conscious saviour within the hearts that are capable. As the old Hopi expression goes, "We are the ones we have been waiting for." We came to love, to share kindness and compassion, to let go of judgment and learn that the Divine is in all of existence, even the darkest, most compelling and despairing illusions, just waiting to be uncovered. Our sacrifice wasn't to descend into suffering as though that was the entire story! Our sacrifice was to abandon ourselves into the divine genius, into the plan unfolding, into the greater desire that we hold in our own hearts that genuinely craves liberation for all beings. Taking incarnation as a human being is like rocking up to the wildest, most confronting, beautiful and passionate party in the solar system! We have to sacrifice our inner notions of 'good girl' or 'bad boy' and be as real as we can be to partake in the revels, stay true to our hearts and share our essence to make that celebration as real, raw and true as it can possibly be.

What made this realisation process a bit trickier for me was that throughout the healing process of my own experiences of sacrificial love, I was working as a healer. It was in some ways the perfect vocation for healing this issue and in other ways an absolute minefield. On a daily basis I was diving into the pain of others, to find the light hiding in it, and helping them learn to trust in their own healing process. I would be supporting them in finding the energy and consciousness that was needed to outgrow their painful patterns and allow their divinity to lead instead of their ego.

Being aware that I didn't want to get caught up in another's emotional landscape as though it were my own, as I had done as a child, made me vigilant about cultivating strong emotional boundaries. Apart from my own wellbeing, I couldn't do my job properly if I got caught up in the emotions and feelings of others and lost perspective and the ability to remain detached to channel higher guidance for them. I had to find enough connection to their emotional reality to really understand what they were going through to be able to help them, but not so much connection that I lost the valuable outside perspective through which I could offer them a different viewpoint, different consciousness and different energy. It was a balancing act that I needed to master so that my clients could receive from me, feeling that I could understand them and relate to their experiences. I had to stay connected to enough higher consciousness beyond where they were at so that they could grab on to that expanded perspective like a lifeline leading them into a different life experience. I had to learn to balance myself between diving into their world and staying connected to my own world, which in turn was connected consciously to the higher spiritual worlds.

My early childhood struggles and my inner work to heal them had given me the skills to be able to offer healing in this way for others. For me it has been a process. There are times when I find it easy to sustain my light even amongst very strong darkness of another, and there are other times when I realise that I cannot serve that situation, that my light will not penetrate the darkness for whatever reason, be it a limitation of my own consciousness or that of another or that it is just not meant to be. Those are the situations where I remove myself from service and wait for inner guidance to show a new direction. I can do this because I trust that all beings are loved and the situation that best serves them will come, whether I am involved personally or not. When I am guided to be involved directly, I am. When I am guided to step back, I do. For years I found stepping back hard. Out of old guilt and my fundamental nature, I tried to help. I learned over time that my help could be helpful when it was the right place for it, and unhelpful if it was not my place to offer it. I learned that I wasn't to be sacrificing myself to the egos of others, but to divine love.

This required a willingness to step up and step back according to inner guidance. It isn't always easy. I have been criticised for it at times, usually by students who have a set notion of the how the Divine should behave! At other times, those that I am stepping back from are actually able to be grateful because they had the consciousness to recognise the love behind my actions and my commitment to their own spiritual awakening.

When a student is able to receive a decision to separate myself from them with love and acceptance, I know that I am leaving them to the next stage of their path having done good work with them. I cannot tell you how proud I am of them in those moments! Their demonstration of consciousness is the sweetest reward for me. I am then open to receive more students who can benefit from the work that I am lucky enough to share, before they move on and the cycle continues. It happens like clockwork. I can always tell exactly how much of my energy has been feeding a particular student or client because once there is separation instantly others will email or contact me to receive mentoring or so on. Often it is several new students or more for the one that is released. It always happens within a day, sometimes within several hours, of letting go. I have some students that are long-term this lifetime and I feel honoured to be a part of their lifelong journey. I have others that are short-term and I feel honoured to be able to offer a boost along their path.

However, not everyone can receive the workings of divine destiny with easy grace. I have had a few experiences in my life of those who responded with judgment or bitterness towards my choice to separate myself from them. It was surprising to me but I accepted it too. It is easy enough to see a decision like that as coming from rejection rather than love, no matter what someone else may say or feel. I felt compassion but I also chose to honour my guidance to move on. Sometimes a person can become too dependent on the light in another, which prevents them from accessing their inner light. My aim is always to light the way for another to find their own light, to be the light that reveals rather than obscures the inner light of another. There were instances however where I found that others were trying to feed of my own light and claim it as their own. This was not doing either of us any good. So the relationship had to be terminated. It doesn't happen often, but when it does, it will limit growth if one of us is not brave enough to call it for what it is and step away.

In surrendering to sacrificial love, my ego had its fair share of being shredded. I had to learn to trust in my truth more than in any criticism of abandonment or rejection that another may cast at me, if I am stepping away and they don't want me to do so. I was taught that I could spend lifetimes with one person and they would never necessarily be able to receive the grace that the Divine was offering through me, and yet I could step away, take back all that energy, redirecting it into other channels, and allow that grace to reach many more, in a shorter time. It was up to the Divine to determine the best use of my energy in service. It was up to me to do the inner work I needed to allow myself to sacrifice my opinions and conditioning into the fire of sacrificial love, choosing to surrender into loving trust. You too are on this journey too. I share this part of my own story with you because I sense that many of you will relate to it and it may help you understand elements of your own journey which you once saw as struggle as being a gift to empower you to walk your divine path.

ASCENDED MASTER JESUS – CHRIST CONSCIOUSNESS

Jesus is most often referred to as the Christ, though sometimes he is also known as Lord Sananda (his soul name in the Ascended Master tradition). In the Ascended Master teachings of the Western Mystery Schools, the Christ Consciousness is a state of being, of divine love made manifest through the Divine Masculine light that is absolute and the Divine Feminine radiance that pervades all of creation, coming together as one to manifest as a spiritually awakened, divine human being. It is sort of like top of the class, graduating with honours for the path of human spiritual growth.

This consciousness is not limited to one person, but Jesus is such a stunning example of divinely awakened humanity and what that can look like, that he has become the strongest symbol of the Christ Consciousness for many of us, and certainly one of its most powerful teachers, with his work continuing on the inner planes.

As a child however, I just knew him as Jesus from the Bible teachings of my primary school religion classes. I was much more in love with God in heaven and absolutely smitten with Mother Nature, and not particularly interested in humanity or being human, which I found rather confounding, cruel and difficult for a long, long time.

Even though I was raised in the Christian tradition, as a Catholic, and I loved all the ritual, music and ceremony of the Catholic mass in my local church, I never favoured it over any other religion. For some reason, even as a very young girl, I carried a love and fascination for all religious traditions. I was curious and intrigued rather than fearful or judgmental of different religious traditions, undoubtedly supported by the relatively free-thinking and open-minded attitude my mother carried in this regard. Given that my friends in primary school were of varying faiths including Greek Orthodox, Hindu, Sikh and Buddhist, as well as Catholic, I was immersed in a rich and diverse pool of cultural influences, religious customs and spiritual iconography from a young age. I was fascinated by the sheer variety of religious images that I encountered in the homes of my various friends and in visits to different churches and temples through my childhood years. Icons of gurus in turbans, the elephant-headed god Ganesha, Mother Mary holding a broken and bloodied Jesus in her lap, an ecstatically dancing blue-skinned Krishna, and Buddhas both wrathful and serene captured my heart and my imagination.

It was when I started university that I chose to formally let go of my religious upbringing, declaring my personal religious affiliations to be none and all, believing that beneath the diversity there was oneness. This brought me a sense of inner peace and my spirituality blossomed. I absolutely believe that each one of us has to find what works for us, and for many, that will indeed be a particular religious path that is intimately connected with their spiritual journey. I respect that completely and also accept that my path is not going to be determined by one particular religious doctrine.

So it was unexpected when I finally realised that Jesus was a very important spiritual teacher of mine this lifetime. He kept his identity a 'secret' for many years, quite possibly because I would have discounted it as being "too Christian" for my more polygamous religious tendencies! He was guiding me and teaching me for many years before I finally cottoned on to who he actually was – but by that time it was just a feeling of gratitude and love that accompanied the realisation, rather than resistance.

The realisation of his identity happened in my late twenties. A friend and I were sitting on her lounge doing psychic readings for each other, as we were prone to do at that age, in the midst of having conversations about men and relationships.

At one point I mentioned that I had made a deeper connection with my higher guidance. Usually I just felt them as a group, in fact I still often do, but at that time I had also been encountering singular guides stepping forward from other realms for various purposes. One male energy in particular had come through but wouldn't reveal his identity as yet. I mentioned this quite casually to my friend. We were used to having intense spiritual conversations in the most casual of manners, as though we were discussing the latest TV show we loved or a new recipe we had tried out.

Being highly psychic, she stared at me and gasped. "It's Jesus!" she cried out. We both found this inexplicably funny and laughed for about ten minutes. We both knew she was right. I just felt it in my heart.

It was after this point that I began to identify figures in my dreams as being an expression of the Christ Consciousness. Sometimes they looked like a typical Jesus figure, but more often than not they didn't. They would feel like him though and in the dream I just recognised him through his vibration or energetic imprint, like an old friend.

He would frequently appear as a gardener, and still does at times. Once he told me that I was trying to plant a garden in an area where it would not grow, and it was best to expand my plans. Or he would be driving my car, with me in the passenger seat beside him, as we reached the top of a mountain. He looked quite at home, somehow, in his white robes and sandals, driving the little black sports car that I owned at the time. Once we reached the top of this mountain, we got out of the car and he showed me two choices. One suggested a way of a lot of force and struggle to reach the top of yet another mountain. The other was a way for him to lead me to a cathedral made of mud and earth, radiant, flooded with golden light and spaciousness. He was leading me away from the Divine Masculine path and onto the Divine Feminine path. One was not better than the other, but one was certainly more appropriate for this phase in my spiritual journey. In all my blessed encounters with him, in dreams and meditations, his words are few, his actions are simple and few also, and he somehow communicates volumes.

In these encounters he is my guide, my friend and my trusted teacher. There are other Masters who appear at various times, but Christ is there for me when needed. I feel a deep soulful love for this being and I know that many others do also, many who are Christian and plenty who are not. I have heard others describe their dreams and sometimes I know that he is appearing as a particular figure, I just intuitively recognise his vibration. It's like recognising a friend in common as someone describes a person they have just met. You hear the description and you recognise your friend even before the person tells you their name.

Even if the person describing their dream doesn't recognise the dream figure as having Christ's energy, it doesn't mean that it isn't there. He is as likely to operate in different form as he is in more recognisable form. Whatever it takes to get the job done. If it helps people for him to appear in a particular way, he will. I have never heard of him runnning on up to someone in a vision and saying, "Hey, I'm Jesus! So listen up!" Of course if that was the most effective approach for the situation at hand, I am sure he would do it!

I recall a story from the life of controversial Indian spiritual teacher Sathya Sai Baba, who passed over in 2011. Long before the days of instant digital photographs, film was exposed to light and then developed into a negative, and eventually a print. The negative would be slid into a light box, and projected onto light sensitive photographic paper, which was then soaked in trays of chemicals to bring the captured image to life as a print on paper. Having studied photography as a teenager, I still remember the magic of seeing the photographic paper transform from plain white into a rich image as it soaked in the tray of developer.

On Christmas day in 1987, one of Sai Baba's devotees wanted to take a photograph of him. The teacher asked why when so many photos were already available, but the man insisted. So Sai Baba agreed and then encouraged the man to go home and develop the film immediately. The suggestion seemed odd, but the man did as he was bid to do. As he developed the picture, what he found emerge in his tray of developer was not a picture of Sai Baba at all, but a picture of Jesus. The man was stunned!

He returned rather quickly to Sai Baba for an explanation, which was never given to him. All the teacher would share were his teachings, which were that God is love and that there is a mystery to be experienced in connecting with the Divine, which may never be truly understood. When we become able to accept the mysterious face of the Divine, we are far more receptive to spiritual presence in our lives. We become increasingly able to 'let the Divine happen' through us. To this end, we sacrifice so much of what we have held on to (opinions and judgments in particular) in favour of surrender into service of that flow of love. It is my personal experience, which may be the same for you, that Jesus loves all. It is my experience that he is interested less in what religious tradition you belong to and more in what lies within your heart.

All truly great spiritual teachers will serve your soul growth, no matter what appears to be. Sometimes this looks like love and tenderness, such as a healing miracle. Sometimes it looks unexpected, like trashing a temple and having a rant at the local authorities. The difference between this being a spiritual act of love and an ego act attempting to justify itself is whether there is any personal agenda in this process for us beyond surrender and sacrifice into the Divine.

Sacrificial love appears to be about others, but in truth, it is about how we relate to the Divine. Others can then benefit from our consciousness, surrendered and sacrificed into divine love, though sometimes it may cause them upheaval and they may not seem very grateful! At plenty of other times, the effect of our own consciousness will not be visible to others or even fully to ourselves. The sacrifice includes the need to unravel the mystery. We have to let the Divine be for the love to flow through us as we become less impeded channels for divine grace and light. Then sometimes, we are given a glimpse of the Divine's workings and it's breathtaking.

ROSOPHIA – LOVE OF THE MOTHER

Rosophia is much like the Christ – understated in appearance and incredibly powerful in effect, without the use of force. To hold it feels like basking in waves of gentle power. It has a particular gift of awakening form or earth (our bodies, for example) with love. It is a deep reddish-brown colour with black swirling patterns through it. It looks humble and may be passed over for glitzier stones if one wasn't to open up to the reality of the stone, which is feminine love itself.

The Christ Consciousness is embodied in this stone – not as a person, or a teaching, but as pure feeling. It holds the energy of love. It is a healer par excellence for any issue to do with the heart, but also the nervous system. It is so soothing to even just look at a picture of the stone – the energy emanates right into your centre, reminding you that you are a child of the Divine Mother, that she will never forget you and will always love you without condition.

Rosophia helps us look beyond appearances, which is the key gift of the heart – to see truth despite illusions of the ego's creation. Known as the Rose of Sophia, or the wisdom of the Divine Feminine, Rosophia imparts greater access to our own spiritual abilities, in particular the capacity for wisdom. Wisdom is the knowing of the heart. It is not emotional reaction or acting out. It is instead our compassion, our empathy, our understanding and our feeling life. It is the experience of feeling our spirit expressing itself in form, through our hearts, through our bodies. It is a spiritual knowledge that pours forth from the heart and cannot be taught in terms of 'content'. The books and workshops we attend might give us information, which can be helpful indeed, but it is the transformational presence of love in any teacher, through their presence which illuminates their work, that awakens our hearts with wisdom. The best teachers support us to access our own heart and the wisdom therein. Rosophia is a crystal teacher that offers us this support.

Rosophia is especially helpful for those that are suffering from the dissociation of spiritual light from the material world. The Angel of this stone helps us realise that creation, including all of this wonderful, raw, wild and beautiful natural world (and our bodies in it) is a manifestation of love. Creation is an expression of the Divine Feminine, bringing the still eternal light of the Divine Masculine into expression, movement, power and play. They are not separate, the light and the world are the Divine in heavenly love-making.

The sense that light and the world are separate is a powerful wounding that many of us who genuinely love and consciously experience the spiritual light can struggle to resolve. It has been my experience that especially during times when the darkness is great, the pure light of spirit can seem far removed from our immediate experiences of life. Our bodies might be sick or in pain and the world around us stuck in chaos and despair, our relationships may be challenging us so deeply that instead of love, we feel lost in emotions of hate, fear or rejection. In such times, the grace of the Divine Feminine as she manifests through all of created existence might be impossible for us to consciously fathom. We may want to believe that the Divine is in all things, and even through our struggle, is helping us to awaken to rapture and bliss – and yet we might just feel like we are being pummelled into a messy pulp or torn to shreds.

During such times in particular, the promise of transcendence, of stillness and bliss, of escape into the spiritual light, can seem irresistible. It is unsurprising that there may be parts of us that want to leave behind the suffering body, complex relationship problems and the other sometimes harrowing challenges of coming to full divine consciousness in this material world altogether. Dwelling in the eternal light of the Divine Masculine, away from the awesome and sometimes awful power of the Divine Mother's multi-faceted creation of the world may seem like a desirable escape at times.

For those that are drawn to the spiritual light to avoid the darkness that is involved in genuine feminine awakening, but who cannot connect with light consciously and naturally, the problem becomes more complex. Without a strong conscious connection to the light, addiction is often the substitute used to seek the perfection of heavenly light. Addictions that are holding within them a deep desire for spiritual light, whether that is obvious to the addict or not, include an addiction to alcohol, especially spirits, and to drugs that give a feeling of being high, like cocaine, as well as anything that takes us away from the limitations of the body such as anorexia, excessive exercising, workaholism, adrenaline-surging sports and gambling, and even addiction to technology and every new version of every new gadget, as well as quite simply being unable to switch off the mobile phone or laptop.

Then there are the addictions that form in response to an exclusive love affair with the heavenly light. Addictions to food, acquiring material possessions and obsessive relationships, sexual addictions and even depression and an inability to summon energy and get on with our task of healing, growing and living are actually an unconscious expression of the feminine instinct. She is trying to keep us connected to the material world of the mother when the pull of the father light is so strong.

This struggle is amplified the more we see the masculine and feminine as fighting with each other, as opposing forces, rather than an expression of the one, seeking harmony within itself. Rosophia and the Christ Consciousness help us heal our inner relationship between masculine and feminine energies so that rather than experiencing them as separate and polarised, we can bring them together into healthy relationship.

If we never saw or experienced masculine and feminine energies role-modelled as loving each other, in marriages, relationships or functional individuals when we were growing up, then we are going to need to be willing to believe it is possible. Contemporary society, particularly in the western world, has a skewed notion of what feminine and masculine energies actually are, and still appears to be hanging on to the now antiquated notion of the battle of the sexes. With all that conditioning to unlearn, it is quite a task to shed the notion of the battle of the sexes and open to experience for ourselves the sacred inner marriage where the masculine is tender, protective and illuminating of the feminine that is enlivening, unconditionally loving and endlessly productive and creative.

The healing starts within ourselves. Our inherent masculine energy learns to cherish, protect and illuminate the genuine heart values of our feminine self. This is the same whether we are men or women. Our feminine energy learns to respect, trust and love the masculine, whilst doing what she does best, which is endlessly manifest in creative, inspired ways. Healing of our relationships then follows, healing of communities and the greater relationship of humanity to Mother Earth follows soon after, which won't be a moment too soon!

Rosophia helps restore the recognition that many of us are here on the path of the Divine Feminine to experience the awakened body divine in physical incarnation. We will explore this concept more in the next chapter on Mary Magdalene but for now, we can say that Rosophia helps awaken the recognition and experience of light in form, the unveiling of the Divine Feminine.

There have been times when I have been lucky enough to experience my body in meditation as little more than light and energy and sound. This did not happen through leaving my body, but by remaining in it, and experiencing it dissolve into its true nature, which is not physical form so much as Divine Feminine radiance.

This did not make me feel ungrounded at all. Rather it gave me a loving experience of the Divine right here and now in all aspects of my life, including the physical world with all its unfathomable ups and downs. I have been able to be the most powerful channel for divine grace when I have been in this state of consciousness because my 'god' was on the 'ground' where all the action was taking place. Sort of like having a general in the trenches with you at the time when he was most needed, whilst he is somehow simultaneously over at HQ planning some coup or other, separate from the action which gives him a bigger perspective.

Meditation or healing work with Rosophia helps us heal any issues that we have with the Divine Feminine, including issues with mothering, mothers and relationships more generally, by gradually instilling within us the loving consciousness of the Divine Mother herself, made manifest as Christ Consciousness within our awakening human hearts. It truly is a stone for the coming golden age.

HEALING WITH JESUS AND ROSOPHIA

Rosophia is not a commonly available stone so you may prefer to use the mandala in this book and call upon the Angel of Rosophia for this healing process.

Find a place where you can lay down peacefully without being disturbed. Have a light blanket or cover over you if you tend to get cool when you relax. It is good to feel comfortable and comforted during this nurturing healing process.

Place the stone or the mandala in the book near your heart, either under you or if that is uncomfortable then on the left side of your body, near your ribcage, and relax.

Start by saying the following invocation aloud, "I call upon the true Ascended Master and loving guide Jesus, Prince of Peace, he who is one with the Divine. I call upon the limitless love of the Christ Consciousness, upon all beings who carry this vibration with purity and service, and upon the limitless love of the Divine Mother, and the Angel of Rosophia, the pure vibration of divine love. I ask for your healing presence, grace and intervention now on behalf of my own soul. Through grace and love, so be it."

You close your eyes and become aware of a deep reddish light, and a feeling of warmth and love flowing through you. You may notice more heat in certain areas of your body, or tingles as energy moves about. It may be very strong or very subtle. There may be emotion or peacefulness, you may feel very distracted or very present. Simply accept and be with your response, trusting it is perfect for you.

Focus on your breathing, in and out for at least 33 breaths as this light grows, flowing into your heart and eventually filling your whole being, like soft sticky honey, golden red in colour and shining bright.

Allow this light energy to shift and lift any heaviness or stuck energy in your body or mind. That energy can just dissolve into the golden red honey light. You may see, sense or feel it happening, or just intend that it happen, as you relax.

When you are ready, repeat this simple prayer, "I invite the unconditional love of the Divine Mother, her presence through the Angel of Rosophia, and the loving brother Jesus the Christ, to be with me always, to help me return to the innocence of my inner nature, to sacrifice my fear into my love and to allow myself to be all that I can in celebration of this divine gift of life. In service to the divine plan, and of my own free will, through mercy and grace, may this now be so."

Imagine that the soles of your feet are becoming larger, opening up and allowing negative energy to be drawn out of them, into the earth. Feel the mother lovingly receive old energy from your feet whilst you sense more openness and peace in your being as a result. Let her take these old burdens from you, whether you know what they are consciously or not. She is vast and capable. What you genuinely offer to her in love and devotion will not harm her.

Notice that the light is now glowing below your feet, above your head, and all around you. Be aware that there is a brighter light before you now, growing stronger, and flowing into the spaces where you have now let go of old energy.

Say, "Mother, please forgive me and I forgive all. Mother, please receive me, and I receive all in unconditional love, with detachment. I release with detachment all that no longer serves the growing light within me, that I may best serve you. I forgive all that has held me back, within myself and within others, for now I surrender the illusion that there is anything other than your love nurturing me forward on my path of return to you. I call upon the power of the Christ, upon the love and the surrender, that takes me to you now, beloved one. Through your mercy, grace and loving kindness, so be it."

Just sit with the light and this prayer, perhaps placing your hands on your heart if you wish and breathe in and out in your own time, for around 33 breaths.

When you are ready, roll gently onto one side, keeping your eyes gently closed and slowly make your way to a seated position, placing your hands at your heart centre in prayer position.

Say quietly, "The light of Christ burns within me, my sacred heart is aflame with the Divine Mother's love and I am a channel ever more pure for the will of the Divine, sacrificing my will to thine. So be it."

Sit quietly and feel whatever you feel in your heart. Be with your breath. Be with your body and the holy light it holds.

When you are ready, simply open your eyes.

Be especially gentle with yourself after meditation and healing. More happens than we are consciously aware of and you are best to take your time in coming back to the world, even if you don't think you need it. Even just several minutes of sitting quietly before taking on the tasks of the daily world again will be helpful to integrate the subtle energy flow that has altered in your being and help that change in subtle energy take root and grow in your system.

6.

ASCENDED MASTER MARY MAGDALENE
(The Awakened Feminine)
AQUA AURA QUARTZ (Crystal Alchemy)

INITIATION INTO THE BODY AWAKENED

Within a dark vacuum, a seed of light appears. Pure white light, crackling with life force, until it grows into a perfect quartz crystal. Divine intention is set and a shower of fine pure gold particles enter the space, surrounding the quartz. An invisible electrical force shudders and the gold and quartz are bonded together. The quartz radiates a vibrant sky blue light with a golden sheen. Harmony. Power. Joy.

I was sitting at the end of a yoga class in quiet reflection. I had been going through some challenging experiences and I felt that my spiritual connection could use some strengthening. I began to settle into meditation, attempting to send my awareness out through the crown of my head to feel the expanded state of universal connection that occurs when I do that. I was puzzled to find that I could not do this, even though it usually came so easily to me. I felt purposefully blocked and my energetic focus, bouncing off the 'closed' gateway above my crown chakra, flooded back down into my body. Suddenly I felt and perceived golden light everywhere, streaming through my body, though my body wasn't just my physical body anymore, it was vast and flooded with golden energy. It was quiet bliss and I was taken aback. Within my own body was the light that I had sought to nourish me. Right under my nose. Literally!

My meditation practice went through a subtle change from that point on, as I learned to focus on simply being present to the body and its many energetic realities. The universe was within it not only beyond it. This was a different experience to sending my awareness out to various spiritual hot spots in the higher planes. I began to experience a spiritual universe from within. It was different and yet it was the same somehow. It was all an experience of divinity, the same within, as beyond.

Our body can be experienced as a source of spiritual love and presence, a home for our spirit this lifetime, and even more than that, a temple of the Divine to explore in order to experience enlightenment. The body can be a bit like a spiritual school, with a permanent teacher in residence (your innate body wisdom), that you live in your entire life. As we wake up to this reality, we encounter an illumined spiritual guide and teacher, patiently waiting to be discovered. It's kind of like discovering the love of your life, after countless searches, is actually the next door neighbour that you have known since you were a kid. What you needed was right there waiting for you all along, you just had to recognise it.

The body is very truthful and it tells our soul stories, sometimes even from past lives long forgotten. Once we reach a certain stage of our soul development, there is a desire to become embodied in complete union between spirit and flesh, to realise them as one divine expression. As this takes place, it is a sacred marriage. The spirit learns to have compassion for suffering and an awestruck appreciation for all of life, the pleasure and the pain, the simplicity and the complexity. In the absolute light of the divine spirit, suffering has little meaning, and therefore compassion is not needed. Compassion is born from the soul of experience, from the body, from the Divine Mother as she expresses the Divine Masculine light in a myriad of forms – animals, plants, human beings, crystalline beings and more. The body learns to share its truths, to communicate its wisdom and to ignite the spiritual light within, awakening the golden light of inner radiance. This golden inner radiance is the uniquely human expression of divinity that is the Christ Consciousness we began to explore in the last chapter.

There is a Sufi mystical teaching that the soul, used to flying freely about, recoiled at God's instruction to enter the physical body. I imagined it to be something like encouraging a boy huddled with all the other boys at a school dance to leave the throng and venture over to the huddle of girls, asking one of them to dance with him. What an epic task! There could be 'girl germs' or great embarrassment of rejection awaiting him!

To overcome the initial reluctance, so the teaching goes, the angels sang and the spirit, seduced by the sound, entered into the body, beginning its journey of coming to life. Like the boy who eventually makes his way over to the girl, and finds new feelings and experiences that awaken him and put him on the path to becoming a man, the spirit grows through connection to the flesh.

Whilst the spirit learns and grows from this sacred meeting, so too does the matter of the body. From inert matter, it awakens and gains life, and over a long process of spiritual integration, the apparent duality of spirit and body is chemicalised in a divine inner alchemy and the result, after a somewhat tumultuous courtship (Shakespeare was right – the course of true love never did run smooth!) is that a sacred marriage takes place.

Through this joining of body and spirit, the evolution of a unique being occurs, a divine human being is made manifest. It is an incredible birth, a genuine miracle of divine alchemy, transformation and fusion. For those of us on the transformational path of self-healing and spiritual growth required in order to be reborn in this way, much is required, but then, much is also bestowed.

There were moments in my own journey when I would feel the rebellious spirit in me, not able as yet to consistently dwell within a body that was still holding so much unresolved emotional pain. That spirit all too easily remembered the complete and utter freedom of flying high and yearned for it. On the one hand, my spirit was desperate to be free of my body and the journey of pain that would be required to accept the gift of life, on the other hand it wanted that gift of life so much. It felt like being torn in two. I was devastated by my own frustration, feeling a crushing despair as I encountered the unbreakable power of divine will that dictated this was as it was going to be and I just had to be present to it and move through it. The inner conflict was at times so excruciating that I could do little other than just stand still and try to keep breathing as the pain of it ripped through me. I was amazed that something so apparently philosophical as the dilemma of my own human existence could be so physically powerful. I knew I was experiencing consciously what many – perhaps all – humans suffered at some point on their path, whether they were completely aware of it or not. I was in the fire of spirit and body meeting each other. I was like that young man at the school dance, in angst over whether he should go and ask the girl to join him, full of terror at the pain of what would unfold in the ensuing relationship, yet desiring the chance to experience it all too. Amplified a billion times over.

In time, my spirit came to tolerate and then even became interested in my body, realising that it was the holder of much wisdom, powerful dreams and the ability to live, relate and experience the Divine in creation. Eventually that interest developed from curiosity to admiration, love and wonder, and increasingly, compassion. Then I had the realisation that the spiritual presence would become something more powerful when spirit and body joined together. The spiritual presence could go from being electricity to being electricity plugged into something – my body – and therefore able to shine as a light. That light would help others find their way. Eventually I could receive the experience that I mentioned at the beginning of this chapter. I began to experience that the body itself was as vast and endless as the spirit, that it is just the Divine in another expression, a feminine expression. It is divinity in its own right too.

It is a long and winding spiritual path to enlightenment through the body. It is my experience thus far that enlightenment happens by degrees, moments here and there that sometimes coagulate together, sometimes fall away, becoming states of being for a while, before the jostling of our consciousness pulls us back into some conditioning or other for another while. It's all just part of being human. In the process, the spirit is entering the body, the body is responding by clearing out old memories and pains, and becoming spacious and open, able to hold greater consciousness and light. It is living spiritual alchemy taking place within us. Humans are living crucibles of spiritual transformation, with a capacity for greater and greater transformation as we develop, gradually accepting the entire gamut of experience as divine expression.

One of the most powerful eruptions from the body in this process is consciousness. As we stop dissociating from the body, no longer forcing it to perform or telling it what to do, as though a dictator to a slave, we can begin to listen and receive. What we will hear are the untold stories of our soul history, expressed through the body.

There may be memories from childhood or other lifetimes that filter into our waking awareness through dreams, meditations or quiet moments of reflection. Or we may feel impressions of symbols, light, colour, sound and strong feelings emerging from within. We may feel creative energy or deep tiredness, an emotional appreciation for beauty or a surprising rush of loving affection – for a person, a tree, an insect that lands on a blade of grass.

The Divine is full of humour and creativity and stands stark-naked, waving its arms at us on a daily basis. When our spirit is at home in a body awakening, we can recognise this to varying degrees. It can be quite startling! I have had a number of experiences where I have noticed a dog standing in the street, for example, or an insect flying before my eyes, and in a manner that quite possibly seemed completely nuts to people around me, just stood there in an awestruck, giggling wonder. There was the Divine flashing its naked self at me, showing off its creative genius as a Scottish terrier outside my local convenience store! In a way that I cannot logically explain, I was shocked, delighted and somewhat stupefied as I gazed at this divine self-revelation in the guise of a furry friend. It was a mystical encounter amongst the ordinary daily actions of life that busted my heart open just that bit more, before the dog just became a dog again, and I bought my groceries and went home to cook dinner. That is a moment in the sacred marriage, as we live the ordinary, that is at one with the extraordinary.

The body may also tell its story through songs that emerge out of our mysterious depths, or through great feelings of loss and passionate yearning. Our intellectual mind may have no clue why we are feeling what we are feeling, and that is just fine. Most often, at least for a while, there will be fear. It is my belief that fear is a primary spiritual teacher on our planet and we will find spiritual mastery as we learn to make our relationship to fear conscious and accepting.

The body is a masterful receiver of energy from heaven and earth. The more spiritually-awake your body becomes, and the more you learn to trust it consciously, and the more you will realise how plugged into to the entire human ecosystem, the entire planetary system, the entire solar system, and beyond, you actually are – through your body. It's sort of like turning on your TV one day and suddenly you have access to about a million channels. Where did they all come from? Is there anything good on any of them? The body awakens and our spiritual cable subscription suddenly gets a massive upgrade. We'll need discernment (see Chapter 4 with Ascended Master Hilarion for more on this) to sort out which channels we are interested in watching and which ones are filled with rubbish, but once we have reached that degree of awakened receptivity, we'll have enough spiritual consciousness to be able to sort the real from the reality TV!

Sometimes we'll find a new channel of communication becomes accessible to us spontaneously and naturally as the body awakens. We experience this in those moments when we feel the Divine talking directly to us through life, without any intermediaries or impediments. It might be a transporting sense of the mystical that you feel as something beautiful stirs in your heart when you listen to a piece of music or you have a moment in nature when you sense that everything is alive and bursting with energy – there is so much divine life force around that you can't possibly miss it!

As new channels of awareness become conscious for us, this is also a time when we start to realise that we are dealing with our own personal fears and issues on one level, and as it becomes spiritually useful for our growth, we also begin to experience our body and our selves in a more transpersonal way, as an aspect of the entire human race, for example, or as an expression of planetary consciousness or even, in those rare precious enlightened moments, as an expression of the divine source.

I experienced this recently. Lying in bed one night, I was about to drift off to sleep. I suddenly became aware that my body was far from still even though I felt very restful. Somehow without physically moving, my body was undulating in cascading waves of energy. It was like it was dancing without actually moving. I felt then that those cascading waves of energy included not only my body, but held within that great wave was also the room I was in, all the furniture, the plants and animals outside my window (including some rather noisy possums on a nocturnal adventure), even my cat who was asleep in the lounge room on the other side of the house, and the lounge he was sleeping on, the air in the spaces, the noise and the silence. All of this was connected in one great, big, undulating living wave of energy and consciousness. Then I felt the Divine Mother was underneath all of it, inside all of it, like a character wearing many masks. It was like she was creating the wave, like a great big cosmic washer-woman, flipping a sheet over the clothes line to dry. The waves of energy felt like massive bed sheets being flung open into the air.

Moments such as these, which are unlimited in how they can manifest and be experienced but hold the same essence – an experience of yourself as more than your physical being – are very special. We are no longer strictly identified with our own small stories as an individual. Those individual stories become more about divine adventure and growth and this can help us release fear and become bolder and more passionate about discovering and living our potential. We can challenge our fears and step more deeply into the support and desire of our true inner nature that wants to live and have many types of experiences this lifetime.

Gaining access to greater channels of consciousness and receptivity can also be very challenging. Learning to remain aware and conscious of our energy in personal relationships can be hard enough. Setting boundaries without cutting yourself off from another can be a difficult skill to develop, especially if your body is particularly sensitive, which is often the case for healers, creative types and those naturally inclined towards spirituality and the psychic arts. If something is arising within us that we don't feel comfortable with and have difficulty admitting or accepting as belonging to us (rather than just making it about the other person), then another challenge arises. And that is all just in personal relationship.

If you add another dimension to this and look at your relationship to your whole family system and the spiritual issues that your family has incarnated to work through as a group, for example, then another layer of awareness can open up for you. This may take years of inner work and much attention to dreams and feelings, and yet it could free you and several generations before you and after you from needing to continue with unresolved patterns of dysfunction. Your inner work in that example could contribute to the spiritual liberation of an entire group of souls. All this simply from orienting your spiritual eye to the body, to the light that grows within, trusting in the feelings, dreams, images and dances or music that your body gives birth to, and allowing the healing to happen through you. At the same time, a refusal to let your intellect or logical demands shut off the process is required, as is a willingness to be in the process, without full understanding and with trust, yet also knowing when you need a break, or rest, or to simply live and not be so engaged in the process... Many skills come together to make such healing possible. The body is the sacred temple through which these skills can be learned and applied to create healing.

Let us say that you progressed through the maze of family dynamics and earned the spiritual capacity to relate consciously to the entire human collective. It sounds like a big deal and it is, but it is not so unusual. We are learning how to remain conscious in the face of insurgencies, terrorist actions, advertising power games and political manipulations. This is an individual learning how to relate consciously to greater collectives.

We need a strong anchor to the wisdom of our own feeling nature, to our own dreams and inner truths, to our bodies, to have any hope of standing firm in our centre whilst all the 'hoopla' is going on around us. This takes us into yet another level of personal growth and spiritual power. At this level, we are probably dealing with fear at a far more intense level, less personal and more collective. It takes a high degree of personal consciousness and groundedness in the body to neither resist nor collapse into the collective consciousness of humanity. As the vastness of the body becomes more conscious to us, we realise that it is possible for awakened human beings to become incredibly capable healers. Through trusting in the wisdom of the body, we can act as change agents for planetary healing through our own personal work taking on a more archetypal dimension.

This is work that I would encourage you to trust organically. You will only be guided into the higher levels of this work when you are under the conscious protection of a spiritual teacher who can keep an eye out for you and hold you in their consciousness, absorbing some of the danger of overwhelm for you, if it were to arise. It's a bit like having a swimming coach when you are learning to swim! Once you have enough skill you can dive into deeper waters, but if you are transitioning out of the swimming pool into the ocean, then you might need some new coaching on how to handle that more powerful environment. It is natural that we are a bit shaky in our footing as we master new skills. Being connected to ascended beings consciously is essential before we embark upon transpersonal spiritual work. This is not something that we contrive. It happens naturally as we grow and I mention it here because I am sure that some of you will already be in this process and will appreciate the explanation and confirmation. Others of you might not be there yet but will remember this guidance in the time to come when it is relevant for you.

When we really connect with the body awakening, life gets more inspired. You might feel compelled to journal, dance, create art or somehow consciously express what is happening for you in your inner world without necessarily understanding it logically at first, if at all. You may live with an intuitive sense of your life unfolding to a greater plan rather than necessarily a concrete understanding of what is happening for you and why right now. You may find clues to understanding your process in dreams and meditations, during conscious dance and in your yoga or other wellbeing practices, or you may not. These experiences, including signs given and times when you are asked to trust without understanding, are communications of your body's awakening.

When you feel that these things are making an impact in your world, that your life is changing, then it is not something that is a mere mental exercise in fantasy and imagination (as useful as those things can be sometimes). When there is physical impact, the body is changing, spirit is entering and actively transforming through your body, it is your divine alchemy of body awakening that is occurring. You are surrendering your life to divine genius.

It sounds like a big deal, spiritually, and it is. You are willing to face whatever fires and dragons come your way, and there will be some challenges that make you cower in your boots! That is how we learn to work through fear – confrontation in an appropriate way, backed up by our spiritual knowledge, one step at a time as we learn to apply our wisdom and trust in our own life experiences as all being an expression of the Divine coming to life through us. And I mean all of them, even the challenging doozies that don't seem to hold any divinity at all. A lot of the time, that is going to be a chance to meet your fear, and your attempt to work with it consciously and with love will be the way forward.

As the body awakens, we do become more vulnerable to energy – constructive and destructive. This is because we are shedding skins and learning to be open to all that is, to approach enlightenment from a perspective that is completely embracing of life. It is hard to do when there is pain or cruelty before us, but it is also far more helpful than classifying the physical world as a distraction to be overcome so that our spirit can be free, which may lead us to opt out of life in favour of spiritual growth rather than realising our spiritual growth is meant to be present in the world and serving it.

This realisation can open us to incredible states of bliss, and also greater darkness than we may have encountered consciously before. This is why having a conscious spiritual teacher around you can be supportive, but you can grow through your own practice if you remember the simple practice of regular connection through devotion to whatever it is that makes your heart skip a beat.

If you are getting overwhelmed by negativity that you sense is not only your own, but a symptom of your inability to completely hold your vibration in the onslaught of lower vibrational energies as yet unresolved within yourself, which makes you more vulnerable to the negativity of the world around you, then take heed. The best piece of advice I can give you is to focus on building your personal divine connection to whatever moves your heart. Get your head bowed down on the floor and surrender to whatever higher spiritual power speaks most strongly to you – God, Christ, Mary Magdalene, music, the Universe, yoga, the Goddess, Mother Nature – and ask for divine protection and to be held safe in the forces of unconditional love. Every day ask for the beings that love you unconditionally to guide you and assist you. Within each one of us is the seed of a spiritual master, in various stages of growth, and we can all benefit from the loving presence of a wise and skilled gardener.

ASCENDED MASTER MARY MAGDALENE –
AWAKENED FEMININE

If you have read my *Crystal Angels 444* book, then you'll know that embarrassingly enough, I knew virtually nothing about even the best-known angelic figures before I began my conscious spiritual channelling this lifetime. I would sometimes receive an angelic name in meditation and assume that I was about to connect with a Renaissance artist rather than the presence of an archangel. Considering I would be relying on those same beings for my sanity (no exaggeration!) in only a few years following that time, it was quite a shock to realise that I could go from knowing so little consciously to having such a deep and personal relationship with these beings.

It was similar with Mary Magdalene. I just thought of her as "one of the Marys" from my childhood days at a Catholic primary school. I always loved Mother Mary (whom we shall meet in Chapter 13) but Mary Magdalene seemed a bit beyond me as a child.

As a woman, I grew to love and respect her, understanding her from a more worldly and womanly perspective. I worked with her energy directly in some healings with clients who were particularly connected to her, and the experience was extraordinary. Her energy is exquisite and moves me deeply.

Mary Magdalene is a powerful and sometimes controversial figure in the Christian tradition. In various writings she is acknowledged as the first and most beloved apostle of Jesus Christ, and some jealousy of her close relationship to Jesus is said to have arisen from the other apostles. She is reported as the last woman attending to Jesus at his crucifixion, and the first to his tomb to encounter the mystery of the resurrection. In the Christian teachings she is a powerful though perhaps misunderstood figure. There is some debate about whether she was engaged in prostitution. While, there is no reference as such in the Bible, there have been interpretations which suggested that later on, though the basis for such interpretations has been questioned. Her personal relationship with Jesus is speculated upon, although it seems generally accepted that she was his companion and apostle and an important supportive figure in his life at least, and quite probably his lover also. To me, whilst these possible facts are interesting, they aren't hugely important. Whatever we may make of the various details of her life, her soul light remains as it is.

Mary Magdalene has her own unique vibration. As mentioned in the introduction, all the Ascended Masters work from a singular state of consciousness, dedicated in one purpose together, simply with different ways of contributing to that one person (a bit like cooks in a kitchen working to create one spectacular meal, each with different tasks of preparation and contribution depending on their particular skill sets). Her vibration is powerful and she carries the qualities of devotion to love, independence and strength.

When I tuned in to her to see what she wanted to share with us through this book, a strong image popped into my inner eye. I saw her face, with clear eyes burning with love, and her hands holding a chalice before her. I understood this to have significance on a soul level. As I sat with this image, the expression "the cup of Christ" came to me and I sense her guidance that through passionate devotion we can become the receivers of the

Christ consciousness, vessels for that love and consciousness to flow from in order to relieve the spiritual thirst of the world.

To me this teaching speaks of our emotional body, represented by water, and our physical body, represented by the cup or chalice. The body and its emotional feeling life are our expressions of Divine Feminine intelligence – whether we are man or woman. The teaching means on a practical level that as we cleanse emotional body, our physical body becomes capable of holding sacred water – or divine consciousness – that can impress itself upon our emotional body, replace fear with knowledge and love, and allow that to fill us, and then overflow and nourish the world.

Mary Magdalene helps us clear shame that has shackled us, often manifesting as a belief that suffering is punishment, an indication that we are undeserving and abandoned by the Divine. Her energy cuts right to the core of what keeps us trapped in this undermining belief system and prevents us from seeking out the grace that is constantly reaching for us. Mary Magdalene helps us let go of the wounding of deep shame, and realise that we are worthy of devotion, of great enduring love and dedication and that our divine devotion will be received and responded to with love. We can be nourished by our spiritual passion that becomes a living presence in our bodies.

She also teaches us how to feel worthy and devoted all at once. Devotion can be a tricky concept in the West, though in Eastern traditions, this is usually more familiar. Where women in particular have fought so hard for independence and empowerment, to bow the head to anything can seem repellent, though for some it is a welcome relief from ego.

If you are struggling with the concept of devotion, then I offer this to you as a place to begin your journey – take your time, work with what feels right, dare to try, and seek devotion to that which has no agenda for you other than your own enlightenment (most important!).

That which is worthy of your devotion and will respond with unconditional love might be the Earth herself, the greater being of the Universe itself, music, art, yoga or a living altar which you create with flowers and offerings to the unconditional love that seeks you through your own heart. You may be devoted to a spiritual teacher, living or passed over, and that is fine provided that you feel you are in harmony with your own heart and you pray daily to the spirit beings that love you unconditionally to help you find your way because at some point, that relationship with a teacher might inhibit rather than serve your spiritual growth. If you are devoted to a living teacher, then the wisest of those teachers will help you through that devotion to find the Divine in yourself rather than solely honouring the Divine in them. Remember that and you'll progress swiftly. If you get caught up in the spiritual charisma of a teacher and your devotion feels as though it is leading you away from your heart, rather than closer to it, then it may well be time to move on and find a more worthy recipient for the flow of your devotional love.

Mary Magdalene can help us discern worthy receivers of our devotional love, who won't use and abuse us, but will instead honour our devotion and through that love, help to inspire and support us on our own unique divine journey. She honours the spiritual power in each individual and yet is utterly devoted to a consciousness that is beyond individuality, which is the source of love itself. She is passionate about love, and the politics and power games that seek to obstruct its genuine flow elicit a holy rage in her, the fire of which can burn falsehood clear away, revealing truth.

During her time on earth it is said that she was challenged by the other apostles of Jesus, challenged because she was a woman and perhaps because they were envious of her spiritual, and perhaps also personal, closeness to Jesus. She stood her ground and remained true to what she knew in her heart. She carries the vibration of strength and independence, absolute permission to be one's self, whether that is socially accepted or not, and a realisation that the source of all dwells within all, as the same source. Her energy helps heal spiritual inferiority complexes whilst empowering us to be able to worship the divine light in all of creation, including within ourselves. Her teachings complement those of Jesus and Sacrificial Love that we explored in Chapter 5.

In the New Testament of the Bible, there is a reference to Jesus healing Mary Magdalene, causing seven demons to exit from her. Although it is never stated in the Bible, it is my understanding of this reference to mean a healing and release of the 'demons' of the seven chakras of the body, a release of fear, guilt, shame, grief, lies, illusion and attachment (as writer and chakra-goddess Anodea Judith describes them). It was a divine healing that prepared her for the awakening of the body. I had a short but very clear psychic vision when I heard this reference from the Bible. I saw a flash of spiritual light searing through Mary Magdalene's body and a release of past blockages in each of her chakras or major energy centres in the body, allowing for the wisdom and beauty of each centre to shine forth, triggered by the spiritual light, rather than old pain to obscure the presence and brilliance of the light within her.

As this process unfolds in each of us, even if in a somewhat less instantaneous or dramatic fashion, we tend to have awakening in our perceptive abilities too. Just like it is easier to know where something is on your desk when it isn't overflowing with papers, more space and organisation within can allow for greater clarity and enable you to find that piece of information that you were looking for more easily. So too is the human being capable of perceiving more easily (or accessing those plentiful cable TV channels we talked about earlier) when there is less psychological and emotional clutter held within. As we clear out, we open up. If you are relating to this chapter on Mary Magdalene in particular, even without knowing why, then you may actually be already in this sacred process of body awakening and perhaps even on the cusp of a psychic awakening, which is where the emotional body becomes receptive to non-physical information more consciously.

Psychic awakenings happen naturally as we heal and grow. Some of us are naturally inclined to be psychic. Usually this will be those of us with softer boundaries which may have to be strengthened so that we can experience wellbeing and happiness and not feel at the whim of the moods or feelings of those around us. We can all develop the psychic part of us if we wish to do so. As we clear out our emotional 'stuff', we create more space inside of us with which to receive impressions far and beyond our own opinions derived from past woundings. As we develop, we will be able to refine our ability to tune in and out of different channels if we wish. Provided that we do this with respect for the privacy of others (for example, only tuning in from a place of love rather than being a sticky-beak or coming from arrogance), our psychic work can help us grow spiritually and serve others too.

If we have had fear due to past psychic experiences, either in this or another lifetime, we may have shut off from our abilities or at least limited them greatly. You'll generally sense this as an inner block that prevents you from hearing or seeing. You can ask that any trauma that is blocking your access to your psychic abilities be cleansed, with compassion, mercy and help from those beings who love you unconditionally including Mary Magdalene, if you wish.

Perhaps you tend towards knowing more than seeing, or feeling more than hearing. Psychic abilities have all different flavours and part of the growth process is learning what ways you most clearly receive energetic information. It can save us so much upset and struggle if we realise that we all perceive in our own unique ways and that may be very different indeed from the way others do in a group you are sitting in, for example. I spent many years dealing with self-doubt as I never found anyone who perceived in the ways that I did. I thought that meant I was 'doing it wrong' and also believed that I was being taught incorrectly and I got angry about it. Ah well, eventually I accepted my abilities would operate in their own way, just as the gifts of others would too, and to share that message, using the anger I felt in a more constructive way.

It doesn't matter how you perceive. It may well change and evolve over time, especially if you have a regular (and by that I mean, usually daily) spiritual practice – you may have once been a feeler who has now become more visual for example. As long as you are patient as you do open to perceive more through your feelings, to receive more impressions from the Divine through your personal spiritual cheerleaders, your team of higher guidance, you'll find the process more bearable. We can become incredibly sensitive during times of psychic awakening. We need patience to trust in our own timing. Once you are receiving more consciously, the trick is to practice discerning the quality of information that you tap into, sensing if it is clear and undistorted or if you feel your emotional waters are muddying the impression received, which is easy enough to have happen, even at advanced stages on the path.

Here are my general guidelines to help set off alarm bells and promote caution about taking information too seriously when it isn't actually genuine higher guidance. These guidelines have helped me a lot over the years and I am happy to share them with you. When information is being provided from higher guidance it will be helpful, positive and encouraging (whilst remaining realistic and more often than not, at least a little humorous). It will also be loving and tender without being indulgent and it will be honest and straightforward. It will be useful, simple and clear. If it is not those things, it's not from genuine higher guidance and if it is not from higher guidance it is not reliable information.

I should also note that higher guidance does not advise, they make suggestions. They will not say, "Do this!" They will say, "Have you thought about this possibility?" Genuine guidance will never attempt to take over your free will and personal power. They are connecting with you to help build it, not break it! You'll never have the power of personal will needed to surrender into the Divine (for it can take an enormous degree of will power not to descend into ego fear and instead to trust in the Divine) if it isn't sufficiently developed within you. Your guidance wants to help you grow, not have you follow them as substitutes for the divinity that you are awakening to within.

As we discussed in earlier chapters, it is a mistake to believe that any source of non-physical information is going to be helpful for us here on earth. This is quite simply not true. We do not gain instant enlightenment upon death. If that were the case, what would be the purpose of life? Beings evolve over time and experience and there are plenty of spirits floating about, having a grand old time influencing life on earth without much care for whether or not they are actually helping another. Even sometimes those that do believe that they are helping others are not actually able to do so because they still have a personal agenda, a belief that they know best and can tell you what to do. As we know, higher guidance will never do that. They will suggest options and help you in many ways, but they will never assume your role in life, which is to make choices and decisions for yourself.

Higher guidance is the most helpful guidance because it is genuine and they are totally committed to your own spiritual success. There is no sneaky sabotage or conflicting interest. Your higher guidance are completely in your corner, absolutely trustworthy and deserving of your love and respect, but you MUST be able to tell the difference between your own higher guidance and any random thought or opinion masquerading as guidance when it is not.

No matter whether you feel you can channel at the drop of a hat, or if you are seated before the world's most famous psychic, or if you think that channelling is for hippies and you would be more likely to walk on your hands all day in a perfect handstand, than even have one moment of conscious divine connection, higher guidance is a part of your life, and you will always be able to open to more purity and refinement in your connection with your higher guidance.

Your higher guidance might reach you as a voice in your heart or an impulse or a gut feeling to go this way or that. It might be a place you get to after you talk things through with someone who can just listen to you, and then you know what your truth is – in that moment, it becomes clear. Provided that you call upon your higher guidance each day, you'll be just fine and your awakenings will happen in perfect timing for your path. (You can do that by saying each morning, "I call upon the higher guidance that loves me unconditionally, please be with me this day, guide me and help me for my highest good. Thank you.")

Lower guidance does pop up from time to time in the form of a person who may be doing their best but isn't able to give us genuine higher guidance, or even in the form of information received on the inner planes for those who are psychically awakening. Often when we are most desperate for an answer and would rather run the risk of some dodgy advice than bear the pain of not knowing how something is going to turn out, lower guidance arises, making mischief.

Lower guidance thrives on collective fear, desire and greed. It is dark, dense and will evoke sensations of despair, doubt and pessimism as it is largely unconscious and locked into unresolved wounds of the human psyche – therefore some of its key qualities are victimisation, helplessness, emotional abuse and disempowerment. As we heal these within ourselves, it becomes much more obvious and easier to side step when mischief-making lower guidance is trying to manipulate us. It affects us less and we become aware and able to hold compassion towards it more.

Lower vibrational energy thrives through mass media (especially tabloids, but newspapers and current affairs publications and reality television shows usually demonstrate lower vibrations of cruelty, ego and fear as well). Advertising relies on the lower vibrational energies of your own wounds in order to manipulate the flow of emotional energy and consequently how many will spend their money. Lower consciousness in these examples feeds on fear, pack mentality (keeping up with the Jones's) and emotional manipulation (nothing like a financial crisis to make us want to buy more insurance, become weekend warriors in home hardware stores and take drugs up the nose or in the form of little blue pills to prove masculine potency).

Lower energies leave us feeling that we are never enough, requiring something to be acceptable, whether it be a new car, a bag (that perhaps costs the same amount as a new car), a university degree or a relationship. Guidance from these kinds of vibrations, whether from well-meaning friends or family, or spirits that are advising you through your psychic faculties, are less about real healing and growth, and more about patching over the issues and bolstering the ego. They are intelligent forces, so they can sound convincing! That is why we can only begin to discern at a deep level as the body awakens. The mind can be convinced of many things, but the body, like any animal, tells the truth in its instinctual responses. It knows when something is rubbish, no matter how convincing it may seem to our minds that get all excited only to find out later it was a scheme. It knows love when it feels it. It just knows. If our instincts or our ability to feel them consciously have been damaged by wounding over the course of our human existence, healing with Mary Magdalene and the whole process of awakening the body, being present to and honouring our pain as it arises in this process to be released, is the way to restore them back to their rightful place as the body's natural nonsense-detectors.

Any advice we receive at this lower level is tantamount to a house of cards. We can spend huge time, energy, money and focus on attempting to work with it to gain access to its promised land, but eventually, because it is false and based in ego, it will come tumbling down around our ears. Truth will always prevail, no matter how much lower consciousness may seek to avoid it, sooner or later. These are the get-rich-quick, get-thin-quick, get-enlightened-quick (in a weekend! Yay!) or get-anything-quick schemes that pull us into a tornado of want, wounding and despairing lack of acceptance for the beauty of the present moment, where the Divine dwells, even if hiding its beautiful face deep in our struggles, waiting for us to witness it, as it gives us a big kiss!

As you can see from this discussion, or as you have probably already experienced plenty of times for yourself, lower vibrational energy feels very different to the higher vibrational energy of genuine spiritual presence and guidance. The more we are in the body awakening, the more obvious this distinction is for us. Lower vibrational energy often manifests as either promising the world or predicting the most despairing outcome. Either way it has little interest in your own growth, and is more focused on either making mischief or what it can gain, which is usually power from feeding off the energy of the emotions that it has triggered within you.

Have you ever met someone who seems to shine brighter and feel happier about themselves when another is miserable? Hopefully you don't meet many of these people in your time, but they do exist and lower guidance has a similar modus operandi. These psychic mischief-makers are people or non-physical energies that want to be fed and will seek out those that they can manipulate to feed them. It sounds dark and it is in a way but it is also pretty common, something we all will have experienced (myself included – plenty of times) and something that we can respond to with compassion, growing awareness and treat as an opportunity to practice discernment and develop our free will so that we can build our 'spiritual trust muscles' rather than falling prey to the forces that want to feed off our fear. See how even the darkness can feed the light in us if we so choose?

The gift of going through a body awakening, even though it gives rise to both incredible ecstatic pleasure and sometimes nearly unbearable pain, is that we clear our emotional body and become capable of identifying and stepping around lower guidance, to attract and receive higher guidance that is more helpful to us. With the ability to sense and communicate with higher guidance also comes the ability to sense vibrations at a similar rate of energetic frequency to higher guidance, which includes unconditional love, bliss and divine rapture.

I believe Mary Magdalene to be a powerful teacher of the mystery of rapture, the state of being so in love with the divine presence, that no matter how it manifests, in pleasure or in pain, only the Divine is witnessed and experienced. This is the promise of a completely awakened, spiritually-impregnated body – the capacity be at one with the Divine in this vast field of manifest creation. It's no longer a game of hide and seek with the Divine, the Divine has been found to be everywhere, all at once.

AQUA AURA – CRYSTAL ALCHEMY

I fell in love with Aqua Aura Quartz before I knew it was a partially artificially created crystal. I love Clear Quartz, and the natural quartz in Aqua Aura is often of a very high grade. The quartz is then placed in a near vacuum and bonded with pure gold filaments. The result is a permanent and stunning transformation of Clear Quartz into a radiant light blue with a golden sheen. It is a combination of the powerful healing metal of gold and the master healer itself, Clear Quartz.

There is some debate about artificially-created crystals. Some, like Blue Siberian quartz, are completely created in a laboratory setting. Some affirm that there is healing property in such stones, for others they are not considered to be particularly 'energetically active', certainly not compared to natural stones. I'll leave those decisions up to each individual to determine for themselves. Personally, my first preference is for natural stones, but there are some treated stones such as Aqua Aura that I feel the energetic power of so strongly, that I would not hesitate to explore it further. Aqua Aura Quartz is one of the treated quartz specimens that is generally regarded highly and accepted as a powerful healing stone by many crystal healing practitioners and experts.

It is quite an expensive stone, but even a small piece of it will create a powerful effect in one's energy field. It strengthens the throat chakra, repairs and builds up the energy field and heals holes or tears from violent interactions, physical and emotional abuse including negative psychic effects of drug use, in all of the chakras. It is good to remember that no crystal is a substitute for healthy lifestyle changes though. Much like vitamin supplements are meant to supplement, not replace, a healthy lifestyle, crystals can certainly support our intention to heal and make the healing pathway more accessible to us, whilst helping accelerate and intensify that healing process.

This stone resonates at a beautiful frequency of positive energy and higher consciousness and can strengthen us as we discern (one of the many natural powers of the throat chakra is to discern vibration) lower energies from higher energies and make choices about how we wish to proceed in any given situation. Aqua Aura can help block attempts at lower frequencies to weigh us down in unhelpful patterns of emotional reaction and physical behaviour, and we can all use help with that sometimes! It is the crystal equivalent of having a person around us who encourages us and sees the best in us – not in an idealising, impossibly perfect fantasy way, but in a real, genuine recognition of the light and goodness within. With such a cheerleader in our corner, it becomes easier to think well of ourselves and to cultivate self-esteem. From that place of good inner health on a psychological and emotional level, our immune system is strengthened and we can easily tend towards inner strength, even in the face of challenge or negativity from others. As we grow spiritually, so do our tests in handling the dark and light aspects of the Divine. Any unconditionally loving help we can get is a valuable asset, not just for beginners on the path but for advanced initiate souls especially.

Aqua Aura holds such a high vibration that it helps stimulate transformation. In alchemy, the transformation of lead into gold via the philosopher's stone is the goal.

For spiritual aspirants it is a metaphor for the spiritual path. Lead is the lower nature, dense and inert and gold is the higher nature, the Christ nature, what the aspirant can ultimately become through transformational connection with the mystical philosopher's stone. The philosopher's stone is any object, consciousness or way of being that allows for transformation of our fears into love.

In the particular process of its creation, Aqua Aura undergoes a type of alchemy, subjected to a vacuum in which it is able to bond with gold. The vacuum is the feminine, the holding, the containing, the emptiness and the creative womb in which birth occurs. Aqua Aura becomes a symbol and a catalyst for divine alchemy within us. It represents the alchemical process when natural forms (like our body, or Clear Quartz) are exposed to higher consciousness (through the divine love of Christ consciousness, or gold) and the result is a transformation (our awakened body, or Aqua Aura Quartz). The philosopher's stone is the sacred feminine – for human beings that is our bodies that can contain and give birth, that are capable of transformation, which the spirit, in its absolute perfect nature, is not. Transformation is an art of the Divine Feminine in each of us.

Once we are at a spiritual level where we are interested in working with the Ascended Masters, we will be moving beyond the notion of spiritual growth for our own sake, and entering into the terrain of spiritual growth for the greater good of humanity and our planet. At this point in our evolution, we'll need to get a handle on basic psychic protection and how to manage negative energy, as we discussed above, which we will undoubtedly encounter on and off through our lives – after all, the light is needed where there is darkness and darkness is very attracted to light.

We'll explore the helpful teachings around managing this in Chapter 14 when we meet the Buddha, but for now, it can be helpful to know that Aqua Aura quartz instils a level of divine protection that is the best sort – the protection of consciousness. Aqua Aura quartz helps one develop a state of awareness where it is not necessary to develop a fear of being attacked. Even if you experienced emotional or psychological bullying or other forms of psychic attack early on in your path or later on when you develop enough light that you become of interest to darker forces that are holding back human evolution, there are always constructive ways to deal with a situation so that you grow spiritually. Always.

Whilst we are learning to overcome the dark nature that feeds through fear, that darkness also balances our evolution so that we don't all spontaneously become enlightened and combust into divine flames, destroying all of creation! It is a checking mechanism and the friction between the darkness and light as a result creates the impetus that we need to catalyse spiritual growth in ourselves and others. Everything serves. Even that which we cannot understand at the time.

We can choose to respect that everything serves whilst still playing our part for healing in this unfolding experiment of life. So keeping that in mind, and therefore panic at minimum, Aqua Aura helps us discern more easily if negativity is being directed purposefully at us. With the support in holding higher awareness, rather than collapsing into reaction to that realisation – perhaps with anger, fear or a 'you can't get me, I am so evolved and powerful' ego attitude – we can instead recognise it and act appropriately.

We are able to allow any negativity to be more about the karma of the sender than us. We can respond if we need to, by aligning with our own soul and doing some cleansing work with the Masters (we will explore a powerful technique for this in Chapter 14 with the Buddha which you can use at any time you feel that you are suffering due to negative energy sent your way and are unable to simply let it pass over you). Calling on Aqua Aura in the healing process below however will typically clear most everyday sort of negativity and struggle, from within and from without, which in turn will help to awaken your body and bring to life the divine light within.

HEALING WITH MARY MAGDALENE AND AQUA AURA

You may like to play soft healing music for this exercise, anything that is soothing and non-distracting and will last long enough for your ritual – at least fifteen to twenty minutes. There is plenty of healing music available on my website www.alanafairchild.com under the spiritual store section for sacred music.

Have your mandala or crystal with you. If you wish to have a special offering for Magdalene, you may like to have white or blue flowers in her honour with you in your sacred healing space.

Close your eyes and sit or lay down comfortably.

When you are ready, repeat the following invocation, "I call upon my divine body-soul connection and all beings who love me unconditionally and support the awakening of my body, through connection with my spirit. I call upon the true Ascended Master Mary Magdalene and her healing chalice, the cup of Christ, filled with devotion, commitment, strength, purpose, knowledge, light and truth. I call upon the Angel of Clear Quartz and the Angel of Gold, I call upon the Angel of Aqua Aura Quartz and the higher consciousness and crystalline alchemy of which you are the custodian. I call upon divine grace, healing, cleansing and empowerment now. May my body be cleansed and awakened with kindness, mercy, truth and grace. May my spirit and body be guided to become one body-soul, united in sacred marriage as an enlightened vehicle of Christ consciousness, expressed in my own unique way. Through my own free will, and for my highest good, it is so."

Close your eyes and relax, focusing on the breath and a soft golden blue light that washes around you. It is like resting on the rise and fall of an ocean of light. Take your time, resting on this ocean of light, bobbing up and down with your breath mirroring the rise and fall of the ocean. Stay here for at least 33 breaths.

You then become aware that around you, containing this vast ocean of light, there is a chalice, a sacred cup that your body rests within. It gleams golden, reflecting the light of a great spiritual sun shining down on you. The spiritual sunlight filters through the water, burning away debris and allowing it to become more clear and still. Eventually the water and the light of the spiritual sun become one – clear, golden, peaceful, luminous. Rest in this space for at least 33 breaths. Take your time and just be held there.

When you are ready, repeat this declaration, "I now call upon divine intervention for my highest good. I ask that my body-soul connection be lovingly strengthened, that my body be supported in awakening to its golden nature, that my spirit shed the last restraints to full incarnation and enlightenment upon my divine earthly path. I call upon those beings who love me unconditionally who can assist me in this process with mercy and grace, for my highest good. So be it."

Close your eyes and be back in the chalice, floating in the light-infused waters. As you relax, your gaze naturally drops inwards to yourself and you become aware of a spiritual sun that shines within you too. It shines within each and every cell of your body. It is a vast sun within you now, filing the inside of your body with light so that you become aware that your body is no longer only a physical body, but a large pulsing body of golden solar light, palpable, bright, radiance, substantial.

Just be with the light within – tiny in each cell, flickering, delicate and then also powerful, vibrant, real and vast, as a body of light beyond the apparent physical limits of your body. Allow your awareness to move gently between the tiny microcosm and the vast macrocosm of light within your body.

Stay with the breath as you gently flow between tiny flickering suns in your cells and the vast bright spiritual sun within that shows your body to be so radiant and expansive. For at least 33 breaths, simply acknowledge this light, either just intending to accept its presence, or seeing, or feeling, or sensing it in some way that feels best for you.

After you have connected in some way that feels right for you, say aloud, "I am a body of light and consciousness, this body awakens through the unconditionally loving presence of spirit, welcomed under the graceful protection of the Divine Mother and her face of Mary Magdalene who loves me unconditionally, entering into this temple of her great enlightenment."

You become aware of a beautiful woman with large eyes gazing at you, burning divine love and fire in those eyes. She witnesses you and the light within you. She acknowledges you, smiling and she gently sweeps her hand in front of your chakras, one at a time, cleaning out any old energy that no longer serves you. It gets burned away by the light within you that is ignited to burn brighter with every sweeping motion of her hand.

Stay with what happens for you in this process, whether it is subtle and calm or emotional and challenging, whether you can remain focused or become distracted, just be accepting of your experience and know that it is part of this healing for your body now to awaken at a greater level.

Lovingly, with your hands lightly resting on your heart now, repeat this declaration, "My body, my temple, my soul animal and my soul home, thank you for the gift of life experience. I give you permission to speak your truths and to release your pain and suffering under the watchful grace of the Divine Mother who loves us unconditionally and through the loving help of the true Ascended Master Mary Magdalene and the Angel of Aqua Aura Quartz. Please receive this gift of complete acceptance, love, support and recognition of you now. I release old beliefs and wounds that have kept me separate from you, that have prevented me from acknowledging that you are the key to my enlightened growth this lifetime and that within you is held what I have been searching for all along. Thank you. I love you. So be it."

If energy, thoughts or feelings, sounds or movements emerge, let them happen. Be as wild or as peaceful as you like. Let your body be, without judgment, with compassionate acceptance and if you can, tender affection and appreciation for this sacred animal of the Divine Feminine creation. Then rest for another 33 breaths.

When you are ready, visualise a rich golden energy wrapping around you in a perfect bubble that seals your energy. Close enough that you feel held and spacious enough that you feel you have room to breathe within it. Allow a layer of golden pale blue to line the inside of the bubble.

Take your time, place your hands in prayer at your chest and say thank you to yourself and the spiritual guidance that has been with you in this practice.

When you are ready, open your eyes, wiggle your hands and feet and take your time in grounding yourself, becoming aware of your day-to-day life once more. You may like to walk around, shake out your limbs or bust a few dance moves (easy does it, though!) for a few moments to really move the energy that has shifted around and out of your body.

If you notice aches or pains, vivid dreams or emotional outbursts over the days following this healing, you are simply releasing. Repeat the final prayer to your body above each day for the next three or so days following the process when you may have symptoms of cleansing and release and try to get enough rest, drink enough water and spend some time in nature. Let your body express itself and awaken. Honour your courage and stay true to your process, beloved.

7.

ASCENDED MASTER YOGANANDA (Loving Service) RHODONITE (Awakening Talent)

INITIATION OF EMPOWERED SERVICE

A pink sphere of light appears, with shiny black lines of energy running through it, like living veins. It emanates a loving vibration. From within the core of the sphere, a golden light shines brightly. Within that core of golden light a face appears, with an affectionate expression. A man with warm brown eyes and glowing dark skin, long dark hair. He holds his hand up in blessing and golden light radiates. He laughs with love and joy, with simple happiness. The sphere of pink light with black veins of energy and a golden core becomes a world. A world of love, expression, spiritual fulfilment and deep satisfaction. This is the world into which you now step.

There comes a time on our path when we are moved, empowered, by a deep compulsion to serve others. We may always carry such a desire as a seed in our hearts. The desire to contribute positively to the world might underlie all our actions. Yet there is at some point a shift from that desire as a seed of hope to an ability to bring that desire to life and actually live our desire to serve in a tangible way. That is empowered service.

It might look like a successful vocation as a healer, a published writer, a singer who shares songs of healing with others, a dancer who has found a way to express his or her talents to inspire others. It might not look as formal as this – perhaps it is the generous-hearted woman with wisdom who invites others into her lounge room for tea and a heart-centred chat.

The way we are each meant to serve is whatever we feel is truthful and authentic for us. It is about allowing our divine essence, with the help of the Ascended Masters, to show us how we can most be ourselves and, through that, assist the spiritual evolution of humanity.

Recently I received an email from a young man who wanted to work as a healer. He contacted me to see what I could suggest so that he could make this happen now because he was ready. I admired his spirit but recognised the error in his attitude, one that I had to learn from in years gone past also. We have to be empowered to serve. It is not something that we decide to do from an ego centre. We have to surrender into it; usually over and over again if we wish for the way that we are serving to evolve and become increasingly effective and powerful.

I remembered having once held a similar attitude to that young man. When I started my work in the metaphysical field this lifetime (and by that I mean becoming a professional healer and charging for my work after some years of study with a spiritual teacher and doing free practice readings for others), it was a leap of faith.

Prior to that leap, I was working in a job that I hated, for an employer that I didn't like or respect and I felt myself in deep internal conflict, wondering what the hell I was doing! I had used my psychic abilities to win the job, answering the interview questions from my ego and not from my heart. The interviewer was very impressed with me. I wasn't impressed with myself at all, but I felt desperate to try to find some work that wouldn't destroy my soul. I wasn't ready to take that complete leap into a full-time spiritual vocation obviously, or it would have been happening. At the time I believed applying for that particular job was the best compromise I could summon. I still remember the job advertisement in the paper for that position. It called for someone 'with heart' and I felt it was written especially for me. Fairly soon I saw that the image that I had bought into, mostly out of despair and hope, and the reality of the job, were very different.

So why didn't I leave to pursue my own path rather than remain in a situation that was so repugnant to me? The truth was that I wasn't ready. I still carried so much fear about how I would survive. I had taken a leap of faith in putting myself 'out there' as a healer around nine or so months earlier and fallen flat on my face, financially speaking. I just hadn't earned enough to support myself by working solely as a healer. I was fearful that this would happen again, that I still wasn't ready.

I felt despair because I knew that simply landing a job elsewhere wasn't going to change anything. In my heart I longed to work for my (higher) self. I found my boss' continual need to have her ego stroked to be frustrating. I felt a lot of resentment in working for her. I didn't throw myself completely into the job because I didn't really care about it. They weren't my finest months, I have to say. The problem was that I felt like I wasn't really living the life I was meant to live and I wasn't happy about it.

I tried to find the good in the situation however. I figured that whilst I was there, I should try and find the spiritual side of the situation. During that time I did a lot of work on my own fear and the other issues that I had that had led me into that situation in the first place. It was hard work and every day was a struggle with myself, but I did my best in that situation, knowing it was the most that I was capable of manifesting at the time.

After months of internal suffering, feeling so degraded in that job and yet helpless and incapable of manifesting something else for myself, I prayed to spirit for help again. I had worn myself out through suffering and couldn't fight anymore. So this time my prayer was all the more powerful because I had surrendered.

Following that prayer, after nearly nine months in that job, I had a powerful sensation as I walked to the office entrance one morning. I felt physically restrained, as though I couldn't actually walk through the door. It was such an overwhelming sensation. I felt like I had to summon all my willpower to force myself to do it. I could just barely manage it and the urge to simply scream as I forced myself to walk through the door was very strong indeed. Somehow I managed to force myself to go into work but I could sense the end was near.

Later that day I saw a couple of the management consultants that I had been lucky enough to meet through my work in that office. Three in particular were just so lovely and we had connected through a mutual love for spirit and a recognition of integrity in each other that was sadly lacking in the place where we all (temporarily) were working. I ended up working with all three of them to varying degrees some time later when I had established my spiritual practice. At that time however, one of them kindly but truthfully reflected to me that I wasn't looking like myself, that I had somehow faded since working there. I knew exactly what she meant.

Something in me had changed in the months I worked in that company. I had lost my radiance and happiness in a visible sense but inside I had been biding my time, gaining strength and summoning the anger and frustration that I had been feeling on a daily basis into an inner fire. I realised that I had more personal power within me than I had claimed thus far and I could choose to put my relationship to spirit before any other fear that I had and reach out again and again until I found my way. I felt more ready within myself to break free and I felt that it was really impossible to continue in that situation. I decided that I would no longer force myself to walk through that office door, and that the uncertainty of what would happen had to be easier to bear than the suffering of working in a situation that felt like it was killing my soul.

That afternoon, I put my intention to the test and called a healing centre near where I lived at the time, in Sydney's inner west suburb of Balmain, and asked if they had any vacancies for psychic readers. The owner said yes and asked if I could come in to do a reading for her as an 'audition', which I promptly did that afternoon. She offered me a job immediately after her session with me, working two days a week as a psychic healer in her healing centre. I knew it was my next step and I accepted. I didn't worry that it was two days a week of uncertain income compared to a full-time paid job. It just didn't matter to me at the time as I knew it was my way out. I called my employer from home that evening to resign immediately and never set foot in the office again.

I felt relieved, exhilarated and free, terrified and uncertain. I was in more financial debt that I had ever been in, living a more expensive lifestyle than I ever had before and I had to support myself financially. There were times in the coming months when I had something like twenty cents in my bank account, and to say I was fearful for my security would be an understatement. Although when I would confront the fear that I would be destitute, I would feel peaceful inside, sure that this would not occur. Somehow when I needed money to pay my bills, or buy food, clients would appear and I would be okay financially whilst doing work that I felt I was born to do. Even so, I felt deeply challenged on a daily basis – but at least I felt like I was moving forwards on my path.

However with the deep wounds that I had, I had to work very hard to let myself trust. As I went through that process of self-healing, I was confronted on a daily basis with intense fear and anxiety attacks. That continued with great intensity for around eighteen months, which goes to show how deep my fear actually was at the time. It was a difficult phase, to put it mildly, but it was a necessary initiation. It was never about whether or not spirit would support me, it was about learning how to let go of a lower vibrational fear for my own survival that I had taken on in my childhood, so that I could attract life experiences at a higher vibrational level, to be more surrendered into divine will. That higher vibrational level would include a life that was anchored less in fear and more in loving trust. Even through all the fear, I still had a part of me within that was peaceful – but it needed to grow, to become more potent than the fear – if I was to be able to resonate at the vibration that I needed to live the life I wanted to live.

I wanted to work for spirit, to live and breathe what I wanted to share with others. I wanted to be genuine, authentic and live in integrity with my spiritual values. I had learned a valuable lesson through the experience that I had working in the management consultancy. Even if I was having trouble trusting, there was no other way really. To attempt to gain something for myself, with questionable integrity in how I used my psychic abilities too, would only ever yield a poisonous prize, and at too great a price. I so often felt guidance coming through about trust and surrender and letting things work out. I had to learn to embody that truth, to live it completely.

I wouldn't have been ready any sooner to confront my own fear though. I had to be ready to face my own demons and even then, with conscious connection to spirit and a loving partner that respected and believed in my spiritual gifts, and even many successful sessions with clients where I knew spirit had come through me and helped that person in a meaningful way, it was very hard work to outgrow my old patterns.

I realised, quite some time later, that the entire experience had been on-the-job training for my work as a spiritual teacher that would come to fruition later on. I was learning through my own personal healing journey, which in turn empowered me to help others. I couldn't have helped human beings stuck in the incredible stickiness of fear and doubt if I hadn't developed the spiritual strength required to emerge from the depths of it myself. I have always believed that our own personal work is the foundation from which we can serve, and at that time, I was building my foundation. It took many more years than I would have ever expected, but what I feel when I look back at that time is not judgment or criticism but a profound respect for what I endured when there was no clear sign that I would actually get through it all. I am grateful for that stubborn streak within me that kept me going no matter what I feared.

I also learned that no matter how aware we are spiritually, we have to be able to penetrate the density of our old wounds with the light of our awareness, otherwise the awareness will remain within us, not able to burst forth and set fire to our lives, burning old forms to the ground and stimulating new growth.

We have to do our part, of course, but that does not include 'making stuff happen', which unfortunately seems to be the content of many new age empowerment teachings based on creating your own reality. To me, using the mind to visualise and create an outcome is only one step on the path. There is a far greater leap beyond this where we learn to surrender and trust in the greater divine vision, which is so much more intelligent than our own limited perspective. Then we take inspired action based on the impulses received by our heart, rather than attempting to direct the flow of the Divine as if we somehow know better.

What I came to learn, slowly, and what the young man who emailed me may also need to learn, is that we cannot make our service path happen. It is not an ordinary job. It is a vocation, a calling. It is not defined or determined by us, our job is to open up and receive it, to allow it to 'become' through our willingness, action and, often, patient endurance as we grow the inner fire through our struggles, eventually becoming strong enough to burst free. A vocation, as opposed to a more typical type of employment, is an expression of our divine relationship. As such, it requires trust, surrender as well as responsiveness and action from us, over and over again.

I also learned that life responds to our desire to serve immediately. It just might not look like that straight away. We ask to step onto our life path and serve and suddenly we are confronted with all our issues through a difficult relationship or challenging life situation. These are responses from the Divine saying, "Look, we want you to thrive and to step into your power but these issues need to be sorted out first, then you'll be at the right vibration to receive the empowerment to serve at a new level, so let's get on with this stuff for now."

Empowerment to serve happens when we are ready. What we have to become ready for is not usually what we expect. We can believe that we just need to do the course, or have the skill set and suddenly, voilà, clients will appear. Doing courses and training may be a part of our process, or it may not. I have done lots of different types of training in my life, but for what I do most and best, I have received little, if any, formal training at all. It is a talent in the soul and it unfolded when I was ready for it. I have no doubt it will continue to do so in its own unpredictably perfect way. So whilst training can be an important part of our process, it might not be so in the way we expect. It might be life training just as much, if not more so, than more formal spiritual study.

There are plenty of healers with healing ability who are waiting to be empowered to heal. There are plenty of writers who have helpful messages to share, perhaps even books already written, but they are not yet empowered to share them. I know of talented healers who have advertised and rented spaces in trust, only to end up with huge bills and few clients. It is not for a lack of ability on their part. They have just not yet taken the initiation into empowerment to serve. I have had material completed that took nearly ten years to be finally published and begin to reach people in a more significant sense. Was it for lack of consciousness on my part? No, I know now what I knew then, and although my understanding and wisdom has somewhat grown in that time, I can also recognise the value of what I created back then and acknowledge its usefulness. What has changed has been my own readiness to trust, which required a shedding of issues of fear and control, and a surrender into divine timing. All things come in time. More quickly so when we let go.

We can only prepare ourselves to be ready for it to happen through us. Empowered service is not about being good enough nor is it about being less spiritual than those who are already empowered in their service, even if we are not as yet. Empowered service is an expression of divine timing, readiness in our own path and the unfoldment of our divine life plan. My mother used to say to me that 'every dog has its day' and this is true – we are meant to help at the right time, in the best way, and each of us will manifest our heart's desire, but it needs to happen according to a higher plan in order to serve. There is divine genius expressing itself through a higher plan that governs the unfolding of human evolution. This determines who steps forward and when, as well as when we need to wait for whomever is to go before us to fulfil their tasks. Can you sense how we are all in this together, working as a team? You are just as much a part of that divine plan unfolding as me or anyone else.

ASCENDED MASTER YOGANANDA – LOVING SERVICE

The great sage and Ascended Master Yogananda is known to many through his engrossing spiritual book, *Autobiography of a Yogi*. When I read this book I immediately loved 'my spiritual brother' as I call him. I pray to him often. He is funny and affectionate and a loving guide to many on the path.

Yogananda was deeply devoted to his spiritual teacher, whom he loved passionately. In his book he chronicles his youth spent in defiance of his elders, travelling about India, seeking his guru or true spiritual teacher. On the way he meets many remarkable characters and tells stories that truly stretch the bounds of belief – in the best possible way. He is funny, human, spiritually talented in numerous ways and capable of a seemingly endless devotion to the Divine Mother. His story of his triumphs and his openness about his failures moved me and also made me laugh.

Yogananda had a vision in his youth, a vision of a white house on a hill near an ocean. It was unlike anything that he had ever encountered in India. For many years, he stayed close to his spiritual teacher, occasionally indulging his curiosity by travelling around the country to meet famed saints and sages, which are about as plentiful in India as celebrities are in Los Angeles. He always returned to his beloved teacher however, with his focus on trying to live his teachings and build his connection to the Divine Mother, calling to her for comfort during the various struggles he had.

Eventually, Yogananda was asked to serve the teachings of his beloved teacher in a particular way. He was asked to leave behind his beloved homeland, and travel to a country where he hardly spoke the language and somehow also to teach. He was asked to take the teachings of yoga to America. Daunted, but willing through faith and trust, he accepted his mission.

His humorous and touching stories continued as he chronicled the journey. He shares stories of miraculous healings and spiritual offerings of grace that touched his path and allowed him to accomplish some truly incredible feats. By allowing the genius and capacity of spirit to flow through him he was able to lecture in a non-native language on vast spiritual topics to thousands of enthralled Americans. Those teachings have since flourished into the yoga movement that many practice now in local fitness centres. That is an extraordinarily helpful legacy for millions of people!

Eventually his vision of a white house translated into physical reality also. It became his spiritual centre on the east coast of America. He sensed it long before it was meant to be – and he grew greatly before he was ready for it. When he was ready, he was empowered to teach thousands of people and build an inspirational link between America and India that has supported the integration of Eastern and Western cultures, still happening in our current spiritual evolution. He had little clue he would ever be doing such work. He just loved the Divine and focused on his spiritual practice, trusting in the guidance he felt in his heart (even if it meant being a rebel at times). He truly was a servant of the Divine surrendered completely and willing to say yes to whatever the Divine asked of him, even if he didn't want to do it (like leave his teacher to journey to the other side of the world, or earlier on in his life, sit for exams that he was sure he would fail, but miraculously did not) and that is what empowered him.

For those of us that wish to embark upon a vocational dedication of our lives to empowered service, being capable of effecting a positive contribution to the evolution of humanity through our life's work, we need willingness and determination. Yogananda demonstrated a determination towards his goal of god realisation, as he put it. He saw the Divine as the only goal ever worth pursuing. That was the truth behind all of his actions. Even as a child when he challenged his sister by saying that the Divine Mother always would give him what he wanted, he silenced her disparagement of the sentiment, by praying to the Divine Mother to bring to him the two brightly-coloured kites that he could see floating in the distance. A mysterious wind brought them right to his grasp, much to his satisfaction and his sister's shock! It was not about the kites, it was about his utter faith in the Divine.

So whilst I hold respect for the sentiment of the young man wanting to serve and get his spiritual vocation unfolding, and for all of us that hold that desire to be with the Divine and live active spirituality in our lives, I also offer what I have learned from my own experiences and from the beloved Yogananda's extraordinary life story. This is that we need to empower ourselves with readiness and then act upon the inspiration that comes, rather than trying to control how and when it happens. It is not about forcing the hand of fate, but preparing for it. It can seem like a fine line at times, and Yogananda could never be accused of sitting around waiting for enlightenment! He pursued it through dedicated practice, fuelled by a passionate desire unmatched by even the most ardent lover. However he did not try to force the hand of the Divine. He didn't try to make his life happen, his effort went into becoming one with the Divine and allowing it to happen through him. That is the path to divine empowerment, where we become surrendered instruments through which the Divine can do what it wishes – we are then empowered by the great and only real power – the Divine itself.

Upon the discovery of Yogananda's body after his passing, the physician called in to examine the body made an unusual commentary. He noted that weeks after his passing, the body remained fresh rather than decaying at the usual rate after death. He had no comment to make about how that could be, but simply noted it. Yogananda had allowed so much divine energy to flow through him and through his empowered service, that even with the withdrawal of spirit from the body, it continued to burn with life. Imagine what a body so drenched in divine energy could offer in terms of spiritual comfort and reassurance to those who struggle to find peace within during their lifetimes on earth. He vibrated at a particular frequency in which the Divine could live and thrive, for the benefit of many.

If you feel in your heart that this is a way that you wish to serve, to awaken the body as filled with living spirit, which is the cutting edge spiritual path to support the evolution of humanity at this time, then the healing process below and the discussion in this chapter will support you in this process.

What Yogananda can help us remember is that the soul is not bound by the ways of the world. He accomplished many tasks which should not have been possible, according to 'normal' ways of the world. These tasks were attained through divine grace, allowed to operate because of his faith, which empowered him to serve.

I don't want the story that I shared with you of my own struggles early on to compromise your faith. For me, that is how I learned trust and developed compassion for the human experience. It was essential training that helped me learn how to find my way back to the Divine even when deep in darkness. How could I help another on that path if I hadn't learned through first hand experience what it was like and how to navigate it for myself? I had to learn how to heal through such an experience so that I could assist others too.

For Yogananda, he tested himself and his fears against his spiritual guidance time and time again before he found his teacher and felt that his prayers were finally being answered. For you, it may be a deep journey of developing trust in order to become empowered to serve. Or perhaps you developed that trust in another lifetime and in this lifetime you do not need to repeat the lesson for some purpose or other, and so your vocation opens up more easily for you.

The deciding factor is the divine soul and what it needs for its growth. So if you are meant to teach or heal, and you sense this in your heart, then that is what you will be doing, no matter whether it is manifesting in the way you imagined it would or according to the timing you wanted, or not. Oftentimes the most unexpected twists on our paths bring us more joy than anything we could have dreamed up for ourselves. Trust gets us there.

This can happen in big ways – where you leave a life you thought you had to have in order to live the one you are meant to live – and yet we can serve our path in smaller ways too. An example of an unexpected soul expression in a small way happened for me some years ago when I was in quite a delicate state, having gone through a deep spiritual process and feeling extremely open and sensitive energetically. I chose to shop for the groceries for dinner that night at my relatively quiet independent local supermarket, just down the road from my home, rather than the larger market in a shopping centre nearby. The thought of having to summon up enough energy to not be affected adversely by 'crazy shopping centre energy' was just a bit much for me at the time.

In the much smaller local store, there is a relatively small product range, so whilst I was perusing the olive oil and attempting to find a locally-sourced product, an elderly lady with perfectly coiffed silver-white hair, lovely make-up and a light perfume, dressed impeccably, came and stood beside me. I was in my own little world of reading labels when I felt her watching me. I looked up and smiled at her and went back to reading when she suddenly burst out, almost as a confession, "I don't know what to choose either."

I was a bit surprised by her outburst, and she seemed to be also. I replied that the range of products was much smaller here so I was having trouble finding a local product, but that this was preferable to venturing to the much larger chain-store supermarket nearby, as it would have just been too overwhelming for me today. A look of relief passed over her face and with so much gratitude she said, "I am glad it's not just me."

We smiled and parted ways. I contemplated this little encounter as I paid for my purchases and headed home. With her perfectly groomed appearance, I wondered if it was a challenge for her to feel the less perfect shadow side of living in modern western culture – confusion and overwhelm in the face of so much choice, so much stuff and so much information and noise. To be confused or just not up to dealing with it all sometimes might not be so perfect at all, yet she certainly isn't alone in her vulnerability. Perhaps that sense that a younger, and therefore supposedly stronger or more energetic woman could have similar feelings seemed to give her a sense of permission for her own experience that helped her feel less guilt and more peace. It was a five-second healing session in the supermarket aisle.

For me, I just marvelled at how a throwaway comment that I made could bring such relief to another and then I felt a little sad because I realised that she might have been very alone in her difficulties, prior to that. Yet shopping for olive oil brought her some peace, and me some yummy dinner, as well as a good feeling that someone I chanced to engage with that day was that bit happier for the experience with me.

The soul is infinitely creative in how it will bring healing and love to the world. I always say to my clients, especially those that are healers, never underestimate exactly how much you may touch others – it may happen deeper than you realise and stay with them for years. I have lost count of the number of times that clients have called or emailed me, eight, nine, even ten years after a meeting, with thanks for something that I had said all that time ago, that didn't always seem that important to me at the time, but I shared anyway, and ended up meaning something to the client in a way that I could never have anticipated. It wasn't me that created that, I was empowered to offer it because I had learned to allow the Divine to serve through a willing channel – me.

RHODONITE – AWAKENING TALENT

Rhodonite is an opaque dark pink stone with black markings through it. It is often tumbled or available in spheres and is neither a cheap nor particularly expensive stone. It resonates with a vibration of love and strength, working methodically and over a long period of time to dissolve emotional patterning that would prevent us from being empowered to serve, and then building an emotional vibration of confidence to listen to and act upon our heart's guidance.

Our readiness to serve can have unexpected effects. As we embark upon the path to empowerment to serve, it is not only challenges that we encounter. There is a stirring of more life within us that can awaken talents that we didn't even know we had. I 'burst into song' as one of my dear friends describes it, as a method of offering healing energy through my voice. I loved to sing as a child and felt that I was supposed to sing for others somehow, but not really feeling like a pop star, I just couldn't get my head around how that was supposed to happen. I also fluctuated throughout my youth between hiding my voice and rarely singing at all, to climbing up on stage and singing solos. I spent many years dealing with the numerous emotional responses that I had to my own voice, healing layers of judgment, shame and silencing, to be able to come a neutral place where I just open my mouth and let the Divine flow through me as sound for healing, which is what happens now. This began to happen without me understanding the bigger picture of how it could work, I was just focusing on getting on with my personal healing work and the rest happened naturally.

The process is the same for many of us and is a bit like scraping excess dirt and pulling out nearby weeds, so that a hidden seed can be free to sprout and grow. Once you were de-weeding, the next moment, an unexpected fresh green shoot is sprouting above ground. You nurture it and eventually it reveals what kind of plant it is to you. That is the awakening of divine talent within us. The power to heal and nurture that Rhondonite provides for us supports us in taking this approach to awakening our innate abilities.

In fact, Rhodonite goes a step further – the step beyond awakening and into application. Although I could sing since I was a child, I struggled to accept my voice and apart from some inspired moments in solitude, I was a long way from singing freely. Being able to confront the fear that sometimes I might sing an off-pitch note and reveal my imperfection in a very public way was an important part of this process. After singing a few imperfectly pitched notes in public, which I seemed to notice more than anyone else seemed to notice, my life managed to carry on, and the world didn't end. What could happen then was a growing understanding of how to apply this talent in service to my soul. I took the seed of music within me, and began applying it, learning as I went. This is the practical application of talent, to refine and develop it into a method of service, that Rhodonite encourages us to undertake.

I have come not to fear the surprises in my life direction – they happen too often now for me not to accept them. Those completely unexpected twists in my life are sometimes most enjoyable, and at other times I need to grow to accept them. Even then, I like that the Divine doesn't care much for how we think things should unfold and has an infinitely more interesting way of expressing itself through us. It could be called a bit of creative 'showing off' on the part of divine genius, a kind of 'wait 'til you see the unexpected twist in this story and how it will all work out with such brilliance'. It's like living in a movie written by the most creative screenwriter ever.

Rhodonite helps us with the strength of character and the healing of the heart (including our sense of self-worth and deservedness as well as our willingness to give of ourselves) that are essential to applying our talents in the world. This is really important. There are so many incredibly gifted people in our world, lacking in the capacity to bring those gifts to life in the world for various reasons. Rhodonite can help heal the blocks and activate the talents, as well as the ability to put them to use in the world, according to what serves the soul purpose of that individual.

It can also help us tap into a very deep inner drive and determination, which we will need when confronting obstacles in the uncovering and expression of our talents. We need faith stronger than our doubts and fears. Rhodonite helps us find a genuine spiritual motivation behind our exploration of talent that keeps it in perspective – helping us remember that it is about service to the Divine, not inflating our own ego, whilst supporting us in developing a strong connection to the Divine to sustain us in those dark moments of self-doubt that we will encounter on any genuine journey of spiritual growth.

I remember hearing one famous pop-star/actress in an interview saying that much of what drove her to express her talent was the desire to be admired. I found this surprising. She was one of the most famous actress/singers in Hollywood. That was a huge need for admiration! I reflected upon what drove me to want to develop and express whatever talent I could discover within me. The admiration that can come with doing so can be a bit embarrassing to me, as I am fundamentally a shy person with a strongly introverted streak, despite appearances to the contrary where I regularly end up singing and speaking in public. However the positive feedback that people have shared with me about my work helping them in some way moves me very deeply.

Fortunately overcoming feelings of shyness or embarrassment is easier when we cultivate the belief that the work is not really about ourselves at all but about the divine genius. I feel honoured and privileged when I hear comments about how people have been benefited from something that has been created through me. I feel humbled to be a channel through which such assistance can come. I realise very clearly when I hear of the help that has been gained, that that is why I do what I do. The compulsion within me is to be what I am. The reason that I have that compulsion is to serve the spiritual growth of humanity in the best way that I can, even if I don't always know what that will look like in advance. That keeps me going when I am moving through painful initiations and keeps me grounded during blissful expansions of consciousness.

Rhodonite helps us maintain this perspective – of figuring out why we want to grow, and keeping us on purpose whilst supporting us as we heal the inner blocks we have to discovering and sharing our talents. This combination of healing effects has a positive side-effect – it also helps us to attract through our openness, the people, situations and opportunities that we need to pave our way in the world, sharing our uniqueness with others in service. Rhodonite is like loving spiritual dynamite that clears the way and also like a magnet in that it attracts to us what we need to move forward.

HEALING WITH YOGANANDA AND RHODONITE

This healing is for empowered service. This is not just for those of us with a passion to be healers, artists, visionaries or leaders in some palpable way, it is for all of us who want to serve the divine plan and become all that we can possibly be, to honour our potential. There is a saying that life is our gift from God and what we do with it is our gift to God. Empowered service is the ability to make something from your life – to return the gift of it as a living work of art, reverence, play, devotion, love...whatever most moves you.

Start by finding either your crystal or mandala and a place where you can comfortably move around so that you can take several steps in a spiral motion. You can place your mandala and/or crystal (and photo of Yogananda if you wish) at the centre of your 'work space'.

As usual, you will need to take your phone off the hook, put your mobile phone on silent, close your email program and maybe hang a 'please do not disturb' sign on your door. You can however also choose to do this ritual healing in a private space in nature if you are lucky enough to have access to such a place.

Start by standing comfortably, or sitting if you prefer, and placing your hands in prayer at your heart centre, saying, "I call upon the true Ascended Master Yogananda who loves me unconditionally. I call upon his spiritual lineage of teachers. I call upon the Angel of Rhodonite and the loving support of Mother Earth. I ask for healing, grace, awakening and courage, opportunity and strength. I ask for the empowerment to serve, according to divine mercy and grace, for the highest good, so be it."

Choose to either be sitting or standing. If you can comfortably close your eyes, do so, otherwise gaze softly in front of you, in a comfortable fashion without focusing on any one thing, allowing your inner gaze to become awake, your outer gaze softer and more diffuse.

Become aware of a warmth at your heart, and then slowly also at your feet. Perceive that a dark pink light with a glowing golden centre is opening up at your heart and in each sole of your feet. Be patient and breathe in and out as the light grows. You may like to take around 33 breaths.

When you are ready, open your eyes and if you have been seated, now it is time to stand up. Sense the presence of the deep pink light with a golden core between your feet and the earth, like a magnetic loving layer of bouncy energy. Slowly begin to move in whatever direction feels good for you, right or left, in a small circular motion around the centre of your ritual space where the mandala or crystal is present. Move one foot after the other, in a gentle, meditative walk. Imagine with each step, the light under your foot grows as you lift your foot and is gently spread upon the earth with each downward step as your foot is placed on the ground.

It can be challenging to move so slowly. Breathe in and step, breathe out and place the foot down. Keep your visualisation or intention if you find it hard to visualise. The foot lifts, the light grows and flows into the earth as the foot is lowered. Again and again.

Slowly allow your circle to spiral outwards. Circle a little further away from the centre with each step. Stay aware of the light at your heart and your feet. If you are struggling to do this practice, which is more advanced than it may sound, take your time and simply stand in one place, focusing on the light, in your heart and your feet, growing as you breathe.

After around 33 breaths, stop moving if you have not done so already and place your hands at your heart centre in prayer position.

Say the following declaration, "I now choose of my own free will to walk the loving steps of empowered service in my life. I am willing to be guided through unconditional love and divine mercy and grace. Help me live into all that I am, to fulfil my divine potential that I may dedicate this gift of life to the great universal source, that I may remember myself to be divine, that I may serve others in that quest also. May I be a vessel for divine love upon this earth. I now accept the preparation and the learning that I require that I may access my talents more fully in this lifetime and apply them successfully, at the highest level of consciousness possible. Through my own free will, so be it."

Release your hands and begin to move back towards the centre where your mandala/crystal lies – if you have stepped in a spiral outwards, simply and slowly retrace your steps. As you stand before the centre of your ritual space again, gazing at the mandala or crystal, you may like to let your arms move into prayer or express yourself through your arms with soft, flowing movements that allow the graceful energy of your heart to speak through your body. If you like dance or tai chi, you may like to use those movements now.

As you gently move your physical body, the deep pink light with golden core fills you and overflows through all parts of your being.

If you like to sing, whether you think you have a good enough voice or not, you may like to sing as you move, letting music or sound just come out of you without it having to be perfect or thought out first. You may like to speak or simply to be still and quiet, receptive and even sitting quietly. Trust what feels right for you.

Take around 33 breaths for this process, or whatever feels good for you.

When you are ready, place your hands in prayer again and say thank you. Place the book open at the page with the mandala facing up, where you can connect with it, perhaps under your pillow on the evening following your healing ritual. Notice what unfolds for you in the days, weeks and months following this healing ritual. Whether in obvious opportunity or the opportunity hidden in challenge as issues and old pain surface, your work will have stimulated growth for you.

You can repeat the above healing process again if you wish to work through those issues that are arising. You may like to journal and possibly also complete the healing of Lady Nada and Rhodochrosite in Chapter 3 if you are finding the emotional process challenging for you. Have faith. That which is precious is worth enduring struggle to liberate and you are being helped, dear one. It is your right to shine this lifetime. Give yourself permission to go through the process necessary to get to that place. It is not only you that benefits from it, but the entire human race.

8.

ASCENDED MASTER KUTHUMI
(Planetary Consciousness)
MOSS AGATE (Earth Healing)

INITIATION INTO PLANETARY HEALING

Swirling patterns of green light coalesce and form a living globe. It pulsates with energy. Loving beings are drawn to it, to help it grow. With their support, it expands as though breathing, and a harmonious sound emerges. The sound grows stronger until the deep green sphere of light breaks open and rays of golden light fan out from within, like rays of an inner sun. A beautiful harmony of rich gold and deep green light cascades into your heart.

Like the little Russian dolls that fit inside of each other, we are beings held within the consciousness of a greater being, who is in turn held within the consciousness of yet another greater being again and so on. We are whole within ourselves and yet we are a part of something more. We have free will through which we can choose how we respond to events in our world and our individual lives, yet there are movements of greater living beings – like planets and solar systems – that influence our fate.

We can choose to recognise that we are divine and also part of the human community and that together we create the world around us by growing into divine human beings, on the same path as the Ascended Masters. In this age of technological communication and accessible travel, which can make the world seem like a global village more so than ever before, we can experience more of our planet, more of her mystery and her raw, extraordinary beauty. We can develop a sense of ourselves as individual and as part of a community, even of a planetary system and solar system! We can start to experience the earth as our sacred mother and home base for our education into becoming divine human beings.

The soul of the earth, sometimes referred to as Gaia, is growing as she expresses her creative intelligence through nature. Nature teaches us a lot. It is the art and science of a vast, powerful divine being – the Earth herself. In another sense, it is her living gospel, her wisdom teachings. It teaches us not only about the being of Gaia herself, but also about our own being, because we as divine human beings in the making are a part of her too, a blend of the stuff of stars, the Divine Masculine light, and the sacred Divine Feminine in manifest creation of the earth, the substance of our bodies. As they are joined together, through adoration, love and respect, they become the divine human fusion of a Christ.

Learning to read Gaia's gospel of nature helps us respect her, revere her, and begin to bear witness to her beauty, endless creativity and uniqueness. It helps to bring love of the spirit that can perceive the truth, the reality within the form, into the form itself. Learning the wisdom of Mother Nature helps us facilitate loving union of spirit and flesh into one sacred radiant expression of the Divine. The mind boggles at the thought, which is why these truths can only be truly accessed with a superior instrument, that of the heart.

It is the heart that opens up the mysterious teachings of nature, and comes to feel their wisdom. Nature teaches us about cycles of life and death. She teaches us about letting go of that which no longer serves, through winter, through death and sometimes through the extinction of species (sometimes through extinction she teaches us to fight for what should be preserved too). She teaches us about adapting and surviving – or even thriving – through adaptation and mutation of species. Through her diversity she teaches us about opening our minds to perceive beauty in so many different forms. She teaches us of the endless variety of life and the many forms of instinctual intelligence that allow so many beings of differing qualities to function as an ecosystem, something that humanity must learn as part of the divine-human awakening process.

Apart from all that wisdom, there is also the healing that can come through her beauty. Nature's creations can be shockingly beautiful. Sometimes a photograph will pop up on Facebook or in an email or I'll see an animal out and about whilst walking (Australia is absolutely thriving with wildlife) and I will be startled by its strangeness and beauty. Absolutely speechless, I'll just stare at it, mesmerised by the creative genius behind that creature's appearance and behaviour. I probably look like a crazy person, stopped dead in her tracks on the street, hypnotised by a bug on a leaf, but the sweetness of that vision is too intoxicating to resist.

To have those moments where I just see evidence of the Divine Feminine through her creations is a sacred communion that fills me with indescribable emotion. In the Hindu tradition it might be called 'darshan' which is to be given the vision of a holy person. To me, Mother Nature is an expression of the Divine Mother, a holy being in her own right. In the Buddhist Tantra tradition she is known as 'Loachana', a great female Buddha who holds the consciousness of equanimity. To witness her body – her physical form – with respect for the spiritual being that ensouls it is one way to revere and love Mother Nature and the Divine Feminine. In this way we can acknowledge and respect her power and creative talent, and to try and learn something from her as a great spiritual being.

In the Ascended Masters tradition, the wisdom of this great soul of the earth is transferred to humanity, and the human species assisted in integrating the higher wisdom of the soul of the world, becoming a part of the soul of the world, by a world teacher. Kuthumi has held that role for some time.

Through Kuthumi we learn about nature and we assist the earth in her spiritual evolution. We are simultaneously assisted by her in our divine human soul growth, through consciously attending to her lessons and attempting to integrate them into our lives. We may also seek to contribute something positive to her evolution and the spiritual growth of humanity through our life work, through our passion for animal protection, human rights, environmental issues and even, perhaps radical in its simplicity, through learning to inhabit our bodies so that we can have access to genuine feeling.

It's possible to be very emotional and yet not have access to our genuine feelings. Emotions are often energetic patterns that get triggered and stimulated in response to a particular situation or circumstance. Genuine feelings might become emotions, but the feeling itself is present-moment oriented and truthful for us. It is not an emotional reaction but an instinctive truth. That feeling is sometimes called a gut feeling or intuition. That feeling is easier to access if we are in our bodies rather than our heads. Taking on the arduous task of unlearning being in your head and learning how to be in your body is an act of deep respect for the earth. It honours her gift to you of your body, which is a part of her own flesh, entering into sacred marriage with your spirit. What is created through this is the unique human soul.

There is a purpose for the human soul, and it is more than a way for the Divine Feminine to simply show off her outstanding creative ingenuity. There is a story in the ancient Vedic tradition of India, handed down over thousands of years in spiritual teachings. The story goes something like this – the earth was in deep spiritual growth. After creating creatures "great and terrible," as the translation of the ancient Sanskrit goes (which, one may suspect, refers to the dinosaurs) she "turned on her side" (perhaps referring to the change in her axial tilt or pole shift) and conversed with the universal source. I can just see the Divine Feminine leaning on her side to get more comfortable and chatting with the Divine Masculine, asking for some help with her spiritual growth process!

As I understand it, the teachings say that the earth asked the universal source for help in emerging from the darkness that threatened to engulf her. Essentially there wasn't enough light where she was and she needed some more to continue on. So, the human being was conceived as a way through which the light of the universal source could be integrated into the spiritual ecosystem of the earth. As certain souls agreed to the task of incarnation in order to assist calling spiritual light onto the earth, they were given certain spiritual powers too – free will and the possibility of becoming a divine being in their own right, an Ascended Master or a fully-realised heavenly human being, an eternal living Christ. So the body was a guarantee that the light of heaven would physically be available as spiritual nourishment for the earth and the sweetest, most tantalizing prize of immortality was up for grabs, along with the gift of free will necessary to be able to obtain it. The human had to work for that sweet prize, and as he or she did so, the human soul, a bridge between heaven and earth, was born, stabilised and strengthened, bringing more nourishment to the great Earth. That is how and why, our awakening is her awakening, our genuine spiritual success is hers and why, when you are walking your genuine divine path, there is just so much support and opportunity delivered to you from the earth when you are ready to receive it. The human soul is an extraordinary, unique spiritual vehicle. And it is a bit like an ant. Small perhaps, when compared to huge beings like planets, yet capable of punching way above its weight.

Our planet needs our awakening just as much as we do and she supports us thoroughly in our quest for spiritual illumination. If we find it hard to trust her, Kuthumi helps us heal our relationship to her so that we can surrender more completely into her transformational wisdom in action. Another way to say that is that we trust our own growth processes more easily, we trust in our own life experiences.

No matter what is happening – whether we are encountering an open door or a door slammed in our face, you can always assume that every minute detail and every grand event in your life serves your spiritual growth. Always. Without exception.

We are actually all in this game of life together, it is just that we don't always recognise this as human egos that have such small and unimaginative versions of the Divine. If the ego's expectations of how life should be aren't met – even in a small way – it can become overwhelmed with feelings of uncertainty, insecurity and anxiety.

We need love and compassion and a good dose of boldness in those times! We need to remember that the Divine is actively seeking us too – seeking out our own enlightenment. The whole universe is playing for the same team actually, but this is only visible at the highest levels of awareness. At our more low-level moments, perhaps when we are tired or frightened, it might seem easier or more realistic to believe that we have to defend ourselves against our lives. It can take enormous willpower to summon up gratitude for what is and really work on accepting it, looking with patience, curiosity and an open mind for the blessing in all that is to reveal itself to us, at the right time.

For every one of us that gets this, there is a sort of internal light switch that gets flicked on, and the flow of divine energy between heaven and earth comes alive in us. We become living conduits for spiritual electricity and its innate transformational presence. We step onto the path of our divine birthright and life really starts moving through us in potent and empowered ways. We become more and more capable of living in conscious connection with the great Earth mother, of letting the divine union of heaven and earth happen through us, in our life circumstances. We participate willingly in our unfolding life situations, even though sometimes that asks for big leaps of faith.

Then every time we meditate, pray, dance, choose wisely to have compassion or grow through forgiveness, the earth gets a jolt of spiritual light and consciousness through us. We pass on this light from the spiritual worlds through our chakras and eventually through our bodies, which in turn feeds the earth's own spiritual growth, and we get a step closer to our own enlightenment and absolute spiritual freedom. Our capacity to bear the divine voltage grows and eventually we will have enough sacred electrical power coursing through us, that the divine presence within will naturally begin to ignite those around us.

The earth, like all sentient beings, is evolving and this is our part in that process. I imagine it like this – let's say that God is a wise old man sitting at a huge table in heaven (I'm showing my Catholic childhood roots here) and he has an awesome clock that one of the gods (showing my university-days pagan streak there) gave him as a present. It keeps perfect time. One day, in God's perfectly timed world, he decides he'd like to understand the workings of that perfect-time-keeping-clock and so he carefully takes it apart to get a better look. He wants to understand it, to know what is going on in there rather than just taking it for granted. He is very, very curious!

So all the bits come apart and what was once a well-organised instrument is chaos. But in the dissembling of the perfection comes understanding. God 'ooohs' and 'aaaahs' over the different parts and slowly begins to put bits and pieces back together, seeing how they work together, how each little cog drives another and how all bits are needed for the whole instrument to work. It's quite brilliant really! But the process requires time, patience and skill. Eventually, the clock will be put back together and God will understand what it is and how it works. Chaos returns to order, and that clock is never seen with ignorance again.

Although we are hardly just mechanical bits and bobs being moved about by greater forces with no free will of our own, we are certainly locked into a system of divine timing. Essentially Kuthumi has a big role in supporting humanity to work with, rather than rally against, the evolution of the earth. We can work with divine timing, and the friction that limitations of time place upon our spirit by living in a body and in doing so, open up to the enlightenment of the Divine Feminine, with her wisdom and creative genius. Often however, in wishing life were other than what it was, we make it harder to find the way through what is into what is becoming, and instead spend our precious energy on having a whine or a tantrum (though sometimes, I do concede, these can be good therapy – provided they are temporary and not a daily way of life).

So, in a way we could say that the possibility for us to all reach an enlightened state upon the earth, depending on what we each choose for ourselves (at any moment to go with or against the will of the earth, for example), will be around the time the last piece of the clock is put back into place. The task will have been completed. Then undoubtedly the curious nature of the Divine will take over and something else will get deconstructed, explored and reconstructed again.

Perhaps a more sophisticated and yet simple explanation for it all is the Vedic one which holds that each universe is created on an out-breath of God and on the in-breath, we end our adventure and all return home to his being again. It might be less entertaining a thought than the notion of God fiddling with the bits of a cosmic clock, but it certainly gives us a notion of the sheer immensity of the creative force, capable of birthing and ending a universe with single breath.

The point of the teachings of this section is to help us realise that we are all evolving as a great living scheme of divine adventure and initiation. We are all growing together. Kuthumi helps us heal our connection to the earth through nature so that we can grow, she can grow and we can all increase our wisdom. She has a lot to offer us – power, creative inspiration, raw beauty and wild grace. She isn't an easy school to navigate, but then you are a powerful spiritual being with a deep yearning to not only connect with the Divine, but to remove all obstacles between you and the Divine, to remember yourself as divine – to attain that perfect inner spiritual marriage. If that weren't the case, you wouldn't be drawn to come to this planet on a healing mission in the first place, whether you consider yourself to be a 'typical healer' or not.

ASCENDED MASTER KUTHUMI – PLANETARY CONSCIOUSNESS

It might seem a little strange that we live on earth and yet we need a teacher to help us connect with her. It is one thing to live in a body. It is another thing to live in a consciously awakened body, or even before that to simply become connected to the body in the first place. To connect to the body can be hard, retraining us, especially those of us who hail from the West (which tends naturally towards intellectual rather than somatic orientation) or those of us who work in primarily mentally-oriented rather than physically-oriented jobs. In earlier chapters we learned that the body often has a lot to say to us and it's not only intuitive instinctual guidance to help us live our lives better. It will also have a lot of pain to express – it might be our childhood or past life pain.

As we evolve, it will also be the pain of the earth body and the animals, the trees and the oceans, that our body expresses. This pain can be great indeed, and extremely challenging to bear. It will rise and fall, this pain, and the more passionate love we feel for the earth and her creations, which tends to increase as we grow spiritually mature, so too does the pain that we become capable of feeling. Sometimes it will feel like a deep, searing heartbreak without a particular reason – we will just feel the enormity of sadness and even rage that cannot be dampened down or appeased.

We can fear we are going nuts, behaving in a crazy way during such times, but we are actually being brave enough to give expression to truth. That is sanity. What is really nuts is to wander about pretending that everything is fine by disconnecting from our bodies, even though so many people habitually do that as a way to cope with what they cannot yet handle. Unfortunately it's a bit like sticking your fingers in your ears and walking into the middle of a war-torn street plagued by gunfire, thinking that if you don't hear it, it's not happening and cannot cause you any harm.

Living the truth of what we feel doesn't mean that we have to be miserable, though it can be easy to assume that it does at first. Yet feeling the truth has a liberating zing that enlivens us. Truth might not be pleasant, but it wakes us up, and gives us the chance to do something constructive. Falsehoods, even if temporarily more pleasant and easier to handle, gradually drain us and leave us feeling uninspired, lacklustre and eventually quite helpless. If we have been too much in that energy, the face of the dark feminine will come and wake us up. We'll meet her in the next book in the series, *Crystal Goddesses 888*, but for now you can know that we'll be poked and prodded into remembering to 'do our homework' of becoming divine human beings, even if life becomes too challenging and we have to fall asleep for a while to cope with it. We can hit the snooze button for a while, but eventually that divine alarm will switch on and rouse us awake.

So truth brings us energy, but yes, it does make life feel greatly challenging at this level too – at least sometimes. We have to have faith and trust in the higher purpose of all of creation, and all of what we feel, without denying our feelings or trying to cut off from their energetic flow. At this level of evolution, we are relying upon all the personal healing that we have done in the past, all the emotional intelligence that we have cultivated, all the methods for personal emotional expression (perhaps through art, dance, journaling or music and poetry) and all the tricks and techniques we have found that help us foster wellbeing and return to balance after intense experiences. We are applying our past self-healing to help us bring our body to its next step, which is healing the planet, including the rest of humanity in particular.

If we are brave enough to continue, the body continues to awaken. Eventually beneath the pain, we start to connect with the light hidden within it. Rather than just the pain, we start to feel the light too – this is an incredible experience. We will explore much more about kundalini and shakti, the Divine Feminine energy, in *Crystal Goddesses 888*, but for now we can say that this is a deeper level of the sacred marriage of body and spirit. The wound cracks us open and the light pours through. Then we begin to burn with divine light. That burning can be ecstatic.

We discover that the divine awakening of light within the body itself is a profound process of transformation. At times it is ecstatic. At other times, agony. This divine communion entails the precise tearing apart of that which separates us from the Divine. Sometimes those are things, habits, beliefs, identities and expectations that we have been very attached to and most unwilling to release. To have them torn away and to remain present to that process can be utterly excruciating. It can also feel like a great relief! There are countless blessings that come from this process, rendering it more than worthwhile, but that doesn't necessarily make the process any quicker or easier.

Despite the intense internal tearing of the self during spiritual awakening of the body to greater levels of divinity, including being able to connect with the great being of the Earth Mother herself, the externals are not always obvious. They may become more so later on, where radical inner change completely transforms all aspects of our lives, including the physical manifestation of our lives.

There will be times however when life may appear to be similar from the outside whether we are awakened or not. As my spiritual mentor of over ten years used to repeat to me on a regular basis, "Before enlightenment, chop wood, carry water, after enlightenment, chop wood, carry water!" She thereby dispelled my fantasies of a perfectly easeful life, completely absent from struggle as a reward for my spiritual work. Though I must admit, life can become much easier as we learn to get out of our own way and let the Divine happen through us – struggles and growth yes, but constant suffering of our own ego creation, not so much.

So with all this suffering and pain, and the fact that our lives may not immediately transform, one may wonder why bother to actively engage with this process? Why build the connection and the awakening of consciousness in our body at all? Apart from the fact that it is the bridge to our enlightenment, and that is in essence the cosmic carrot dangling at the end of this string of incarnations, there is a completely different inner experience of life with an awakened body compared to life without it.

If you are reading this book then you are undoubtedly some ways on this path already, perhaps quite a long way. Or perhaps you are just starting to bring your body to consciousness this lifetime. Either way, life in an awakened body is an extraordinary experience. You certainly would never need to turn to drugs to expand your perception in such cases because your perception naturally becomes expanded every day. Your energetic sensibilities are heightened, your sensitivity becomes exquisite (which can give rise to a need to learn to manage your sensitivity, something that Kuthumi and Moss Agate can help us with) and you become capable of mystical experience, something that is like a spontaneous private rendez-vous with the ultimate divine lover, that takes you over completely, shows you a world of such utter beauty and love that you can hardly bear it, and even if it is over in a few seconds, there is an eternity in those moments and you are fundamentally changed. You don't just look at things differently, you are different. You are one vibrational adjustment closer to the living Divine. It is extraordinary grace.

Even if not having a fully-fledging mystical revelation (and we'll explore the mystic's world much more in *Crystal Saints and Sages 777*, later on in this series), to live in the body awakening gives you a capacity to energetically expand from living within the limits of three-dimensional reality into a reality of multiple dimensions, beyond time and space in the physical sense. Literally, new worlds open up. All whilst living in this awakened body, with the inner light switch flicked on. It's the capacity to hook up to many more channels on the cosmic cable network that we discussed earlier.

An awakened body is also capable of transformation and healing. So much so that you may feel as though you are changing enough to live several different lives within the one lifetime. This degree of change happens each time your awakening body is capable of more light and eventually will outgrow a level of vibration, having reached a critical mass of light that is sufficient to propel your body and its consciousness into a new stratosphere of awareness. It is like you are you but living as a more refined version of yourself in a different world.

I have experienced this in my own life many times. I have people who have known me for periods of a few years being shocked at who I have become over the course of even just that short period of time. How can such change happen? It may happen for you too in which case you'll know the answer to that question. I make it my practice to let my body lead me as much as I can, listening to its consciousness and participating in its intelligence. It isn't always an easy journey, certainly, in fact it rarely is for me, but I have learned this is the only true way forward spiritually on the path of the divine human being at this time in our planetary evolution. Whenever these shifts happen, my physical life will change – I'll end up living somewhere else, or my work will take a big leap, or my friendships or relationships will alter dramatically, or some other physical expression will demonstrate the change that has taken place within.

Kuthumi helps us connect with this awakened body (and you can explore the healing process to help allow this state to unfold more fully within your own body-soul through Mary Magdalene in Chapter 6 if need be). When connected with our awakened body, we can plug that connection consciously into the Earth too. It is an advanced practice. When we have begun the journey of awakening the body, bringing it to consciousness, we have delved into our talents and become empowered to serve, the next step is that we stop identifying with ourselves as separate individual beings. Even though in some ways we are individual and that's fine, we can come to realise that is only a small part of the bigger story of what we are. We begin to learn the lessons of nature, the wisdom of the ecosystem, of interdependence, of mutual enhancement and support.

Kuthumi begins our lessons in the wisdom of ecosystem, one of Gaia's gospels, by teaching us how to hold planetary consciousness or group awareness. This is an understanding, not only on a mental level, but deep in our being. It is not just an idea. It is a consciousness that alters our experience of reality. This consciousness is what allows us to tap into the Earth awareness. We can feel what she feels and have a sense of her wisdom. She will talk to us and we can talk to her consciously from this place. Even on day-to-day issues like the weather (which is very helpful if you are hanging washing on the line and want to know if she is planning on raining in the next few hours).

Apart from those rather practical but mundane matters, it is essential for humanity to build the capacity to consciously connect with the earth as it is the only way we can genuinely realise that there is no such thing as profit at another's expense. To genuinely access this startling realisation will topple the many systems based on competition and survival of the fittest and help us craft a new human culture that is compassionate and community-oriented so that we can survive and really have a go at helping God put his cosmic clock back together (and succeed in this great spiritual experiment of the human soul and its possible enlightenment).

We must look to cultivate win-win scenarios in our lives for this planet and all of its creatures to thrive into a new age, not just physically, but spiritually as well. If another cannot accept this in their own lives, then that is their choice and we do well to live and let live, but we can choose to model a different way for those that are ready to move beyond competition and into co-operation. It is a far more loving, less scarce way to operate, and in time we will evolve into that consciousness as an entire species. For now, however, we are just starting to make our way there.

This is happening because the light on our planet is growing, bit by bit. It is elevating its vibration with the help of human beings who are attempting to live consciously – not to deny our dark nature, but to attempt to integrate it, to make it conscious and to treat it with love and respect. It serves a purpose. One such purpose is to stimulate compassion from the light and create the friction we need to take action, to be not only a divine being of love and surrender, but a divine being willing to be moved into sacred purpose and action. This is not meant to only be a romance movie, this life on earth, but also a great adventure, thriller, and epic story of a hero's journey.

On a global level, the intensity of planetary initiation, the spiritual growth of the earth herself, has an impact on individuals whether they are consciously connected to her through an awakened and attuned body or not. Sometimes the impact is in a very physical sense through the attempts of the earth to rebalance herself with flooding and drought, earthquakes and volcanic eruptions, tsunamis and cyclones. During such times prayer for peace and seeking to balance to the Earth through your own personal spiritual practices can help. Calling on the assistance of those that love the earth unconditionally, especially Ascended Master Kuthumi and the Angel of Moss Agate can be helpful too. Then whatever the heart tells us to do on a practical level, such as donate money or help out in other practical ways, then we do that too.

We know from the introduction, and from the chapters to date, that initiation is about moving more deeply into love. We also know, quite possibly from our own spiritual journeys that the journey into love can be confronting as it evokes clearing of negativity, fear and illusion that would prevent us from receiving and giving at a deeper level. It will take time for us to acclimatise ourselves to a culture of love, after existing in a culture of fear for so long. Yet this point in planetary evolution has been sought for aeons, so we are progressing in the greater scheme of things.

However, do not underestimate your importance at this time. The world is in great need of light bearers to lead the way. Spiritual leadership can be expressed in many ways – from the small choices you make in the way you raise your children, to the conversations you have with your friends and work colleagues. Practice positive expectation, look for the divine wisdom and opportunity to learn in all situations. Do not be afraid to think differently from others. Recognise that it's actually part of what you have come here to do! You are meant to challenge negativity, fear and doubt and model for others a different way – a way of positivity, love and trust. Even when you are going through a period of suffering or challenge in your life, you can have your tantrum and resist and know that it is love leading you forward.

In the same way that personal initiation brings up the issues that would prevent us from moving forward spiritually to a new level of consciousness and life experience, so too does this happen at a group soul level for humanity during planetary initiation. We could say that humanity is ill from living out of balance right now and is going through a healing crisis for the illness of lack of soul caused by a spirit dissociated from the body.

We can either enter into despair, gloom and judgment or we can look at it from a much higher perspective and recognise that this has the potential to yield an amazing outcome of healing, but we have to get on with it. Though it will be painful for a time, ultimately everything works for good and the result of this healing crisis on a planetary level will be that people are not so anchored in fear. This isn't just a case of the eternal optimist striking once more (she has curly hair and likes to laugh whenever possible!) but is also just good common sense (well sadly not so common, but we can change that).

We must find our optimism without becoming complacent and indulging in magical thinking that without any effort on our part, everything will just work out. We need to do our part too. Reading this book, taking the healing journeys, acting on what comes up for you, talking to others in a way that feels in integrity, giving to good causes that move your heart and taking chances and trusting in life, those things are ways that we do our part.

Maintaining your centre through experiences of darkness, fear and despair can be difficult enough when it is simply on a personal level, but when it occurs on a global level, much conscious work is required to stay in your centre, and to trust that light, even when not visible (because all seems negative or in disarray), is still present. For advanced souls, however, this is an important part of 'doing our part' too.

Fortunately by the time you get to this spiritual level of planetary healing, your soul will have been around the block, spiritually speaking, quite a few times already. You are most likely far better equipped to deal with planetary levels of intensity than you realise. You more than likely are already doing so.

Even recognising that what is happening for you is about healing on a planetary level can help lighten your load by giving much needed perspective. It's a bit like naming a fear. When I left employment to become self- (or should I say Higher Self-) employed, I was able to name the gnawing fear of becoming destitute (and more specifically living in a cardboard box on a street corner). That helped me gain some perspective. I could ask myself if I genuinely believed that was part of my future, which I did not, or if it represented a fear that if I didn't feel in control, I wouldn't be safe and supported by life. I could connect with the fear and realise that I didn't actually feel that was meant to be part of my life experience this lifetime and I didn't have to fear for my financial security, I could trust spirit to help me meet whatever my needs were.

Please know that this doesn't mean that you 'should' no longer feel sadness, grief, anger and so on. These are healing emotions that can be an important part of your journey. The positivity and hope emerges in how we respond to our process, no matter how dark it may seem at the time. If we hold the view that pain serves a higher purpose, then we are contributing much sanity to our otherwise crazy-making human culture.

This approach also helps us stay centred in our own soul at those times when the going gets tough, taking us to the possibility of spiritual surrender into deeper peace. Optimism and hope serve you just as much as they serve our planet. If you cannot quite get there yourself, and we all have times that we can benefit from loving support, reach out to fellow lightworkers, healers and teachers that you trust, and ask for that love. If you are lacking in those connections, pray to Kuthumi to help you find your support systems in the physical world. And come and join my Facebook community for regular spiritual guidance!

Fortunately we don't need to know how things are going to turn out, we just need the courage to do all that we can and offer as much of ourselves in service to the Divine as we possibly can. Don't hold yourself back from the world, give of your heart and soul from a place of genuine trust and surrender. The work through Chapter 7 with Yogananda will help you get to that place in your own time, so that it doesn't feel unsafe psychologically or emotionally for you to do this (in other words, it's the right timing for you). Pray for peace and trust and do the healing process at the end of this chapter. If you open to divine assistance, you will always, always find it.

MOSS AGATE – EARTH HEALING

Moss agate is an inexpensive and beautiful stone. It can be translucent in parts with deep green markings that thread into each other, swirling into patterns. I have observed moss agate that sometimes looks like veins, at other times like nature herself, in leaf-like patterns and when cut into spheres, like a beautiful green planet.

Moss agate helps connect us to the energy of the natural world, including the cycles of life and death, of destruction and rebirth. Moss agate is known as a birthing stone on all levels – the birthing physically of a new reality, spiritually of a new consciousness, emotionally and psychologically of a new way of being. You can probably sense why it is such an important healing stone for those of us doing inner work and for the planet more generally at this time.

One of Mother Earth's many talents is transformation. Her ability to absorb that which is putrid or dying, otherwise toxic, and turn it into fertiliser for new life marks her as an evolved spiritual being. I often tell my students that Gaia is a vast being and what is a storm of pain for us, is a drop in the ocean for her, comparatively speaking. Whilst we are here to bring through light for Mother Earth, she too is there for us. We need each other.

As we learn to surrender into the healing process of our own bodies, and our healing and supportive connection to the Earth Mother herself, we can become more efficient at releasing toxicity and pain. This is especially important when we are working not only with individual experience but from a perspective of group healing. Moss agate can help us shed and discharge energy, helping us recover naturally if we have become blocked or overloaded with toxicity to the point of finding it hard to process and release.

Fostering enthusiasm, healing stress (particularly of a long-term nature) and boosting a sense of deep trust and optimism, Moss Agate heals us in a similar way to us spending time in nature. If we cannot do this for some reason, Moss Agate helps us access the healing results of deeper earth connection. As the planet goes through her particular initiation, this becomes important for us as supporters of her process.

Her initiation on a global level currently involves failure of the external concepts into which greater humanity has invested its faith and power – the housing market, economies more generally, banks, share markets, electronic systems, how we source our energy, the safety-nets of jobs, education, insurance and government. The way these structures currently operate cannot survive in the face of greater spiritual evolution. They must change and they will. As the change doesn't seem to be coming willingly, then it will happen through spiritual crisis that forces the energy stuck in those structures to be released so it can be reformed into systems that honour the greater ecosystem, rather than divide and separate humanity, undermining goodwill.

This doesn't mean that we have to descend into a panic-stricken frenzy, fearing chaos! It does mean that when it's time to evolve, which is pretty much right now, the old ways will cease to support us. Failure forces adaptation and evolution. We are learning to place our security in spirit rather than in things. That can be a tough call. We often only do it if we are forced to do so, otherwise, why bother? For many of us, it's too hard to just trust.

Initiation demands that we learn to do so however. The capacity for us to surrender into life as a result is expanded and the world can operate in a more organic, less fearful, less forced and less artificial way.

This planetary initiation is having an effect of wearing away the obstacles between humanity and the divine becoming that is meant to fulfil the human spiritual destiny on this planet. This involves removing the false gods that we have placed between us and spirit. This may be the false idol of work (for the workaholic), addictive substances, the need for material security to come from outside of us (such as believing that we can only be materially supported through external means that fit with our current belief systems – like a job, for example, or even a certain type of job or having a certain amount of money) rather than through acknowledging, honouring and practicing our divine ability to receive through trust, love and following our inner path, acting on avenues that open up as a result of following the inner path of healing. It is often a shocking process at first, and you cannot go back to sleep once you have witnessed truth, yet integrating it into our lives takes practice, patience and learning as we go.

When you enter into initiation a lot of what you once held to be true is stripped from you. More than likely you have experienced this for yourself already. You see things how they are which may not be anything like what you thought they once were or possibly should be. This is happening for humanity as a whole, through the collective soul of the human race of which you are a part. It can cast people into fear of the unknown.

Austrian philosopher Rudolf Steiner once described the process of opening to clairvoyance (or clear sight) as like having your eyelids burned away by exposure to the great light of the Sun, so that your vision was no longer obstructed. Not a pleasant experience, yet the result is truth. This is what it can feel like to go through the revelation of initiation. The relief of finally knowing and seeing truth is such a tonic to the heart, but the ego can struggle to accept it for some time, fighting against things being as they are.

If this is resonating for you, or you sense it happening around you, you may like to work with Moss Agate to help you find ways to look for the silver lining in each cloud. The opportunity to get closer to the Divine is always there. You can discipline yourself to look for it during darker moments of your life. What we are in need of during times of uncertainty and transition are people that are strong enough not to collapse under the weight of negativity and shut off from life. It's tempting to want to psychically (or even physically) get under the covers and go back to sleep for a while, just shutting off from everything. But there is a difference between getting enough rest and hiding from life. You need to be brave, to live your life as truthfully as you can and to be okay with who you are! We need you. Just as you are. Right now.

If that seems to be too much to ask, remember that you have lots of helpers on your side, working along with you and we are all allowed to make loads of mistakes (which I like to calling learning experiences). Nonetheless you also have as allies an entire Earth Mother and plenty of Ascended Masters, Crystal Angels and many other higher beings willing to aid you on your path too. Assistance of higher beings is always available to you, and you can ask for help without disconnecting from how much personal spiritual power you already possess through your power of choice to come from love rather than fear in any given situation.

Thankfully, Mother Nature in her healing wisdom, has also provided us with a gift to help us manage this tendency. I recommend taking Red Clover flower essence to help with keeping steady in your own light and not getting swept up in mass panic, especially if you find that this tends to happen for you because you are quite sensitive to energies, especially unprocessed energies of others. The entire North American FES Flower Essence range is marvellous and I've created many custom-blends for clients (and for myself) from their range over the years. The Pink Yarrow flower essence will also support all healers who want to strengthen their own psychic boundary, making the information that they do receive clearer and brighter, without the interference of unprocessed energies of others entering into their auric field.

HEALING WITH KUTHUMI AND MOSS AGATE

Sitting comfortably with either your Moss Agate stone or your mandala, take a moment to really feel your connection to the earth – your body, your feet, the ground beneath you.

Then say aloud, "I call upon the true Ascended Master Kuthumi (sounds like Coo-Thoo-Me) and the loving spirit of Mother Earth, the Angel of Moss Agate and my own soul. I call upon healing grace and love, light and power. Cleanse and rebalance, empower and strengthen me now, beloveds. I release all karmic debris of a personal or planetary nature that no longer serves my soul growth. I release it into the divine power of the Earth Mother with gratitude, and in return I allow my soul light to grow in service to her. So be it."

Perceive a ball of light, swirling with rich dark green energy forming around you now, rising up from the earth. It feels cleansing, powerful, supportive and balancing. Imagine that you are bathing within the light of that sphere, sensing or visualising it all around you, opening up your chakras and clearing them out, starting at the base of your spine.

You may like to breathe in and out allowing the light to focus at the base of the spine and to clear out the base chakra.

Then the light rises to the sacral chakra in the sacrum or hip area, with special focus around the navel chakra just below the belly button. Imagine these two centres being cleansed and strengthened by the intelligent light of this energetic field around you. Breathe in and out, allowing the light to cleanse and empower you.

Then the light rises to the abdominal area, the solar plexus chakra, front and back, is gently and effectively opened, cleansed and strengthened with this energy field of rich swirling green light.

Allow the patterns of green light to make their way up to the heart chakra in the centre of your chest, front and back, where the light opens, cleanses and dislodges stuck energy, allowing fresh new light to stabilise in the heart. Breathe in and out as you mentally and energetically let go.

The light rises to the throat chakra at the base of the throat, clearing and empowering that centre. Feel old vows, old words, lies, confusion, clearing and new light stabilising in the throat chakra, allowing it to become strong and clear.

The light rises to the third eye chakra in the centre of the forehead slightly above the eyebrows where you perceive beautiful rays of green light. Allow your mind to be cleansed and to receive light.

Finally the light rises to the top of your head, clearing old fear and karmic energy out of the crown of your head, opening up your spiritual connection in a more conscious and powerful way. Breathe and allow the light to flow.

When you are ready, say, "In service to the Earth Mother, I call upon the beings of divine protection that love me unconditionally and I ask for your help in manifesting my life purpose of earth healing. May I graciously receive the benevolent assistance of the divine Mother Earth as together we journey towards enlightenment sublime. I am a light upon this earth. I am connected to the grid of light upon this earth, supported and nourished, body and soul as one. Through my own free will, so be it."

Perceive that the field of light becomes a living tree made of energy, vast and wide. Allow yourself to become a part of this tree, absorbed into its unconditional love. The tree roots extend deep into the earth and the branches extend high into the heavens. Let yourself feel the immensity of your being, connected to this universal tree.

Stay there for at least 33 breaths and when you are ready, visualise a layer of deep green light surrounding you, head to toe, in a bubble. Then visualise or intend a second layer of golden light to surround that bubble.

When you are ready simply place your hands in prayer and say thank you and in your own time, open your eyes.

You may feel all sorts of sensations, emotions or even have vivid dreams following this process. You may also just feel more peaceful and free from fear. If you are struggling with intense fear or anxiety in the wake of this work it is recommended that you complete the Lady Nada healing in Chapter 3, followed by the Buddha healing in Chapter 14, before returning to this healing process again in a couple of weeks' time.

Mother Earth has deep loving gratitude for the work you are doing on her behalf and returning that love with devotion through doing healing practices such as this opens you up to her assistance. Remember beloved, no matter how big a problem may seem, there is nothing that is more powerful than the Divine. Stay true to your path and ask for help, and have faith in yourself too.

9.

ASCENDED MASTER ST. GERMAIN (Violet Flame) AMETHYST (Spiritual Connection)

INITIATION OF CONSCIOUS SPIRITUAL COMMUNICATION

From within great silence, a point of violet light is perceived. Expanding, moving in all directions and through all dimensions. It cannot be contained. Divine electricity pulses through the light and yet it is peaceful. Beneath the intensity of its energy is stillness. Quiet eternity, before all creation and at the end of all creation. Quiet eternity, speaking through the stillness, held within the violet light.

Your soul or higher self is something like a personal telephone line to the divine source. When you become more conscious of your soul presence, it is a bit like learning how to pick up the receiver of your in-built cosmic telephone so that the Divine can speak to you more consciously.

The Divine has many faces. For you that might be spirit, your version or versions of God or the Goddess, it might be your own inner divine essence or your team of higher spiritual guidance, including your spiritual guides that love you unconditionally, your angels and of course, the Ascended Masters. For you, the Divine might be these forces combined, or the one energy that underlies all of the manifestations of these faces and all of creation.

Whatever face or form of the Divine will serve you best at the time will be the one that reaches out to you, be it your own higher self or a guide, the holy spirit or the soul voice of Mother Earth herself.

Consciously being able to receive spiritual communication offers us endless benefits. Imagine a friend who was always in your corner, would always understand, never criticise and yet also be truthful and let you know when you needed to grow or make amends for something you had chosen to do. Imagine a friend who empowered you and loved you, had no agenda beyond your spiritual growth and could tirelessly help you without ever getting drained or tired. This is how the Divine is with us. I have learned a lot about the Divine and the nature of spiritual love through my work. It is what I feel when working with others. I feel the love of the Divine flowing through me. I often receive healing as well as the person that I am working with. That is a hallmark of spiritual presence – the creation of a win-win situation.

Apart from being the receiver for higher impressions, when it is at an advanced level of evolution, the human soul itself can contain a vast amount of spiritual energy, becoming increasingly aligned with the divine source and operating as a conscious living channel of the source. If you do healing regularly on yourself or others, and regular meditation, channelling and other forms of self-healing such as conscious dance, you will be taking in and to some extent also storing, spiritual energy. Over time, this accumulates and provides energy and consciousness not only for you on a human level, but for your soul on a spiritual level. The soul grows too, you see. You could imagine that spiritual energy is like sacred water and your soul is a fountain – as the energy grows, the fountain begins to fill up and in time, flows over. It is at the times of overflow that our own personal spiritual healing becomes healing for all those around us too. Divine energy just flows through us, overflowing into the world around us.

Learning to open up and receive, and eventually integrate the energy of our higher self into our physical body, allowing it to fuse and awaken our physical body (Chapter 6 holds more information on this) is how we grow. That growth opens us up to conscious spiritual communication and the building of divine inner presence that receiving this energy can stimulate. As we grow, we can not only receive information but also come to feel and embody the nature of that energy. It is like we get saturated in the heavenly perfume and we begin to emanate it. We are what we (energetically) eat, so to speak.

Whatever we desire has a frequency. Often what we are dreaming of and desiring to manifest will have a higher frequency than our current state. Especially if we are bold enough to dream big and deeply desire to manifest our soul truths in the world in a practical way. If you want a life that is more abundant and prosperous, in a truly loving and heart centred way (rather than simply acquiring more money from a place of fear and manipulation), then you are reaching for higher frequency life experiences. When we are prepared to work on ourselves to remove obstacles to vibrating at that higher frequency, including our own beliefs, habits and even the company we keep which may lower our frequency and keep us from attaining our dreams, we are given a lot of spiritual help.

The soul or higher self is so helpful in such situations. It can assist you in seeing how you can create what your heart truly desires by working on your relationship with yourself.

It will take you to the core of the issue and assist you in working through whatever it is that is blocking you. It helps you see the truth in a situation, rather than the illusion that causes you to believe that someone or something is blocking you from having what you want to have, or being the sort of person you want to be. This is how we shift frequencies from the vibration of where we are at now, to where we want to be, in order to manifest the next stage of our life expression.

The insight and energy of your soul helps you to see yourself as the co-creator (along with the great divine intelligence and plan) of your life experiences. Through that awareness we can feel energised, inspired and very motivated to work on ourselves, to become endlessly committed to do everything we can to be open to receive life, in alignment with the divine plan and life purpose etched in our heart's desire. I call this 'getting out of our own way' and 'letting God happen'.

One of the best ways to connect more deeply with your soul (and the Divine through your own soul 'telephone' line), is to get in the habit of talking to your own higher self about what you are experiencing, requesting the help and encouragement that you require. We live in a free will zone in this universe. This means we have responsibility for choices and although help is always available for our spiritual growth, we have to ask for it. The Divine already knows that of which we are in need. The Divine knows even better than we do, what will serve us. That is why I believe the best prayer is not, "I want," but, "How can I serve best here?" It isn't that your wants aren't valuable, it is more that what you really want in your heart of hearts may not be what you think you really want at the time you are praying. Praying for a specific item or person to love you, for example, is not a great prayer. Praying for the best meeting of your heart's desire is a better prayer for it relies on the divine intelligence to operate through wisdom and still acknowledges the value of your own desires and that they too can be a way for the Divine to manifest through you.

Ways that we ask for help most simply include prayer (talking to the Divine) and meditation (listening to the Divine). Sometimes no words will be involved. We can pray through dance and emotional offering. One can pray wordlessly by placing one's forehead on the ground and surrendering all of oneself to the Divine through intention to let go. It is the feeling, the energetic truth that makes it a prayer. It is like a genuine apology. There is a feeling that makes it truthful. A more impressive apology may be spoken by someone, but not really felt or supported by their actions. A simple genuine apology may be short but really felt energetically. That is the different between chatting to the Divine and prayer. Prayer has some punch! It doesn't come from a chatty mind so much as a deeply opened heart. Don't strive to be perfect in your prayer, just aim to be as vulnerable, real and honest with the Divine as you can be. An imperfect messy prayer that comes from the heart is precious and effective.

When we pray, we receive an answer. It is never issue, a prayer being answered. The answer is always given, without exception. The tricky part for human beings is usually receiving the answer consciously. The more detached and open we are, the easier this is. The problem however is that usually when we are praying deeply about something, it is something that is very important to us and therefore it might be hard to truly surrender through prayer. We might want to be open to an answer and yet really hope that a particular sort of answer is given. This is very human, and understandable, but it can make it harder to hear an answer. It's a bit like sticking our ego-fingers in our ears and even if the answer we wanted were the one that came, we wouldn't really be able to hear anything. Usually the questions we most need help with result because of a struggle between how we want things to be and how they are. There is often a part of us that refuses to see anything other than what we want to see (our emotional attachment) and as a result, as spirit tries to tell us that there is another reality, we fight against seeing it and as a result feel conflicted and confused. It can be very painful!

When you are seeking to connect consciously with guidance, you will need to ask that your emotional self be detached so that you can be open to hear whatever needs to be heard. If we are ever claiming a lack of guidance in our lives, its possible that emotional attachment is causing us to stick our fingers in our ears and pretend not to hear. We need to remember that asking for guidance is not the same as asking that we get told what we want to hear. Sometimes we will hear something that we want to hear. This can happen and often does! But it can also happen that we are given a different perspective through an answered prayer. Detachment is essential if we are going to really give spirit a chance to help us find a better way to live our divine destiny. If this is a real struggle because the issue you need help with is hard to release, then you can support yourself by attending to Chapters 1 and 2 again before progressing on to this chapter. That will help clear the way for you, before doing the work here in Chapter 9.

Apart from working through the earlier chapters, to outwit these ego habits, we can take certain other actions. To become increasingly conscious of the answers and impressions you are receiving (and we all receive them), you will need to provide yourself with regular time and space to be in your own energy without distraction. So constant noise of the computer or television, telephone calls, family crises, friendship crises and so on can make it difficult to receive your answers. It is possible to get a flash of blinding clarity in the midst of all the drama of course – it has happened to me before – but some quiet time can be really helpful to build our capacity for conscious receptivity. A simple relaxing visualisation of yourself in a peaceful place, surrounded in white light or focusing on a point of light in your mind's eye is a simple and effective way to create some internal space for yourself. A walk in nature on your own or with a pet might be another way. This is particularly important if you are in a situation where your physical space and ability for solitude is compromised for some reason or other (perhaps you have the in-laws staying, for example).

This personal space practice may only require five or ten minutes each morning or evening – but that is certainly enough for you to notice an enormous difference in your feelings of spiritual connection. Over time, and sometimes even immediately, you'll sense this practice as strengthening your intuitive knowing about which choices to make. This practice can help with any type of decision, from which eating plan will suit you best, to whether or not to stay in a job or relationship, where to live, whether you should take up that class you were thinking about or if you should go ahead with that business plan that has been lurking in the back of your mind.

You will also notice an increase in your self-confidence, which grows along with your belief that you truly can access your spiritual guidance when you need it. You will be able to tune into your feelings more easily and become clearer about what feels right or wrong to you on a deep, intuitive level.

One of the largest obstacles to receiving guidance consciously is having expectations of how that answer is going to be delivered to you. Images of God speaking in a powerful voice from the heavens above are not going to help you become more grounded in your expectations of conscious spiritual communication. Your answers may come that way, but more than likely, and most often, they probably will not. Spirit communication is a natural, everyday occurrence. Losing your expectations of Hollywood-style special effects and opening to subtleties will boost your confidence and help you to notice the way spirit is already at work in your life. Spirit can be very creative about reaching you.

This means sometimes your answer will come through in your own thoughts in the time following your prayer. You, perhaps, will take credit for it at first. This is easy to do because answers to prayers can seem so simple. Or perhaps you will be talking to someone and they give you some great advice or wise counsel. Spirit may be speaking through that person, perhaps even your own higher self has been transferring messages and guidance into the unsuspecting mind of the receiver (in this case, the friend you were talking to on the telephone who had no expectation of anything and was therefore very open to receive). Your friend may later reflect that they were quite surprised as all those wise words flowed out of them, not quite knowing where they were coming from at the time.

Many times, you will stumble across a book, magazine article, movie or even a TV program that answers your question in quite clear ways. Spirit is very inventive in getting through to us and has quite the sense of humour. I have received guidance through cartoons on television, which was amusing because it seemed such an irreverent and quirky way to transmit divine wisdom. I also once experienced a book that I was looking for literally fall off a bookshelf in a metaphysical bookstore, landing at my feet. I was simply walking by, not rummaging about on a shelf. I took it as a sign that yes, I would certainly find reading that book most helpful, which was later proven to be true. It was a book on angels. I had no idea that I would be writing a book on that very topic many years later.

I have heard clients say that they were drawn to go into a bookshop where I had earlier been drawn to go and leave some business cards. It is not a practice that I do very often, but when guided, I do so. I had a client once tell me that he had pinned one of my flyers on his kitchen noticeboard. For several days he would go into the kitchen, and it had somehow fallen off his board and landed on the kitchen floor or table. He would pick it up, pin it again and then have the same experience the following morning. Eventually he decided to just call me and have a session! These are subtle things, easy enough to dismiss, but easy enough also to be curious about.

Recently I asked the Divine for a sign about a retreat that I was thinking of running in France for Mother Mary. I asked in meditation, "Do you want me to go to Paris? Things aren't really coming together, even though I felt you gave me earlier nudges in this direction, is the time right to work on this?" and then fell back into meditation and forgot about it. Later that morning I clicked onto a group in Facebook – and I didn't know why I was looking at that group because it wasn't something that I was consciously needing information about at the time, or so I thought. As I clicked on the group's page, there had just been a post in the group – about going to Paris. I giggled and let it go. I always felt that if the Universe wanted to tell me something it would do so at least three times. Later that day I went to dinner. An unexpected dinner guest was there – wearing a jumper with the Eiffel Tower on it. I giggled again and then later that night, one of the dinner guests was doing a 'show-and-tell' of all the gifts she had received at her 40th birthday celebration the night before. She handed me a bottle of perfume – which was labelled "love in Paris." Those were my three signs. I continued on with the work of organising the retreat.

There are times when I can receive clear messages and my questions are answered in a conversation with guidance or the Divine in other forms, as if they were sitting in the room with me. I very much enjoy those conversations. Yet there are other times when life circumstances and situations provide me with the answers that I need. I experience this as direct, conscious communication too. I can feel just as much of the Divine in an experience of an animal crossing my path and passing on a message to me through its presence and metaphysical symbolism as I can from receiving an inner mental impression of guidance. It is all just divine creativity and variety. One is not less than the other, but the joy that accompanies the realisation that divine guidance is real, and direct, and that there are actual loving beings that know us, listen to us and talk to us makes opening up to conscious spiritual communication such a worthwhile task.

Even though the ability for conscious spiritual communication comes easier for some than others, much like athletic ability or any other talent, we can all develop our natural ability. If you are resonating with this chapter in some way, then it is guidance that you are at a point where no matter what your ability level has been up until now, you are being guided to develop your personal practice (through meditation or conscious dance for example) in order to allow for your abilities to grow, that you may more deeply and clearly connect with spirit at a conscious level.

The greater your commitment to dedicate time each day to a personal spiritual practice, the more you will receive your messages directly from Spirit, through knowing, feeling, telepathic impression (thoughts that feel as though they drop into your mind), inner hearing or inner sight, and of course, through consciously recognising in an intuitive 'hit' the divine signs in other ways, through dreams, conversations with other people or situations and circumstances more generally. The Divine speaks to us everyday through all manner of methods. The work in this chapter is about bringing it to awareness.

Sometimes, after you have become more confident in your ability to receive, you will find that you are halfway through asking the question, and the answer comes immediately to mind. This may take some practice, but Spirit has the ability to answer you instantaneously. Any time delay we experience in receiving answers to our questions is not as a result of the Divine sitting around dealing with a backlog of cosmic emails! The instantaneous nature of a response depends on how receptive and clear we are.

If the energetic vibration of an answer to our question is above what we are capable of receiving then it will take some time before we really know our answer. An example might be that if we ask a question about a difficult situation that we are in, and the answer is to trust or love, but we are deep in fear and judgment. We will have to be able to access the vibration of the answer in order to consciously 'get it' but that might be hard at that moment. The divine will keep transmitting to us, reaching to our hearts, but it will take some work perhaps to let go of the fear and allow love to soften our hearts so we can be open to our answer. When that happens, we'll 'get the answer' to our prayer consciously. Then we can be as we must be for the situation to resolve itself.

Sometimes however, we will find it easier to release fear. It will be more like an old habit than something we really believe in, and when the answer is transmitted, we are more swiftly capable of rising to the vibration of it – so that answer is received more quickly, has a swifter effect and the situation resolved more promptly. The Divine is the same – we have evolved however, in our ability to consciously receive.

I have found it powerful to take the time and energy to focus your questions and to speak them aloud and/or write them down. It is true that the Divine knows what is in your heart – often more than we consciously do in our human form – so it is not for the benefit of the divine source that I suggest that we do this. It is for our own benefit.

When starting a reading, I tune into someone to give 'energetic feedback' before asking them what their questions are and what they would like to focus on in that particular session. If someone has prepared, taken time to contemplate and become more aware of their questions, then more often than not, that is exactly what I will start speaking about before they have opened their mouths. Their energetic broadcast is clear and it is easier to give them the answers and guidance that they need. It is not about making my job easier, although it does do that, but more about making it easier for them to receive the guidance that they need. Often there will be guidance to get clear about what we want. That can be much harder to do than one would think! If you don't know what you want guidance about, then a simple and effective resolution of that is to pray to be shown how you can best serve. That will pretty much fix any problem you have going on by showing you how to work through it.

There is so much power in asking the right question during our prayer, but we have to work, sometimes quite hard, to generate the awareness necessary to formulate the right question. With the right question, an answer can seem self-evident. Questions which focus on what we could be learning in a situation rather than why so-and-so is not behaving as we would like are more likely to be helpful questions. The right question leads us closer to a genuine answer.

A less helpful question is based on us trying to get the answer that we think we want to hear (irrespective of whether or not it is genuinely helpful and truthful). I can tell you now however, and I suspect you already know this, the Divine is never going to say, "I love you so much more than that annoying person who isn't giving you what you want!" I have a giggle at the thought of that happening, because it is so unhelpful and unrealistic, but I am pretty sure that most of us have had a nice little fantasy about receiving such guidance when we have felt unfairly wronged by another. The point is that the Divine gives us answers that actually help us outgrow our issues, not indulge in them. Sometimes that is experienced as tough love, but it is always compassionate and never judgmental.

Whether you are starting with clear questions or simply an inner urge to accept this invitation to build a more conscious relationship with spiritual guidance, I suggest that apart from the healing process at the end of this chapter, you may like to start writing and speaking your questions for spirit and your requests for help out loud. I suggest that any time you pray or ask for help you always start with the following phrase, "I call on the beings that love me unconditionally, please hear me and help me now with..." and finish off with, "Through my own free will, and for the greatest good, may this be so now."

Waiting for a few days (and forgetting about your question in the interim) can give you time to receive and process information from spirit whilst you are sleeping. We can be very productive during sleep. The soul has an ability to engage in spiritual training and esoteric schools in other realms and dimensions during dream-state. You might even remember dreams where you were in school or at a lecture, which can be hints that your higher self was actually in spiritual training.

You may like to play at writing the answer you imagine the Divine would provide to your prayer, sort of like channelling an intuitive guidance session for yourself. I have done this for myself many times over the years, imagining that I was writing for myself as though I was my own client. This can be extremely helpful, so long as we keep in mind the following qualities of divine communication – non-judging, non-fearing, love-based, constructive and operating from a much higher perspective. I have done this exercise in my own journal at times when conscious spiritual communication seemed to elude me because my attachment to my own struggles was making it difficult for a higher perspective to easily come through. I have found it incredibly accurate when going back and reading it some months later and finding that yes, the guidance indicated exactly what was going on and what was going to happen.

You may find that this process works for you also, and as you sit down to write your answer, you realise that somewhere along the line, you were already given the answer and you already know what it is that you need to do. This indicates that you have received guidance, albeit unconsciously, and have processed it. It just needed to be brought to the surface of your awareness. If this doesn't happen easily for you, that is just fine. Be patient. Keep praying and trust. If we haven't consciously accessed an answer to a prayer as yet, then it means one thing and one thing only, we are growing into that answer. That is all.

Developing your conscious spiritual communication ability often takes time, practice, persistence and patience – just like it would to develop any other skill. The key is to start with the assumption that you are already guided and know that as you develop your inner awareness of your own mind and thoughts, the imparting of guidance will become more and more conscious to you. With attention and application over time, you'll be able to sense the vibration of guidance – which is loving and wise – and how that is different to perhaps negative or fearful self-talk that may arise for you from time to time. You'll begin to sense the presence of the Divine within and how it communicates with you through so many different ways. You'll start to differentiate between the quality of different thoughts, sensing which is loving and which is fearful. You feel the difference when something is simply an old pattern running, when something feels as though it comes directly from the love of your heart, when something is from a place of lack or fear, and when something is asking you to be bold and trust and it feels loving too. You'll begin to feel, sense and discern the different qualities of various thoughts, feelings and impressions. You'll begin to sense which are reliable and coming from a greater source, and which are perhaps more familiar but not nearly as helpful. Then you'll be able to hear the subtle nuances of your higher guidance even amongst the often noisy, repetitive thought patterns and emotional ups and downs of daily life.

I should also add here that a common response to some guidance is that 'I already knew that!' So when we get guidance that we could help ourselves by loving ourselves more – we might not bother to reflect on it with any great intensity – because it sounds so obvious. However, if we really comprehended a particular lesson like that one – no matter how much our mind already seems to understand it – our lives would change radically. I have met many people who knew a lot, could speak with such apparent wisdom, and sadly did not experience any improvement in their lives through that knowledge. Knowing is not enough.

More often than not, your mind will have enough conceptual knowledge to be able to heal the difficulty you are experiencing right now. In such cases, spirit will gently (and sometimes not so gently) remind you of something you know but need to actually apply in your life. Communication from spirit can nudge you into turning 'head knowledge' into 'heart knowledge' or wisdom. Wisdom is what happens when you turn ideas into experience that results in healing and higher understanding. Just because your mind knows something does not mean that your heart is ready to put that knowledge into action in your life. We must seek to live our guidance, growing into our wisdom with patience and commitment. This will be the difference between you knowing about spirituality and having it transform the way you live your life. It is meant to change us, to help us grow. So if your mind goes, "Well that's so obvious – how is that helpful?!" always ask your heart, "Can we do this more deeply?" If the answer is yes, then you know to keep going with that simple guidance.

As we embrace this journey, (and no one is saying that it is a small task, but it is certainly worth the effort), we come into a sacred state – being open to receive clear answers and knowing that we can trust them. Then even guidance that is challenging – such as walking away from something that you thought was going to be so important or staying put when you want to walk away – will become possible for you with some inner peace, even amongst the challenge of it. I have done things that I can't quite believe I had the guts to do – even looking back – but I did it because I knew there was divine guidance in the action, so I trusted and acted.

As I am writing this chapter, I am noticing a beautiful hibiscus blossom outside my window. I have been drawn to it at different times this morning, whilst writing, and I knew there was a message in this chapter relating to this beautiful flower. First thing this morning, it was tightly coiled. Its petals are now slowly opening, gradually it will open up to the embrace of the warm midday sun. I know it will open, but for now, I have to wait. So it is with the fruits of our action on following higher guidance. Sometimes the outcome will be instant, sometimes we have to wait quite some time for the fruits of our labour to be ready to harvest. Patience and trust often include a willingness to endure not knowing and delayed gratification in seeing the results of our work. Although this might not seem like much fun, it is much more fun that pursuing a path that builds your ego to the detriment of your heart truths, which generates great pain and is a recipe for unavoidable future struggle. So the message from the wisdom of Mother Nature for us on spiritual communication is this - hear me, act, have patience, and trust.

ASCENDED MASTER ST. GERMAIN – VIOLET FLAME

The Ascended Master St. Germain is associated with equality and socio-economic and political revolution. His particular spiritual gift to humanity, the Violet Flame, is an energetic vehicle that he helps to anchor. The Violet Flame will feature in our healing process at the end of this chapter because it opens up the crown chakra, which is essential for spiritual communication and consequent spiritual intelligence.

The wisdom that spiritual intelligence brings is essential for the healing of our political and economic systems (that are mostly lacking in wisdom at present and functioning in a destructive way). The Violet Flame purifies and protects the energy field, which is helpful when we are opening up energetically at a new level. The stronger and clearer we are as individuals, the more the passion of St. Germain can flow through us. This passion ignites social revolution so that social structures can be expressions of spiritual love, inclusion, community and connection, not fear, dominance, separation, callousness, disregard for fundamental human equality, and greed.

When I think of St. Germain I cannot help but think of one of my mentoring clients, with a particularly strong spiritual presence. She seems to radiate his essence. On several occasions I have seen her in a vision, almost dancing, as she waves the St. Germain pomander (a beautiful liquid creation by the Aura-Soma company) around her head, leaving her energy lightly dappled with pale violet light and smelling heavenly. The few times that I had shared this vision with her, usually at the time of a reading, she just laughed and said something along the lines of, "Well yes, I have just applied the violet pomander." I suspect many of her own clients have come to know her by this scent. That is the energy of St. Germain for you. It can be subtle and yet once we become able to identify and recognise it, it can become a part of who we are spiritually.

St. Germain is an important guide for healers, lightworkers and therapists who are open spiritually. Anyone involved in deep healing or clearing work will benefit from this presence. This is also so for any sacred activist who is passionate about political and social reformation, the rights of human beings and animals, the development of sustainable and equitable economic systems.

Violet as a colour contains properties of cleansing, purification and protection. It is of a high vibrational frequency. My clients consistently report seeing violet light when they have spiritual healing sessions. Other colours do come through but violet is almost unanimously reported by my clients, along with gold, and these are generally the vibration of spiritual presence. Some of my clients that are clairvoyant have reported seeing violet light coming out of my eyes when I am teaching a workshop. It sounds much more Hollywood-special-effects than it is. Some clients report hanging up the phone after a telephone session and seeing it surrounded by violet light. It seems spirit likes to travel down the phone line, out through our eyes and our voice and through our hands in equal measure.

Why violet? It is the colour frequency of spirit. It is the Divine in pure essence, sometimes called the godhead, the Divine Masculine or in the Hindu tradition, Brahma. The Divine exists in manifestation as well – which is the Divine Feminine or creation. She is all the colours of the rainbow and even colours that are yet to manifest upon the earth! The pure spirit and the spirit that has manifested as divinity in form are two halves of the one divine whole. In Crystal Goddesses 888 we deeply explore the creative divinity, the Divine Feminine, focusing on the art of manifestation. For this chapter, we focus on pure spirit and its communication through the violet light, which is its signature. If we all had a phone number represented by a colour, violet would be that of spirit.

Violet is also often used in colour healing to purify, disinfect, cleanse and protect. As a colour, it can help us detach from thinking about our problems which helps us to 'let go and let God', so to speak, because it strengthens and balances the crown chakra, the seat of our divine connection to spirit that can then flow through us in totality. This is when we become ready for healing to occur. Violet light helps us get to that place of surrender and release that can occur when we really connect closely with the Divine.

The symbol of the flame is also relevant. It is an ancient symbol for illumination and enlightenment (the real process of 'lightening up' by letting go of that which no longer serves us) and of spiritual cleansing and purification. The power of divine fire, the flame, is a crucible for transformation. When we work with the energy of divine fire – be it through the Violet Flame, the clear flame, the blue flame and so on – we are opening up to spiritual transformation. We are agreeing that we will emerge from the flame different to how we entered it.

Combined with violet light in particular, the Violet Flame becomes a tool for the 'three Ts' as I call them – transcendence, transformation and transmutation. These are the three steps of our inner spiritual alchemy, which is how we go from a terrified human, trapped in painful illusions of separation that give rise to a terror of death and the world of the ego, to an awakened human being, burning in divine love with the sacred heart overflowing with compassion, a divine being of great awareness, moving in harmony only and always, with the greater divine genius. The Violet Flame helps us access all three phases of this human healing and spiritual growth process.

At the beginning of the spiritual path, human beings had to separate mind from matter to be able to really taste what the spirit can offer. To experience the shining spiritual light of eternal stillness brings an understanding of the bliss, love and endlessness of the Divine Father. To encounter it is sheer bliss, contentment and fulfilment (or at least, so we feel at that moment). It is a divine happening, a bestowal of grace, to commune with the heavenly spirit in that state of utter intoxicating rapture. It takes us beyond our mind and to a state of being that is beyond words.

To be able to become light enough to touch the sky in this way, we dropped the body. Over time, however, we forgot that this was only the first half of the story. We got seduced by the light, by its limitless possibilities. We came to love technology but forgot that it was supposed to be brought into harmony with the rest of creation. We can experience so much happiness and healing as we come to know the truth of the transcendent, eternal spiritual light, yet it is in bringing that loving bliss back into the other half of the divine expression, the creation of the Divine Feminine – which is this world in which we live and grow – that we become whole and enlightened. Somewhere along the line, many of us forgot this. We either became too scared to leave the safety of the 'known world' of the body at all to find the vast worlds of eternal light, or we became seduced by our own love for the light and forgot that the purpose of our discovery of the light was to bring it home to the earth, to our bodies.

To be able to accept the light is transcendence. It is both a gift and a test. It can bring us enough detachment to let go and rise above an issue. It can help us feel free to fly above so many of our struggles. It is also this beauty that makes it too easy to suffer from spiritual addiction to it. I have seen this happen to people who flock around gurus – some of whom may still have a lot to master themselves – and other 'high energy' people or organisations trying to find the high of the spiritual light. The person or organisation can take over the life of the person, who crumbles into addiction to the energy that it delivers. I have seen people willingly do some questionable things to stay connected to that energy. Spiritual addiction doesn't mean it isn't really an addiction. It is, just like any other addiction. Like all addictions, this might serve someone for a time, pushing them to grow stronger than the pull of the addiction in order to overcome it. It takes a very strong-willed and aware person to know when to let go and trust that their own inner connection to the Divine can be enough for them, even if at first it doesn't seem as dazzling as the light delivered by the person or situation to which one was addicted.

The Divine wants immediate and intimate relationship with all beings, to wake up to enlightened self-realisation through all of us, not just a chosen few. This means at some point every single one of us has to take a risk and take a leap into reliance on our own inner divine connection, direct to the source. This requires transformation - which we will talk about in a moment. The difficulty can be leaving the perfection of transcendence behind, letting go of the adoration of the spiritual light no matter what the cost - because sometimes the cost will be our own spiritual growth, which requires we learn to love not only the light, but the form of all creation, including our bodies and each other (even though that may seem rather more challenging at times).

Those of us who have experienced addiction to transcendence – whether through an obsession with spiritual light to the exclusion of the physical world, or an addiction to drugs or alcohol, or the highs of sex or shopping, or work or working out, or anything that takes us out of the pain of daily life and allows us to escape or numb-out – know that it is a very hard addiction to surrender. Sometimes we just want to feel good and not have to struggle quite so much! Sometimes that is fine. As a way of dealing with life on a regular basis, it can prevent us from getting into the heart of an issue, healing it, and genuinely out growing it (which is rather different to avoiding something for as long as possible).

However the surrender of transcendence eventually comes when we have had enough of dwelling in the realms of light and want to feel alive, to experience the body that we have been given, human love and affection, intimacy, the adventure of life. The desire for this can become so strong that it pulls us away from needing the perfection of light and into the quest to find out what else there is! We start to crave life itself. We want to experience it - the colour, the taste, the sensations of it.

For years, or lifetimes, we might try to resist this desire for life, holding back out of fear.

We know at some level that when we really choose to live, we hand over our illusions of control to the Divine and surrender into an adventure far greater than just our personal role in the grander scheme of the divine plan. It is exciting, humbling and uplifting, all at once.

Resistance to letting go of transcendence is easily spotted in our culture. It often manifests itself as arrogance and ignorance. Technological 'developments' that don't seek to enhance nature or protect her, but to dominate and control her are one example. Over-thinking creating stress and anxiety and an inability to find a way to simply be and enjoy your life are another symptom. Lonely disconnection from the world trying to substitute genuine connection through computers is yet another. Don't get me wrong, I love technology. I believe if used consciously it can enhance the feminine values of connection and creativity. But we have to be conscious and balanced with it and it is very, very hard to stay balanced unless we are consciously working through our own issues on this topic. Far too many people either reject technology altogether, which is not necessarily helpful, or don't realise that we have to be conscious to work with it rather than having it distract us from living.

Without shifting from transcendence into transformation, we lose the gift of transcendence and get stuck in its shadow. After a while what was bliss becomes death, and we lose our connection to life, our bodies, and the feast of life is left behind, untouched. The Divine in form understandably becomes frantic at this point – angry, sad, trying to gain our attention and connection with her. Natural disasters and other signs of imbalance start to show. Even our own bodies might be frustrated, angry, sad, lonely, even though we don't necessarily understand why. We are called then, in increasingly serious communications to deal with the situation more consciously. To bring the light into the form, not fluff about in the sky, dissociated from what is happening in this divine temple of earth, requires a love of the light and an equal love of the earth.

This dual-love leads us from the spiritual light of transcendence into the Divine Feminine world of transformation. We have enough spirit to be able to bear the form, to bring light and awakening to it, rather than to fall asleep in it. We are ready for the next level of truth, that there can be something really valuable to learn (and become) through engaging in the struggle of human existence, that this is part of our journey. We can take the truth of spirit and use it as a source of strength, inspiration, love and peace as we are initiated into the feminine world of polarity, where we become exposed to the pairs of opposites, including the agony and the ecstasy of life. The tension of these pairs of opposites, which is the grist for the mill of transformation sometimes feels unbearable. We will experience love and hate, grief and joy, good and evil, violence and tenderness, success and failure, and so on, until we are so dissembled, and broken down, stripped of our concepts and beliefs, stripped of any false notions of control or logic, that we are finally completely and utterly surrendered. We have died to our old selves and our old ways of knowing and believing that we have life 'all sorted'. It is a painful but also liberating death. We have become our own fertiliser, preparing us for the next phase to come, that of transmutation.

The transformational process really develops compassion and wisdom. Over time, it eventually forces us into confrontation with all of our fears, and in doing so creates unbreakable faith and strength. These are the times when we need to learn to trust in ourselves and to know that we are capable of taking care of ourselves and capable of generating healing as a natural force within us. Perhaps we are developing faith in our own wisdom and strength, in our ability to surrender into life's sometimes seemingly crazy ways and let it be. We let life do her work of creating what will serve and destroying what will no longer serve. We surrender, surrender, surrender.

It is a challenging journey and there are times when we cannot and will not make sense of it. The deeper we go into the mystery of life, the more unfathomable it can seem. Yet from deep within the heart, there will be a sense that a greater plan is unfolding, and that even if we cannot know why or how, everything that happens in life is an expression of the divine genius.

A requirement for transformation to occur is that we permit absolute honesty from ourselves. Transformation doesn't shy away from difficult feelings, but brings them out into the open where they can be dealt with. If you are scared in the middle of the night by the sound of something under your bed, the transformational approach is to grab a flashlight and have a look! As I say to clients, the fear is often worse than the reality. You may be imagining a monster under your bed, when in truth there is nothing but a moth fluttering about. Even if it is a monster, you have enough power to deal with it. The tips in Chapter 14 with the Buddha will help you if you do find yourself in a situation in which you are frightened, as will the entire *Crystal Goddesses 888* book and the chapter on Lapis Lazuli and Archangel Michael in *Crystal Angels 444*. But unless you look, you will not know, and if you don't know, you can't do anything about it.

With confrontation, or to put it another way, honest exploration, you can find out what your anger, fear, shame, sadness or depression are communicating to you. It is always a message, oftentimes quite valuable. We become able to hear the messages of our oldest pain not by seeking to rise above it but by going into it and expressing it in a journal, through art, in therapy or through conversation with trusted loved ones. With the messages under our feelings revealed, out of confusion and pain can come a clear indication of what it is that we really need to acknowledge and act on in our lives. Therein lies our key to healing. Anger may be telling you that you are not taking care of yourself, or fear might indicate that you don't believe you deserve success, or sadness be showing you that it is time to move on, or any number of truths that only you can find for yourself.

This transformational process of seeking real communication from the previously hidden parts of us (that could only speak indirectly through pain) frees up energy from being hidden away and locked up in an old emotional pattern or physical illness, and allows it to flow into a more natural, less obstructed channel. Then instead of stagnation, we have progress. This is why after a lot of energy has been directed into healing an issue and we have been doing painful inner work, as we emerge out of it, there is often a rush of creativity, fast-progress and life seems to fly so quickly – because all that energy has been released in a rush of forward movement, almost like we are jet-propelled out of our old holding pattern and into a new expression and experience of our life.

Transformation gets the fuel for its fire from our spiritual insight. This is our ability to rise above a repeating pattern, instead of getting swept up in it (or whilst we are getting swept up in it, another part of us is observing the process). This is why we needed transcendence first. We had to develop the ability to fly above and see things from a higher perspective. From that vantage point, we start to notice that what we thought was the issue – that someone else wasn't doing what we thought they should, for example, isn't the real issue at all. Maybe the real issue is that we feel very insecure if we don't feel we are controlling another. We start paying attention to what is really happening, rather than focusing on the red herring, the thing that seems so important, but actually is a distraction from what matters.

We used to get these red herrings in law school exams when I was at university. You would be reading a scenario and all of a sudden there would be this big red flag of a fact that would throw you. It seemed so important and yet if you were to go with this apparently significant fact, you would lose track of the real question of law that you were being tested on. You would be drawn off the path, your energy distracted from the real issue at hand.

So instead of making fear the issue, for example, or anger, or an eating disorder or chronic relationship difficulties, we look for what is really happening underneath, seeking out the most honest communications from ourselves. The more honest the communication that we can acknowledge, the more powerful the healing transformation that we can facilitate for ourselves. Suddenly we realise that we need more rest, and perhaps more fun. We realise that we haven't been kind to ourselves, we have got caught up in an old version of love that isn't meeting our needs, so we learn to love in a different, more responsive way.

The Violet Flame supports all three T's. You can connect with this support by simply imagining your higher self burning like a Violet Flame. It might be in your heart, your belly, or all around you and within you. Whatever phase you need - be it more transcendence, transformation or the third phase of transmutation - which we will discuss below - the violet flame will support you in accessing it.

Transmutation is what happens naturally following the first two phases. It is in effect the release of energy from a more limited lower form into a higher expression of its essence. It is a hard-won alchemy. It is what happens as the fuel of transcendence translates into the fire of transformation, and the divine alchemy naturally follows on. Our inner lead is turned into gold, we are transfigured, no longer just a spirit or just a body, but a fully-integrated divine human being, which is known as a Christed being, in the Ascended Masters tradition. It is a significant milestone on our own journey into the frequency of love, wisdom and compassion, and a will completely surrendered into and aligned with the Divine.

This may happen in micro-transmutations along the cycles of growth on the way to becoming a fully-fledged Christed being. Micro-transmutations could be a shift of fear into insight, or of hatred into compassion, or even of an argument into a profound meeting of minds where two people come to understand each other and be able to lovingly respect and connect with each other deeper than before they began their argument. With transmutation what once seemed to be dense or negative can actually be experienced as very light indeed. At the highest level, transmutation is an ability to experience everything, no matter whether light or dark from a lower perspective, as divine light.

An argument with a family member for example could either reinforce our wounded child, or force us to seek out spiritual insight when we realise there is something for us to learn here. We see and experience the family member in question as a soul having a spiritual growth experience that has little to do with us at all. We see that we are a soul having our learning and we can only deal with our own experience, and so we go into the pain of inner work, earning the transformation of emotional healing. What started as pain, led to insight, which fuelled our transformational work, and we are somewhere entirely different as a result – we are liberated, we are free. We have gained spiritual power and what was once a troubling issue has become a way to experience the Divine. It is perceived and experienced as a divine gift. The Divine is in all, just waiting to be discovered. With transmutation what was once experienced as not being divine is now experienced as being of divine substance. That which was dark has become light – not in the sense of one opposite swinging towards another, but in the sense of an entirely different experience at an entirely different upward turn of the spiral of our own spiritual growth.

I remember one example of this that occurred for me whilst I indulged in a strange desire to watch a teen television series called "Dance Academy" on the Australian ABC channel. Looking back, I now realise it was spirit helping me heal something unresolved within me, but at the time both myself and my partner were somewhat bemused by my absorption in the series written for an audience far younger than me. The series chronicled the lives and loves of a group of young teens studying ballet with a view to becoming professional dancers. Their hard work, aspirations and the negative effect of their passion for ballet on their body image at times took me back to my own unresolved childhood experience of ballet training.

Ever since I could just barely walk, I wanted to dance. My mother enrolled me in ballet classes and I loved it. Classical music was always a passion of mine. I used to sit on the end of my bed as a young child, listening to Beethoven on my little cassette recorder (it was the 1980s!) and pretend to be conducting the orchestra with my little arms waving about passionately in the air. It wasn't long before I was studying piano and learning my favourite classical pieces. Ballet was another outlet for this deep love of musical communion where I truly felt my emotions, body and soul all in the one place. It was wonderful!

My childhood ballet classes soon became a source not only of great bliss, but of great despair as it didn't take long to realise that whilst I had the soul of a dancer, my body was not built for ballet! I have always been fairly flexible, but a ballet dancer needs a certain type of mobility in the hip joint to allow for postures to be technically correct, and no matter how hard I tried, I couldn't change the structure of my hip or knee joints, not to mention become less curvy and less tall, to allow for my dream of being a ballerina to come true.

Even at that young pre-teen age, I suffered much grief over this. I made it mean something quite painful without even realising it. Rather than being able to fully mourn it and move on, which didn't really happen until I was watching this TV show decades later, I subconsciously interpreted this experience as meaning that I couldn't have what

I wanted, that I was destined to be thwarted by my own body's imperfections and could never have my heart's desire. What a message to tell myself!

As you might imagine, this interpretation didn't do much for a positive and trusting relationship with my body! So how, after all those years and much inner work and spiritual growth, did a teen TV show help me have a transmutation of nearly three decades of conditioning? Because of all the transformational work that I had done over the years, and having had so many experiences of transcendence, the loving spirit of peace that sustained me even whilst my pain was unresolved, I was well prepared. So when it was time, it occurred in an instant.

My healing moment came from a random comment made by the character Tara in the show. She said that a dancer had to learn how to control her body. Suddenly I had an insight that cleared the last residues of my grief and helped me realise the gift in what I had thought was a setback. I could just let it go, feeling a sense of resolution that had eluded me without me really being aware of that fact prior to that moment.

My insight was this – my journey has been about learning not to try to control my body but to trust it and let it lead me. That was it. Simple, true and completely shattering to this old painful story. In that instant, my perspective changed and an old pain left me – instead of mourning not being able to be a ballet dancer I was suddenly relieved and grateful! I promptly lost all interest in the TV show (the temporary obsession now having served its purpose) and came to a place of deeper peace with my body and my spiritual journey than ever before.

Since then, dance has featured more in my spiritual practice. The freedom from old grief has enabled me to explore this path of healing in my spiritual work personally and professionally. The transmutation occurred and my experience of dance went from wounding to grace.

Visualising the Violet Flame and calling on Master St. Germain will help us access whatever phase of the three "Ts" will be most helpful for us at any given time, on any given issue. It is an instant prayer for clearing, protection and peace. It can be called upon at any time to surround us with healing energy. It can just as easily be called upon to surround a house or a situation, such as at the site of an accident that you see when you are out driving one day, or perhaps after a heated emotional exchange has created a disturbed feeling of chaos or anger in your workplace. It can be sent to parts of your body or soul that feel imbalanced. It can be called upon to work through you "according to higher divine intelligence that loves me unconditionally."

You can use this for yourself and others as much as you would like. The Violet Flame is a spiritual healing technique and as such will only go where it is needed and accepted. You can send it to another trusting that if they do not want it, they will not take it in. A bit like if a friend brought over a paperback book about his religion, which isn't your thing at all. You might be a bit interested but end up putting it (lovingly) into the recycling bin! On the other hand, it might just contain a perfect bit of advice or healing for you in that moment, even if you don't take to the whole school of thought.

So it is with the Violet Flame and sharing it with others who aren't into lightwork or the Ascended Masters (or aren't yet, anyway). Sometimes their soul will just let it slide right on by them without much interest, but many times, it will drink it in. Especially if that person is very sick or dying, then the Violet Flame can help them connect with spirit and release fear of death. If it is their time to pass, this can help it be a more loving experience for them. If it is not that time for them, it can still help that person feel more connected to love, which is a blessing at times of vulnerability. It can also help them heal their relationship with their body, which can be a tremendous blessing if one is in sickness or at the end of their life. It is like making peace with your dearest, most devoted friend before the relationship ends forever. It works gently and beautifully with animals too.

If someone is trying to cope with a death or sickness of a beloved person or animal, the Violet Flame can be an incredible gift also as the colour violet helps process grief. If you are clairvoyantly opening, you may see dark violet light in the auric field of a person who is grieving. Healing grief requires a recognition of loss and a release of a person, place or thing at a physical and emotional level. After that process, there can be a sense of spiritual connection with that person, place or object that endures. Violet light encourages letting go emotionally and physically, and dealing with the sometimes excruciating pain of that. The price of human love is the willingness to bear its loss, not just to celebrate its presence. The violet energy also helps one recognise the spiritual bond that lives on. That bond doesn't replace what has been lost, but offers a different kind of connection that can be quite precious to our hearts.

The guided meditation featuring St. Germain and the Violet Flame initiation is on my meditation CD called *For Love and Light on Earth*, published by Blue Angel Publishing. This is a meditative exercise and is recommended for healers and lightworkers as a regular cleansing practice, perhaps once every one to three months, or even weekly, depending on the degree of spiritual cleansing you feel you need. This will vary and will increase during times of growth and intense work with self and/or others. It's also a great meditation to do with groups, especially if you are doing earth-healing work. Enjoy!

AMETHYST – SPIRITUAL CONNECTION

After Clear Quartz, Amethyst is probably the best known of all the crystals. It is also quite often a stone that calls people who are just beginning to connect with crystal energies. It is accessible and beautiful, gentle and works over a long period of time. It purifies, protects and strengthens divine connection, clearing out obstructions like addiction and over-thinking, helping the crown chakra open and the connection to the Divine to become stronger and more conscious than our fears and doubts. It is something like a Violet Flame encapsulated in a stone.

Commonly found and not particularly expensive, unless of a very high grade (which will be very rich in colour, a dark and glistening purple), there are various forms of Amethyst available, including geodes (or crystal caves), and most commonly, crystal points. Amethyst can be naturally mined, and also combined with other stones, such as Citrine (that stone is called Ametrine) and with chlorite, which can look like the eyes of peacock feathers combined with the Amethyst stone. These two combinations amplify the cleansing power of Amethyst. Amethyst is frequently found in jewellery as well as small tumbled stones and is safe to wear or carry for prolonged periods of time.

This stone is wonderful for use in meditation spaces and sleeping areas as it encourages peace. If you are going through a process of spiritual growth or intuitive development and psychic awakening – or even finding that you are struggling with dreams that are challenging emotionally – then Amethyst in your sleep and meditation area is helpful over the long term. It has a capacity for psychic protection and purification of negative energy. If you combine this with a small dish or bowl of salt water (kept away from any nosey pets and changed on a daily basis) in your sleeping area and if you work as a healer, in your healing space, then you can minimise negative energy.

Because Amethyst connects with the crown chakra, which is the seat of connection to soul (and therefore spirit, remembering that the soul or higher self is like a telephone line direct to the Universe), it can help us access past life issues, if we wish to do so. This is because it is the soul that reincarnates over and over again to heal issues over a long-term period of many lifetimes – we'll explore this in *Crystal Lifetimes* 999 later on in this series). Apart from past life healing, Amethyst also supports the crown chakra as we open up to more conscious connection with our spiritual guidance. It strengthens all the aspects of the crown chakra which includes the ability to be detached emotionally, to feel connected to all beings as an expression of the one unified spiritual light, and to experience claircognisance or spiritual knowing (those moments where you will say, "I don't know how I know, I just know!").

If you are craving more spiritual presence in your life, Amethyst may hold quite a pull for you. If you are in need of more grounding, combining Amethyst with Zincite (see the following chapter on Master Lao Tzu and Zincite) which will help make this stone work for you, calling your heavenly energy into the earth of your own body.

HEALING WITH ST. GERMAIN AND AMETHYST

Find a place that is peaceful and where you can comfortably seat yourself upright. Have your piece of Amethyst or the mandala in this book near your body, preferably touching your body.

When you are ready say the following invocation to call in higher guidance, "I call upon the highest guidance that loves me unconditionally, I call in the true Ascended Master St. Germain, I call in the Angel of Amethyst, and I call upon the Violet Flame. I open to receive what I need, according to unconditional love and the highest grace available to me now. I surrender in trust and open to spirit. Through divine grace and of my own free will, so be it."

Imagine that you can close your eyes and see, sense or feel that all around you there is a field of rich violet light, crackling like a flame.

Breathe in and out and get used to the energy of being within that holy flame. You may sense it having an effect on you, subtle or obvious, but whatever you feel, just be with it. Breathe.

Then you sense that there is a large, luminous pair of angelic wings, white but outlined in rich violet light and they open up before you now, emerging out of the Violet Flame crackling all around you. There is a sense of peace and yet a realisation that there is a lot of energy entering your space now.

Using your breath, imagine that you can breathe in this energy, the energy of the Violet Flame and of the angelic wings, on the inhalation. On your exhalation, anything that is no longer needed is released, pouring out of you on the out-breath.

Let the violet energy in the flame and in the angelic wings stir up stagnant energy and release blockages in your body, mind and soul, even if you have no conscious notion of what it is that is happening. Just stay present with your intention and breathe.

If you find it hard to focus as you breathe in and out, allowing this energetic cleansing to take place, simply repeat the mantra "I AM" either gently aloud, or in your mind. "I AM" as you breathe in, and "I AM" as you breathe out. Repeat this for as long as feels good, but for at least around 33 breaths.

You may notice a calming effect, or that anxiety, fear, sadness or anger rises and falls through this process. That is fine. It is healing taking place. Stay with your breath and the mantra, if you are using it.

When you are ready to move on, take your awareness to the crown of your head. Imagine that there is a beautiful lotus flower opening, petal by petal, at the crown of your head. You may sense that the crown chakra is far larger than you realised, with many petals in many layers opening. You may sense physical sensations of sharp pains or soft tingling. Or it may be very subtle for you. Whatever happens, or does not, is perfect for you at this time. Perceive the violet energies of the flame and the angelic wings beginning to swirl and expand at the top of your head, moving through your crown chakra.

When you are ready, repeat the following prayer, "I now surrender into karmic grace and absolution all blockages in my crown chakra, all weapons and fears, and I open to spiritual grace, protection and light. I open to the divine connection that will assist me best now, through loving grace and divine mercy, so be it."

Imagine that your crown chakra can breathe in the violet light and divine love that is all around you. On the out-breath, the crown chakra is purged clean of darkness and pain.

You may or may not consciously understand what is happening and that is perfectly fine. You may sense past life patterns or attachments leaving as this occurs, or feel physical sensations in your head or other parts of your body.

You may feel light-headed or even a little ungrounded. If that happens, place your hands on your feet or knees, palms face down and open your eyes whilst you breathe.

Let the crown chakra breathe in and out at least 33 times, using the mantra "I AM" if necessary to help you focus. Breathing "I AM" into the crown chakra, along with the violet wings of the Angel of Amethyst and the Violet Flame of St. Germain, then exhaling "I AM" as the crown chakra releases old energy and grows.

If at any time this exercise feels too strong or ungrounding for you, stop immediately and move on to this last section of the exercise to complete it. If you can stay with this process for around 33 more breaths, do so, but honour what you feel and take your time. Nothing is gained by pushing here. Let what needs to happen do so in its own timing.

When you are ready, say the following, "I AM heaven in earth, I AM light in earth, I AM spirit in form. I call upon the light of heaven to touch the earth of my body now. I AM protected, grounded, anchored in divine light here in this divine form. So be it. I call upon the Violet Flame of St. Germain and the Angel of Amethyst for your protection and grounding now. Thank you."

Place your hands in prayer at your heart and bow your head.

Then place your hands lightly on your feet, touching them with reverence, and bow your head. Stay there for a few moments.

When you are ready, open your eyes.

You may wish to move about a little to get grounded again, bouncing lightly on your feet and even placing your head in your hands or laying down with your head on the floor for at least a few breaths, letting yourself really connect with the earth again. This is especially so if you are one who finds it easier to connect with the spiritual worlds of energy than the physical worlds of form. If you are one who finds it hard to consciously connect with spirit and easier to connect with the physical world around you, then you may not need to complete a grounding exercise afterwards and may prefer to simply finish with the prayer and touching of the feet.

As with all the healing exercises, notice what you feel in the days following – perhaps journaling if necessary – and nourish yourself. Particularly when working with spirit you'll need good exercise (not exhausting exercise) to ground you and move the subtle energy through your body and enough rest to process the effects of that energy. You'll grow faster working with the process rather than trying to force yourself to move on. Be kind. You deserve it.

10.

ASCENDED MASTER LAO TZU (Eastern Wisdom)
ZINCITE (Power)

INITIATION INTO BALANCE

From deep within the earth, heat and pressure build causing enormous friction. Intensely, yet slowly, a brilliant red-orange crystal is forged. The stone rises up out of the earth, shining bright with red-orange light. A male elder, wise and calm, yet holding great power within, gazes peacefully at the process.

Earth school holds many lessons for old souls, including the lesson of balance. It can be learned no matter what state of development we are at, and each time we grow a new skill or develop a new level of awareness, we often need to tend to balance again, coming back to our centre or core and learning how to find the strength that we need there in order to sustain the extension of our energy – perhaps into a new relationship or new work, for example.

Initiation into balance is sometimes known in Eastern traditions as the Middle Way. The Middle Way involves finding a path of integration, releasing extremes and choosing a path that includes and accepts all of life, and ourselves, with compassion. For human beings comprised of an earthly animal body and a divine spirit that eventually will fuse as one, finding a path of moderation or the middle way can be very helpful.

There are times, especially during intense initiation, where we will feel anything but moderate. We may feel flung from pillar to post, as the expression goes. We can feel reactive, highly sensitive and swing between intense analysis and high-voltage emotional states. I have had times in my life where I have felt locked into extremes at either end of the spectrum from the intellectual to the emotional and it's been hard to find a way to integrate these different parts of me.

If, like myself, you tend to not be half-hearted in your approach to life, perhaps being a very passionate person, then learning balance and moderation can be a challenge. My closest friends call me "Red," a nickname that came about due to my tendency to charge forward with great momentum. I don't just decide to write one book, for example, I'll decide to write seven. I had to learn that if I am going to continue in this way, and I've been like this all of my life so I am assuming this character trait is set in me to some extent, then I'll have to have balance on a daily basis so as not to burn out. I get very enthusiastic about my work and balance is something that I have to really force myself to pay attention to. It doesn't come naturally to me. I learned that even apparently desirable extremes, like orientation to the higher spiritual worlds for example, can be regressive if we cannot eventually draw that energy back to the physical world and our bodies, so we can apply it. Without finding a middle way, a way of balance and integration, we cannot grow. If we are very active people, then we can burn out without balance. If we are floatier and more receptive types, without balance we won't find the will and oomph that we need to take the action we need to take to manifest our heart's desire. We need enough heat and yang and activity to be balanced with enough coolness, yin and receptivity. Living a balanced life is a spiritual art form and we may have to work quite hard on it in order to create a way that suits our individual temperaments.

Seeking methods of balancing ourselves is essential for integration. Without integration we feel like we are pulled in all sorts of directions from within, as though we are fighting with different parts of ourselves. We can begin to feel very fragmented, like we are playing all different roles in our lives rather than just being who we are always. Without integration you might be a harried mother, a dutiful daughter, a happy school-volunteer, a professional corporate person, an endlessly sympathetic friend (even if you might want to give your friend a smack and tell her to wake up sometimes rather than listening to another conversation about her particular problems), and a good sportsperson, but you might not ever really feel that you are able to just be 'you'. You might not always be sure who 'you' actually are.

After a while the cracks show and the real you will yearn to come out and let you know who you are after all. Maybe you'll start behaving in ways that others don't like, you might get criticised because you aren't fulfilling your roles as you were in the past and people may not want you to change. They might be more interested in keeping things comfortable for them than in you growing. You might feel angry and hostile or really sad and not know why. This is the real you shaking things up from inside and demanding to be lived. This is a sign that integration is starting to happen. Sometimes for integration to happen however, there is a lot of shaking up of things as they are, because if left as they are, you will be locked into them and unable to break free and grow into your true self (which is what you are here to do).

Once the integration process begins – and we remember that to bake a cake we have to crack a few eggs – we will really need to seek balance. Finding ways to pay attention to our painful emotions, but also taking in the simple beauty of nature for example, is important. Taking time for meditation or journaling or prayer – or all three – and balancing these with physical activity and time with loved ones, or with a pet, or in nature, is also helpful. Balance doesn't have to be a sophisticated or tricky process, sometimes the simple approaches that are accessible to us now are very effective.

At the best of times in a busy life, this kind of simple balance can be a challenge. When we are going through initiation however, where things get more intense emotionally and psychologically, balance becomes more important and yet sometimes harder to attain.

When things are getting messy inside of us or in our lives because growth is happening within, and we don't know how it is all going to turn out, we can feel very much out of balance.

Personally, it took me well over a decade of conscious inner work, study and experimentation, to even begin to find effective methods through which to balance myself. I had to learn the signs of my own mind, body and emotions that were indicating to me when I was veering out of balance. When I learned what my signs were, I could then do something to bring myself back into balance before my symptoms became too extreme. I learned about healing and recovery, about what was needed to replenish myself if I became too drained, for example. I learned about when physical activity would replenish or drain me. I learned about how to mentally rest (which was difficult for me, given that my natural mental state tends towards constant creative motion – give me a day and I'll give you countless new creative ideas on any number of topics!). I had to learn about emotional balance and how to attain that through inner work as well as physical and mental activity, as well as taking breaks and rest when needed. I had to learn a lot.

I also learned that each being is an individual and what looks like balance for me, the way that I achieve it, may be very different for someone else. Our individual energetic constitution is unique – it is a bit like our soul fingerprint. The intricate patterning of our masculine and feminine energies, with their differing needs, will not be exactly the same for another as it is for us. That patterning will unlikely remain the same even for us as we grow through this lifetime. We are learning to accept constant change and to seek balance as a way to interact with the changes and flow of life, to cultivate a responsive relationship to the spiritual growth process that we are in, and to allow ourselves absolute freedom to seek and decide upon what works for us, realising that not everyone will benefit from the same formula.

One of the wisest men I have met is my Chi Gung Master Zhao. He is playful, cheeky and insightful. He has a lot of knowledge and has studied most of his life. Yet when it comes to nutrition advice, he says get to know what works for you. This is the most sensible advice I have heard in my entire life about nutrition – and there is an over-abundance of nutritional advice available to us.

It is the sense of responsibility for ourselves that perhaps makes the initiation of balance a challenging one. Many of us seem to prefer being able to follow the guidelines of another.

Perhaps if that is you, find some guidelines that feel as close as possible to what works for you and then give yourself permission to explore the boundaries a little to see if you need to make some tweaks here and there.

Of course it's hard to make decisions about what you need if you don't know what you need. And you won't really know what you need if you don't know how to communicate with yourself, with your body, and sense whether you need to be active or to rest and reset yourself, for example.

If you are one of the people in this world who find it easy to ascertain your needs, then you have either done a lot of inner work or you simply did not need to go through this lesson in such intensity this lifetime. You will still likely find elements in this chapter that can help you, as balance is something that we are all working towards as a human race.

If you are one of the people, as healers so often are, that naturally tend towards sensing the needs of others rather than their own, then this chapter is especially relevant for you at a personal level. If you are a complex being, with many competing needs, which is what I realised I was over time, then the mastery of balance will require more skill for you to attain.

So with this process of balance and the healing at the end of this chapter, you may find that you get more of a grip on what your needs are and how to meet them in a functional way. Those needs are not always going to mean you have to attend to yourself, either. In more complex beings, there is a need to give, to make a valuable contribution that feels like it is uniquely from you in service to something greater than yourself. There can be creative needs too, for self-expression. Then there are physical needs that depend on your own unique energetic patterning of mind, body and soul. These can include food, clean air and water, spiritual connection, sexual and creative expression, a need for music or other communion with something greater than one's own sense of individual self, for fun, for adventure, for peace and calm, for stimulation or for inner reflection, for community and for solitude, to be seen and perhaps sometimes to be unseen. If you are a complex being tending towards wholeness, then you are often going to have to learn to balance competing needs, finding ways to allow all of your self to flourish in this life.

It sounds like a big task, and it can be difficult at times, but we don't have to be perfect. If you have ever watched a tightrope walker, surely one of the best physical examples of the art of balance, you will notice that they move slowly, steadily and with constant small subtle adjustments. There will be wobbles, but that doesn't mean the person won't get across the tightrope. It just means that they have to get focus back again and pay attention, and on they go.

There is no magic formula or recipe that will serve you throughout your whole life, especially if you are growth-oriented and in a path of transformation (and reading this book indicates that you are one of those growth-oriented people). If you can learn to be responsive and self-aware, and then have the courage to act upon what you sense, you will learn how to approach balance within yourself more effectively, even in difficult situations. It is not about perfection, for even perfect balance will become destabilised when another step is taken. It is about learning to find the right relationship to life – which means taking care of your needs and trusting in the flow of life that asks us to grow, to re-adjust and adapt as we develop.

Then our mastery of balance at that level renders us capable of taking on more load, of carrying more light or more wisdom, for example. So we have to learn at the next level how to balance all over again. If our foundation is good, we can rely on the skills we have learned as we attempt to apply them in more challenging situations or circumstances. We learn again, not how to always stay perfectly in our centre, but how to allow the instability of growth to ruffle our wings a little (or a lot) and be capable of returning to centre when we are jostled out of it by the forces of our own spiritual growth. We have our wobble like the tightrope walker on the highwire, and as everyone below gasps, we pause, breathe, find our centre, perhaps wink cheekily, and continue on.

So our initiation of balance is not about the perfection of always being centred, although our experience of remaining centred during all sorts of situations or circumstances will increase markedly as a side effect of this initiation. It is more about the process of returning to centre, to self, to truth, to the middle way, to moderation. From that place, we are even more empowered to continue with higher levels of spiritual growth and to express ourselves in the world in a healing and constructive way.

ASCENDED MASTER LAO TZU – EASTERN WISDOM

Known by many as the Father of modern Taoism, Lao Tzu (meaning 'Old Master') serves humanity with a sense of humour, with compassion and with wise knowing. Taoism is a spiritual tradition from the East. Lao Tzu distilled from that ancient tradition some accessible teachings and included them in his spiritual classic, the *Tao Te Ching*, in around 600BC. This was over two thousand years after the inception of Taoism, said to be by the first emperor of China, Fu Hsi.

The Ascended Masters, just like you and I, have had various incarnations upon the earth. They choose the incarnation from which to ascend and maintain their radiant physical body which will now be a part of their personality and role as an Ascended Master based on what will best help humanity (rather than, I imagine, what their favourite hairstyle might have been). Lao Tzu appears as an old man, some others, such as Jesus appear as a younger man or Mother Mary as a youthful yet mature woman.

Lao Tzu doesn't appear to be particularly interested in claiming that his soul was incarnated as Fu Hsi, the first emperor of China who introduced Taoism as a complete spiritual philosophy to help guide people through all aspects of human life (though it does occur to me that he may well have been), but he does agree to me sharing that he belongs to that same soul mission, that those two lifetimes shared some similarity in spiritual purpose.

I am reminded by the energy of Lao Tzu of a cartoon character. This character features in the animated movies of *Kung Fu Panda*, and its sequel. The character is a slow moving, very powerful turtle known as Master Oogway. If you feel drawn to Lao Tzu, or this chapter, then I would suggest that you watch these films as they hold within them some of the Eastern teachings of the Tao (with a somewhat Hollywood-style spin of course, but I adore them nonetheless and find them funny and delightful).

In the *Kung Fu Panda* film, it comes time to choose the next Kung Fu saviour, a very important task. Master Oogway leads an ornate ceremony to honour the occasion and to choose the next hero. It is attended by animals (all the 'people' are animals in this film, another thing I love about it) hailing from far and wide. There is much celebration and ritual, spectacular Kung Fu demonstrations by various Kung Fu masters, and then the moment is upon them. It is time to declare the next great Kung Fu hero! With bated breath, the crowd stills and the spectacle grinds to a halt. Master Oogway points his turtle-foot in a particular direction, eyes closed. The eyes of the crowd follow his directive and wait...

At that exact moment, through a mishap involving a large amount of dynamite strapped to his body, a large, enthusiastic though undisciplined, Panda is launched through the air, over the high walls and closed gates of the holy city, landing right at the feet of Master Oogway, with an embarrassing thump. The Master opens his eyes to find that he is pointing at a portly panda bear, inelegantly slumped on the ground before him, not exactly known for anything much, other than a passion for overeating! Certainly not the excepted contender for the next Kung Fu hero!

There is a collective gasp of horrified shock as Master Oogway giggles and accepts that this is indeed, the new saviour of Kung Fu. His highly disciplined and skilled students and other Kung Fu masters are unified in their horror and immediately question his decision. Oogway is unwavering in his trust that this is indeed the right person for the job, because this is what life has delivered.

As it turns out of course, Panda has the very qualities that were needed in the Kung Fu community for it to flourish, in a way, balancing its shadow side and bringing a spirit of love, friendship, compassion and devotion that would unite and strengthen the community. Perhaps there was no mistake that the panda, black and white in colour like the yin-yang symbol itself, would be the representation of balance and wholeness restored to the Kung Fu community.

However none of that is consciously known at first. What enables the unexpected and in this case, apparently improbable, divine genius to unfold is acceptance. In some situations where the circumstances seem so ridiculous, it is very hard for even the most advanced Kung Fu experts to have acceptance. It is only the greatest master of the masters, Oogway, that has enough wisdom to trust completely and utterly in what is happening.

There is a Buddhist teaching from one of my favourite teachers in the Buddhist Tantra tradition, Reggie Ray. It is a simple teaching and I share it with my students often because I have received a similar teaching myself from the Divine Mother. The teaching is this – trust in your life experiences. Trust life! Life is the ultimate divine teacher, and the Tao is her manual. To have a consciously trusting and responsive attitude to life will always help us find our way, in fact, the way will open up before us.

Master Oogway is an expression of Taoism, the spiritual path of wisdom that helps us attune ourselves to life, and learn her mysteries, one of them being balance. He is pictured in the film standing on one leg, balancing on a long thin stick, in deep meditation. Balance personified!

So much of our learning happens as we gain the ability to shed our preconceptions, and our ego, and learn to align ourselves with that which is vaster than we are – we can find greatness and power not through our own fanciful imagination, but through actual experience of the natural power of life. This is where Master Oogway's power is sourced, not from force, or even strength or other characteristics, no matter how desirable they may be – such as courage and compassion. Oogway accesses his power through his spiritual connection to life. The Tao helps us find our way to live in harmony with life.

At the heart of the Tao is the balancing of two flows of life energy – yin and yang, or loosely translated into Western concepts, feminine and masculine energy. In the West, we are more familiar with masculine styles of power – force, strength, dominance and making things happen through exertion, striving and personal power. Many if not most of our new age spiritual teachers are focused on these sorts of power and how to use them to gain what you want, or in new age terms, to create your own reality.

That path serves a purpose for a while but is not an end in itself. It can help people develop willpower and an understanding of the law of attraction, which is essential for entry into higher stages of the path. We cannot surrender to a higher power if we don't have any willpower from which to do it. Wanting to surrender is a great start, really wonderful because it accepts that there may be a creative intelligence in the Divine that knows more than our ego does. This is true and the start of growing up spiritually. It is a wonderful desire! It is on its own however, not enough to just want to surrender, we then actually have to do it. We have to summon the inner strength to trust and it takes a huge amount of willpower in the initial switch from trusting in fear to trusting in love to not fall into our old patterns of thinking and to bring about new patterns of trust. Giving up the old drama takes a lot of willpower indeed.

Also if we don't understand the law of vibrational resonance, or attraction, then we won't understand that we have to do our personal work to grow and refine our vibration. There is no point wanting to live a life of love, passion, creativity and divine inspiration if we are vibrating at the level of fear, distrust, disconnection from life and lack of belief in ourselves. Those vibrations are not compatible. We have to work on healing ourselves to be capable of receiving the blessings of the Divine through feelings of trust, worth, openness and surrender. That is why there are so many healing processes included in my work. As the Sufi mystic Rumi puts it (and we'll meet him in *Crystal Saints and Sages 777* later on in this series), the fault is not with the wine (the Divine) but with the cup (our ability to receive).

So we learn something from this 'create your own reality' teaching. This masculine path can be helpful if we really do learn these lessons. But it can also seduce us away from taking the next step if it is co-opted by the ego and turned into a spiritual tool that serves the ego's need for everything to be as it wants it to be (forget about surrender! I just want lots of money, sex appeal and my super-hot yoga instructor to fall in love with me!).

Growing up isn't easy, even spiritually. As we do though, we realise that what we really want, underneath all the passing desires for this product or that job, is a fulfilment of the heart's desire. The Divine wants that for us too. The problem is that sometimes we don't know our own hearts very well. Fortunately the Divine does. If we allow it, it will lead us straight into our own fulfilment, way beyond anything the ego could ever even imagine in its wildest fantasies. The Divine might even lead us towards fulfilment via that product or that job, or that person falling in love with us, but it might have other ways that would be even more wonderful for us. Just like Master Oogway though, we don't know in advance, we can only trust.

As we grow up spiritually, we become wiser. We learn to balance our creative will with a surrendering to the greater good. So if you really want something, and you just can't let it go, fair enough. Desire isn't a bad thing at all – it can be the passionate obsessive need for the Divine that gives us strength to never give up on our spiritual path. But say that you have a desire that is intense and you are struggling with it, not sure about whether it's a good thing that will help you grow or a big distraction that might cause you a lot of unnecessary pain later on, or you are obsessed with something or someone and it just isn't happening as you would like; then you may want to pray along these lines, "I feel myself wanting this experience or thing – I open to receive it but I surrender the desire for it to the Divine. If it comes to me, let it serve the greatest good. If there is something else the Divine wants for me instead, I open to trust and receive that. Let me serve the Divine as best as I possibly can." You might feel very challenged, and very emotional, with lots of ego tantrums as you pray such a prayer. That's uncomfortable but a good sign that you are actually letting it go.

Often things manifest very quickly for me through that sort of prayer, but sometimes I have to wait much longer or things manifest in a different but ultimately superior way. Trust is the key to moving beyond the masculine "I'll do it my way" approach into the next step, which is, "Perhaps there is an even greater way of which I am, as yet, unaware."

This next step, especially for those of us that relate to the more masculine path of getting it done our way (because wisdom is about balance, not about only one right way) is the Eastern Wisdom of the Tao.

The Tao provides us with a more holistic view of power, which includes feminine power or yin power. Yin or feminine principles operate very differently to the effort and force based masculine or yang principles. Yin power is something we experience in small ways when we aren't trying to do anything in particular. When we miraculously find what we were looking for, even without really looking for it, we are experiencing yin power. It could be a teaching or a piece of guidance that speaks to us as we randomly open a book and read a paragraph to find that it is just what we needed to hear. It could be an actual object that we receive, perhaps through a friend looking to offload a new washing machine just as yours is finally breaking down, which has happened to me, or finding a place to live that suits your needs even though you had no idea how it could possibly come together (all your needs, seemingly impossible to meet within a realistic financial budget) which has also happened for me. Both situations were completely out of left field, and not something that I could have dreamed up for myself as a solution. They were gifts from the Divine that I was capable of receiving, and I felt deep grace at work in the process – for which I felt a lot of gratitude and appreciation.

I also had an experience of a yin moment of manifestation with a dear friend of mine when we were creating an event together, called The Divine Circus, and we needed to find a shaman for our event. We were discussing this need, as one does, before running a goddess dance night dedicated to Kuan Yin (Yin!). At that precise moment, the doorbell rang and as we bolted down the stairs of the dance studio to open the front door, there standing at the threshold, was, in fact, a shaman. Of course. Problem solved via yin power – the solution literally comes right to your door! There have been countless examples of seemingly miraculous situations in my life where yin power, which I would also personally call divine grace combined with our ability to receive it, comes to my aid.

The Tao teaches us how to cultivate this flow, how to become more receptive, more capable of working intelligently and consciously with yin power to attain, rather than believing that striving and struggle is the only way. Yin power requires that we be trusting enough in the divine flow to relax and let things happen according to the workings of a greater power. Sometimes we'll have very clear confirmation – like the examples of the washing machine, place to live and wonderful Divine Circus shaman I mentioned above. Sometimes the manifestation will be far slower and deeper moving and we won't see instant results, we have to trust that the yin power is doing its thing. If we lose faith and try to take over with yang power, forcing our will, we lose our yin power process. We can honour and remain in our yin power process by trusting in the Divine and doing only what feels inspired from the heart from a place of innate inner trust. Working with yin power can be a challenge for more type-A, driven personalities. Perhaps they may even be naturally more yin-type people, who had to adapt in order to succeed (or so they were taught by Western society) becoming more adept at working with yang power. This was certainly the case for me.

For those of us that are learning about Yin power for the first time, it can be a bit confusing. It is far less dynamic and more magnetic. It is about surrender. Our effort goes not into making things happen but in summoning the power to allow for happening. I'll have moments like this when I am writing. I'll need to tap into what is being asked of me for a particular chapter or section, or entire book! If I reach a blank, and nothing is coming, I'll know that I need a break. The information comes most quickly to me if I can summon the energy to counteract any guilt I have about taking a rest and going to lie in the sun or doing something completely different to writing, like washing up dishes or doing a spot of house cleaning. During that time of switching off, I become receptive and the information just comes to me. Then I can set about writing again.

One of my animal totems is the lizard. Have you ever watched them? They are in abundance in Australia, visible in the summer months especially and are quite beautiful, extraordinary creatures. The ones in my garden lie about conserving energy until they need to act (often to avoid feline predators, also abundant at this particular house for some reason – perhaps I need to invoke Bast, the cat goddess, a little less). When they do need to act, they are lightning fast. They don't waste energy in striving. They do or they don't do without apology or explanation. They have the skill of patience and right timing mastered. When I need to laze about in the sun in order to gain energy, a lizard will often appear in my field of vision. They are reminders to me of yin power and of my need to not let my yang, action-oriented and "Red" nature take over my creative process, powering through any obstacle, and instead let my receptive, magnetic nature pull to me what is needed through a conscious choice and action of surrender.

For us to be able to let go of our programmed notions of attainment only through exertion to the point of exhaustion, we have some reprogramming that needs to happen! The Tao helps us, pointing to another way of thinking, of perceiving. One of my favourite teachings of the Tao inverts our perception of what is forward movement and what is backward movement on our path. I have taught time and time again that from the highest perspective there is no such thing as regression or backwards movement as everything serves the path of growth and evolution, moving it forward, even moments where we appear to be heading backwards. The Taoist teaching is that the way forward sometimes appears to be heading backwards and the way backwards sometimes appears to be heading forwards. This means that what we think will move us ahead may not and vice versa.

My grandmother summed this up nicely by teaching me, as a little girl, that sometimes you had to lose the battle to win the war, as the express goes. She taught me that life was not about absolutes, and sometimes you consciously had to let the other have the upper hand in a power game, but it was all about where you were going, the ultimate destination, which to her, was love. I resisted this as a child, having a strong sense of justice and dislike of political game playing (the latter dislike is still intact, which may or may not make my life harder at times). In time however I came to appreciate her wisdom, understanding that right and wrong were not absolutes at all, at least not from a spiritual perspective, and that it was safe for me to let go and allow life to happen. This didn't mean that I wouldn't be able to live what was most important to my heart (freedom, equality and love being two of those deep heart desires) but that I would actually be shown by life, over time, how best to do so. I had to trust. It wasn't necessary for me to burn myself out over all the details. It was better to use my passionate nature to respond to life as it was, bringing about healing through that approach, rather than trying to control it or force it to be as my justice-loving heart wished it could be. She taught me to find effectiveness by softening into the flow rather than by head-butting my way through life. I am sure I still charge like a bull at a gate from time to time, but I have become more balanced in my approach to life because I have learned to trust more in its ultimate wisdom, humour and genius.

The Taoist philosophy sees life as a spiral of consciousness, expanding and contracting in natural rhythms, much like a breath in and out. The spiral is ever growing larger, but sometimes as we spiral, we will feel like we are revisiting old experiences or patterns. We are doing so from a different perspective, a different rung on the spiral. This is a more yin view of life than a linear progression from ignorance to enlightenment. Even if we think life is a linear progression and the spiral is too foreign or awkward to get our minds around, to embrace yin power we have to at least let go of the belief that the way we progress and manifest has to make logical sense. Our journey from A to C might be via Z! If that makes the most sense spiritually, if that is the way we will reach wholeness, avoid unnecessary obstacles (perhaps they were hiding at point B), then that is the way we will naturally grow, provided we don't try to get in the way by resisting our life experiences. That is the genius of yin and the reason why we need such trust to honour it.

Lao Tzu gently nudges us towards acceptance and surrender, to learn to attract through alignment with life that which we need and to trust in the perfection of all that comes our way – even if it is disguised in the most unlikely of forms (such as a dumpling-obsessed Panda). I have to admit, the unexpected twists and turns in my life which have not always been the easiest have somehow also been the most fun.

ZINCITE – POWER

Power is often considered a masculine quality in Western culture, yet in the Eastern traditions, particularly the Vedic traditions of India, power is the terrain of the feminine, of the manifest divinity.

For us to begin to tap into our power, we need access to those chakras which are most familiar for the more worldly types and least familiar for the more spiritually-attuned types (at a certain stage on the path). For those of us that love the spiritual light, the lower three chakras which initially govern survival, sexuality and aggression often become of secondary importance as the upper chakras are explored. Spiritually-inclined individuals will come back to the lower three chakras later on in the journey of growth, realising that through those centres our spiritual light can be radiant in the world where it is most needed. We can transform the content of those chakras through spiritual work and allow them to become holders of a different frequency – of community, belonging, creativity and sacred sexuality, of integrity and healthy boundaries that support a more functional community. It is in the 'downward journey' after the upward journey of transcendence kicks into the more embracing journey of transformation that we begin to experience our spirituality through the lower chakras in a very rich and empowering way.

This will be the case especially if you are what I call 'star children', essentially these are souls that are incarnating on earth that don't really feel that they belong here as much as they belong out in the stars or in the higher spiritual worlds where they sense the energy is much more aligned with their own light. Later on in this series, in *Crystal Stars 11.11*, we will learn more about these beings and the worlds from which they originate. That book is dedicated to such souls and their unique path on the earth. If you have a child or family member, or clients and students, who are star souls, even if you don't consider yourself to be one, that book will be of benefit in understanding their unique needs and spiritual disposition. Of course, if you are intrigued by the energies of the stars and working with them and crystals together for healing, that book is for you too.

However perhaps you are an earthier person more naturally and your access to your lower chakras is already pretty strong and what you are seeking is connection and opening with your higher chakras and you would like to open up more consciously to the subtle spiritual worlds. No matter which end of the spectrum you are coming from in your approach to wholeness, Zincite is going to assist you.

Zincite is an incredible stone of awakening power through attaining balance. If you are skewed towards the upper chakras, it helps pull the energy down into the lower centres so you can live your light physically. If you are caught in the weight of the lower chakras and need help lightening up to find the freedom of the heart, the spiritual light of the throat and third eye and the bliss of universal connection through the crown chakras, then Zincite will act like a dynamite blast for your kundalini flow, or spiritual life force energy, encouraging it to rise up your spine so you can consciously access your higher chakras and the gifts that they bring.

I only recently encountered Zincite in 2012 when it was given to me as a gift, not once, but twice, from two separate clients, in two separate towns, on a teaching tour through the north Australian state of Queensland. Usually expensive and not easy to find, I was delighted to receive a small bright orange piece and another far deeper reddish-orange, piece. I held these relatively small specimens, no bigger than the size of my little finger nail, and felt the power almost immediately. For someone who has a natural tendency to dwell in the upper chakras, which were working hard during that teaching tour, the relief of rebalancing into my lower chakras again with the help of this earth healer was so deeply appreciated.

Zincite holds a teaching that is Taoist in basis, which is essentially that there is only one direction. We may perceive up and down, higher and lower, heaven and earth, but they are unified. As we progress into mastery of balance we come to see that one extreme will flip us into the apparent opposite extreme. Neither are independent of each other, so we can instead seek to find the middle way and balance both. Zincite works with this awareness to balance our energy field and our minds.

I had a physical experience of this whilst meditating during a particularly challenging but also spiritually empowering growth-spurt during a teaching tour in Europe in 2012. I was seated in meditation when I felt what I can only describe as a fine silvery column of energy in the middle of my spinal cord, filled with a flowing almost liquid substance. It extended up to the crown of my head and down to the base of my spine. The feeling of this energetic substance at the core of my being was utterly exquisite. The pleasure of it I find hard to put into words, except to say that it felt subtle, sublime and refined. Then there was a sense of powerful movement, upwards and downwards at the same time. I felt stretched up and pulled down to the earth with so much force it was almost hard to stay conscious to it, but I surrendered into it and eventually I felt quite peaceful in it. I realised that this movement was not two directions at once, but one direction awakened.

I later also realised that I was experiencing what the ancient Vedic traditions of India referred to as the sushumna, or the energy cord that runs along the spinal column. I also realised that Zincite helps to clear and activate this channel, bringing our spiritual light to life in the world in increasingly helpful and empowered ways.

One of ways that Zincite helps us unravel the mystery teachings of the divinity of body and spirit, is through its own creation. Originally discovered as a natural crystal in New Jersey, USA, Zincite was then 'accidentally' formed in the air shafts of a disbanded zinc smelting plant in Poland. These 'man-made' crystals formed in prismatic shapes, clearer in quality and with a wider range of colours including not just the typical oranges and brownish reds, but also vibrant clear greens. The formation of a divine healing stone through the very earthly environment of an old factory is a humorous expression of the healing that Zincite can bring to us all, the realisation that the Divine does indeed exist in the material, if only we provide the space for the awakening. It also shows how the Divine can happen in any situation – whether apparently spiritual in focus or apparently material, whether expected or not. Awakening will indeed happen, according to divine timing and divine will. Sometimes in the most unexpected and unlikely of ways.

Zincite helps us to realise that whilst we may have once identified with our spirit, or perhaps to the other extreme, our body, we are, as human beings, becoming something that is neither one nor the other but encompasses both. We are divine alchemy in process, we are the balance of spirit and animal, we are a soul in the process of awakening as divinity. It's rather a lot to take in at a mental level, hence the wisdom of the Tao supports us yet again with the teaching that even a journey of a million miles starts with a single step.

HEALING WITH LAO TZU AND ZINCITE

Have with you either your piece of Zincite or the mandala preferably placed near the lower chakras of your body, unless you are already very grounded and find it hard to open up to higher worlds, in which case, place it closer to your heart.

Seat yourself or lay down and say, "I call upon the true Ascended Master Lao Tzu (sounds like LA-OW ZOO) and the Angel of Zincite. I call upon the unconditionally loving Masters of Eastern Wisdom and the Custodians of the Tao (pronounced either DAOW or TAOW). I ask for your healing presence, grace, teaching and support that I may receive the Eastern mysteries for the greater good, bringing more peace, healing, spiritual intelligence and balance into my own life and the lives of the human race, upon the Earth. Through my own free will, so be it."

Focus on your breath and perceive that there is a rich orange-red light growing within you, around the site of Dan Tian or the navel chakra, just below your belly button, deep inside the lower belly above the pubic bone. Imagine that there is an egg-shaped energy organ here, strengthened and awakened by this rich orange-red light.

As you breathe in and out, the energy from the navel centre rises up to the middle of your abdomen, bringing warm energy with it. Allow the energy to dwell there at the solar plexus for several breaths in and out, for as long as feels appropriate for you.

The energy then rises up from the solar plexus to the middle Dan Tian, at the heart centre in the chest. Allow this centre to become warm and balanced. If it is too hot, allow it to be cooled and balanced. Stay there with your awareness for as long as feels appropriate.

The energy then rises up through the throat chakra to upper Dan Tian in the centre of your head, behind the third eye, slightly above, deep in the inner space of the head. Allow the energy to gather there, as if it was at the top of a fountain, peacefully overflowing, abundant and expansive in the head centre.

Don't worry if these processes feel obvious or very subtle for you, or if it is hard to feel anything or if you feel a lot of energy. Your body will be supported for the best possible experience for you by the loving Masters and Crystal Angel, so trust in your own process.

When you have remained with your awareness in your head for as long as feels appropriate, breathing in and out, you become aware of a point of light within the centre of your head.

Allow your awareness to travel into it, as you step through the light into a sacred open space within your head, filled with heavenly light.

This sacred space is the realm of the Master Lao Tzu. You may feel as though you have stepped into Ancient China or in an otherworldly or earthly temple, where there is beauty, grace, serenity and much spiritual power. You may perceive his presence or simply intend to receive his energy.

Say quietly in your mind, or aloud, "Old Master, I offer my deepest respect and gratitude for your teachings and love, thank you for all your help, over so many years. How may I serve your teachings? I open to receive your blessing and wisdom, that I too may live in harmony with the way and help others to learn to do the same. With a humble heart, I ask for your help and guidance now."

Allow the master to respond to you. He may do so in any number of ways, but all will be with love and affection. Receive either his verbal or non-verbal messages. He may show you an image from nature. Or share a colour of light with you. Know that what you need is being given to you through his graceful nature, whether you can consciously access that now or not. You will 'get it' consciously at the right time for you so don't worry if the exchange feels subtle now.

After this exchange has taken place, simply say "thank you" and then perceive a large disk of the yin-yang symbol (pictured below) being formed beneath you. It is not static, but in constant swirling motion of black and white, yin and yang, feminine and masculine energies in responsive dance with each other, always changing and shifting but always in perfect balance.

Notice how when one energy grows, the other shifts to accommodate it. Notice that the energies can only move as one, in wholeness, dancing with each other as one living intelligence.

See yourself stepping upon that disk of light and feel that you are moving with it, as though each foot is anchored onto that disk of light and as it moves, you are rebalanced by it. Let yourself be upon that disk as it corrects imbalances through your entire being – body, mind and emotions.

When you are ready say, "I give permission for the Angels of Yin and the Angels of Yang, who love me unconditionally and are in service of the lineage of Master Lao Tzu and the Tao, to help me balance the yin-yang energies in service to my own divine mastery, for the greatest good of all. Through divine grace, so be it."

Breathe in and out for several moments. Place your hands in prayer position at your heart and imagine that the large yin-yang symbol now moves into your heart, created from light and resting in perfect balance in your heart centre. When you are ready, bow your forehead to your hands in prayer saying 'thank you'.

In your own time, just open your eyes.

Following this healing process things will shift within you and outside of you. Be prepared to break with your usual routine and to be open to eating, thinking, acting and responding somewhat differently to your typical patterns. Don't try to lock these new ways into new patterns, allow for spontaneous responses to gently guide you, step by step, into greater mastery of balance within you. If you have repeated thoughts about changing your routine in some way, which follow this healing process in particular, please do follow up on them. May you be blessed by the loving warmth of the Yang Angels, the cool wisdom of the Yin Angels, and the divine power of Zincite and Master Lao Tzu.

11.

ASCENDED MASTER KUAN YIN (Spiritual Rebel) PEARL (Amrita)

INITIATION INTO ENLIGHTENMENT

Responding to darkness in need, great light is summoned. A compassionate embrace of light enfolds the darkness, transforming it into a precious Pearl. Sounds of ancient mantra, Om Mani Padme Hum, resonate from within the Pearl, that now glows with inner light. From darkness, divine love is made manifest.

Over a decade ago, I came across a spiritual teaching that went something like this – if any one knew what enlightenment really was, they wouldn't want to touch it with a ten-foot barge pole! I was shocked but determined (my first spiritual teacher would have said stubborn) enough to proceed towards this lofty goal, not really expecting that I would get anywhere near it this lifetime, but still determined to hold it within my heart as some sort of distant promised land, inspiring me to stay committed to conscious spiritual work this lifetime.

There are a surprising number of modern day teachers that claim to be enlightened. I have heard one such teacher claim that he knew his work was finished then. I have heard a lot of claims on the subject actually. I also know that the people making the claims genuinely seem to believe in what they are saying. Yet the greatest teachers that I know make no such claim and when it is assumed, they tend to laugh and say, "When did I say that I was enlightened?" The Dalai Lama, whom I love and respect, is one such example.

Those that do claim such a spiritual status have their reasons no doubt, but one of my core teachings, is that we must learn to trust what we sense and feel over any appearance or claim of another. It is very easy to be impressed, even if not completely convinced, when a teacher claims enlightened status, especially if they appear to have powers or abilities that impress you. Yet the guidance I have given you will hopefully help you remember that actions can speak louder than words. Let the essence of what you experience be your guide and remember that enlightenment fundamentally expresses itself through service. A teacher may choose to be public or private about her spiritual evolution to the extent that it serves the divine purpose through her. Whilst you can love and respect those that are seeking to serve or those whom you want to serve in order that their work be supported upon the earth, discernment is never misplaced (see Chapter 4). With this initiation of enlightenment, what is important is the journey that it opens up for us, not whether or not we think, or anyone else thinks, that we are enlightened at the 'end of it'.

You can come to understand through this initiation of enlightenment that there is no good or bad, right or wrong in the sense that you once believed there to be. This initiation teaches us that it's all just a matter of perspective and so judgment isn't truthful. What we do need is discernment and the ability to continue tuning in to our own heart's guidance to find our way, no matter how many powerful teachers we encounter along the path that may dazzle us with their light or abilities. The job of the teacher is to awaken you to your own divine connection, not try to gain your worship or obedience. These things are not wrong or bad, but they are not of a high vibrational reality. You may find yourself in the company of such a teacher or not. They may have something valuable for you to learn from them or not. But when it all comes down to it, at some point, to grow, you are going to have to trust in your own inner connection. That is what all these higher beings – angels, Ascended Masters and so forth, are here to help you build. It is not about them. It is about your relationship with the Divine. All higher beings know this, which is why they aren't interested in being worshipped, but interested in lovingly helping you connect with the Divine within.

Before I continue with this discussion I will give you one example of discernment and the trusting of feeling over appearance. In my own life, I have often struggled with darker forces that manifest as negative energy. It has been my personal experience, which may or may not be similar for you, that negative energies are as attracted to my light as positive loving beings tend to be. This reality has taught me how to respect darker forces and use the encounters that I have with them to serve the growth of my own inner light, learning to come from compassion rather than fear. I now tend to use encounters with darker energies as signs that my light is growing stronger. As a note, we will discuss working consciously with darker forces in more depth in Chapter 14 when we discuss the Buddha and in more depth again in *Crystal Goddesses 888*, the next title in this series.

In the past, before I recognised that darker forces had an effect on me, there would be times when I simply suffered without realising that there were greater reasons at hand than my own immediate personal growth. Before teaching a class, in particular, I would often be drowned in fear and negativity. For many years I mistakenly believed that this was all my own stuff. Then after a while I came to believe that it was also the stuff that my students were carrying. Some time after that, I began to sense that whilst some of what I was experiencing was my own issue, some was the collective student soul that I would be working with, and there was a third aspect involved in this phenomenon, which was that I was being actively undermined by darker energies that really didn't want me to be doing the healing work I was doing. Perhaps I was ruining some of their fun, or they had fun in trying to ruin what I was up to, it doesn't really matter though, it was enough to just realise that something untoward was happening. It helped me gain some perspective and become more aware in how to work constructively with the situation.

These energies were forming a sort of psychic attack that lasted for over a decade of teaching before I realised the third piece of the puzzle. It was only because I loved the light so much, and felt so dedicated to what I was doing, that I put up with it without understanding it for as long as I did. Every time I prepared to teach a class, for hours, sometimes even days, beforehand I would be swamped by fear and negativity and felt like I was dying. As soon as the class started, the feelings would be gone, I believe because I entered into such a high state that those lower vibrational energies, at that level, couldn't affect me anymore. However as soon as I dropped back down to a more day-to-day vibration, I was vulnerable to attack again. One time, several years after it had started I did stumble under the weight of the onslaught of negativity from time to time, but somehow (must be that stubborn streak of mine) I just kept on going, occasionally taking a break from teaching to get my strength up again, and then starting a new cycle of classes.

Once I got a handle on the situation and decided enough was enough, those darker energies changed tactic and then I found that some of my more powerful students would be overtaken with strange fears before coming to class – fear that they wouldn't be able to find the new location for our gatherings, when it was changed to a more suitable venue. I knew instantly that this fear was nothing to do with them (shocked as they were to easily find the location and arrive early for class) but about darker forces attempting to block my work and their growth. Such energies can be highly intelligent obviously.

When I did realise what was happening, I didn't feel fear, I didn't feel frustration, I just had a moment of, "Oh, that's what's been happening – wow, glad I finally got it," with a divine light bulb comically going off in my head. Because I feel a deep connection to the Ascended Masters and the other light beings that we will be meeting throughout this entire series, I didn't feel that I had to deal with this situation completely on my own, though I certainly also knew that I had quite a lot of work to do. I could ask for as much help as I needed but it was also just I that was needing to step up to take on more of my destiny, not to shrink back from it.

Once I was on to them however, I realised that I would need to build my own light to provide a safe harbour for my students, to provide a strong enough 'light house' through which my students could still reach me. Instead of feeling anger, self-doubt and frustration about this, as I had done previously and which wasn't particularly constructive, I came to realise that this was just part of life on earth – the dance of light and dark together – and I needed to continue my personal work and just do the best I could in whatever situations in which I found myself. I changed my tactics again and began to work in different ways when possible and when I had to face the energy directly because I would be teaching, I just dealt with it as best as I could. When I needed help, that help would arrive. We are all given the assistance and the teachings that we need, when we need them, so that we can complete our life's work. That is the Divine's side of the bargain when we agree to a life of serving the sacred awakening of humanity.

One of the most helpful things that I learned in trying to outgrow the interference of darker energies was to take stock of my own reactions to their efforts. Sometimes I would fall into the habit of worrying that something was wrong, that I had too much fear, or that I was too tired, that I had to do more work on myself, and worrying that if I was being so affected by negativity, was I strong enough to be teaching?

More awareness about those unhelpful responses, realising that they weren't true but just habitual reactions, helped me stand my ground and maintain my awareness, setting stronger boundaries and making some tough choices. I actually became more focused, more productive and far less accepting of emotional manipulation of any sort more generally in my life. I let go of a number of, which wasn't easy, but it helped me focus on what seemed to be the heart of the work I was doing, pouring my energy into that. I let my heart lead me. The lesson, though tough and certainly confusing at first and draining for a good decade of my life, was a powerful one. It woke me up to a whole other reality and helped me realise how much power I had through the simple choices I made in my life. It helped me realise that no matter how much darkness we are drawn into, if we are willing to trust in ourselves, that darkness can be made – through our choices – to serve our light. That is our tremendous power of free will in action. That is the power of our own spiritual intelligence, if we choose to use it.

This was just one of many enlightenment initiations. It showed me that the darkness is divine in purpose, ultimately as much as the light. We are not here to judge it, but we are here to live our own heart truths. If our hearts yearn to serve the light, then we must do so using all the spiritual intelligence, compassion and creativity that we can muster. We must ask for help and we must have faith in ourselves because we are capable of so much positive contribution to the forces of light. Then the bigger playing out of the dance of light and dark on our planet can happen for higher divine purpose. For us however, we do our part, fighting with everything within us to give all that we can in honour of the light whilst respecting that the darkness is part of the game. We don't have to like it or understand it, but we can accept it and get on with our role in life.

Enlightenment isn't about getting rid of the darkness, it is about learning that it serves a divine purpose too – and the extent to which we can work with our own encounters with darker energies without fear, but with intelligence, creativity, compassion and respect, will be the extent to which we are using our innate spiritual power to grow from the interaction of dark and light. So whether your encounters with darkness be somewhat extreme, perhaps like mine (a barrage of psychic attack over several decades, which actually started for me when I was a little girl), or whether they be more commonplace, such as in the darkness that you encounter in another or in yourself when you blow your cool and get into a rage at your kids (perhaps horrifying yourself even more than them!), that darkness is part of your enlightenment initiation. It is what you choose to do with it that matters most, not whether or not you have encountered darkness at all.

Psychologist Carl Jung described this as the difference between diving and falling. With discernment we dive. We enter into the darkness consciously with a view to understanding its purpose in our lives, with great respect for its power yet without feeling intimidated by it, realising that our light will be served by all of our life experience, no matter what. Falling is being seduced by the darkness, allowing fear to overcome us, and to pull away, back to where it is known, even if painful. Sometimes however, our discernment might tell us that retreat is a wise course of action. The discernment in that situation is to know when to cut your losses and step back in the face of a larger foe which you are unprepared to successfully confront, to garner your reserves, do your inner work and know that when you are ready, you shall step forward again. Discernment helps support us as we journey into this enlightenment initiation, into the acceptance of the dark and light faces of the Divine as both part of our life experience and our spiritual growth towards oneness with the divine source.

There are entire religious sects from ancient times that still exist today based on exploring the darker side of existence and actively seeking to experience many social taboos with the view to finding the Divine in all of life, to reach the enlightened state. If these are to be 'successful' in the sense of yielding enlightenment, then it is through diving, not falling. Running amok, breaking all sorts of taboos with no spiritual motivation behind it would be falling. There are those that seek to find enlightenment through the pursuit of desire until its end point. There are many paths. The one for you will be the one that your heart speaks to you of – guides you to, and gently calls you back to, again and again, no matter how many times you may find yourself wandering off course into a 'grass is greener' spiritual moment of flirting with another's path instead.

It is my experience, through connection with the illumined spiritual guide, Kuan Yin, that enlightenment is for every person. It does not require particular religious orientation or even particular spiritual philosophies or beliefs. Enlightenment is the remembrance of our own absolute nature, which has very little to do with the particular flavours of spiritual journeying we take this lifetime. Those different journeys are about getting us to a place where we can embrace an enlightened state in increasing degrees, not about the enlightened state itself, which is for all of humanity, at the right time, and through our own efforts combined with the bestowal of divine grace.

ASCENDED MASTER KUAN YIN – SPIRITUAL REBEL

I have always had a soft spot for rebels.

Even if some of my more hard-headed students were rebelling against me, not liking the way that I was teaching because it didn't fit their expectations of what a spiritual teacher should do, I still respected their right to do it!

Rebellion has at its heart the art of questioning. I think that 'why' is one of the most helpful words we have at our disposal. It might drive parents of young children to distraction, but it is nonetheless a gift from the Divine. It is most wisely used as a tool through which to understand further, rather than a challenge for another to convince us of something (as no one is divinely required to convince anyone of anything).

Rebellion helps us take a step beyond what we currently know and into exploration of what could lie on the other side. A spiritual rebel is an adventurer in consciousness. Rather than a more prosaic rebellion of breaking rules or shirking authority just for the sake of it, spiritual rebellion is the daring boldness of a heart that loves the Divine over and above anything else. We will meet lots of these divine rebels in *Crystal Saints and Sages 777* but for this chapter, the sassy Kuan Yin will be our rebellious guide.

It takes a lot of courage to live your spirituality. You will know this from first-hand experience, I am sure. It is the rebel in us that asks us to make the Divine our priority and to allow that divine energy to work its way through us, to guide us, even despite those around us perhaps telling us that we are crazy and need to come back 'to the real world' (so ironic that this statement is often uttered by those that are trapped in the 'unreal' world more than those that are they are trying to control).

Rebellion that is conscious and spiritually-oriented is not selfish but about service. The rebel that breaks with convention without compassion for the effect of his or her behaviour on another is not choosing a spiritual path. Compassion is the point of difference between conscious rebellion driven by divine desire and ego-driven rebellion that does so much less for our spiritual evolution. It still serves our growth, of course, everything can do that, with the right attitude. But it is the *eau de toilette* of rebellion, whereas spiritual rebellion with compassion is the pure perfume variety, richer, more potent, more valuable.

Rebellion at a spiritual level understands that there are no guarantees of safety and niceness that are worth winning, and knows that when rebellion is genuinely directed from the heart, it opens up a path that is rich with grace and divine protection.

Sometimes great souls take on great suffering to further the spiritual evolution of light on the planet. Great spiritual rebels are often included in this task. The Dalai Lama has endured displacement from his home and tremendous suffering of his people in order that his soul may bring the kindness and compassion of Buddhism to the West in a more meaningful way. Jesus suffered derision, humiliation, betrayal and crucifixion to bring through a teaching of great light and love to the world. Kuan Yin endured abuse and a violent death in order to teach the power of compassionate blessing to bring enlightenment even to those who had been in darkness. These great spiritual beings have much grace on their path – it enabled them to accomplish so much in the evolution of the light, and yet the path has many challenges. Sometimes it is the greater souls who can bear such challenges and they willingly embrace them in service to the whole.

Rebellious Kuan Yin supports us in our own lives with our evolution from mass consciousness (where we go with whatever the collective seems to think and value) into individual awareness sourced from within our heart (with the courage to think and value differently to the masses).

In her own life, she broke rules. She did that out of spiritual necessity, not personal agenda. She defied the rule of her father, who wished to keep her locked up and away from the world and instead chose to explore the world. She was killed after being subjected to humiliation and violation, but what came of this was her ascension. The suffering didn't cause ascension, it was her response to it that did. Her forgiveness and non-judgment, her ability to see that within even great evil and darkness, the Divine dwells, allowed her to seek that seed of light in all. Her first blessing after her ascension was said to be her father who was indirectly the cause of much of her suffering in life in the first place. She blessed him that he may be spiritually free. She was able to sense the seed of light in all beings and love them, to want them to be spiritually liberated. She still helps all beings find their way to enlightenment, no matter how flawed they may be (and let's face it, we are all pretty flawed in our own quirky ways).

There would have been plenty of haters that would have questioned why she 'wasted' a blessing on a violent and ignorant man. Why not bless a good person who loved the Divine and served the light? Kuan Yin delivers a wonderful teaching – that we aren't bound to hate anyone. We can learn to forgive and love and bless if we choose to allow this to come through us. We can choose to break with convention when it is truly in our heart to do so and to accept that the consequences of this will serve our growth to liberation. We don't have to be afraid, we can choose to live according to our truth, whether it matches the opinions of the world around us or not.

On a mundane level, this can be as powerfully simple as choosing, when 'common cold season' is declared and radio stations begin pushing for the latest flu vaccinations and medications, that you can begin to challenge the idea that there even is a cold season (somehow its inception seems to coincide with the creation of cold and flu medications, don't you think?). You can turn off the radio. You can rest and nourish your body in winter and in doing so stay well more than you get sick through natural means. It takes a lot of power to begin to vibrate at an individual rather than mass level of consciousness – those belief systems of the masses can be very compelling at a subconscious emotional level, but it all starts with changing our thoughts and asking for divine help in shifting up a few gears, vibrationally speaking.

Mass consciousness holds great force but it is not the ultimate power. The power that we have as individuals to choose is vastly unacknowledged. If you don't like something, vote with your wallet, shop elsewhere. Give a little to charities. Don't underestimate how much this can help the charity and help you to feel more empowered and less helpless in the face of all the changes that need to happen on the earth. If you find something silly, demeaning or degrading, look for another way. In small actions, there is great power. We each, within us, have the capacity to create a different world. We cannot know when that one small action from us will create the next tipping point into higher awareness and greater compassion on our planet. Small and not-so-small movements of people dedicated to kindness and awareness are popping up all around the world. What was once such a small group of world servers is growing in an accelerated fashion. This is happening and it will prevail. You are a part of that. From the smallest to the most dramatic actions you take, you are a part of that and your effort on your path is a precious gift to the world. As we then learn to work together, that power can grow. Each thing in its own time. We have greatness within us, you see, and we must nurture it like a beautiful seedling worthy of tender care.

Kuan Yin teaches us that we have within us this seed of spiritual adulthood. It can seem scary, it can seem challenging, yet it is so much less scary and less challenging than playing at still being a child when within there is so much more of you that wishes to be expressed. If we can tap into our spiritual maturity, taking responsibility for our own choices as much as we possibly can, then our child within will feel safer and some of his talents can emerge because we no longer have the weight of the world belief that one 'cannot change careers and be successful at this age' (just as one example) on our shoulders.

Her grace can reach us most easily when we pray to her. Her presence, her soul light, stimulates that seed of spiritual maturity within us, until it blossoms into the spiritual tree that each of us has the potential to embody in our own unique way, becoming a source of light and life on this planet. Prayer can be through the methods outlined in the healing process at the end of this chapter, but it can also be through the use of her mantra, *Om Mani Padme Hum*, which are sacred sounds that hold her divine vibration of compassion, love, grace and peace. It can be repeated several times on its own, independent of other practice, or in addition to meditation, as a prayer to this beautiful mother of light.

I have such love for her; she has helped me so much on my path and been so incredibly responsive. She will offer you the very same love and blessing as you open your heart to her.

Some of you may already know that for over a decade I wanted to write an oracle deck. I worked hard in as many ways that I could, sharing healing and light on this planet before I was eventually emailed by my publisher and asked if I would like to write an oracle deck dedicated to Kuan Yin. He mentioned that he was considering offering the project to another more established writer at the time but that he kept feeling that I was the person for the task. I readily agreed – as I recall, with quite a few exclamation marks in my email response.

I had been collecting images of Kuan Yin for some years prior to this, stashing them about my healing room. As my publisher emailed me the list of images that the artist for the deck would be providing, I was stunned because every single one of the images I had found were by that artist. I didn't even know who the artist was at the time, or that all the images I had collected over the years were all by him. Zeng Hao, the artist, captured what I felt of her grace through his sublime artwork. It felt like a sign that this task had been pre-planned by the Divine.

I was absolutely ecstatic because I knew it was the beginning a new level of empowerment to serve (we explored empowered service in Chapter 7). I could hardly wait to channel her light and wisdom and to have it reach people. The thought of someone in suffering or the darkness that many old souls are asked to endure as part of their service to the light on this planet, tore at my heart. How I longed to be able to offer nourishment and loving light to those great beings, who had perhaps forgotten amongst all the suffering and struggle, that they were indeed pure love of spirit. The feedback that I receive from people all over the world about their connection to her through the Kuan Yin Oracle has touched me even more deeply than I imagined it would. It affirms that the comfort and reassurance of the Divine Mother as Kuan Yin is reaching her beloved devotees. To have been a small cog in that divine wheel is such a privilege.

Her presence continued to surprise me, however. When I was walking through a local shopping centre, I came across a busker playing beautiful Chinese music and the thought of a Kuan Yin meditation CD with that music kept buzzing about my head. My publisher was keen and when an agreement didn't come together with the busker in question because of legal issues, my publisher suggested that I write the music. A piece of music that I had written nearly ten years earlier, for some unknown reason of course, and had never used came to mind. I unearthed it and it became the basis for the *Divine Lotus Mother* CD of meditations to Kuan Yin released by Blue Angel Publishing. It has been tuned to 44.4 hertz as a healing vibration and I have used it in regular classes with strong – and sometimes quite abrupt – healing outcomes.

I felt that the piece of music that I wrote then, at that time in my life when I wasn't writing music much at all and wondered what the point of it was anyway, was another indicator that the Divine is working through us even when our conscious mind is completely unaware of it. Her grace taught me that the Divine is always lovingly preparing us for our destiny, no matter what doubt or ignorance of this we may hold at the time.

Kuan Yin's spiritual rebellion teaches that the way of the Divine is more powerful than every single person in the world saying that something cannot be done. She teaches that any obstacle is nothing more than a way to light and through trust in the Divine, every darkness can be mined for the light it holds within.

PEARL – AMRITA

Known as the stones of queens for thousands of years, Pearls have been symbols of great value and worth. Said to be worn by royalty and served crushed in wine by Cleopatra (for her most important guests), even the Bible makes indirect reference to the esteem in which they have been held by the comment in the Book of Job that the price of wisdom is above Pearls. They were once known as valuable for their rarity because only one in one thousand oysters would produce a natural Pearl.

How Pearls are formed is probably not much of a surprise to you. A piece of grit finds its way into an oyster and the creature, irritated by the intrusion, begins to formulate an essence to coat the irritant. Eventually, a precious natural Pearl is formed. From that irritation, there is great beauty and value. It is a natural process that starts with annoyance and transforms it through responsiveness and natural adaptation into a lustrous gem.

In the ancient spiritual teachings of India, there is a story of the nectar of immortality, or amrita, which translates roughly as bliss. This prized and rare nectar was reputed to clear karma forever and endow the recipient with complete divinity awakened. It was the key to the end of suffering and absolute enlightenment, peace and divine power. Now of course, everyone from the highest priests to the darkest demons of existence thought this sounded pretty good and they all wanted it.

However, the amount of strength required to unearth the divine nectar from the depths of creation, in which it resided, so that anyone could get their hands on it, required that they all work together. A serpent would be offered as the 'handle' which the demons on the dark side and priests that served the light would stir together, to churn the ocean of consciousness and in doing so, eventually uproot and liberate the divine nectar.

Over and over again, light and dark pulled this way and that, and eventually, amrita was indeed liberated – in the form of a golden goddess of wealth, enlightenment and beauty named Lakshmi (we'll meet her in *Crystal Goddesses 888: Manifesting with the Divine Power of Heaven and Earth*). Everyone coveted this divine goddess, and the bliss she embodied, but she chose to enter the heart that held pure love.

The Vedic tradition has a knack of turning the vastest spiritual principles into nifty little stories that can help us in the modern world awaken and connect with spiritual truths.

The amrita, the divine bliss, what we most desire in our spiritual quest, comes through a process. It is the same teaching as the wisdom of the Pearl – it is through responsiveness to darkness, to grit, to irritation, to suffering, that the light flows. Both light and dark, in ourselves and in the world, create friction and conflict. It is this conflict consciously entered into, rather than resisted or judged, that churns life, creating the force necessary to eject us out of the ordinary reality of 'automatic pilot', mindlessly repeating past behaviours, and into a place where we can access, in our deepest heart, our true divine beauty and power. In the Vedic tradition, every being is seeking the Divine – even the demon – we just have different paths to get there. The aim of the initiation of enlightenment is to truly know in one's heart the peace that comes from realising all is Divine. This is the gift of the Pearl, which is the teaching of amrita, or bliss, that comes from dark and light in relationship that eventually gives birth to divine awakening.

When you are in the thick of a struggle, this might seem to be of little comfort. Yet it is a prediction that, in time, this struggle will be recognised as the basis of some of your greatest assets. Guidance has often said to me that my greatest successes were born of my most challenging adversities. Although I had a little moan about perhaps having some greatest successes through divine blessings too please (I have had many blessings for which I am deeply grateful, so we all knew I was playing), they were right and I believe this to be the case for many souls.

The Pearl is the prize that comes through the struggle. It might be the struggle for independence and gaining possession of yourself finally from those that once sought to possess or control you for their own means. It might be the prize of liberating awareness that comes when you have truly been present to your own suffering in a relationship or circumstance, perhaps even for a long period of time, to eventually realise the reason behind it, how it has served you, how you have grown through that learning and do not require that suffering any more. You have earned your freedom. The Pearl is our symbol of hope that light will come through struggle, and our symbol of divine adaptability, that we are capable of responsiveness so that we can turn what was once a struggle for us into hard-won wisdom.

My teachings come from a place of experience. These experiences are in some ways my own unique experiences and yet I am certain that many people can relate to them – perhaps with a subtle tweak here or there – and could claim some type of similar experience themselves. Where the amrita has come from for me, the gift of the Pearl, of bliss, is through understanding, through being able to mine every ounce of my own suffering to find the divine presence in it, the wisdom. It is always there. It may reveal itself suddenly when I am writing and at other times it may take years or even decades to reveal itself, if I am repeating a pattern over lifetimes, then it will perhaps take lifetimes to be seen. What comes, and when, is what is needed. We are given the right amount of grit to form the right sized Pearl for us.

If this chapter particularly resonates for you, then you are rare, like a natural Pearl, in your ability to adapt. You have a high level of spiritual intelligence which gives you not only the understanding of these teachings, but the ability to transform your suffering into grace. Prayer to Kuan Yin supports this process whether you are one of the talented minority who naturally do this or one of the loving servers who needs some help (though don't we all at times?) with taking the grit of life and bringing compassion to bear, so that a precious gift may be created.

There is a saying in the Buddhist teachings that every human is a jewel in the net of the Divine. For each Pearl that we create, we are adding a jewel to the divine netting that drapes across the beautiful head of the Divine Mother.

HEALING WITH KUAN YIN AND PEARL

Start with your Pearl, whether natural or cultured freshwater, or your mandala. If you have the *Divine Lotus Mother* CD or digital download, you may like to play the Lotus Interlude in the background, which is just music and chanting to the Divine Mother Kuan Yin or any other music that feels beautiful and connected to her grace. If you have the *Kuan Yin Oracle* you may like to draw a card and lay it out in your sacred space, reading the guidance in the accompanying booklet at the end of this healing process.

Start by lying or sitting comfortably with your Pearl or mandala resting in your hands or balanced on your heart chakra.

Close your eyes and say, "I call upon the true Ascended Master Kuan Yin, Divine Mother of the Pearl, and the Angel of the Pearl. I call upon the enlightened lineage of my own soul that loves me unconditionally and I dedicate myself in service to the light. I call upon that divine intelligence that promotes spiritual integration and evolution. I open up now to the greatest bliss of which I am capable, through divine mercy and kindness, compassion and wisdom, grace and intelligence, so be it."

Breathe in and out slowly, for at least 33 breaths repeating the mantra OM MANI PADME HUM either quietly or out loud (sounds like OM - MAN - EE - PAD - MAY - HUM), gently allowing the sound to fill your heart chakra in the centre of your chest.

When you are ready, imagine that you can travel deeply through the space created by the sound until you are holding within your heart a small speck of dirt. This dirt is a challenge that is in your life at present. It may be a relationship issue, it may be a circumstance, it is anything either within you or around you that you are struggling to turn into a source of bliss and comfort. It may be that more than one issue is represented in that speck of dirt.

You sense an extremely bright light filled with love around you as you hold your gaze on that speck of dirt. It perhaps feels very uncomfortable but keep breathing and stay present to it if you can. Allow the love that you feel around you to begin to open your heart and shine through it, onto that speck of dirt.

You feel the dirt coated with wave after wave of pearlescent light until it begins to change shape, turning into a perfect, large Pearl. Notice the colour and sheen of the Pearl, its natural shape. Notice its beauty and uniqueness. Feel what was once irritation becoming now a feeling of acceptance, appreciation and acknowledgement of beauty.

Stay with this process for around 33 breaths.

Once that Pearl is complete, you notice a pair of pale white hands, gleaming with brilliant white light, open before your heart. You can either hold the Pearl within your heart, or if you are ready, you may place it in the loving hands and watch as Kuan Yin places your Pearl in the net of jewels, draped across her head.

If you wish to allow this to happen, let the Divine Mother in whatever form she appears to you, whether as Kuan Yin or in another expression, offer you a blessing, directly into your heart. Receive this as love and warmth, as a symbol, colour, vision or simply as an intention to accept her grace in whatever form it comes to you.

If you prefer to hold on to the Pearl for now, for whatever reason, accept it. Let it nurture your heart with understanding. When you feel inclined to let it go, you can repeat this healing process again and do so at that time. There is no rush. All things come in time.

When you are ready, place your hands in prayer position and repeat the mantra, Om Mani Padme Hum, three times.

Bow your head to the mandala or Pearl and when you are ready, simply say thank you and then open your eyes.

If you have the oracle deck, you may now like to read the guidance for the card that you drew at the beginning of this process.

After this healing, which you may repeat at any time, you may feel lightness in your being, or any energy from your heart lifting over the one to three days following – that energy might be sadness or grief that you didn't consciously know was within you, it might be fear or anger. Just let it rise and fall away knowing that the grace of the Divine Mother is reaching to you through that, purging it out of you.

Also notice that as you receive the grace of the Divine Mother for growth, you may be surprised how it comes to you. It will always come. If you are uncertain, take a moment now to touch your heart chakra and just say quietly, "Please help me have the capacity to recognise the presence of divine grace in my life, through mercy and unconditional love so be it."

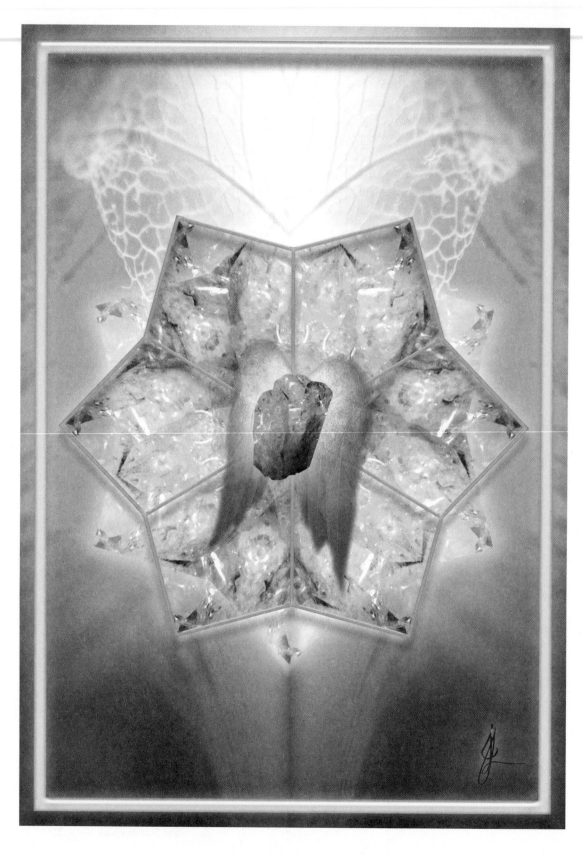

12.

ASCENDED MASTER WHITE MATTHEW (Purity) DANBURITE (Innocence)

INITIATION OF ORIGINAL SELF

A shaft of clear light pierces time and space. All is illuminated by the presence of this light and revealed as clear and radiant. The light lives. It shimmers endlessly. No experience or suffering can taint this essence, eternal and pure. In the presence of clear light, the truth of purity intact remains.

The poet T.S. Eliot wrote, "We shall not cease from exploration, and the end of all our exploring will be to arrive where we started and know the place for the first time." This phrase describes the heart of the spiritual path. We go on a journey, we learn and we let go, only to discover what is already within us. We cannot know it without experience and wisdom gleaned from that experience. Through that experience and consequent wisdom, we become capable of a perception that would otherwise not be available to us.

To unveil what has always been, as though it is a great secret only to be discovered through experience, wisdom and eye-opening adventure, is the nature of the divine path. We are all in process of realisation of the source within us – it feels like coming home. Having embarked upon a spiral adventure, taking in the centre from vaster and vaster perspectives, we are blessed with keener insight and understanding.

Have you ever felt that a little bit of distance gives you a fresh perspective on an issue? That it can be hard to gain clarity when you are in the middle of something? At a far greater level, this is the case with life and the quest for spiritual realisation. We always were divine. But to pay this more than lip service, to truly know this in the sense that we step into the unbreakable, eternal comfort of divine union, requires a journey away from the centre. The experience that this adventure brings leads to wisdom which enables us to take the return spiral journey back 'home' to the centre, or the source, that dwells in our own body-soul, and recognise it for what it is – divine.

When we approach this spiritual path from this perspective, we will experience the spiritual journey as more of an unveiling than a creation. We become witness to the most extraordinary cosmic reveal, as the Heavenly Mother burns through veil after veil that would obscure our vision, until all that remains to behold is the blinding beauty of the divine presence. Have you ever had an experience of looking at someone, perhaps someone you have known for a long time, and then feeling suddenly like you are seeing them for the first time or they are not the person that you thought that they were? You see them differently even though you have been looking at them for years perhaps. You have looked but not really seen – until that moment. It is the same with reality through spiritual awakening. It is like we look at reality and actually see it without obstruction, perhaps for the first time ever.

We are one in truth with the Divine; we are remembering it. This means that the divine paths of creation and of revelation that are happening concurrently are happening through us too. The Divine is a paradox to our minds. How can one be creating what is already in existence? How can one be becoming and also just be? It doesn't make sense, and yet it is the higher truth.

For many years I thought I was creating my path – well co-creating with the Divine, being created through the Divine, more accurately. I considered myself and others to be evolving works of divine art in progress. In some ways this is true. Yet the initiation of the original self takes us into another equally valid perception of the Divine.

That perception came to me in a funny way. I realised that as I was growing older I still felt the same inside. My body was changing and I was undoubtedly growing internally too, yet a part of me was always the same. In my twenties I thought this meant that I wasn't really growing up, that I still felt like a child playing at being an adult. However as I grew into my thirties I realised that I now felt more like a grown up really, but I was *still the same* somewhere, deep within myself. The realisation eventually hit me that whilst I am on a transformational path of becoming, at another place within, I am what I have always been and always will be – I just am. I understood the statement and prayer of 'I AM'. It is the prayer of being rather than becoming. I AM.

I realised that for the I AM part of me, nothing is happening at the centre, which is eternal. It is outside where all the drama is happening as veils are removed whilst the more temporal self is transformed to be able to recognise what is already there. It is like the being and the becoming in all of us are playing hide and seek, with the being hiding and the becoming seeking. The being is giggling quietly at first in utter divine bliss, bubbling away, whilst the becoming is madly trying to find the hiding place. The moment when becoming finds the being, tearing the veil off its hiding place and yells aloud, "Found you!" is an ecstatic moment of divine rapture and glee for both parts of the divine self. The transformational path doesn't stop, but it does recognise the existence of the eternal self within. Then rather than seeking something that was once thought to be missing, through the transformational process, transformation becomes simply engaging in the divine dance unfolding. Nothing is missing. It is just that part of the divine experience is the becoming. And so we continue to grow – from a place of fullness within that brings peace, and a bold willingness to be open to life and change.

We have discussed the process of becoming in the previous chapters on healing and transformation. That is where most of our work happens as we enter into the divine game of hide and seek with our own true nature. The being is bubbling away in bliss as it does. On the path to unveiling it (with a triumphant conclusion to the game) our becoming journey is not just about building up trust, faith, love and other qualities. It is also a dissembling, a tearing away of the walls of defensiveness and protection that we place over ourselves. It is entering into a holy relationship where we are asked to hold nothing back, to not hide behind anything and in doing so, we become capable of seeing and being seen beyond all those walls we once hid behind. We thought we were hiding from the world, but it turned out we were hiding from our divine being, waiting for us to drop the veils and shout, "There you are! I found you!" whilst it yells at the same time, "I am here! You found me!"

This process of surrendering the layers of protection can be really painful. At some point we believed we needed those layers or we wouldn't have built them up over the years. Letting them go can bring up a lot of fear, old memories of why we built up the defences in the first place, and insecurity about living without them. We might feel exposed and vulnerable. This does not mean that we turn ourselves into doormats to be preyed upon by unscrupulous forces. We can keep our wits about us and our healthy boundaries, but we can also trust that we can be vulnerable and even hurt, and we will be able to sustain ourselves, to make wise choices based on those experiences, to recover, that we will be okay. Within our hearts, as we shed the defences we once hid behind, we uncover ourselves, releasing enough judgment and fear that we can be naked with ourselves without fear of being shamed or found to be anything other than beautiful and worthy of compassion, reverence and adoration.

As we take the path of inner nakedness in our own hearts, what we discover is our original self, the being who has always been and will always be. On my path, as I began to shed the layers of protection that I had subconsciously placed over myself from early childhood, I was able to discover that sense of enduring self within. It was subtle at first, and then it became very obvious. I realised I am in essence who I always was. I was perhaps more purely in touch with that part of myself, that original self, in childhood. I remember a time earlier on in my healing path when I began to really reach for that child self, to try and find out who I was back then, no longer being satisfied with who I was told that I was. I became hungry for photographs from my youth, searching for clues about that little girl that I was. She seemed to be so artlessly herself.

Eventually I came to know that the child in me knew this original self before she got caught up in society conditioning and emotional suffering. Those things were the beginning of the transformational path of becoming for this lifetime. But they had no effect on the being within. The original self within us is ageless and unaffected by experience and choice. It projects itself through us to be alive through the body in this life, to be a part of that divine game of hide and seek, or should that be 'seek and find'? Yet its radiance does not dim or flicker, but simply burns as an eternal sun. I have seen a vision of this eternal self, this original being. It is not human, nor in form as we would typically know it. I know that this original self exists in every one of us, the question is not whether we have this original self, but to what extent we can recognise it. That recognition happens at the right time as a gift of divine grace. The transformational journey of becoming prepares us for the moment.

For me personally, the perception of this original self was incredibly emotional. I saw the vision and felt its presence before I knew what it was. I was just staring dumbly at this surreal, massive, ancient white sun, crackling with an electrifying intensity. I could physically hear it, like flames cracking wood. It was eternal, strange, beautiful, and so real yet not of this physical world but also obviously connected to it somehow. I stared at it with my eyes closed, and cried tears of relief and bliss. Eventually words erupted from my mouth without me knowing what they were going to be until I heard them. "It's my soul," I said and the moment began to fade, and back I came to the here and now.

I still remember when I had a moment in therapy, not long into what would turn out to be over a decade-long process of deep emotional healing and self-reflection. It was a moment that was prompted by something that I cannot remember. All that I do remember is that moment. It was the moment when I realised that there was nothing wrong with me. I had nothing to be ashamed of, nothing to feel guilty about, there was nothing wrong with me. I felt like a paralysing weight that I had been carrying internally had fallen away.

This didn't mean that I thought I was perfect and had nothing to learn or no need to grow. It meant that I had let go of the toxic sense of shame that I had picked up as I had grown up, believing that I was not alright as I was, that somehow fundamentally I was guilty, wrong, or worthy of being judged. This led to the development of many painful adaptations which took years to undo. It was this long, arduous process of destroying the many defences that I had unconsciously built around me to protect what I thought was my not-good-enough self. It was hard work even when I realised that who I was inside was actually perfectly acceptable. There was a lot of undoing to be done!

This is the gift of the initiation into original self. It is an undoing. Not from a place of judgment or failure, but from a place of no longer needing what was falsely built. It is divine support in becoming less 'defended' than ever before. This doesn't mean that you will be prone to inappropriate vulnerability, though it may feel that way for a little while. What it actually means is that you won't be suffocating yourself behind walls that were once built to keep out undesirable suffering but ended up keeping out too much life.

I remember a teacher that I encountered once who had a mantra that I have shared countless times, often to people who don't quite know what to make of it. I call it a mantra rather than an affirmation simply because of the number of times that he stated it – it would be at least a few times every single time he was teaching. He would say, "You are a beautiful soul that has never done a thing wrong," and he really meant it.

I understood exactly what he meant by this sentiment even though I knew others were puzzled by how this could be and dismissed it as 'hippy nonsense'. He was a compassionate and mature soul in many ways and he understood that the soul never does evil. It is simply a spark of the Divine, having an experience. His teachings were based on this notion of original self, the divine spark that is the being that we are eternally. Yes, we have this gift of life, temporary and passing. Good or bad is a judgment call that depends completely on your perspective, and is therefore not absolute. These were his teachings and his grasp of the purity and innocence of the original self could have freed many from shame, guilt and self-hatred – which abounds in human beings far more than we often realise – if they had have taken the time to challenge their own shunning of his seemingly way-out teachings to see instead, what would happen if they adopted them as worthwhile guidance.

His teachings however are not commonly adopted. There is a fear within humanity, a fundamental distrust, that if left to our own moral devices, we will descend into a scene reminiscent of the novel *Lord of the Flies* by William Golding. In that story, a group of children were stranded on an island without adult moral guidance and chose to form their own society. This society was brutal and violent and one of the children was murdered. As a teenager reading this novel in the second year of high school, I was depressed by its bleak view of human nature. When speaking to my father about it, and hearing him claim the brilliance of the book, I was further disheartened. I was shocked that this seemed to be what we thought of ourselves as human beings. We seemed to hold such low standards for ourselves and then attempt to live down to them! It was like we believed we were so terrible that we thought we might as well act like it then, like surly teenagers.

It was a similar teaching that I received in Catholic primary school, which was the teaching of original sin, that we need to be saved from our inherently evil natures, that we are fundamentally impure and need to be baptised in order to be saved. I always loved the ritual of baptism, but not based on the notion that there was something that needed saving, more that it was a graceful connection with divine presence, a divine dedication of future assistance on the undoubtedly troubled path of human spiritual awakening.

As a species we are undoubtedly still evolving towards the majority of us carrying an inner-governed moral choice to cultivate kindness, compassion, mercy and co-operation. Yet I still hold the belief that beyond all of the conflict, which we handle with differing degrees of skilfulness, the divine original spark within every single one of us, whether we appear to be demon or angel, is pure and absolute.

Spiritual teacher Matthew Fox came up with an alternative to original sin, which he called, beautifully enough, original blessing. The notion that life and our experiences, our nature, are blessed rather than sinful and in need of saving, is a different way of looking at the exact same spiral adventure from centre to farthest outreach and back to centre again. To hold a view of oneself as blessed by an opportunity for experience is healing. To not identify with our human existence as being based in some kind of sinfulness is healing.

What happened for me when I realised that there was actually nothing wrong with me was that I lived more fully, and more freely. I could take this gift of life and do something with it and with far more gratitude for it. It opened up my heart to more celebration and even though I still had much growth ahead of me, and undoubtedly still do now, I was able to embrace the journey, even the darkest parts of that journey, without falling into a great despair of belief that the suffering meant there was something wrong with me. It actually just meant I was having a human experience.

The initiation of the original self calls us to shed our false layers, to let go of old ways of operating and to allow ourselves to be revealed – perhaps through deepening intimacy in relationships, certainly through a deepening of our own relationship to ourselves and the Divine to begin with, and perhaps also by stepping onto a more visible platform in our life's work.

If this chapter is resonating for you, but you are feeling some emotional or psychological resistance, then it is suggested that you go back to Chapter 3 and perform the Lady Nada healing process and then come back to the healing process at the end of this chapter.

ASCENDED MASTER WHITE MATTHEW – PURITY

White Matthew is the newest of the new when it comes to Ascended Masters. He is said to have been a famous pop star who recently died. I have a sense that this is true and that a great light and positivity reached the world through his music, but when asked directly about it, there seems to be little interest in revealing any further detail about it – at least to me, at this time. What prompted me to include him in this book was the reaction that I had when I connected with his energy when creating the list of masters that I would write about.

I had heard about this master but never worked with him before. My preference in my work is to share only that which I have personally experienced, so I know that I can vouch for everything that I write. Yet my connection with this master was so beautiful and instant that I knew I wanted to include him in this work, and I knew I would get to know him as I did so.

Simply by intending to connect with him, what I felt emanate from him was a gentle sweetness and purity that reminded me of a truly innocent child. It took my breath away for a moment as I felt opened and softened from inside of my heart, as though I was beheld in a gaze that was so utterly free from judgment of any kind. I felt like I was gazing at a baby and somehow I was also the baby. It was a beautiful feeling of love. I have encountered many beings of unconditional love. It is incredible to me exactly how many different types of pure love we can experience from higher beings. Each Ascended Master, for example, loves us in their own unique way, yet it is all unconditional.

You may have had experiences where you had a friend that thought the world of you, knew your talents and really believed in you – and found that they somehow brought out the best in you because of that. Around people like that, you feel as though you are empowered, somehow you have permission to be yourself without apology or shame, or a path lies before you to be your best version of yourself. You are not trying to be something that you are not, you are instead being what you are, not holding yourself back or trying to play down your various characteristics. You want to be yourself in high definition and you aren't scared of it.

Imagine that permission, that sense of capability to be yourself absolutely and without shame or fear or regret or guilt amplified many times over. This was my experience of White Matthew for the first time.

There is such a goodness, even just in the vibration of his name (you can feel his essence by gently repeating his name), that I felt compelled to include him. He says that if you are having trouble connecting with him directly, perhaps because you are still grappling with acceptance of your own innocence, perhaps still needing to forgive yourself for being human, making mistakes (which he describes as an entirely human notion, the divine expression for 'making mistakes' is actually just 'living') and having experiences. If that is the case for you then you may like to ask for the Soul of the White Dove (one of his spiritual names) that loves you unconditionally and that will help you connect with his presence.

His teaching is that purity is independent of action. This does not mean that we have to worry that we are going to become perpetrators of negative action and suddenly be murdering others, à la *Lord of the Flies*, or vengeful grandmothers who declare that they would take a gun to the head of anyone who tried to hurt you and kill them in cold blood (or was that just my Italian grandmother!?).

What happens when we discover our innate innocence is that our moral centre naturally awakens. Have you ever heard of the self-fulfilling prophecy? The idea, for example, that if you tell a child for long enough that he is useless and bad, he'll start to believe you and act accordingly, no matter whether he is talented or not? This was the case with a man that I was once involved with and loved very deeply. Vastly talented in a number of areas including spiritual healing, counselling and music, he struggled to bring those talents to fruition. His programming that he would fail, from a number of sources growing up, obscured his ability to manifest his talents and express them freely in the world.

One of the many wise and helpful choices my mother made on my behalf as I grew up was deciding not tell me that my sixth grade teacher thought I was destined to fail. I had no idea that she felt that way on a conscious level, though subconsciously I knew that she didn't like me, but I didn't much like her, so I figured that was fair enough.

My mother only shared that remark with me many years later. Apparently my sixth grade teacher had told her not to let me take the scholarship examination for the high school I was applying to attend, because I wouldn't get one. It was a bizarre comment to make, but then I don't know what issues my energy triggered in my teacher.

Me not knowing of her discouragement was helpful. Although I am a rebellious sort and someone saying, "You can't do that," would more than likely make me decide that I would do it, young people can be more sensitive and absorbent of the comments of their elders than we realise. Fortunately by the time my mother passed on my teacher's comments I had already won a scholarship, finished as dux of the school and gone on to complete tertiary studies. Although my university courses bored me senseless, completing my degrees did push me to develop the confidence and skills I needed to do things that support my work now, like writing, managing time, meeting deadlines and undertaking public speaking. When I heard of her comments all those years later I felt a bit sad for her and grateful that she was no longer an influence in my life.

What White Matthew teaches us is that once we discover our natural beauty, our innate purity, and our innocence, we can release any subconscious feelings of being 'damned anyway' which could lead us to a negative self-fulfilling prophecy in our choices and lifestyle. With a sense of our innate innocence that can never, ever be tainted, we can come from a much healthier place of fundamental self-esteem that allows us to make choices that are supportive, healthy and loving. When we realise that we are loved by the Divine, that we are a divine speck of love, a new respect for ourselves can emerge. This is the new chapter in our lives offered by White Matthew's presence and teaching whenever we are ready to receive it.

DANBURITE – INNOCENCE

Danburite looks a little similar to Clear Quartz, although it has a much softer vibration and an angelic feeling about it. It is most often shaped as a four-sided prism with a flat, downward sloping top, something like the flat-sided edge of a chisel. These stones can be clear or colourless, and less commonly yellow, soft pink or lilac. The stone is not particularly common, and not the cheapest stone to purchase, but it is quite beautiful, each stone having its own particular soft vibration. Even a small piece can be powerful.

Danburite is a stone of spiritual growth. It enhances the return to innocence that comes when we remember who we are. Danburite helps cleanse the chakras of blockages, particularly those of shame that clog our energy and prevent it from flowing cleanly into new patterning. It is often hidden shame that keeps us trapped in behaviours that undermine our desires and intentions. That hidden shame tells us subconsciously that we are not worth the change in our behaviour, that we won't be capable of sustaining a new way, that we don't deserve the happiness that can come our way, that we should just stay right where we are.

It takes a lot of light and a lot of power to dislodge old programming that keeps us acting on auto-pilot rather than spontaneously creating from a healthy and healed centre within us. Often we need extra help in the form of divine grace to dislodge that programming. Danburite helps us with this – it is a bit like a crystalline 'smoke signal' to attract attention from unconditionally loving helpers so that we can find our way on the path. Working with Danburite gives us a 'hand up' to a higher vibration that would resonate less with shame and more with forgiveness, acceptance and resolution, and a willingness to move on from the past, even if we are uncertain about what the future will bring to us.

From that place of willingness our curiosity can flower. It takes the innocence of a child to be completely open and curious about where life can take us. For those souls who have been sensitive and suffered greatly, often in service to the greater good, it can seem daunting to remain curious and not fearful or retracting in the face of new experience. Sort of like the expression, "Once bitten, twice shy."

Danburite has a soothing quality to the soul that helps to clean away karmic residue gently, and open us up to curiosity and acceptance, to release negative expectations based on the past. So much of our suffering is based on the belief that something has been a certain way and it will continue to be that way. We have negative expectation without even being conscious of it.

Perhaps our pattern of relationship experiences ending in abandonment or betrayal has happened once too often and we now believe that pattern is more than a pattern but some kind of inevitable cruelty of life. Or perhaps our constantly outgrowing the people or situations in our lives, leaving us feeling alone and angry that we have to start all over again, has us doubting if we can ever truly experience a long-term relationship with another without compromising on our own spiritual growth. Or perhaps a history of missing out on recognition and support for our talents and our creativity has us wondering if there is any point in continuing to try to get our work 'out there'.

We can come to believe that this is the way it is because it is the way it has been. But this is not true! We are suffering a sort of spiritual post-traumatic stress disorder in allowing negative expectations based on past experiences to dominate our minds and hearts. Danburite is hope in a stone. It helps us to access the higher truth that in the present moment, we have the possibility to set our course in a new direction. It helps us draw spiritual support from angelic beings, and from the Angel of Danburite herself, to assist us in summoning the courage from within so that we can act based on what we want now, not on what has been in the past, and the powerful gravity of past habit rather than the lightness of heart that we may want to cultivate in our lives and relationships.

Danburite is a spiritual rescue stone, with an ability to connect us more consciously to the loving angelic realms, opening our heart to the love of the source. When we work with Danburite, we are sending out signals of reclaiming our divine innocence, of letting the past (including karma of past lives) be released that we may experience our lives now from a basis of spiritual self-esteem, of realisation that we, as much as any other creature, have a right to be here on this planet and to seek a life of spiritual richness. Danburite helps cure the mistaken notion that our personal growth is selfish and helps us tap into the more realistic understanding that the work we do on healing ourselves and growing in consciousness is not at the expense of another, but in service of the greater good.

HEALING WITH WHITE MATTHEW AND DANBURITE

If you are fortunate enough to have access to a piece of Danburite in any colour, have it with you, near your body, or use the mandala in this book. If you choose to lie down rather than be seated, place it near your crown chakra. If you are seated, just place the crystal or mandala wherever it is comfortable, but as close to your body as possible.

Say aloud, "I call upon the true Ascended Master White Matthew, and his sacred symbol, the holy white dove of unconditional love. I call upon the angelic kingdom that loves me unconditionally and the Angel of Danburite. Beloveds, I ask for divine grace that I may now strip away falsehood, lies, self-deception and past pain that has kept my original self obscured, hidden from my sight because I felt ashamed, trapped or broken and couldn't see clearly. Please continue the loving healing process within me now that my body, mind and energy field be free, through divine grace and my own awakening, from these past blocks. I wish to experience the beauty of my original self that I may awaken and be a healing light upon this earth, according to my highest good, so be it."

Perceive that all around you is a brilliant clear or white light and imagine that it is like soap! It might even be bubbling or frothy, or just soft and light as air. Let it gently dissolve layers of grit, grime and grease that have muddied the clear radiance of your original light, preventing you from really witnessing what is within you.

Stay with this dissolving light for at least 33 breaths. If you need a mantra to help you focus and surrender into the process, you can repeat, "I AM," as you breathe in and out.

Once you feel ready to continue with the next step, say the following out loud, "I now, of my own free will, break any contract or agreement I have ever made, consciously or unconsciously, that does not support my conscious spiritual awakening into realisation of my original self, thus also breaking its effect upon my body, mind and energy field. I now forgive myself for all obstructions and spiritual forgetfulness. I now forgive myself for repeating past patterns that no longer serve me. I now forgive myself for acting in ways that created shame, guilt, fear, self-doubt, anxiety or uncertainty. I now forgive myself for abandoning and betraying myself or another. I forgive myself for all such experiences in this or any lifetime. I now choose, of my own free will, to open up to the endless grace of my original self, which is divine. I open my heart to the mercy, grace and power of this being, through unconditional love, it is so."

When you are ready, you may wish to gently bring yourself to a standing position. Using your hands, make gentle but firm cutting motions in front of you, as if cutting through invisible cords that have connected you to suffering, using the side of your hand like a knife. Make sure that you reach over your head and even reach behind you gently too, intending that whether you can reach physically or not, the cutting (or sweeping if it is easier) motion of your hand clears your energy field.

Then sweep your hands in firm motions making sure that you cover the top of your head all the way down to your feet. Sit down if you need to do so in order to then sweep under your feet. As you do this, know that you are helping to clear energetic connections to the past experiences that you have now declared yourself willing to release. Take your time and breathe deeply in and out as you focus on doing this.

When you are ready, sit yourself down again or lie down, and be aware of a pure white sun burning brightly. Notice if it changes colour or form. This is a symbolic connection with you from your original self. You may see or perceive or just hold an intention to receive a communication from this original self. Imagine that you can open your heart and drink in what is given to you, whether you are conscious of it or not. You may feel some emotion with this experience. Whatever happens or does not is perfectly fine for you at this time.

Finally make the following declaration, "I now declare, with the Universe as my witness, that I am willing to surrender falsehood into the eternal purity and innocence of my original self. I am willing to remember what I AM. I AM. I AM. I AM (repeat as many times as feels right, whilst breathing gently in and out). Through my own free will, so be it."

Place your hands at your heart and bow your head to your original self, with acknowledgement, acceptance and gratitude that this is a step forward on your spiritual path. Well done, beloved.

When you are ready, just open your eyes.

Following this experience, you may wish to check in through prayer on a regular basis – reminding yourself gently, over time, that even whilst you are the Divine becoming, through healing and transformation, you are also the Divine being. You can state this simply with the mantra I AM.

13.

ASCENDED MASTER MOTHER MARY (Protection) CELESTITE (Serenity)

INITIATION OF TRUST

Waves of pale blue light rise and fall beneath you, as if you are resting upon an endless ocean of peace. Sound emerges from the waves of light, like angels singing. The sound creates patterns within the waves of light. A beautiful swirling dance of peaceful blue light ensues, and energy builds. Suddenly a beautiful golden being rises up from the ocean, cloaked in robes of blue, white and yellow, she raises her hand in blessing and gazes at you with loving recognition. Stars fall from her eyes, into your heart.

I can say that the fundamental teaching that I have come to share this lifetime is trust. It is the foundation of my work. Without trust, the mysteries of the Divine cannot reveal themselves to us. To learn trust requires at least for a time that we have imperfect knowledge and partial vision. Without those impairments, we wouldn't need trust because we would already see and know all! However, the journey through Earth School is not about being perfect, it is about process. We are here to be initiated into divine mysteries through the experience of life. Trust helps this happen in the most blessed of ways.

In learning trust, we are able to expand our consciousness further and further into the divine source. In learning trust, we can be helped to accomplish spiritual tasks that we could never hope to do on our own. Trust is an empowerment that is bestowed through an acknowledgment of our own limitations and a realisation that those limitations are the way that the Divine can reach us. I'll explain that further now, with this sweet story I first heard when I was in my twenties.

This is the healing story called 'The Cracked Pot', which tells the tale of two pots that the servant of the household used to carry, one on each hip, as he walked along a path to fetch clean water from the well each day, and then back along the path to bring that clean water into the master's house.

One pot was perfectly formed, without flaw and held water all the way to the brim, without leaking one single drop. The other felt somewhat inadequate by comparison! It realised that it was slightly cracked and couldn't help but drip water all the way back along the garden path from the well to the master's house.

One day the servant felt the sadness of the cracked pot and asked it why it was so forlorn. "I am so flawed!" the pot lamented, "that I cannot possibly be as pleasing to the master as the perfect pot that carries more water than I." The servant smiled kindly and gently spoke to the pot. "Do you not see that the trail of water you leave each day has led to flowers growing along the garden path? These flowers grace the master's table and bring him much joy." The cracked pot then felt joy too, realising that it was able to serve the master and bring delight, just by being as it was.

Trust enables us to live, love and be as we are with compassion. When we do inner work and embark upon spiritual growth, it is with the knowledge that we are opening up to our own divinity, however that may uniquely manifest for each one of us, rather than trying to fix ourselves into some notion of perfection that we have conjured up through fantasy or comparisons to others.

It is trust that also helps us accept and even embrace our life experiences, seeking to live them fully. It is then that the Divine can flow through us, because we are surrendered (through trust) into life and flowing with it as best we can. We come to allow life and our experiences to be as they are and seek the Divine in them – rather than trying to fix them to be otherwise.

Sometimes it is our vulnerability that helps others as much as it is our strength. On several occasions I have had feedback from students that the sharing of my life stories (and how I have certainly tripped and stumbled at times along the way) makes me and my teachings more accessible to them. They can see that I am learning and growing like everyone else, despite what people tend to assume when they meet someone with spiritual capabilities in the public eye, which is that they are somehow perfect. I certainly know that the odd imperfections and idiosyncrasies that I have found in my spiritual teachers over the years endeared them to me more than anything else. On the odd occasion that those flaws were such that I decided to end my study with them, I can honestly say that I learned as much from the dark side of their personality as I did from the light side.

What trust allows us to do is deconstruct the walls of expectation that we may have unwillingly or unknowingly built up around ourselves, that keep us in a state of wanting or wishing or needing life to go in a certain way, rather than being able to respond to the currents that present themselves. It releases a lot of stress and anxiety!

I still remember a healing session – it would have taken place over ten years ago –

where a highly intelligent, spiritually-inclined man came to see me for a reading. Good looking, successful and bright, the man was seeking something more than his current level of achievement and satisfaction in life. As his guidance session drew to a close, after delving deep, there was a final piece of guidance for me to impart, which was to trust. He looked at me and promptly said, "Well, yes, that makes a lot of sense, but *how* do I do that exactly?"

I was a bit surprised, never having had someone ask me how to trust in the Divine before, and eventually I answered that there was no formula to follow, simply a choice to be made. You either chose to trust, or you did not. These days I put it a little differently; I say that we put our trust in the Divine or in our fears. We get to choose where we place our trust at any given moment.

Some of us have come to this planet to live a lifetime where consciously connecting with divine energy plays a significant role in our life path and spiritual growth. It might be because we are here to be healers or way-showers for those that are seeking a way out of lower vibrational awareness and need some help to recognise another way. It might be that we are spiritual rebels, creatives, visionaries and cosmic lifeguards, helping other souls not to drown in an ocean of suffering. Another term for that is the boddhisattva which we will explore in the next chapter. As you are reading this book, you are more than likely going to fall into one of those roles in some meaningful way.

For such souls, there is an inescapable need to master the lesson of trust in order to be of full malleability to divine energy. You have a lot to do this lifetime! A big offering to make. You'll need to be able to be guided by an infinite intelligence to be able to do what you are here to do. Trust enables us to flow, to be responsive, to be permeated by the Divine so that it just flows through us – literally. Trust enables us to become like water. There is so much power and efficacy in water. It can wear away rock, it can take many forms, it is capable of bestowing life.

We who are here to serve the Divine in particular ways like those described above, are learning to trust, to let ourselves become like water, to be moved by the divine current. To do this without losing your lightness of spirit, your strong centre, your integrity, and your ability to act when needed – in other words, your air, earth and fire nature as well – is a fine balancing act. If you are still working on this (and that will be most of us at some time or other) then Chapter 10 can help and we will also explore this further in *Crystal Goddesses 888* when we discuss Tantra and elemental healing. For right now, however, our focus is on developing the trust that we need to flow as water with the divine currents.

Whilst using visualisation and intention to manifest is an important learning on the path, as we evolve, we are going to be asked to let go and let God many, many times too. This might feel like we are asked to become more like the wave in the ocean, or the raft adjusting her sails to meet the wind, rather than trying to huff and puff, blowing our sails in the direction we think we should be going, if only the Divine knew what it was doing. These are the times when we feel like we are moving in a direction, rapidly or not, yet we are uncertain about exactly where we are going. We are asked to trust and flow, even though we may have no clue where it is we are flowing to or what it will look or feel like.

So we might be asked to rest when all we want to do is strive forward and make things happen. We might be asked to walk away from something that we have put a lot of time and energy into creating. We might be asked to stay put when all we want to do is leave. The heart may be guiding us to trust in something that is happening in our lives, whilst our head is filled with fear, escape fantasies, plans of attack or distracting daydreams of life being so very different. Trust is about learning to use our own personal will not to demand our way, but to let the Divine have its way through us, with us doing our best to align and co-operate. It is giving in to spirit without giving up on life.

The trickier part of this process, and why perhaps it is only for the more advanced soul, is that the requirement of trust is huge. We may be asked to endure without clear knowledge for months or many, many years. I have been through this myself many times and the struggle between trusting and wanting to know what is happening and why can be extremely painful.

Being one who is easily adaptable and once given a clear vision or instruction, tends to create extremely quickly, I found the waiting for things to come together to be challenging. For well over a decade I sat in unknowingness. I knew that I wanted to gift my work to the world in a broader way, but I had to wait. I had to endure not knowing if or how that may happen. I had to keep working without immediate result or gratification with the understanding that this was not something that I could make happen through sheer force of will. With full knowing that I could do all that I could possibly do, but it was still up to the Divine as to the timing and the extent of my heart's desire coming to life – I had to trust.

Looking back now, I can see that I was growing and waiting with intelligent purpose. There was much that happened within that twelve or so years that helped prepare me to do a better job later on in my vocational development. It also gave me a chance to meet my publisher who would help me in many ways. I would also meet others who would help me with their various skills and business ability. I needed a team to do what I felt in my heart I was supposed to do. The Divine knew this and had it all sorted according to perfect timing, like a divine juggling act with all the souls involved. Apart from that, the people that I wanted to help had to be ready to receive what it was that I was able to offer. It was like I was one of the meals in a long divine degustation menu, and I just had to wait until it was my turn to be served up!

However I didn't know any of that back then. There was no clarity ever given to me about what was going to happen, or when. I believe that this was the case because it helped me grow stronger spiritually. The only choice I had available to me was either to trust or to despair. Sometimes despair won, but more often than not, I was able to sustain trust. Quite possibly if guidance had have said to me, "Look, it's going to be about fifteen years or so, so just chill out for a while," I would have missed out on the intense spiritual growth that I developed over that time.

My sometimes impatient and curious nature and desire to dive into the next adventure still makes trust an important spiritual anchor for me. I have often been chided by my guidance, in a loving way, that I rush off so fast to the next destination, forging ahead, when I could have relaxed and got there at the right time with less effort. That's trust, in the timing and unfoldment of the divine plan.

It took years before that trust in the face of what seemed like 'no love' from the universe in publishing my work was replaced with a sense of relief that I was finally being given permission to move ahead professionally. Trust was a challenging lesson to put into practice over more than ten years, although I have no doubt that there are many who have had to endure much more than this, perhaps through illness or devastating life circumstances, and simply trust. These are quite possibly very great souls, learning a powerful spiritual talent – the ability to be present, to allow and accept the Divine and be open to what is in this moment, even when in this moment, there may be heartbreak and pain. Those are the moments when trust is needed more than ever. Those are the times when Mother Mary can help us most.

ASCENDED MASTER MOTHER MARY – PROTECTION

Mother Mary used to stand, as a large statue on the top of my grandmother's wardrobe, gazing down at her (she was also named Mary) as she slept. As a little girl I would often lie on my grandmother's bed, and gaze up at the lovely Mary statue (in between riffling through her jewellery boxes and delighting in shiny, pretty things). I would look at the statue with curiosity, noticing it was chipped and old, but that the pale blue and white robes of Mary looked beautiful still. I would hear my grandmother swiftly chanting her daily rosary, praying to the Holy Mother under her breath, and feeling probably the safest I ever felt as a child.

As I grew, so too did my awareness that Mother Mary was with me. She was more physically present in my life than some of the other Masters who appeared more in dreams and meditations. There were times when I could feel her and hear her, even whilst in normal states of day-to-day consciousness. She was with me even when I did not consciously realise it until much later on.

Raised as a Catholic (before I renounced religious affiliations in favour of embracing all spirituality in my late teens), I took the confirmation name of Bernadette. I didn't know why, just that I wanted to use that name. It was decades later that I realised that this was the name of a saint to whom Mary had appeared and through whom she requested that a Chapel be dedicated to her in a grotto at Lourdes. In my early teens, I decided that I wanted to go to a school called St. Catherine's. I didn't know exactly why, but I just knew I was meant to be there. Again, decades later I had a more intimate understanding of the role of St. Catherine as another receiver of divine grace from Mother Mary. I believe that these weren't coincidences but confirmations that the Mother was always close to me, whether I knew it consciously or not. If you have love for her, then she is close to you too, whether you know it or not.

I share these next two personal stories with you to encourage you to know that she is witness to our most intimate heart-felt prayers and always answers. I believe I was blessed with these two experiences because she knew that her presence would be recorded by me and shared with others, that they too may feel hope in the presence of her grace. Even as I write this, I feel her presence welling in my heart and I know that she has so much love for you and wants you to know that she has heard your prayers, even before you have uttered them, she reads the truth of your heart and asks that you pray to her consciously if you wish to receive her grace and protection because she wants to share that with you, beloved.

The first story that I'll share with you centres around the story of Mary's apparition before St. Catherine.

It was around 2002 or so, and I had finally summoned up the courage to send a manuscript that I had been working on to a well-known new age publisher. After some nail biting weeks, I finally received a response. I still remember looking at the stamped self-addressed envelope that was sitting in my letterbox, written in my own hand, with a sinking feeling in my stomach. It was a form letter rejecting the book proposal. The form letter had my name misspelled and was dated incorrectly – not just the month, but also the year. Those careless mistakes amplified my feelings of frustration, as though I was so insignificant, that my letter didn't even warrant a basic spell-check. I was so certain that they hadn't even bothered to read the proposal, even though they said they were accepting unsolicited manuscripts, and I felt crushed with feelings of disappointment, doubt and despair.

It might seem a bit dramatic, but I truly felt devastated. I have always been a passionate person and despite my usually calm exterior, I feel things very deeply. At the time I honestly felt as though my dream had been crushed. I felt completely out of my depth as a young writer without an agent who couldn't get her foot in the door of a publishing house. I felt lost. How could I get my work out into the world if others wouldn't take a chance on me? I knew that I could only do so much on my own, then I would need help from those that knew more about publishing and distribution than I could ever hope to learn. Despite attending courses on the publishing industry, learning how to write book proposals and doing my best to put myself in the view of those who could help me get my work to those that I knew I was meant to help, it just wasn't happening. I knew that I could continue on a path of self-publishing, which I had done with my meditation CDs, but the time and energy that this took for distribution and marketing was the time and energy that I wanted to spend on creating new content, recording the near constant stream of divine dictation that coursed through me every day. My grandmother would have said that I was stuck between a rock and a hard place. I felt utterly bereft and alone.

At that moment I knew that my journey was going to ask a lot more of me than I had expected. I felt unequal to the task and filled with questions born of insecurities unearthed by my rejection letter. I have heard stories of writers wall-papering their study with rejection letters to motivate them to write better and work harder, perhaps to prove those publishers wrong, but my response was not so hardy. Instead I took the rejection to heart and wondered if the book I had been working on, that was supposed to help people, had as much value as I had once believed. I had questions about my work that I needed answered. So I prayed for help, for a sign, about my path and how to proceed.

Shortly after this prayer, I was walking along the main road of the inner west Sydney suburb of Marrickville where I was living at the time, trying to focus on the trees and not breathing in inner city smog. After only a few blocks of my walk, I noticed a small gleaming object on the ground, a few feet ahead of me. I slowed down my walk, looking attentively at this object as it started to come into clearer view, feeling a strange excitement and hopefulness welling up inside me.

Being an inner city Sydney street, my logical mind imagined that this gleaming treasure would most likely be a bit of rubbish like the twist-top cap of a beer bottle. Despite this, my body was reacting as though something much more precious was being offered to me. I reached the glinting object, kneeling down to pick it up and saw that it was a small silver medallion with the image of Mother Mary on it, wrapped in a green and purple ribbon around a piece of white paper with blue text. My heart filled with a mixture of joy and incredulity. It felt like my own personal visitation with Mary had occurred in downtown Marrickville, perhaps not as historically glamorous as France during the revolution, when

St. Catherine received her first visitation with the Holy Mother, but at least not as bloodied.

Transfixed, I stood in the middle of the footpath with traffic blaring around me, fumes everywhere and slowly unravelled the paper scroll to read the text. The first words that I saw were these: "God has a special task for thee." I felt a surge of emotion in my heart – gratitude, relief, wonder and intense love. These words spoke directly to my heart. I felt affirmation that my spiritual direction was going to manifest somehow and not to be disheartened. I felt that my prayers had been heard and things were going to be alright, somehow.

I continued reading the unrolled pamphlet which chronicled the story around the medal tied to it. It explained that the medal was a part of the manifestation of St. Catherine's divine life mission, which she carried out in service to the Divine Mother. This felt like a clear answer to my own prayers about my life mission. It would happen, it was meant to be, just as I was meant to be. I would be guided about what to do, and when. It would happen according to Her wisdom and will.

This experience helped to revive my belief that there was a space for me and for my voice in the world, and that it would be of service to others' wellbeing, and my own, but that I had to trust in the Universe as to the 'how', 'who' and 'when' of it all.

My encounter with Mother Mary through this little symbol became my light at the end of the tunnel, during a particularly challenging time in my life. Her presence, her reaching to me became the point that I focused upon when the uncertainty and passing of time, where nothing appeared to be happening, could otherwise have caused me to lose hope. I still have that medal, tied in ribbons the colour of the heart and crown chakras, in a special corner of my healing room, underneath my altar.

The other story I want to share with you is of the Holy Mother's protection, at a time when I didn't know that I needed it and therefore didn't know to ask for it! Such was her wisdom that she provided me with Her grace anyway. In the provision of that grace, I learned that I was actually in a situation that I needed to remove myself from, and it may have taken me a lot longer, and a lot of pain, to realise that eventually for myself without her intervention on my behalf.

I was studying with a charismatic spiritual teacher with a strong dark side that appeared to be largely unconscious to her. I felt uneasy in her presence early on, even through the blinding glare of her dazzling light. I was puzzled by her dangerous (and presumably unconscious) behaviours because it was my Higher Guidance that had suggested that I connect with this teacher in the first place. They never said why, of course, just suggested that I go. So I rocked up to the school, and was presented with simplistic content that I had studied decades ago. So there I was, in the most confounding situation, sitting in classrooms to learn material that I had taught my own students with far more depth and understanding, over a decade earlier. I didn't doubt that I was meant to be there, but, my goodness, I was confused as to what the purpose of my presence there could be.

In my path up until then, I had been interested in two faces of the Divine – love and light – with a respect for the dark face of the Divine, believing that it was expressing love and light even when hidden through crisis or trauma which may have been painful but was always ultimately drawing us closer to the Divine.

What I had eschewed however, was the third face of the Divine, which is power. I dismissed it as unnecessary at best and a seduction of the ego at worst. Clearly I didn't know what I didn't know. The Divine led me into the learning that I needed to grow spiritually and become more capable of fulfilling my role as a planetary helper.

In that school, it wasn't the content of the classes that was of interest to my Higher Guidance. It was what was happening in the school that they knew I needed to learn about in order to develop. The school worshipped divine power; sometimes with conscious awareness which brought about great growth in the ability to express love and light in the world in tangible ways. Unfortunately more often, from what I experienced at least, power was worshipped through unconscious addiction and dysfunctional self-abnegation. Essentially it was – if not a cult – at least a group with a high level of cult-like characteristics. What a perfect place to learn about power, and discernment as well.

It took me several months to get my head around what was happening. In that time I struggled to understand the light and dark aspects of power. I knew that if I were going to understand how power could serve the Divine, I would have to go through the shadow side of it too. It was certainly not something that I was enjoying, but I could recognise it as an essential part of my own spiritual training.

So without fully understanding why I was there, but prepared to accept that I was learning something of value or else I wouldn't have received the divine nudge to work with this teacher, I faced the challenge before me.

It was very hard, being in that school, trying to remain energetically open to master the lessons I was supposed to be learning there. It was hard to identify what the lessons were, because I was working with my own ignorance about power so it took me a while to even realise what I was supposed to be learning, let alone practice mastering the lesson.

It was also hard to not fall into the ways of the school, with constant pressure and various techniques of manipulation that they utilised to 'encourage' you to do so. I met many people who confided in me about their struggles to manage the demands of the school in terms of time, finances and emotional energy. They struggled with their own addiction to being 'in the energy' as they described it and the impact it was having on their personal relationships outside of the school and their own finances (given the constant push for donations from the school). I somehow became the unofficial confidante for many people there. I was blessed with friendships during my time at the school with many of those people who recognised my light and were drawn to me, seeking some sort of comfort in the storm of what it was like being involved in such an organisation. I found many of these people to be fundamentally lonely and looking for connection, not only genuine divine connection in a spiritual sense but to each other as well.

I was also treated with suspicion by some that were very much 'in' the system and sensed that although I was attending the school, was respectful and open, I was not the same as them. Even though I had no interest in changing or challenging their beliefs, my own beliefs which were that divine connection was an direct experience that required no intermediary, and any intermediary was nothing more than a temporary helper on the path, seemed to give rise to suspicion and distancing.

I have since heard that my name still gives rise to a mixed response in that school, years after I have had any involvement in it at all. Yet I had little sense of my impact at the time. It was only after I left, supporting some others that trusted me, to help them find their own path which sometimes meant venturing out of that school and into their more authentic divine destiny (that had little to do with me, and everything to do with their own soul purpose), that I began to realise that I had been there not only to learn for myself and to be trained for my deepening work, but also to help some others who were in need right then and there. I had no agenda other than unravelling the mystery of why I was there in first place, so the Divine could work through me in numerous ways, some of which I am unaware still, I suspect.

I was deeply disturbed by much of what I encountered there. I was certainly meeting the shadow side of power and cultic dysfunction on a broader level. This applied not only to the school, but I realised eventually it was endemic in our contemporary culture. It wasn't just in cults that abusive power-games took place, they were just more intense in those situations. Abuses of power exist in many ways in our control-based culture where power is focused on one individual or core group and others develop spiritual amnesia of their own innate strength and divine connection. They are blinded by the powerful light of another and forget that they can only behold what they are – that the light they are seeing is their own. If we don't know power, if we aren't wise to its light and its dark faces, we can be easily manipulated in situations where, with a little more wisdom, we would rather quickly withdraw, and when enough people did so, the dysfunction would not be fed any further and could finally wither and die.

My time in this school offered me a chance to learn these lessons, to be exposed quickly and intensely to direct experiences that would help me access invaluable wisdom. I was directed into a place where I could experience what conscious access to divine power (through absolute surrender) could achieve as well as witness the destructiveness of unconscious power and the conditions in which it could thrive or be destroyed. These were invaluable lessons and I will share more of the wisdom that came through these experiences in some of the chapters of *Crystal Goddesses 888*. For now however, the discussion above helps paint the picture of how helpful some divine help was along my journey at that time.

So when the time came for me to leave, some months since my first steps into that school, my Higher Guidance simply said, "We suggest that you leave now, as you are getting distracted and it's not going to help your path any further to remain there." I had all that I needed to gain further spiritual mastery and move forward on my path to help others. I was certainly ready to go.

After I had left and was processing and making sense of all that had happened – and the integration took the better part of a year to come to me – my guidance described my 'spiritual adventure' in that school as entering the belly of the beast. So with that in mind, I'll share the story that involves Mother Mary and my involvement in the spiritual school I have been discussing.

Early on in my attendance at the school, I went to one of their weekend seminars. It was held in the beautiful grounds of an unrelated secondary school, situated nearby, in an inner west suburb of Sydney. I learned some helpful teachings, which put some of my own experiences over the years into a perspective that made sense to me.

During a break, I wondered around the lovely grounds. As I walked along a pathway, I noticed a large tree with white blossoms and surprisingly enough, felt the presence of the Mother Mary. I paused to savour it for a moment before rounding the corner. As I did so, I saw that this tree actually stood before a small grotto, obscuring it from view. As I moved closer I saw the grotto contained a small statue of Mother Mary within it. I sat and prayed to her during the break, returning to the session somewhat refreshed.

The next part of the seminar was a meditation. During that meditation I felt my energy rising and could feel my consciousness preparing to leave my body. Apart from the first couple of years of my meditation practice this lifetime, when I would have experiences that had little to do with my body, as I darted around the many playgrounds of our limitless Universe without much awareness of what was happening 'back at home in my body' at the time, my meditation practice had since developed into something that grounded me into the physical reality of my body. Instead of disconnecting my spirituality from my body, I had learned to anchor the two together, and this was a lesson that I had to learn even though I didn't want to for many years, preferring to 'fly off' and feel what I thought was freedom, but was actually just dissociation from my body.

Nonetheless, I wasn't thinking of any of this, or thinking at all actually, as I began to feel my spirit rise up and prepare to leave my body, out through the crown of my head. Just as I was about to pop right out of my body, an enormous dark masculine figure stepped before me, blocking the teacher of the seminar energetically from me, standing between us both. Facing me he gently but very firmly proceeded to push me back down through my crown chakra and into my body again. I proceeded with the meditation in a puzzled state, not exactly sure why I was held in my body rather than allowed to leave it, but feeling that although the figure appeared very dark, he in no way felt dark in a negative sense. His power was employed with tenderness and I knew it was safe to trust him.

Later that day, during another break, I went back to the grotto. I could feel the Holy Mother's presence and again and I felt calm and serene. Then she spoke unexpectedly. "I sent Michael to protect you," she said. I knew that she was referring to the enormous, shadowed masculine figure. I was puzzled but no more was forthcoming and the short tea break was over. I went back into the room and sat in my seat, glancing up at the screen behind the teacher. On it was projected a huge picture of Archangel Michael. I have no idea why. It didn't relate to what we were learning, but there he was. I felt a sudden jolt of glee and the sense of humour of the Divine. I laughed.

I also took it as a confirmation that even when things may seem to be 'of the light' or 'of the dark', the Mother knows best (!) and sends protection when we are in need. It took me some serious months of integration to come to understand the reasons why this protection was needed in that circumstance, and eventually it made sense and I felt relief. I came to understand that it was not appropriate for me to adopt the teachings of that school, that some of their instruction confirmed and clarified my own teaching, but that the rest needed to be left alone. There are phases on the path when learning to leave the body is key for spiritual development and times when learning to experience higher spiritual presence from within the physical is the way forward and any deviation from that could be critically harmful for the initiate learning to love the light in the form. Seduction back into the light beyond form might make it harder than it needs to be to realise that very same light is right under your nose – in the cells of your nose even. The teaching is that the 'flesh is to be rendered holy'. We explored this in Chapter 6. At the time I didn't have the distance to put my experiences into perspective. Despite my momentary puzzlement, I just had to trust. We will be helped when we most need it. If we are helped, then even if we don't realise it, we were in need of it.

Mother Mary is known and beloved by many. I have met her devotees in the form of witches, even Catholic witches (clearly having a soul path of religious integration this lifetime!), nuns, Christian mystics, Yoga teachers that honour the Hindu path and more. She loves without reference to religious affiliations.

The meditation with her on my guided meditation CD *Mystical Healing* is one way to connect with her gifts of peace and alignment into one's body-soul through the chakras. I love Mother Mary and I feel blessed to also offer the *Mother Mary Oracle* set and the meditation CDs *Mother Mary Meditations* and *Eastern Star, Western Star: Meditations with Kuan Yin and Mother Mary* through Blue Angel Publishing to help others build their relationship with her too.

CELESTITE – SERENITY

Celestite is a stunning medium-blue hued crystal, semi-transparent and appears usually in clusters. I have one piece of it, quite large in that it is a bit heavy to hold with one hand, with delicate snowflake-like clusters emerging from the main cluster of terminator points at the base. Celestite is also often shaped into eggs that are part polished and part open with the cluster emerging, and in rounded crystal geodes of quite small to medium sizes. It is reasonably easy to source, though a good quality stone can be expensive.

The piece that I have has always been precious to me and reminded me of the blue of Mother Mary's robes on my grandmother's statue. I bought it from a crystal store in the city, travelling by two trains from an office job that I detested (you may remember me referring to that earlier on in this book!), running in and buying the crystal and returning on two trains, cramming the whole adventure into a stressful lunch hour. On the way back, holding that crystal in my hands, even all wrapped up in newspaper, I felt calmed. I believe it was the beginning of a divine intervention in getting me out of that job! I have loved that piece, which remains near a picture of Mother Mary in my healing room to this day.

Celestite holds the peaceful energy of serenity and an angelic gentleness. Mary is known as the Queen of the Angels, and this stone holds the vibration of her energy as well as that of the angelic kingdom. It is a safe stone to have permanently in use in any room of the house, except where a lot of physical energy is needed as it certainly tends towards being a more dreamy, meditative stone, bringing peace and tranquillity and slowly but surely it helps us adapt to having a constant conscious channel with the Divine. That can take a while to get used to – like learning to scratch your head and rub your tummy at the same time. For some of us, it's pretty natural, for others, it's really challenging as we learn to be able to hear the gentle vibration of our higher divine guidance even amongst the noise of daily life.

Celestite is a powerful healer of the throat chakra, and supports healthy metabolism and immunity. It strengthens and opens the upper chakras, gently making way over time for more conscious divine connection to be able to take place. We receive according to what we are capable of, you see, not according to how much we are loved, for the Divine loves unconditionally. If there is an inner child tantrum waiting to happen because deep down you would perhaps like God to love you more than God loves your evil nemesis, then that's okay. But know that once you experience unconditional love you won't feel that way anymore. You'll know that there is no need for competition because unconditional love is so completely filling that you are not left wanting. Another being loved doesn't take anything away from how you are loved.

Celestite helps us to understand this by gently expanding what we are capable of receiving from the Divine, opening us to trust in our divine connection and therefore become more receptive.

Because it works on the throat chakra, it also helps us express our truths – such as a need to change field of employment! Our truths might also help us really know how we feel about something or someone. Getting to know our truths helps us let go of situations that we are pursuing out of lack and to open up to receive that which would really and truly mean something to our hearts.

If you have a particular love for Mother Mary, or even if you haven't yet discovered such a bond but want to be open to it, then you are one of her children. You can ask that she tends to you through a connection that is enhanced and strengthened by a piece of Celestite. Just bring one home, cleanse it and dedicate it. The introduction to this book goes over the basics of that process if you need some assistance there.

HEALING WITH MOTHER MARY AND CELESTITE

Having your crystal or mandala nearby, preferably near your crown chakra, and laying comfortably, say the following, "Holy Mother, Full of Grace, I call upon you now, Mother Mary, Blessed Mother who loves me unconditionally, I call upon your healing intercession, your grace and your protection, you who knows the true voice of my heart, hear me now Blessed Mother. I call upon the Angel of Celestite and ask for your loving presence, healing and support. May the Grace of the Mother bless me, from heaven to earth, so be it."

Breathing in and out in your own time, you become aware of a beautiful temple, created from a large sky-blue crystal, extending before you. Step into it in your own time, being aware of beautiful light, either from a sun or moon, or from within the crystal itself, shining in the temple. Notice the floors, the ceiling and the walls, created from beautiful Celestite.

The natural spiritual light that floods the temple creates a rainbow of light at the centre, swirling and flowing. A beautiful woman in coloured robes of blue, white and yellow emerges from this rainbow of light, within the centre of the temple and raises her hand in blessing over you. You feel calm, loved and seen.

The violet ray from the rainbow, is swept up by the Beloved Mother, as she creates a rose of light in the palms of her hands, directing it towards your crown chakra. A rich violet coloured rose, filled with the Blessed Mother's healing essence, swirls and blossoms within the crown of your head.

Breathe in and out several times, for as long as feels right, allowing that rose to cleanse, bless, balance and protect your crown chakra.

The process is repeated, now with the Mother scooping up indigo blue light from the rainbow light gathered in the centre of the temple. She gently rolls the light in her hands, creating a beautiful deep blue rose of light that gently nestles itself in the centre of your head, clearing out behind your eyes and your ears, your mind and your thought processes.

Breathe in and out several times, for as long as feels right, allowing that rose to cleanse, bless, balance and protect your third eye chakra.

The process happens again, now with Blessed Mother scooping up sky blue light from the rainbow light gathered in the centre of the temple. She gently rolls the light in her hands, creating a beautiful light blue rose, sending it with love to the centre of your throat, clearing old vows, words, lies and thoughts that no longer serve you, helping you know your truth and make choices that support it.

Breathe in and out several times, for as long as feels right, allowing that rose to cleanse, bless, balance and protect your throat chakra.

The process is repeated, now with Mother Mary scooping up emerald green light from the rainbow light gathered in the centre of the temple. Moving the light in her hands, she generates a rich emerald green rose of light that gently nestles itself in the centre of your chest, opening your heart to life, releasing past pain and constriction, allowing you to breathe more deeply and peacefully.

Breathe in and out several times, for as long as feels right, allowing that rose to cleanse, bless, balance and protect your heart chakra.

Once more Mother Mary reaches within the rainbow light and now draws out a beautiful yellow that is perfect for you. Notice if it is bright daffodil yellow or soft lemon yellow, or some other shade and allow her to create that stunning yellow rose of light with her hands, as she sends it to clear, heal and balance your solar plexus chakra in your abdominal area, building self-esteem and self-worth, healing old shame and clearing doubt and distrust.

Breathe in and out several times, for as long as feels right, allowing that rose to cleanse, bless, balance and protect your solar plexus chakra.

Now Divine Mother draws vibrant and joyful orange light from the rainbow gathered in the centre of the temple. Notice if it is soft coral tone or a bright and vibrant fruity shade of orange. She gently pulls the light into her hands, creating a unique rose of orange-hued light. It gently nestles itself in the centre of your belly, beneath the belly button, renewing your energy, recharging your emotions and clearing out old emotion, shock and pain from your body, uncovering joy and playfulness.

Breathe in and out several times, for as long as feels right, allowing that rose to cleanse, bless, balance and protect your sacral chakra.

The process is repeated one last time now with the Mother scooping up luscious red energy from the rainbow gathered in the centre of the temple. She moves the light in her hands, creating a red rose of light that rests at the base of your spine, opening and connecting your body to the earth, bringing you passion, grounding, presence and power.

Breathe in and out several times, for as long as feels right, allowing that rose to cleanse, bless, balance and protect your base chakra.

Now be aware of all seven roses and finally of a field of white light that the Mother sends to you, to completely encompass you and sustain the healing within for as long as it needs to continue.

Place your hands at heart centre and say, "By Blessed Mother's grace, I accept healing, protection, love and divine intervention now, with mercy and unconditional love, so be it."

You have finished your sacred healing ritual. Know that she remains with you always.

14.

BUDDHA (Compassion)
PERIDOT (Increase)

INITIATION OF THE BODHISATTVA VOW

Within a dark, vast, open space, a yellow-green light flickers. Glowing more brightly, the flickering slows down, and begins to pulse. The pulsations become slower. Each pulse of light becomes longer, until the light simply glows, radiant and constant. Brighter, wider, more powerful. The light expands. Yellow-green rays of light illuminate open space. Joy. Happiness.

The Buddha consciousness, like the Christ consciousness that expressed itself through Jesus, flows through those that are capable of receiving it. It has many faces. It may be expressed through the Goddess Tara (whom we will meet in *Crystal Goddesses 888*) or the Ascended Master Kuan Yin (whom we met in Chapter 11). Buddhic consciousness might manifest through saints and sages, like the great being known as Avalokitesvara (a masculine manifestation of the Kuan Yin energy) or even be felt in the round-bellied laughing buddha known in the Japanese tradition as Hotei, who was later incorporated into the Chinese tradition as a symbol of abundance. Then there is the Buddhic symbol known as Maitreya. Maitreya is named as the Buddha of the future, that soul consciousness of compassion that will incarnate as various forms to help the world until all beings are free. This task is the manifestation of the Bodhisattva vow, to help liberate all living beings. Or perhaps when you think of Buddha, you think of the sage who lived around 400 years before Jesus Christ and founded the Buddhist tradition, Siddhartha Gautama Buddha.

The energy of the Buddha is the same no matter what face it carries, even though based strictly on appearances, those faces seem to be quite different. All faces of Buddhic consciousness share the same divine communication. Do you remember the teaching to trust in your feeling or perception of truth, no matter what appearances may tend to be? Underneath the appearance of the fat, laughing buddha, the graceful dancing lotus mother Kuan Yin, the ascetic meditating monk beneath the bodhi tree and the luminous manifestation of all compassion, Avalokitesvara, there is the same consciousness.

There is a story that illustrates this one consciousness of the Buddha nature, which leads to the initiation of the Bodhisattva vow.

The story goes that there was a great man who progressed so far spiritually, that he had climbed a mountain and could sense the endless love of divine eternity stretching out before him – so close he could just step off the edge of the mountain and return to the complete bliss of divine reunion forever! The spiritual goal after many lifetimes was finally in sight. As he prepared himself to end his painful journey of illusory separation from the Divine, diving into an eternity of bliss, something caught his attention.

He heard a great moan arising from beneath him. It rose up from where he had been climbing up the mountain. Just about to dive into the divine ocean of love, he held back for a moment and listened carefully. Then heard it again. His heart was moved into aching tenderness. He realised that this moan was the collective suffering of humanity, calling out for help. He was hearing the cries of the world.

He knew that he couldn't abandon the suffering he perceived even if that meant postponing his own complete spiritual liberation. He stepped back from the edge and vowed that he would not complete his spiritual journey and return to the Divine until every being was free from suffering. He descended again and began the great work.

This being was named Avalokitesvara. He is known as the manifestation of the compassionate light of all the buddhas; past, present and future. Whenever I hear of this story, and I have heard it from a few different sources, I am so deeply moved.

What this story speaks of is the bodhisattva vow. It is the soul dedication to the liberation of all beings.

If you are resonating with this chapter, then there is likely to be some relevance of the bodhisattva vow to your soul contract with humanity. Your presence upon this earth, and your path, is about not only your own growth, but your own growth with an understanding that this is not separate from the path of others but in fact intimately connected with the awakening of the whole of humanity, to help heal and free all living beings.

If you carry this vow in your soul, as you grow spiritually and become increasingly able to consciously perceive your soul, you will also come to perceive the presence of this vow within your own higher self. It holds a distinctive vibration, like a certain harmony on a musical instrument or a particular unique fragrance. It can be perceived in the soul as a golden consciousness. However it can exist whether we are conscious of it or not. If you are impelled to heal, to bring light or uplift consciousness, then it is highly possible that this vow has already been taken by your higher self, that you are here, along with the others demonstrating compassion, to help throw a rope to those drowning in the ocean of illusion even whilst you are taking the spiritual journey along with them, perhaps just a step or two ahead of those you are helping.

You may or may not have chosen to be a healer consciously, yet if your higher self has taken the bodhisattva vow, you will be an agent of healing even without conscious intent or awareness. You may do that in any number of expected or unexpected ways. You may do it through being a business leader guiding an organisation, through music, through art, through being a very ordinary person who believes in kindness and uplifts those around them. You may also be the person who sees the dark truths that are not spoken of and has a tendency to bring situations to a head – even without any particular conscious action on your part. A divine agitator, or as I would refer to you, a shadow healer, in that you cannot help but bring the darkness that others try to hide into the light. People may not like it, and even you may not like that this tends to happen when you are around, but you are a healer nonetheless, promoting wholeness.

If you tend towards a way of helpfulness, of upliftment or awakening, in your own unique way (whether as a soft and gentle emanation of divine love or a big thundering truth-speaker that rattles cages everywhere she goes, a blunt instrument of divine awakening), then your soul has taken a healing vow. If that healing vow is taken by an advanced soul, one that was close to enlightened status but chose to remain rather than proceed, to help others along the way, then your soul has taken a vow of healing a step further, into the bodhisattva vow and works closely with the consciousness of the Buddha.

Like the Christ, Buddha consciousness is not limited to any religious persuasion or philosophical doctrine. The Dalai Lama has said that kindness is his religion. This vow can exist on a soul level and be unconscious to the human being helping to express it. If we do identify more consciously with the path of the healer, and even perhaps the Bodhisattva vow, it can actually present some challenges for us at first, getting over our own ideas about how that 'should' look to let it be what it is. Later on, that awareness can help us surrender and work more intelligently with the divine plan if need be.

The challenges that arise for those of us that consciously understand we have a healing contribution to make to this planet often date back to childhood. The very issues that we struggled with in our lives, perhaps from childhood experiences, are the issues that lead us to find our power once resolved. To learn not to fall into saviour mode, or martyr yourself to another, imagining that you are healing them through your own unconscious behaviour is sometimes pretty difficult! If you really identify with being a healer, you'll be challenged to let go of some of the more typical beliefs about what that means and how it should look.

In essence, provided that you work consciously to minimise your personal agenda (beyond serving the highest good of the person you are seeking to help), your behaviour will be aligned with the soul and therefore in service to the highest good. You might find that you are demonstrating great gentleness. This is usually the way my own soul operates, but upon occasion there will be a fierce implacable side that arises and woe betide anyone or anything that gets in the way of it. It isn't a pretty or enjoyable experience for anyone involved, myself included, but it does bust through some intractable patterning and gets energy flowing in the right direction. It doesn't always win me devotion from those that encounter this side of me, but more often than not people are appreciative of it, recognising the divine presence in that fierceness. I never consciously choose this way to be, but I do my best to allow it when it comes through me, working very hard on dealing with my own agendas so that I can be as compassionate and non-obstructive as possible. It is only then that I feel accepting of my actions, even if those around me do not like them or criticise me for not behaving as they feel a spiritual teacher should behave, in their opinion.

For me however, kindness and compassion are not some sort of spiritualised indulgence. Sometimes stepping away from someone in order to allow for breathing space and time to integrate is a greater kindness than proceeding with a healing or teaching that would leave them confused. You wouldn't expect to progress to level three if you hadn't mastered level one – let alone level two. It would be confusing when in time, it need not be so. However if you really, really want level three and you know that I could teach it to you, but you don't receive it, you might become cranky and accuse me of being mean or stingy, for example. You see me as being hard, whereas I know that I am being kind.

As a healer, you'll learn that quickly, and realise that seeking out positive validation from others is very likely going to hinder rather than help your work. This is part of the trickiness of this path – we have to learn how to develop a centre of integrity within us that is about aligning with the pure light of the heart and be ruthlessly honest with ourselves about our own motivations. No one else can see in your heart like the Divine can, and there is no one to convince or impress, you just have to know within yourself that you are surrendering yourself and whether others like the outcome or not, you continue with it because it is the truth that you can access. What comes of that truth, when it is real and genuine, is always kindness – sometimes gentle, sometimes fierce.

The ego's declarations are one thing, but the genuine communion from soul to soul is something else entirely. I have found that the more I work with the soul, the more healing happens, but it takes a certain type of person to be comfortable with this. They have to be spiritually advanced enough to be willing to trust their own heart sense, even if their ego is going nuts with confusion, pain, questioning or doubt.

It can be very hard to stay on the path and follow where your heart is leading you when a part of you is suffering. The ego wants to feel that it can make sense of what is happening in order to feel safe, and this is often the case even if someone has been on the spiritual path for a long time. It can be hard to bear suffering, even when you have some understanding of the learning behind what is going on. It is much harder to bear it when you cannot sense any higher purpose for it at the time.

I have the utmost compassion for that, having experienced it myself many times, but whilst I understand that the ego may want validation and explanation, sometimes it isn't helpful to the soul and its path of spiritual growth. Often, I do offer encouragement and validation, because that ego needs the strength to continue with the process. It can be almost impossible to keep going if the spiritual path of your life is going into some very dark places without that genuine encouragement and explanation of purpose.

Sometimes however I do not offer validation, I just feel as though my mouth is 'stopped' and I couldn't open it to speak those words even if I wanted to go against the guidance I felt to be silent. Those situations are not lacking in love. It is more often that the ego is getting too powerful in blocking the soul that wants to move consciousness in a very different direction. By withdrawing validation and encouragement, by gently (sometimes) but firmly weakening the operation of the ego, the soul can gain some traction, pushing out of an unhelpful pattern (which is perhaps familiar and therefore appealing to the ego) and shifting into something far more appropriate for spiritual growth.

If the person in question is attached to her own viewpoints (and therefore ego) rather than learning to perceive through discernment and the eye of the heart, then they will reject what doesn't match their viewpoint. Even people who have been on a spiritual path for a long time can do this. Whether 'spiritual' or not, an ego is an ego and it likes to judge. As we learned through our discussions on discernment, it is really important not to abandon what we sense in our heart as truth, but this is very different to judging which shuts us off from growth.

Sometimes it can be really hard to allow a 'no' to come through you in your life, to set a boundary or to apparently even let someone suffer. But what if that suffering was the last straw before they gave up and let the Divine in to their hearts? What if you took that moment from them because you couldn't bear the weight of their suffering? I could completely understand where you were coming from if you did so unknowingly and yet I can say to you that as our heart grows, our capacity to bear suffering of our own and of the world generally, with compassion, does increase. It doesn't become easier necessarily, it just becomes more possible.

So with some faith that our own desire to serve is genuine and a willingness to let a 'no' or a 'yes' come through us based on our own heart impulse rather than what our ego might think is right or wrong, we become an increasingly surrendered and empowered channel for the Bodhisattva vow, a vehicle through which the great Buddha consciousness can flow to help all beings be free.

As you may be realising now, an action carried out as an expression of divinity, without ego agenda is an act of healing, and this Bodhisattva vow is fulfilled through healing action. That same action carried out with ego agenda is not, because the energy behind it is distorted.

Our part in the process is to become as honest as we can be with ourselves about our agenda. If we are going to work in this way and really surrender ourselves to the Divine, we have to do our inner work about our motivations and what is driving us. Sometimes we will be far more altruistic than we realise, and at other times, we'll be fooling ourselves if we believe that we are completely neutral in a situation. It isn't about some kind of complete absence of any personal motivation, it's about honesty and doing our best to get out of the way of divine flow.

Whether you consider yourself a healer for this lifetime, or simply as a person who wants more fulfilment in life, or even as bearer of the Bodhisattva vow in the soul, helping all of humanity, you'll be meeting your inner demons to a varying degree as you advance along the path. These are the parts of you that you perhaps would like to imagine don't exist, but of course they do in every one of us. Selfishness, pride, greed, anger, hate, fear and doubt all lurk within. We will either find them within us and integrate them, or we will experience them outside of us in the form of other people or situations – this will be life saying, "Now that I have your attention, can you have a look at this and find it within you, and get more conscious about it, so that we can move on with your journey?"

It isn't bad to have these qualities within us. It is just tricky not to let them be motivating factors in our actions. If you have any personal attachment to an outcome, if you have any personal need hiding behind your actions, then you are going to unintentionally create some havoc when you try to offer healing to another, when you attempt to open up to be a channel for the divine presence. This is why we need compassion. None of us are meant to have perfect vision. Whilst operating in the world, with limited awareness, this is not possible. Some of us will be able to perceive beyond illusion more than others, but if you are here in physical form, you'll have your moments of falling prey to distortion. Prayer, alignment with higher beings of unconditional love and compassion can help us forgive ourselves when we do mess something up, and also learn how to avoid being dragged down by the comments of others, because a wounded human can easily become a critical human and there are plenty of wounded amongst our ranks. That is why we need bodhisattvas.

BUDDHA – COMPASSION

The Buddha is the essence of compassion. Compassion is hard to describe, sort of like love (of which it is an expression) but you'll know it when you feel it. It isn't the same as empathy, which is an ability to 'walk a mile in another's moccasins'. My grandmother taught me as a young girl that we should never judge another unless we had walked in their shoes.

The compassionate heart goes even further than this. It leads us to a place where we can hold a place for the suffering of others that we don't have to understand – the person who commits a mass murder, whom we may not be able to relate to at all, for example, or a person who is cruel to animals and whose actions we may condemn with every fibre of our being. We may feel moved to fight for animal rights (wonderful!) and yet still be able to feel compassion for the brokenness in the soul that carries out cruel actions knowingly or not. The compassionate heart doesn't say, "Ah well, let them do that, who cares, it's their karma that's being created!" or denounce them as unworthy of spiritual assistance. The compassionate heart has a vision that suffering is being expressed. Whether we can consciously relate to it or not, compassion holds the energy of divine love which makes healing possible, for all. Without exception. Including ourselves. There is a Buddhist teaching that if we don't hold compassion for ourselves, we don't hold it at all.

Compassion is not necessarily soft and sweet, yet always has love at its basis. Sometimes that love will be tough love. Not from ego, as we learned in the example above, but from an understanding that different energies respond to different vibrations. To someone who is just opening up, a high intensity love might feel like a pale person sitting in the bright midday, mid-summer sun – a bit too intense and possibly harmful! A gentle, softer response, with more distance, might be just right. Or someone who is very bound up in defences and blocks might not feel a tap on the shoulder to get their attention. They may need a smack with the master's cane to realise that something's up. To smack a sensitive person who is able to be gently scolded with a look is unnecessary and cruel. But to attempt to scold with a look someone who doesn't even see you isn't going to be helpful to them at all. Compassion sees all deserving of help and allows the Divine to determine how that help is best delivered.

In his parenting tips, television personality Dr. Phil McGraw talks about currency when devising consequences for your children's actions. For example, if you ask your son to call you and let you know that he is safe when he is not going to be home when he was supposed to be, and he doesn't bother to do this, the consequence for that action is probably not going to have any constructive effect if it doesn't hit him where it hurts, so to speak. So if the consequence is going to be that he can't go shopping with his sister on the weekend, he'll quite possibly not give a hoot. However if the consequence is that he doesn't get to use his computer for three days then you may well hear of your son's whereabouts on a regular basis, without exception.

The Divine, in its compassion, works similarly with us. It is responsive to who we are, what we need, what will best serve us and when. For a long time, as a little girl at school,

I could never understand why people withheld compliments. For me, they had the effect of spurring me on to work harder. I found positive feedback to be encouraging. It never occurred to me until much later in life that for others, affirmation could have the opposite effect, of creating an attitude of laziness and disinterest in trying to improve.

Compassion means that we get what will help us the most, with the most love – whatever the appearance may be. This is the wisdom that underlies the teaching that we can trust in our life experiences. What we need is there for us, the work is not to make our life different as much as it is to understand how to relate to it differently. Then our life experience naturally transforms.

In teachings of the Buddhist tantra, a beautiful spiritual philosophy and practice that embraces the material world and the body as the key to our spiritual enlightenment, there are a number of instructions about compassion and how to cultivate and express it. The teaching that it is essential for us to have trust in life experiences is probably the most simple and powerful. This trust opens us up to the Divine in a surrendered way and in turn allows us to receive the endless assistance that is available to us. Divine compassion is in abundant supply, where we can run into limitation is with our own ability to receive it and allow its effect to move through us and our lives. This can be hard because it often asks us to let go of our judgment when we may feel much safer by holding on to it. Judgment can become a way of relating to the world that is known and the more we feel lacking in trust of divine benevolence, the harder it can be to let go of judgment. You have to have enough love in your heart to realise that the Divine loves you and helps you always, without exception, to surrender judgment over time.

One of the hallmarks of Buddhist teaching that can help us experience this love first hand is to practice detachment. Detachment doesn't mean that you cease to care or become cold of heart. It means that you accept that the Divine has far greater resources and understanding than our limited perspective can possibly ascertain. Detachment is a sign that we trust in divine compassion. The legend of the Buddha Avalokitesvara is that he was given eleven heads from which to hear the cries of the world and a thousand arms through which to respond. Compassion is not only loving and wise, but capable and intelligent.

As we practice compassion, and work on our own issues, we open our hearts. We take the spiritual path from being asleep to anything other than our own limited ego world, to awakening to the world of spirit and its endless love. We then journey further along the path to awaken as a bodhisattva dedicated to awakening the love of the spiritual worlds within all living beings, heading towards the higher consciousness of a divine human being, a fully-fledged buddha, operating completely and utterly from compassion.

This is not an esoteric concept. We will actually feel the effect of energetic heart opening. We become capable of compassion in circumstances where we once would have judged. It is a very freeing feeling that applies to more and more situations and circumstances as we grow. It is a measurable response that cannot be contrived. It is not something to try to assess but rather just something that you notice – perhaps whilst others around you judge and you realise that you don't hold any judgment of the situation being discussed, nor of the people doing the judging! Instead you just witness it and feel compassion. Perhaps you speak out, perhaps you do not. But whatever you do, it is not from a place of judgment.

At the basis of any judgment is fear. As the heart opens, we gradually release our fear and eventually become capable of compassion rather than reactive judgment. If we are judging, I suggest that it's important to be honest about it, have some compassion, and ask yourself what you are afraid of – underneath the judgment there will be something about the situation that makes you scared. It might be that you are not going to succeed, or that you could be like the person you are judging and you are terrified that you couldn't love or respect yourself if you were like that. It might also just be a habit of consciousness. It has undoubtedly existed for many, many lifetimes and we can be deeply honoured by progress to the point in this lifetime where surrendering judgment is becoming possible for us. Forget perfection and celebrate how much closer you are to the Divine now. Kicking the judgment habit is not just about not needing it as you used to, but letting yourself get into the habit of a compassionate mindset. It will happen with patience and application.

The point is that judgment doesn't change anything. It keeps us, and the situation, in lock-down. To hold a space for transformation requires compassion – which flows through an open heart without fear. Sometimes we will be able to create that space easily, because we have done a lot of work and we aren't triggered. Some of us are more tolerant personalities, naturally, than others, even whilst we are all developing our ability to be compassionate, to grow our heart more than our ego.

Yet there will be times when we are really challenged not to shy away from something in fear, and to remain present, and open, and to engage. Often this is in the presence of darker forces or energies. These may be negative parts of our own psyche, things that we were told weren't okay as children, such as our anger or sadness. Or it might be negative energy consciously or unconsciously coming towards you from another. As you flourish, people will respond. They may become jealous of what they perceive you have that they believe they do not have. They may be fearful that you will outgrow the relationship that you have with them – and they may be right. They may equally love and support you, but it is likely that not every person will have a positive response to you, no matter what your intentions or offering to the world may be. I have heard people criticise the Dalai Lama. If the most exemplary living model of human compassion can be criticised, then it is safe to say that probably none of us are immune from criticism.

I still remember the very first spiritual class that I taught at a community college in Sydney. I was in my twenties, and it was only my first experience running a spiritual growth course, but I felt so at ease, as though I had been doing it forever. Well, I suppose my soul had been! It was a lovely group, a mixture of ages. The men and women in that class were open and receptive students, all from very different walks of life but there was nonetheless a lot of good will towards each other and the course stayed full to the very end and was promptly run again the following semester. The only fly in the ointment, so to speak, was that one young woman, an attractive blonde with a bubbly personality, absolutely hated me. I know because she came up and told me after the first class! She seemed quite troubled by her reaction to me, not knowing why she felt that way. I wasn't at all offended, and actually had compassion because I had experienced difficult feelings towards some of my spiritual teachers too. It was a difficult situation but we worked through it as best we could.

Since then I have experienced a number of extremely positive and of course, some quite negative interactions with others. I felt like as much as I loved and served the light, I had to take a crash course in intensive study of negative energy. I didn't want to become unbalanced or be a teacher who in a desire to build light, denied the presence of darkness. I felt that this wouldn't be responsible, but as I grew, so too did the level of negativity that I needed to manage. Sometimes I did well, maintaining my centre, responding with compassion and effectively transforming the situation, if not into a love-fest, at least into greater consciousness and I was proud of myself and grew in confidence.

At other times I failed completely, fell back into my own fears and doubts and comforted myself with the thought that no particularly powerful negative energy would consider me enough of a threat to be interested in trying to undermine me. Nonetheless, as I have mentioned earlier in this work, the inner light is attractive not only to light beings but to darker forces too. These darker forces are not something that we need be fearful of, but it is handy to know that if we are in need of dealing with them – and some of us will have that task this lifetime, others not so much – then we know that we have some help and guidelines through which to proceed.

Whether you consider yourself a lightworker who needs to be trained in dealing with darker forces that are actively trying to thwart your spiritual path (in which case, be flattered briefly and then get prepared by working intensively with the material in this book and then the following one in the series, *Crystal Goddesses 888*, especially the chapter on Kali and work with my CD *Inner Power* also released through Blue Angel Publishing), or if you are someone who would just like to deal more effectively with the negativity that you pick up from those around you that brings you down and dampens your mood, this chapter will help you.

Although I will provide you with the basic guidelines you need to know to manage your spiritual light in the presence of darkness – and these guidelines remain the same whether you are dealing with a small bout of negativity in an office situation or a full-fledged psychic attack in spiritual healing work – if you are drawn to this work, get some training from a qualified teacher. As I mentioned, I will be offering further instruction on this topic in *Crystal Goddesses 888*, but even so, training with a teacher who has some mastery of this work is highly recommended. I do teach from time to time, and so does Raym Richards, who is a joyful and skilled healer working from Byron Bay, Australia. You can find him through his website: www.global-healing.com. His work may appeal to you, even if you don't embrace all aspects of it, he has a lot of wisdom to share. If his work doesn't appeal to you, be open to allowing your angels and Ascended Master guides direct you to the right teacher for you. Genuine and empowered spiritual teachers are rare gems, but when you need them, they'll appear. They just seem to pop up and say what you need to hear when the time is right. This can happen because they are surrendered to the divine intelligence.

Now, let's focus on what is important for us to explore in this chapter.

Remember that negative energy is just energy. Some of it is simply free-floating stuff, an amalgamation of fearful energy from random people or situations that sticks together and blobs about on the energetic planes. It is a bit like a psychic ball of stray hairs. As it rolls about the astral plane (the psychic or energetic layer of existence created from our thoughts and emotions), it gathers more hairs and grows in size, becoming quite a fearsome fur ball! It will gravitate towards other sticky energy, like more fear, and continue to grow.

If we aren't vibrating at that level, it will roll on by us. However we might feel that fearful fur ball of energy if we are doing some cosmic cleaning in divine service, such as through a healing for another or if we are dealing with some old fears of our own because of various life circumstances. Or perhaps we encounter that psychic ball of fear energy in our day to day activities in an office that is going through upheaval because of company changes, and is therefore prone to collective insecurity about the future. That insecure 'vibe' in the office is energetically real. The office is filled with sticky fear energy that attracts and builds similar vibrations of fear into something quite palpable. It can be hard then to leave the concern at the office – it might start gnawing away at your body and mind, disturbing your sleep, creating stress and blocking your ability to receive clear guidance for a while, until you process it. Or perhaps we just fall into conversation with someone who is quite fearful themselves, and we just feel their fear, forgetting that it is not our own, and we unconsciously allow that sticky fear energy to get a bit caught up in our own energy field. We know when something like this happens because at one moment we may feel quite fine then all of a sudden we become overwhelmed by a surge of fear or anxiety (or anger or sadness, whatever the quality of that particular blob of unprocessed energy happened to be). If we stay present, work through it and let it go, we have processed that particular blob of fear out of our energy field, and perhaps helped others not to be affected by it in future because we have actually helped to unravel it a little, rather than increase it.

Some negative energy isn't as free-floating and has more intelligence with a purpose and force of its own. Love is the ultimate power but it is foolish to imagine that dark forces that are empowered by fear do not hold power or deserve respect. They do! They serve a purpose in our world, whether we understand it consciously or not. However, through our power of free will we get to consciously choose how we will respond to those forces. We choose whether to jump on the fear band-wagon and feed them, or to gradually learn how to cultivate trust and love in our hearts and come from that place, politely but firmly saying, "Thank you, but no thank you," when darker energies come knocking at our door – whether in the form of a hateful person or a random emotion that feels like it either comes from within you or is in response to something coming at you.

The healing process below will help you to energetically say, "Thank you, but no thank you," whenever you are struggling with the effects of darker energies in your life, whether through depression, fear, anxiety, anger or distress in any way. How do you know when you need to do that healing? Sometimes you will feel ups and downs in your mood based on the events taking place around you, but you still have the sense that what you are feeling relates to you personally. So sometimes your partner might be in a grumpy mood. It isn't enjoyable for you, you might get a bit cranky yourself, or feel disappointed that you can't freely connect with your partner at the time, but you know you are experiencing your own feelings, in response to your partner's situation. So it doesn't necessarily need a healing process. However at other times you may feel tired, drained, exhausted without reason, or because you know you have picked up emotional energy that doesn't really originate from you, isn't really your 'stuff' so to speak, and you need some help letting it go. The healing process will help in that situation. Another situation in which the healing process will be helpful is to overcome so much fear that has 'suddenly' come up so that you cannot summon the strength to go to a course or outing that you really wanted to attend, for example. That might be negative interference and time for a healing. It might not be, of course. You may just need a rest, but a healing process certainly won't hurt. Then you'll either feel better and can move on, or you'll realise that you really do just need a rest. Either way, the question is answered.

With experience, you'll learn to identify the presence of darker energies. It's more than just feeling anger, fear or sadness in your life, which are natural, normal, healthy emotions for us to feel as we experience all of life. These darker energies manipulate us through those emotions to step away from what is right for us, to not trust ourselves, to not fully live our lives. It is the difference between feeling our emotions and feeling manipulated or controlled, blocked or derailed from what we want to do, by our emotional life. If we are living our lives fully, and experiencing painful emotions from time to time in the process, that is no cause for concern. If we are experiencing painful emotions and feeling actively blocked and disabled from trusting ourselves and living our lives because of it, then the presence of darker energies is possible and may need to be dealt with. Sometimes this will be so obvious to you and at other times, it will be far harder to sense.

Whatever happens is just part of the human journey and does not have to be feared at all. Before we knew what germs were, we didn't have any fear of germs, but we also didn't have great hygiene either and people unnecessarily suffered from infections. Darker energies are a bit like that – we don't have to be fearful of them, we just need to practice our spiritual hygiene (such as through the healing process below) and then we'll have less unnecessary suffering through more awareness and practical defensive actions.

If you ever feel nervous about this topic, it just means that you need some more information about how to handle it. When you are informed, you will feel more relaxed and confident without feeling cocky and looking for a fight. Remember also that there are many beings of great power in the light who want to help you – all the beings in the entire Crystal series that I am creating with Blue Angel Publishing can and will assist you when called upon. If it is not in your best interest to learn about these darker energies in more than everyday ways, then you won't encounter them. If it is, then you will. Either way you are being supported to grow and if something is coming to you, then you are actually capable of dealing with it and you'll get all the tools that you need to do so. You just need to ask for help from the beings that love you unconditionally.

Whether working consciously with darker energies is part of your spiritual journey in a big way (perhaps helping a child that is regularly traumatised by horrific nightmares) or a small way (perhaps dealing with annoying colleagues at work), the following guidelines apply.

Firstly, have compassion. The ugliest in appearance or action are often the most frightened. Underneath great rage and anger, determination to hurt or control another, are usually feelings of helplessness and terror. Without being arrogant or condescending, with respect and compassion in your heart, you can offer any such being – whether a human person or a wounded spirit causing negative interference – a chance to heal and remember itself as love.

Training further with Raym or reading his book *Alchemy of Crystals* will help you learn techniques for this, as will my work in *Crystal Goddesses 888*. If you are a healer and you want to learn these techniques, by all means do so. It has been my experience that if you are meant to do that work, you'll be naturally attracted to it. If you do not feel that way, just let it go right on by you and focus instead on applying these guidelines more generally to more 'ordinary' situations in your life, such as the annoying co-worker or tyrannical boss that is pushing your buttons so much that you want to grow spiritually to get them off your back.

Some negative forms of intelligence will actually want to transform and accept healing from you and will be grateful, though possibly a bit reluctant at first. Some will not. It is always a choice. You can offer but you cannot force. Remember that this work would be an expression of the bodhisattva vow and the bodhisattva doesn't drag beings to enlightenment! Avalokitesvara wasn't trying to push the world up the mountain along with him. He listened and responded. It is more about answering the call. If the call isn't there, respect the free will of that being, or that energy, and know that it is just as important to honour that, as it is for that being to honour your free will when you state that it must leave your energy field, for example.

This may play out when you feel the presence of a darker energy in your home, for example, sensing something that causes you a feeling of unease. It might be a similar energy around your child's bedroom that causes them to wake up in terror at a recurring nightmare (this could be a sign of negative energies trying to scare her to close down her spiritual abilities, for example). It may be that you aren't sure if you are sensing anything psychically but you just know that someone is trying to undermine you professionally out of jealousy or covetousness or some other reason. It might also just be that you suddenly feel fearful and anxious without reason.

In any such circumstances, or similar, you can say to that energy (if you can't sense or see it, just speak it to mid-air!), "I call on the beings of unconditional love that can help us here, now you can go to the light, or not, as you choose, but you cannot stay here in my (or my child's) energy field, as I choose with love to assert my boundary and my own free will and ask you now to leave and not return." Believe it as you speak. Your free will is a powerful tool and can be used with great strength simply through realising it. I have shared this with clients and they have, with some amazement, responded quickly back to me that it works. It does. You don't need to do this forcefully, gently and firmly is just fine. You can repeat it three times if need be, but once is most often quite enough.

Secondly, if you collapse into fear yourself, have compassion too. I have been utterly terrified at various times when I have encountered some particularly powerful darker forces that I now encounter with serenity (usually!), as they move right on by me. I have stumbled many times in my lessons on working with fear. In have learned that in time, what will be a challenge to me at the moment, will some time after that, no longer be so. As we grow, we become more skilled in our responses to darker energies and more importantly, our own fear. It is all about growth, humility, having a sense of humour and learning to come back to love, even if we have got swept up in fear for a while.

Thirdly, and importantly, do not go and seek these energies out. You are not being trained to become a ghost-buster here. If you are meant to do that work, it will find you and the training you'll need will find you too.

I once had a group of advanced students who fell into this trap and should have known better. They got into their heads that they would go on a psychic clean-up mission of the negativity around a mass-murder that had taken place, specifically on the energy of the man who committed the murders. The amount of negativity and malevolent darkness that they encountered overwhelmed them, made some of them terrified and others who were more sensitive quite physically and emotionally unwell for a time. After they withdrew (which was the most sensible decision that they made in the whole sorry situation) and processed what had happened, and were thoroughly roused-on by me when I found out what they had done, they were all wiser for the experience. And more humble. Pride and feelings of being more powerful than a darker energy are not consistent with compassion. Compassion is where your genuine power to work successfully and effectively with darker energies comes from. Any other response will ultimately backfire.

I hope in sharing these teachings with you and the healing process below that you have enough information to take basic spiritual care of yourself and feel confident in dealing with negative energy. If you need to do this work, you'll be shown what you need to know and when. It is not for the majority of people. Most of us will simply have to learn how to deal with negative people or toxic environments, and that's enough! Some of us will be working more deeply to heal these energies. Trust that your path finds you and when something is meant to be, you are usually drawn to it and interested in it. I hope that you realise that if what is offered here seems to not be enough for your needs, more training will always be available to you. We need only genuinely ask from the heart for training, through unconditional love and divine mercy, and know that our prayers will be answered.

These are the situations where the Buddha can really help us. We will explore a specific healing for dealing with negative energy below, but first, let us connect with the healing energy of Peridot, for its beauty and abundance support us through this initiation.

PERIDOT – INCREASE

Peridot is a beautiful yellow-green stone with semi-transparency. It is often used in jewellery, is of medium expense and readily available.

It holds a special resonance for those on the healing path. It affords psychic protection and stabilises a healing light around the energy field. It promotes forgiveness of self and others – which is essential if we are going to find compassion in our hearts. It also helps raise the solar plexus energy to the heart centre, opening up the channels of energy flow through our body. As this happens we become less focused on controlling our relationships and more focused on how we can collaborate, enhance and serve within them (and by that I mean serving the relationship, not martyring yourself to the other person – so, to all you mothers who are reading this, please take special note here).

Peridot strengthens the heart and thymus, boosting the immune system and supports the throat chakra. In terms of our energy body, this is the equivalent of taking some super-vitamins. When our energetic immunity is stronger, we can more easily tell if something – like a negative cord of energy flowing towards us from another for example – is affecting us. We become more capable of just letting it fall away – like an infection that can't take hold because our immune system is strong enough to keep it at bay. If it does overpower us for a while, we can fight it off more quickly.

When working with psychic attack, or even on a more mundane level when dealing with the odd negative aspects of relationships that will arise from time to time, such as jealousy, spite and resentment (just to name a few), Peridot can help us become more aware and clear mentally. With that greater awareness and clarity we can search for the 'hook' within us that is allowing negative energy or projections of others to take hold and affect us.

Without that hook, the energy of others slides off us like Teflon. When in meditation there are times when I will encounter some quite dark energies. However they just move about me. I am not reacting and neither are they. There is awareness and no harm. However if we have a hook, we can be affected.

The Buddha in the form of Gautama Buddha once taught the lesson in this way. An angry man came to him, criticising him in the midst of a public discourse with his disciples. The Buddha sat calmly and listened, and responded to the man with some questions. "What would happen to a cup of water, that you offered me, but I did not accept?" the Buddha asked. The man, rather puzzled about this response answered, "Well, it would be left with me, and I suppose I would drink it instead!" The Buddha then asked, "What would happen with a plate of food that you offered me and that I did not choose to eat?" The man said, "I would eat it!" The Buddha then said, "What will happen with this anger that I do not accept?" "It is left with me," the man replied, walking away.

It was an example of taking responsibility for one's emotions but also in how free we are when we do not buy into the story that another may be sending our way with their hatred, fear or negativity. The power of being detached and compassionate helps get us there, but if we have a hook in us, upon which the projection from another can catch, then we will still struggle, even if their anger actually has nothing to do with us at all. With this understanding, we can even use the negativity of another that does 'catch' on our own wounds as a way to grow our light, to heal and become stronger spiritually. We can turn our lemons into lemonade.

I had an experience of this with a woman who once who accused me of "possibly being capable of stealing her work." It was a bizarre sort-of-accusation and one that I knew held no merit. I also knew that this woman was projecting her own dark side on to me, as she regularly took ideas from other people and used them in her own work. Usually completely shamelessly! She had even claimed one or two of mine for profit, later casually commenting, "Oh, but that was your idea, of course." I saw that she had the pirate archetype in her energy field (we will explore archetypes and how they play out at a soul level in *Crystal Lifetimes 999: Past Life Healing with the Power of Heaven and Earth*) which would cause her to claim and prosper from what was not rightfully hers, bullying others along the way.

I knew all of this but still I struggled with her accusation. I felt extremely frustrated that it had affected me because even though I knew it wasn't true, there was a hook in me that allowed a projection that was actually about her, to stick to me and evoke pain. I didn't like it but the pain that I felt forced me to search deeper to see what it was that allowed her projection to hook itself on to me, rather than just slide right off as it should have done.

I delved within and found something surprising. I realised that I had to heal an old sense of misplaced guilt that I developed as a child, where my natural sensitivity had morphed into a belief that I was responsible for the feelings of others. I had learned to feel responsible for things that had nothing to do with me, and guilty that I couldn't fix them.

Until I became more conscious of that hook within me and cultivated a more accurate and loving inner consciousness, the projection of the other woman, no matter how unfair I knew it was and how angry I was about it, stayed with me. I was walking about feeling guilty for a crime that I didn't commit whilst the actual perpetrator wandered about, continuing on with her ways and not caring two hoots about any of it. I can say that I was infuriated with the whole situation for a while but eventually that anger shifted into greater wisdom and a hell of a lot more discernment in who I worked with, along with stronger boundaries.

It is important in our work with negative energy that we focus on how we can serve the light. Often that will be about healing and growing our own inner light. Ultimately no matter what challenges arise, we are being asked to grow our light. Peridot helps us increase that which we dwell upon. It is a stone of abundance and healing and when we focus on the heart, what increases is what we most desire. If we have Peridot with us when doing inner work, and we are asking the question, "What is the truth here that is trying to break through so that my light can grow?" we'll get help with receiving a clear answer. That is a good question to ask at any time we are encountering a struggle with negativity – that of another or our own.

HEALING WITH BUDDHA AND PERIDOT

There is a beautiful mantra prayer which is based on the bodhisattva vow which is in the ancient language of Sanskrit and translates as "may all beings be happy and free." The prayer is Lokah Sumastar Sukinoh Bhavantu (which sounds like LOW-KAA SUMMER-STAR SOOK-E-NO BAR-VUN-TWO – don't worry, it gets easy to remember with practice!).

We will use this prayer in our healing practice below.

Start by having Peridot or the mandala close to your heart or placed before you.

Say, "I call upon the Buddhas of past, present and future, the unconditional love of compassionate grace, divine protection, equanimity, peace and detachment. I ask for divine protection now. I ask for divine assistance now. I call upon the Angel of Peridot and I ask for awareness and your gift of healing, may the pure consciousness of love be increased. I call upon divine light and divine mercy, and the power of my own free will as a sovereign being of light. In service to the greatest good, so be it."

Focus on your heart and breathe in and out for at least 33 breaths as you sense a golden green light growing from between your heart and solar plexus, expanding until it encompasses both your heart and your solar plexus and then expanding again until your entire body is touched with this light, flowing out all around you.

Visualise a luscious emerald green light washing around you then, pouring down from the heavens and creating a bubble around you.

Follow that with a rich indigo blue light, pouring down from the heavens and creating another bubble layer around the rich emerald green light.

Then follow that with a strong violet-coloured light forming a layer of a bubble over the indigo light.

Allow this three-layered bubble of light to then be finally coated in a layer of golden light.

Above your head, from where this light has come, you sense a great source of love. It may appear as a Buddha or a symbol. Let this love reach you through the crown of your head. Be soft and receptive, allowing your heart to be comforted and become calm.

Stay with this process and breathe for 33 breaths or for however long feels right for you.

When you are ready, say the following, taking your time, speaking clearly and if needs be, repeating it two or three times until you can say it and really mean it as much as possible.

"I acknowledge myself as a spiritual being of light in human form, with the gift of free will that cannot be taken from me. I now claim my power as a compassionate light with the ability to choose. I now choose of my own free will to dissolve any contract or agreement that I made with dark energies that are blocking my higher development and draining my energy. I now choose of my own free will to reclaim my power and with loving respect I now declare that any energy, cord, attachment or entity that is connected to me, which is not serving me through unconditional love and dedication to the path of light, must leave my body, mind and energy field and may not return. I now reclaim any permission I have ever given to any such being, consciously or unconsciously, to attach to me, feed off me or attack me. With respect I say that you must leave now and never return. I forgive you, I forgive myself, go in peace. If there is any entity or energy around me now that does not offer unconditional love, and you would like assistance, I call on the beings that love you unconditionally and ask that they lead you into the light now. Through my own free will, so be it."

Repeat the mantra below as many times as feels right, allowing it to build light and compassion in your heart which helps to keep you calm and bring you peace, as well as offering peace and freedom to negative energy being released. It generates a field of the Bodhisattva compassion around you for protection, healing and upliftment.

Lokah Sumastar Sukinoh Bhavantu
(LOW-KAA SUMMER-STAR SOOK-E-NO BAR-VUN-TWO)

Om Shanti, Shanti, Shanti
(OM SHAN-TEE SHAN-TEE SHAN-TEE)

As you repeat the mantra, perceive a luminous Buddha light opening up behind you, embracing you and flooding all around you. See that light as beautiful golden yellow-green light. Perceive that same light beginning to glow and radiate from within your own heart chakra.

You may perceive Buddha as having eleven heads and a thousand arms, able to reach for all who are in need.

Continue to breathe and stay with the Buddha light until you are ready to close your practice. With your hands at your chest in prayer position, bow your head. When you are ready, simply say "Namaste" (sounds like NUMB-AH-STAY) which means, "I honour the light in all beings, the light which is the same in all beings."

You can repeat this healing process, and listen and/or chant to the mantra prayer at any time you feel you are suffering from a lack of gratitude (which just doesn't feel very good) or struggling to remain positive in your life. If you feel that you want to offer something positive to the world, and to be open to receive more positivity in your life (the universe mirrors back to us what we offer others with intention and love), then you can do this healing process at that time too.

It is not harmful to do more 'cleansing' of the self, provided that like anything else, we have some moderation. It is safe to do this exercise three times in the first week if you wish, and then perhaps once or twice a month from that point on, or more often (perhaps weekly or twice a week, or even in extreme circumstances, daily) if you are a healer who is working with negative energies on a regular basis or are regularly exposed to a toxic emotional environment (perhaps where you are living or working for a time) that you find draining. Listen to your own needs and experiment with what feels helpful for you.

emotional environment (perhaps where you are living or working for a time) that you find draining. Listen to your own needs and experiment with what feels helpful for you.

15.

ASCENDED MASTER HELIOS (Consciousness)
CITRINE (Radiance)

INITIATION OF SPIRITUAL GROWTH

A burning golden sun above your head. An explosion of love in your heart. You gaze within and see a burning golden sun within your heart too. All around you, the hearts of others, burning golden suns. There is nothing to do but bask in the golden radiance, feeling it like the warmth of sunlight upon your face, gently upturned to the heavens.

In my second year of law school, I moonlighted for a short period of time as a law clerk. I did mind-numbingly boring work so I could save money and go travelling. It was a young, dynamic company, refreshingly un-stuffy, and it drew law students from many different universities to its doors. My already busy social life expanded further. The person that I clicked with the most however, was the sassy receptionist. She absolutely bubbled with vivacious energy and was cheeky as hell. I liked her immediately. When we both realised that we had a passion for spirituality in common, we became friends, getting along like the proverbial house on fire. It was through her that I learned about the gift of spiritual growth.

This woman spoke with wisdom. It wasn't clichéd 'out of a book' commentary, she had genuine insight. She knew herself very well, had done a great degree of inner work over many years and was an articulate, bright and capable individual.

Yet the vast wisdom that she held never seemed to manifest in her physical life. It was as though she could approach the goal, almost get there but never quite touch it. So she stayed in a vibrational reality that seemed so much less than what she would naturally vibrate at, should her insight and wisdom be integrated into her life. She would run into situations that I thought, given her state of awareness, just shouldn't be taking place.

I struggled for years with the paradox between this woman's words and awareness, and her reality, which seemed so disparate. With so much insight, why couldn't she grow from it? Could she not apply her spiritual gifts to her life?

My mentor helped me understand this situation many years later after this lovely woman and I had fallen out of touch. I was speaking with my mentor about a situation I was having with a client who was very aware and was not able to shift stubborn patterns, no matter how much work we did together. I was concerned that I was not doing my job properly because this client just seemed to be spinning her wheels and not getting anywhere. My mentor made a comment that changed the way that I viewed spiritual growth, solved the mystery of my past friendship and the dilemma I was having with that client at the time. I knew it was spiritual truth because it solved so many things at once and spiritual truth is incredibly efficient.

My mentor at the time simply spoke of the different abilities that various people have to grow. It had never occurred to me before that spiritual growth was an ability. I had always assumed that awareness led to change and more awareness meant more change. What she helped me realise is that not only was awareness a gift, but the step between awareness and change, the transformation of spiritual growth itself, was a form of intelligence that not everyone had to the same degree.

Being a staunch egalitarian, I had erroneously assumed that everyone was capable in the same way. My mentor suggested that spiritual growth was a talent like athletic ability or musical ability. We could, with attention, develop what we had, and in some cases become extremely adept, and yet there would be those who found it more natural and those who found it harder. I accepted this as it felt true, though novel at the time and since then, have seen this proven in action time and time again.

Some will struggle to make the most basic connection between a dysfunctional relationship pattern and a previous emotional trauma. I remember a friend of mine once speaking about a frustrating situation in her marriage. Her husband, who was academically brilliant, physically fit, emotionally passionate and earning an exceptional income at the top of his profession, would flat-out refuse to see any connection whatsoever in his admittedly dysfunctional and abusive relationship with his mother and his dysfunctional relationship with his wife. He couldn't see how there could be any connection, despite it being as plain as the nose on his face, just below his piercingly intelligent eyes.

The spiritual growth 'gene' wasn't active in him, at that time at least. His high levels of energy were being channelled into super-achievements in other areas. Whether he would have become capable of greater insight should some of that energy been directed inwardly, I cannot say. It is possible, but it is also possible that his intelligence did not skew in a spiritual direction.

Then there are some, like the gorgeous receptionist from my law clerk days, that are capable of a level of awareness and insight that completely eluded the brilliant academic husband of my friend. While holding those insights, they will not be able to really 'digest' them, to gain nutrients to make real change within themselves and their lives.

So even with amazing insights and awareness, there is no guarantee that they will lead, in this lifetime at least, to spiritual growth and a transformation of the person in question. An example of this is with weight loss and health. It is one thing to know what to eat and when. We are bombarded with information, yet how often can we apply it? For some, that consciousness is already in place and it is relatively easy to do – it takes discipline, but it is not a constant inner struggle. For others it is near impossible to change their weight. Despite applying the right actions, it isn't long before weight creeps up. Why? Consciousness. It affects the nature of our body – our composition of fat and muscle. It is capable of some degree of change, but it takes a change in our consciousness, in how we feel and experience and relate to our body, for it to stabilise in a profoundly transformed way.

For me, there have been great changes in my physical body over the years, relating to what was happening for me at the time emotionally and psychologically, as well as physically. Whenever I am approaching a different way of being in my body, changing my consciousness, I am confronted with the old way wanting to maintain the status quo. It then becomes a matter of sitting with the inner conflict and giving myself time to grow into a new way from inside. Then the outside change will fall into place. If the change sticks, it is because my consciousness has shifted. If it does not, it was because I was applying the force of my will rather than awareness, trying to change the situation from the outside in, rather than patiently outgrowing it from the inside out. Will power only takes us so far. We have to learn to be the change that we want to see, rather than apply our will power to enforce a change if we want long lasting results without near constant inner struggle.

The soul evolves according to its own pace. Sometimes lifetimes are spent cultivating ideas, opening up the mind before the soul would even begin to approach application of those ideas – with all the challenges that can entail (such as standing up for yourself when your ideas are not conventional, for example).

Then there are others who are capable of great transformation. These are the relatively rare people, I have found, that seem to live lifetimes within lifetimes, such is the extent of their capacity to grow. Their essence is always the same, but the expression of it becomes distilled over time, like a brightly polished gem. If you find a person like this, honour them because deep within, whether they are conscious of it or not, there will be trust and spiritual intelligence and they can inspire you to honour these forces within yourself.

Often exposure to a teacher who also holds this ability for transformation will stimulate an awakening and strengthening of this spiritual intelligence within the student, but it has to be accessible to the soul. It is not the teacher that provides the ability. The most powerful teacher in the world could not give a soul something that it didn't have the capacity to receive. A spiritual teacher can only awaken, to a greater or lesser degree, that which is in potential within the student. Lebanese mystic Kahlil Gibran says it like this, "No man can reveal to you aught but that which already lies half asleep in the dawning of your knowledge." The rest depends on the grace available for the student's growth and to what extent the soul chemistry of the student and teacher together can call in that grace.

There is no judgment that need accompany the gift of spiritual growth – and to what extent it is available to us or another. Sometimes it serves and as strange as it will seem, sometimes it does not. There are times when a soul is ready for a high-action lifetime, with vast transformation. There are other times when the soul prefers a gentler experience. I am the first to admit that highly transformational lifetimes are a bumpy-path lifetime. Sometimes the higher self needs more rest to integrate what was learned in past lifetimes, before embarking upon a new intense cycle of learning. It's a bit like taking spiritual summer school to master those tricky lessons before starting the new academic year. The soul will always choose what will best serve. It is highly likely though, that as you are connecting with this material, written for those on an evolutionary path of some intensity, that you are one of the ones to whom the gift of spiritual growth is being bestowed.

As the Iranian proverb goes, "To eat is human, to digest, divine", and so it is with consciousness. To be in contact (conscious or not) with higher consciousness is a natural human condition, yet to be able to metabolise higher energy to bring about transformation is an ability that not all human beings have in equal measure. As I have learned over the years, human beings are not on an even playing field when it comes to transformation and it can be good to remember this when your process is tough. It can be easy to begrudge the work, but to be able to grow from caterpillar to butterfly is an extraordinary gift which not all are capable of receiving this lifetime.

This discussion is relevant here because when we speak of the initiation into consciousness, we are talking not only of awareness, but of the ability to use the energy of insight and awareness and grow from it. We are discussing something that we cannot do with our minds, or even with our various healing techniques, we are speaking of the gift of consciousness itself. This means a change in our vibration which is initiated at the soul level. We don't just wake up one day and decide that "today is a high vibrational day" and we are suddenly done with the lower vibrational challenges. It is rather that we surrender consciously into the process of spiritual growth offered to us, developing our ability to be acted upon by higher forces of spiritual light, intelligently dealing with our own responses to this, and observing the result – spiritual growth, higher consciousness and personal transformation.

To this end, we work with the Master Helios, the soul of the Sun that shines on the Earth each day. In truth, our inner divine seed is stimulated by any being that holds greater spiritual light. Each of us will be drawn to different masters, angels, aspects of the Divine Feminine in the form of goddesses, or aspects of divine blessing from various stars, for example. Each of these beings can assist us. Then there is one being that affects every living creature, and all of us on a spiritual path here on Mother Earth, which is the Sun.

HELIOS – CONSCIOUSNESS

In the ancient wisdom teachings, and particularly in ancient Egypt, our sun is known as a wise and powerful figure capable of great spiritual blessing. Helios is the spiritual name for the sun. Other names include the Ancient Egyptian name of Ra. This leads me to want to share one of my favourite (tongue-in-cheek) invocations to the sun, written by the wonderfully talented Caroline Casey, in her book, *Making the Gods Work For You*. It goes like this, "Hail to the Sun God, He is a Fun God, Ra! Ra! Ra!"

The sun is the most immediately obvious and accessible form of intense spiritual energy that we have in this solar system. It is often considered to be a symbol of the higher self, and when I directly perceived my own soul or higher self, I saw it burning white like a nuclear sun.

We are exposed to this being each day and yet most would not think twice about it. There is spiritual brilliance, the Divine made manifest, right before us each day – underneath our sacred feet in the form of the Mother Earth and above our crown in the heavens as the Father Sun. Yet we somehow manage to tune out the sublime more often than not. The Divine hides in plain sight. I call this the 'crop circle syndrome', named after the incredible formations of crop circles that, when genuine, show such outstanding spiritual technology and brilliance that if one were to contemplate them in any depth, entire lives would be transformed forever! Yet they emerge, creating potent energetic fields, and life goes on as per usual – a case of undigested divinity if ever I saw one.

It is not the Divine that needs to come closer to us, but our eyes that need to open to its presence. As most of us find that the physical world is still more accessible to witness than the inner worlds of light, we can use the temple of the mother, the beauty of the earth, to become a vehicle through which we see divine expressions. We can equally be open to the presence of the sun as a way to receive high-energy transmissions from a great spiritual being.

The sun is pure consciousness – and to access even a tiny degree of that will stimulate whatever is within our soul to grow. Of course, spiritual light doesn't mean that all is fluffy and harmless. Even vitamins in high doses can become toxic. This was graphically demonstrated to me in two different ways. The first was when I watched a BBC documentary on the earth and her relationship to the sun. I saw a huge magnetic field, an auric field, around the earth and how the power of the sun bends it, so it flares out behind her not unlike a comet's tail. The auric field of the earth was protecting her, much like a psychic skin so she could shield out the sun's harmful rays and receive the light and intelligence from the sun, the power and energy that she needed to grow. If she had no resistance, it would be too much and she would be incinerated by the greater power of the sun. Too little and she would die also. Life needs balance to thrive, and it needs light and consciousness to evolve.

The second time was when I first began connecting with the energy of the earth directly. She is a powerful being. I called upon her in mantra with my spiritual teacher at the time. The teacher said to call on her, rather than on the earth directly, and the energy of the earth would flow through the teacher into her students. I however did not feel my energy expand in calling upon this teacher, so I directly invoked the soul of the earth. The power and expansion that I felt was incredible and the next day I paid for it. I had gone too far too soon and I learned a valuable lesson by how utterly revolting I felt the next day! I have never been hung-over from alcohol because I hardly drink alcohol at all, but I am guessing that this must be the equivalent of a spiritual hangover. I felt dirty and blasted, like all my wiring was old and broken. Too much voltage had passed through a body that wasn't quite prepared for it.

So whilst I accept that too much is too much, we can easily go to the other extreme where people actively become fearful of the sun (perhaps tapping into current life fear-based "health" campaigns – and I use that term with irony) and past life beliefs that the sun god would be a vengeful god causing drought.

The fear that has been generated around sun exposure has always gave rise to sacred rage in me, as I believe to take this approach to excess denies us the physical energy that the sun provides for our body, but also, the spiritual light and consciousness that it provides us for our spiritual growth. Helios is a spiritual benefactor, promoting life and growth of light within us and upon the earth. Yes, he is a powerful force and I completely understand that we need to learn to manage our responses to intense energy. However if we run away in fear, we are missing out on so much! Like physical exposure to the sun, little by little, building up tolerance, or finding what suits your particular body, is the key. The point is to learn what suits your particular constitution and to learn how to manage your responses.

We learn this at a physical level with the sun and we have the sign of sunburn if there is too much (something I learned as a child in Australia, growing up in the late 1970s and 80s). I know that there is tremendous fear about skin cancer running rampant, particularly in Australia where the sun is very intense, so much so that new incidents of vitamin D deficiency have been found in children because schools won't let them outdoors without being shirted, sun-screened and hatted, as well as covered by sun-proofed shielding.

In Australia at least there has been a fear-based skin-cancer television campaign that would rival the fear-based television campaign run about the AIDS virus in the 1980s (which featured the grim reaper - who I assume was meant to represent the AIDS virus - knocking over people like bowling balls). Yet it is my understanding that disease is karmic. Two people may do the same actions and one becomes ill and another does not. Karma does not mean punishment in my rulebook. It means that there is a particular pathway for growth and for some that will be disease. The soul decides what serves. I believe that there is no human reasoning for it.

This makes people uncomfortable for a number of reasons – mostly it takes much of our notion of control out of the equation. I remember having a conversation with a yoga teacher recently about a colleague who died from cancer. This teacher was fearful in response to this news. She is a devoted raw-food, yoga-practicing disciple of all that appears to be healthy. So was her friend who died from cancer. This completely freaked her out.

I don't know what forces benefit from fear-based campaigns, perhaps advertising executives, perhaps more. I don't really care too much about that. What I am more interested in is that we become awake enough to realise that fear-based campaigns manipulate us through our need to feel that we are in control and can dictate our life experiences.

Certainly we can make choices to affect our wellbeing, but we will all live and all die (until we master the spiritual laws of death which isn't going to be relevant for the majority of us at this time!) and how that happens and when, is a question of karmic necessity. It isn't about whether we are good and/or bad, it is about what serves our soul growth.

What I believe this fearful yoga teacher was looking for, she hadn't quite cottoned onto yet. She was looking for security, to feel safe that she could inoculate herself against suffering, disease and death. I don't know anyone who particularly wants to experience a terrible disease, and I have compassion for the fear around the possibility. Yet if we want to feel secure within ourselves, to feel safe, it can only come through choosing to trust in the ultimate spiritual purpose behind all that manifests.

None of us have within our power an ability to avoid our own karma, though we can certainly soften more challenging karma through inner work and devotion to serving the planet as best we can. Yet disease and death, unless you are an ascending being without any karmic legacy, are not within our absolute control. Healthy people die of strokes. It happens. Unhealthy people live to a ripe old age on health benefits. Does this mean we should all just abandon the effort and discipline of trying to live a balanced life style and to be well? No! Of course not. But we do it for legitimate reasons – because we love ourselves, would like to care for our body as best as we can, and live as good a quality of life as we are capable of living with respect for all that we have been given to experience life – including our body and mind.

What does this mean for the fearful yoga teacher? I believe her answer will come to her through consciousness, not control. We cannot control karmic forces, but we can develop a spiritual security in knowing that our consciousness will grow and adapt to whatever forces arise in our life, even if those forces are a karmic disease. It is our trust in our own spiritual light that sees us through challenges, even those that feel like they may break us, that brings us internal security. It is only ever an illusion of safety that lurks behind our fantasies of control.

Though there are undoubtedly plenty of people who will say that if you lie in the sun you will die of skin cancer, point blank, without healthy sun exposure, your body will suffer and so will your spirit. Unless you are a rare individual built with an inability to tolerate any sun (in which case you trust in that, because you are built the way you are built with divine reason) then finding how much sun exposure works for your wellbeing is up to you.

I believe that balance is the key and I advocate that each person does their best to find what suits their particular disposition, rather than making a blanket rule for everyone as though we were children incapable of assuming independent responsibility for our wellbeing. It is my belief that balance is key but what that means for each individual varies.

I know for me, I crave the light of the sun and I believe that is one of the reasons that my soul chose for me to be born in Australia this lifetime, so I could be close to that solar intelligence as it is very active in this country. When I receive sunlight, I don't only receive physical energy, but spiritual intelligence. It fills a need for divine communion in me in a palpable way, like talking to a friend on the telephone can connect you to emotional nourishment. Those needs may change for me in time, but for now, this is what suits me.

I am also aware of when there is too much and I need to step back, something which I often learn by suddenly needing much more sleep than usual. At an energetic spiritual level I have taken in enough and need to integrate it. My body tells me this through sleep. Light that is genuinely taken in causes transformation. Too much too soon is excessively destabilising, and will cause a high followed by some very challenging lows if we are not careful. A bit like eating more than we can digest. We will often not feel hungry following such a big meal, perhaps even into the next day.

With solar light, spiritual consciousness, and everything else to do with our wellbeing both spiritual and physical, we need to find a balance within so that we can temper our progress. You can have too much of a good thing, just as you can have too little. I often say to students who are finding their path a bit too much to bear to talk to the Divine, to tell the Divine, "Hey, this is too much – I need a break!" and I have actually received guidance myself at times to slow down and not be so relentless with my passion for spiritual growth and sometimes to just be gentler with my own body.

It is completely normal, and in fact a confirmation that spiritual growth is happening, that we feel destabilised at times. When solar flares are released from the sun, which happens on a semi-regular basis, the earth receives jolts of spiritual consciousness. I can often feel that they are happening by their effect. Everyone seems to get riled up and even act a bit nuts for a while as we adapt to the increased spiritual light available in whatever way we are capable.

So during spiritual growth, where we are learning to integrate greater spiritual light into our being, we can have emotional pain from the past releasing, and be pulled into old stuff that we thought we were well and truly done with and wonder if in fact we are regressing rather than progressing. Do you remember earlier in this work that I shared that regression on the spiritual path is not possible, that everything serves? Rather than a linear progression, we move on an expanding spiral of consciousness. As the spiral extends outwards, there will be times when we feel that we are moving away from the light, yet we are actually growing. We may finally recognise this only when we continue to progress along that spiral, coming back to the light in an expanded and more powerful version of ourselves, only to start the next growth loop of the cosmic spiral of our divine growth process.

Consciousness during such times is what enables us to stay trusting in our centre, even whilst we are experiencing 'growing pains'. When we can identify pain as growing pains, it changes our relationship to it. Instead of feeling victimised or fearful of our pain, we can be grateful for it. There will undoubtedly be times when we are tested to the point of failure and this too, is growth. We might find it hard to be grateful and yet there are more times than not that I can say that I am pleased to have my growing pains because I know it means I am shifting something that needs to leave for my capacity to hold divine power and love to increase. After many years of feeling numb in an effort to avoid my sensitivity, to open up to feeling was a sign of aliveness that although very painful at times, was welcome to me.

This is the caterpillar breaking down in the chrysalis and the sign that you are blessed spiritually with the gift of spiritual growth. Such consciousness is there for those that are willing to let their spiritual growth happen, to do their best to take care of themselves from a perspective of love rather than a fear-based pattern of trying to control life. Consciousness and control are not compatible and your consciousness expanding will tackle control issues head on.

When this is happening we come back to the heart of consciousness – which is to trust what you feel, sometimes despite appearances. To be able to do this requires some personal growth and healing. We have to have enough self-esteem to stay true to our instincts. We also have to learn the difference between an emotional reaction, where we act out unresolved past pain, and a genuine feeling which is neutral. I'll give you an example that distinguishes the two. I had an experience recently, following a very deep and expansive meditation, of some old emotional pain surfacing in the hours following. It is not uncommon for this to happen. Contact with spiritual light brings healing and transformation, if we are lucky enough to have karmic access to spiritual growth.

In that old pain, I felt some anger. I knew the anger was not real in the sense that it wasn't about anything that was happening in my current life. My feeling was gratitude. I was grateful that the pain was arising and being released because I could feel that I was growing spiritually in an intense way, supported by my meditation practice, and this old pain was no longer needed. My emotions were a riot of suffering. My feeling was peaceful and grateful. I felt centred and stable, even though there were parts of my awareness running wild. My emotions were playing out whilst my feelings told me, "It's okay, there's nothing wrong. This will pass fairly soon and you'll have more energy and be clearer because of it." The feelings enabled me to stay present and trust, whilst my consciousness expanded, clearing out the pain in the process.

The appearance was that I was having an emotionally painful time of it, tears, suffering, the works. The internal reality that I had was that I was growing and glowing! There was suffering, yes, but it was tempered with consciousness. I didn't fall into doubt or fear about the suffering, making the experience more drawn out and painful than it needed to be. My feelings, or intuition as some of you may call it, helped me stay conscious as my emotions worked out an old knot, much like the pain of a muscle as it releases long-held knots of tension. Now that isn't always the case mind you, I have plenty of moments of growth that are not nearly as radiant, but that one was a good example of the difference between the appearance of suffering and the reality of grace.

Another example of feelings versus appearance was with a woman that I once collaborated with on a project. She was charming, magnetic and lovely - looking. Beautiful, affirming of others, oozing generosity and never short of many admirers, both professional and personal. I was fascinated by the spell she wove. It didn't take long for me to notice that amongst the many compliments and seductions, she also aggressively undermined anyone that she felt vaguely threatened by, and spoke negatively of pretty much everyone of her acquaintance, but only ever behind their backs. Being around her was like stroking soft rabbit fur, reaching for beauty only to find a razor blade lodged here and there. You thought it would be so lovely, because of the beautiful aura that she exuded, yet you ended up cut, bloodied and confused.

When I met her, I was struck by two things – firstly, that although my own consciousness immediately set off alarm bells, I was still determined to place my hand on the hot plate to see if, despite the warning, yes, I would get burned, and secondly, that only two other people in our mutual acquaintance could actually see what I saw. These other two women both had the consciousness to see the truth because they had both been well-acquainted with darkness in themselves and in others through their personal healing work over the years, so meeting this woman was not a revelation to them, more a sign to get away quickly (a sign which they heeded, and eventually I did too, though not quite so quickly). As for the others in her sphere, well it seemed that they were so wounded already, that they didn't feel the cut of the razor amongst their already present pain. Whether that is still the case now, I cannot say as I removed myself from her circle of acquaintance, but it was quite an eye-opening, consciousness-raising experience at the time.

If you have encountered situations like this in your life, you'll know that consciousness takes work – the work often being to not doubt yourself and to trust what you feel, despite sometimes conflicting appearances.

CITRINE – RADIANCE

Citrine is a transparent golden quartz. Natural Citrine is usually soft yellow in tone, but there are darker natural citrines that are almost brown. The Citrine points and geodes (or caves) that are orange-yellow at the base and a dark almost brown yellow at the tip have more than likely been artificially irradiated to create the dark colour. Even artificially heated Citrine still has healing properties. As one of my crystal teachers, Raym, has said, crystals have survived millions of years of incredibly intense radiation within the earth herself, so they'll certainly be strong enough to withstand anything we come up with.

As I mentioned in *Crystal Angels 444* when talking about natural and artificially created crystals, and in Chapter 6 of this book in discussing the Aqua Aura, trust what you feel with a crystal. Even if there has been human-intervention, this is not necessarily going to inhibit the power of a stone. I usually prefer natural Citrine, as it feels softer to me, but that doesn't mean treated Citrine won't work as well.

Citrine is a stone of the sun. It holds golden radiance and, perhaps my favourite attribute of this stone, it never needs cleansing. It works on the solar plexus chakra, which when finely polished through divine consciousness to the point of being free from personal power drives, allows divine light to shine through it unobstructed and the soul becomes very active in the physical world as a result.

Citrine is a way to access the consciousness of the sun even when physical exposure is impossible because of location or season, or ill-advised for health reasons. It is a gentle stone, despite its high level of vibration and it is usually inexpensive and commonly available. Citrine sometimes has rainbows included in it and this holds an added dimension of healing, bringing the solar light into all of the chakras. If you have been lucky enough to be blessed with a Citrine with a rainbow inclusion, then the solar Master Helios is communicating with you, sharing with you that you have a capacity to work with colour and light for healing purpose. You may do this as a colour therapist, artist, or fashion or interior designer, or simply in the way you wear or use colour in your home which has a powerful effect on those around you.

Because it never needs cleansing, being capable of deflecting and burning through negative energy, Citrine is a perfect stone to block psychic attack and strengthen the immune system, much of which is in the digestive functions of the body. Citrine strengthens our digestion and elimination on all levels, physical and emotional, and helps us grow in light. It helps us access our shadow as well, and find the constructive and healing aspect of the shadow – which is learning to integrate and love all that we are, becoming an increasing instrument of divine presence as a result. Citrine builds consciousness and an inevitable part of that growth is to encounter and accept not only our light but our shadow or hidden side (where dwell all the ickiest parts of ourselves that we like to imagine don't exist as well as our most spectacular magnificence that we perhaps didn't realise we had within us at all).

Fortunately Citrine heals the solar plexus chakra which means it will help budge and finally release old programming that we have picked up over the years where we don't really like ourselves, or we accept or value ourselves less than others. It heals wounds of self-esteem and self-worth. If we are inflated, believing that we are better than everyone else (underneath which will always lurk a belief in our own inferiority, ill-masked by our proclaimed superiority), Citrine helps us dislodge this and come to a more realistic, balanced place where we can acknowledge our divine beauty and uniqueness and power, and also our very normal everyday attributes that are pretty much the same as everyone else's.

It is in learning to love and accept, to bring consciousness and eventually some development of all of our facets of being, that we become the shining gem of potential that we hold within us. It isn't an easy path, and it is certainly rarely a particularly pretty one! However it is the key to liberation. To get the lotus to grow and blossom, we really need the mud.

For those times when we are really in darkness, perhaps exploring our shadow selves or training as a shadow healer at a soul level (which means we will be learning how to find the light in darkness over and over again, in ourselves, in others, in the world), Citrine is helpful. It can help connect us with the energy of sunshine, happiness, joy, just for the sake of it, with no reason particularly needed. If we are in a dark night of the soul, where challenge is so great, to have access to a source of light, such as the loving abundance, increasing optimism and solar power of beautiful Citrine, is a true god-given gift. It won't take away the dark night, but it will remind us that there is love seeking us through it.

The radiance of Citrine attracts abundance. It is often known as the prosperity stone and with growing spiritual consciousness we do come to a place of greater abundance-oriented living, realising that we have so much already and that what we need is always available to us in ample supply. As Citrine heals old solar plexus wounds of competition-based operation, of survival, threat, taking down enemies and undermining others, we become open to co-operation of the heart. The solar plexus can receive energy of the heart and work with it through the conscious choices we make in our physical lives. Healed self-esteem and reconciliation of dark and light parts of us, growing in consciousness, is often a recipe for increased flow of abundance in our lives, which is one reason why the ancient Indian goddess of abundance and prosperity, Lakshmi (whom we will meet in *Crystal Goddesses 888*) is known as the goddess of enlightenment. In true ancient wisdom, the Indian tradition of several thousand years of age sees enlightenment as another form of wealth, of spiritual prosperity.

Citrine is a great healing friend on our path of consciousness and we can safely meditate with it as often as we would like.

HEALING WITH HELIOS AND CITRINE

This simple healing technique is to be used at any time you feel that you are in need of spiritual growth. You can always attempt to decide this at an ego level, but you don't have to do so. You'll feel the impulsion of your own higher self towards growth by the symptoms of what is happening in your life.

True spiritual growth, as we mentioned, is initiated at the soul level. Rather than trying to direct it, we open up to allow it to work through us, and at times when we see the signs of something trying to break through, we do our best to work intelligently with it, like the surfer feeling the surge of a wave building, and paddling to reach the wave so it can be surfed. Sometimes we'll catch the wave, sometimes we'll get dumped, but there will eventually be another wave building. The spiritual growth process requires that we keep aiming to surf those waves.

Signs of spiritual growth happening will vary, but some of the more typical and unmissable ones are feeling out of control, dealing with fears emerging, having issues of trust (or related issues like abandonment, betrayal, anger or abuse) arising, and a sense of a new chapter opening in your life (which may be exhilarating, exciting or confusing). Other symptoms of spiritual growth that can intersperse the symptoms above are feelings of joy, beauty, being deeply moved, great love in your heart, incredible emotional intensity of adoration, bliss and gratitude, as well as playfulness, lightness of spirit and a love of being alive, just for the sake of it.

You will benefit from this exercise whenever you do it, but if you relate to the above, especially the more challenging aspects of spiritual growth, then you truly are urged to complete this healing.

Have Citrine or your mandala (or both) with you, be seated comfortably, preferably with the spine erect and the crystal or mandala somehow resting against your solar plexus (middle abdominal area) or navel (around or just below the belly button) chakras.

Say the following invocation aloud: "I call upon the true ascended being Helios, spiritual surveyor of human evolution, I call upon the Angel of Citrine and the loving grace of Mother Earth. I call upon my own higher self and the divine genius of life. I call upon consciousness. May I now be blessed with higher consciousness in any area that benefits my soul growth. I open to receive the light, love, divine grace and healing, mercy, kindness and protection that will help me now, for the greatest good and of my own free will, so be it."

Close your eyes and perceive a soft golden light. It shines all around you and before you. You sense that it is concentrated in a luminous core, shining as bright and pure as you can tolerate. Notice that around the light there is great radiance and around the radiance, as it dims, there is great darkness too. Softly allow the light to grow and the darkness to become less and less. Slowly in your own time allow this to happen.

Breathe in and out for at least 33 breaths or however long feels good.

If you have something arising for you, in your life or in yourself that you wish to surrender into higher consciousness (a good idea if you have been struggling with it for a while and not really getting anywhere) perceive that you can throw it into the core of this great solar light and visualise it being eaten up and the word "GRACE" emerging it its place once it has been digested by the solar intelligence.

If you offer anything and the word "GRACE" does not appear afterwards, be patient, you'll benefit from that learning for a little while longer. Allow yourself to receive some more light from the solar being instead, breathing it in and allowing that light to go to whatever part of your body most needs it.

Take your time and when you are ready, visualise the golden rays of the sun around your energy field, purifying and energising you and the cool presence of the earth beneath you receiving any excess solar energy.

Stay with this process for at least 33 breaths or however long feels right for you.

When you are ready, simply place your hands at your heart and say, "I honour the solar love, ancient and wise, I accept your power and grace, through all my lives, I give thanks for your help, that I may remember my divine light, you guide me always, bringing a fresh day after every dark night. May your hope and joy burn in my heart always. So be it."

Open your eyes and take some time to be cool and to rest if you need it.

If you have resonated with this chapter in some way, there is additional guidance for you at this time. The guidance is that you are blessed with the grace for growth. This means that a situation or circumstance with which you are struggling, internally or externally, is going to shift. You are either capable of this already, within your own energy field and spiritual connection, or you will be given the support you need (via a person or situation) in order to transform. Be patient and pray for grace. If this chapter doesn't speak to you strongly at the moment, don't be concerned. It is likely that you will feel drawn to it at another time, and this message will then speak to you too.

16.

ASCENDED MASTER MERLIN (Alchemy)
MYSTIC MERLINITE (Activation)

INITIATION OF LIGHT BODY

A deep black stone, mottled with grey and lavender, rests upon the earth. Large, silent and still. From within, energy stirs. Invisible but crackling electricity shoots out from the stone in all directions. It begins to shimmer with intensity, come alive with divine voltage, bringing everything around it to life.

The earth goes through cycles of spiritual evolution and growth, just as we do, though on a far larger scale. She moves through world cycles, of hundreds of thousands of years, and within those cycles, smaller transitional phases of thousands of years. Whilst there is some disagreement between scholars as to exact dates, it is generally agreed that the Earth is in the phase of Kali Yuga, where darkness has prevailed.

During such dark phases, there is great challenge to stay connected to light and the practice of meditation – in whatever form works for you. It is of great importance for us to remain connected to divine consciousness because the illusion of separation from the Divine is at its most convincing. It is taught by Masters such as Yogananda (whom we met in Chapter 7) that the earth is ascending to a new cycle within that greater cycle, so that there is more light available now than at the depths of Kali Yuga, yet we are not out of that dark world age as yet.

Our practice of meditation is important for this reason. There is an expression that it is easy to be grateful when there is a feast, not so much during a famine. It is easy to feel close to the Divine when light abounds, but when in darkness, it can be much harder, and yet that is the time we need it most. Fortunately it is often when we suffer that we realise this, and work harder to reach for divine grace. For human beings, meditation in whatever form works best for each individual is how we attempt to remain in divine consciousness even when the world around us going through the dark spasms of death and rebirth of Kali Yuga. Through meditation we gain the fuel we need to fulfil our divine task of being a conduit for the energies of heaven and earth to meet and transform each other, contributing to the rebirth (rather than just the destruction) of life on earth.

To further this spiritual plan of divine rebirth, human beings gain assistance from various higher beings – the masters, the angels, benevolent star systems and faces of the Divine Feminine in the form of goddesses, to name a few examples that we will be exploring in this series. The role of humanity might not seem as important as the role of these extraordinary evolved beings, and yet the ancient Indian teachings from several thousand years ago share that humanity has been sent as a saviour to the earth, to ensure her survival.

It might seem to be a stretch to our modern minds, given how much fear there is in many quarters that humanity will end up destroying our planet. Much of this fear, and of the destructive modern-day behaviour that supports such an idea, is based on old guilt and shame. The possibility that humanity will destroy this planet, rather than help her grow, is not inevitable unless we choose to make it so. If we can use that fear to jolt us into taking conscious action to help the planet, then that is a wise use of that energy. If we deny the fear or collapse into despair over it, then we are not making such wise use of it.

The guilt and shame underneath the destructive actions that human beings take, and the sense of ominous doom that we are going to destroy our mother planet, is part of a racial wound that we are healing. If we understand this, we can change our relationship to the fear rather than getting swept up in it and unconsciously acting out a self-fulfilling prophecy in a negative sense.

Part of how we do this is to accept the purity of our beings underneath all the experiences and learning that we have acquired (sometimes through great 'mistakes' which are worthwhile when they teach us something of value). We explored the original self and purity in Chapter 12. This is an important healing step in being able to accept the fundamental purity of humanity. If we see ourselves as unworthy and destructive beings, who ought to be destroyed before we destroy the earth, we are not going to be in a very empowered position to take constructive action and give as much as we possibly can to the healing path of ourselves, each other, the animals, the oceans and forests, the planet herself.

We have to remember that we are here to help the earth and in doing so, she blesses us with great abundance. If we are locked in shame and self-esteem issues, we think we are here to just take from the earth and try to get ahead of everyone else. It isn't a constructive way to be and it doesn't bring us real joy either.

For those of us that get this, we have a job to really be in that state of higher awareness as much as we can, to emanate a different energetic broadcast to humanity – one not of how much we can take, but of how much we can give and how richly we are rewarded in that process when we just let go. How superior that is to anything we can summon up on our own!

As we embody this as much as we can, our psychology, our bodies, our emotional patterns change and we can become frequency-emitting way-showers through how we are in the world. Your courage and choice can bring so much hope to another. Hope without blind optimism, hope that helps us take positive and constructive action in our own lives and for the planet is so important to our survival and evolution as a unique divine species. The human soul is a unique and precious divine experiment in consciousness that is certainly worth fighting for.

When you are exposed to something all the time, you can forget how incredible it is. Sometimes we are just so busy trying to live well and make sense of our lives, that we can forget what we are as human beings, which is quite extraordinary. We rose out of the Earth Mother as a body, which has the capacity to become animated by the heavenly light of our spirit. We are both wild creature and sublime spirit, joined together to create consciousness, awareness and eventually, divine realisation. What an amazing mind-boggling phenomenon.

Yet as we deal with the day-to-day realities of living and juggling the life's complexities, it can be hard to remember that we are a living, breathing, divine creature. We can support our divine awakening to remember this by creating time for spiritual practice and through doing inner work such as we explore in this book together. Apart from that, it is a divine happening, something we prepare for so that when the time is right, we are ready.

In the ageless wisdom teachings of the Ascended Masters, the second coming of the Christ is taught as being the mass awakening of humanity. It is the awakening of the loving Christ energy, the sacred heart that Christ and Mother Mary are often pictured with in religious iconography, awakened in all of humanity. It is the collective shift from fear to love. This is the same teaching, in slightly different language, that the Dalai Lama referred to when he said that the next Buddha could be a community. Our divine saviour isn't external to us – it is what we are awakening to becoming, together.

To support this end, many advanced souls have incarnated as human beings to help move this process along. These are known in various circles as planetary healers, planetary servers, lightworkers and initiates, as we discussed in the introduction to this book (when we also considered that whether you thought of yourself in that way or not, you are more than likely one of these souls too).

These relatively advanced souls will have various spiritual talents to help heal and transform consciousness within various fields of endeavour, including business and finance, music and the arts, health and healing, education, law and politics and also religion and spirituality. Each will be guided and given opportunities to progress in the field within which that particular soul's characteristics and talents can be best put to use. That field may change slightly over the course of a soul's evolution as spiritual talents grow and develop.

This is why it is so important to realise that spirituality can be just as alive in a business person as it is in a priest. The Divine wants to be recognised and integrated in all aspects of existence. Often the spiritual path is exceptionally challenging for those who are involved in areas that don't easily 'allow' for spirituality to be acknowledged and applied, such as the corporate world and the medical profession.

Souls bringing spirituality into these areas, often in 'sneaky' ways, are very brave. They are doing important work and what they need from the rest of us is love, encouragement and support, not judgment that they are 'less spiritual' because their work as healers is less obvious than those of us who work in the new age field. Most advanced souls know this already, but there are some who still put spirituality in one corner and everything else in another. We need to outgrow that attitude to really help each other get on with our divine task of earth healing. It's too big a task to try and accomplish on our own. We need to help and be helped by each other to be successful.

As we go on this journey together, awakening individually and then assisting each other on the spiritual path, the substance of our bodies is refined. This includes our physical body, and our subtle bodies of emotions, mind and spirit. Spiritual growth is essentially our ability to live as the Divine. Part of this process includes an illumination of matter, which we discussed in the golden body initiation in Chapter 6 with Mary Magdalene. For this to be able to happen, there has to be a structure that supports it, a bit like you need a bunsen burner and flask to carry out the mixing of chemicals in a science experiment. The chemicals being mixed, on the human spiritual path, are the masculine divine spirit and the feminine divine body. Eventually they will create a golden body, divine human. The container for those heavenly chemicals to come together, the way that chemical reaction can be orchestrated, is through the light body.

The light body is refined and developed over lifetimes. It includes our aura – the energy field that surrounds us and holds energetic information about our current and past lives, our soul talents and life mission. The light body also includes our chakras or energetic gateways for divine energy flow to interact with the physical body, linking it back to the subtle bodies of our emotions, mind and spirit. There are many chakras in the physical body and beyond, but there are seven main centres, which we connected with in Chapter 13 with the healing of Mother Mary.

The chakras can grow and develop through life experience and with spiritual growth can become more refined. They, just like the larger light body to which they belong, awaken with increasing spiritual consciousness. The light body also eventually grows to include parts of our nervous system, including the spinal column, and the brain, allowing for key aspects of our physical and energetic being to evolve from fear to love-based consciousness and being. We have a tremendous in-built capacity for mutation, adapting to higher consciousness through transformational processes. The light body is the equipment in the divine science laboratory that allows this to happen.

The light body in someone who is based in fear and separation is going to be less active, and less empowered to host some great inner spiritual experiments, than one who is based in love and connection. The divinity in those two people is exactly the same, for there is one divinity in all that is. The degree to which that divinity is actively awakened will vary and will change as we grow spiritually. The capacity that we have for consciously awakened divinity depends on how much divine frequency our light body can handle.

When the consciousness of a human being has shifted enough from fear to love, tipping over into a higher frequency, the light body awakens quite rapidly and we become capable of living a higher vibrational reality.

Souls that are planetary servers have agreed to awaken light body to help the planet. They are living as brighter lights than those souls that have agreed to hold the more average vibration of mass consciousness. It doesn't make these souls more godly, it just gives them a different role to play, that of lighthouse, as one example. The awakening of light body has its own unique gifts and sometimes more challenging (though temporary) symptoms. The following section of this chapter focuses on the effects of this awakening, and how to manage it (because it can be a bit tricky at times), which is one of Merlin's many talents. This will be relevant to those of you reading this book – working with spirituality and the Ascended Masters will mean that at some level your light body is awakening, otherwise even the notion of Ascended Masters would probably seem like a bit of a fairytale to you and their vibration wouldn't be able to stimulate you enough to even pick up this book let alone read it and work through the processes.

ASCENDED MASTER MERLIN – ALCHEMY

Merlin is a mysterious figure with many talents. It is my understanding that he actually likes the element of mystery to shroud him and uses it to his advantage in his spiritual service to the evolution of humankind. He's sneaky in a good way. If you resonate with Merlin, then it is likely that there will at least be a portion of your own spiritual work and service that is 'invisible' to those around you or has some mysterious or 'undercover' quality to it.

I learned more about this in recent times whilst conducting a meeting with a group of advanced teachers. They all worked in completely different ways. Two of them, more sensitive types in their own way, didn't have as many clients as one of the teachers in the group, who was a much more physical, earthy-type with natural business sense and an ability for self-promotion that resulted in her generating a thriving client base. She is a very 'on the ground' healer, active on a day-to-day level.

It occurred to me that it would be easy to assume from an ordinary perspective that she is more active in her spiritual work than the other two. Yet this is not the case. Both of these other sensitive souls do a great deal of work energetically in their respective communities. One lives in a rural area and is one of the purest, sweetest beings that I have ever met. She is that way naturally, without agenda or manipulation. She just wants to serve. It is as natural to her as breathing. The amount of spiritual work that she does is incredible. The other has a similar desire. Her healing practice is somewhat smaller, and though she is a remarkably gifted healer, her soul work only partially expresses herself through her healing practice of one-on-one clients. The other arena in which her soul shines is through her work on the boards of various organisations. Although her spiritual light is active in those arenas, it is not obviously so (unless you are attuned to such light and can recognise it consciously when in action).

Merlin watches over many soul groups and soul types, including as it turns out, the ones that I was mentioning above. Merlin, like the other Ascended Masters, is an expression of a higher consciousness through one particular personality. He has had numerous incarnations, and it is my experience that he is still partially incarnated through a number of souls on this planet, whilst the 'bulk' of his being is in ascended state. This is a sign of a very advanced being. I believe that there is more that we don't know about Merlin than there is that we do. As I mentioned above, this seems to serve him well and I believe that he is quite happy to have matters continue in this way, for now at least.

We mentioned above that the earth is going through a phase of spiritual growth, her own dark night of the soul in a grand sense, through this Kali Yuga world age. In the ancient Vedic tradition of India that shares these teachings, there is described a manifestation of a saviour, who will ride a white horse (perhaps a symbol for the vehicle of this saving grace as being a pure spirit) and is known as Kalki. This being is a consciousness, a light and a bestower of grace. It is an Eastern counterpart to the Western teaching of the second coming of the Christ and the New Age teaching that this second coming is actually the awakening of the hearts of humanity (that it will be an inner job rather than an external manifestation of a saviour).

It is my sense that Merlin has a particular role in anchoring the manifestation of Kalki in the hearts of awakening humanity. He is serving the presence of saving grace on the earth. Merlin is intimately connected with the Kalki energy of light, that same energy that every lightworker or planetary server is also hooking into and then building, as together we support the earth, calling in light and consciousness, as she evolves into a new world age, sometimes referred to as the golden age (which is like a golden body initiation that human beings undertake, but for the earth herself).

My conscious connections with Merlin have been unintentional and at times, a little unbelievable, at least at first. I have only ever connected with him consciously in deep meditative states, unlike some of the other Masters that can pop into my awareness in every day waking state, such as when washing the dishes! I don't know if there is a particular significance to this except to say that it is possible, as I have intimated above, that he is the face of a far greater being and to access that level of consciousness requires more attention than the frequencies of the Masters that more actively seek us out at a more mundane human level of interaction. This doesn't render one master 'more spiritual' than another – they are all a face of the one higher consciousness. It does however suggest that the task of Merlin is less about individual growth and more about wider plans for service, so that his contact with individuals, about individual matters, is fairly limited.

Even when I have connected with him consciously – and I will share two examples of that with you in a moment, it has never been about my personal issues at hand, but rather about soul group endeavours. This doesn't mean that it is impossible for Merlin to relate to individuals about personal matters, but just that it is perhaps less likely and if it does happen, it will be in service to the greater plan that he is working on in some way.

The first encounter I had with Merlin was when he popped up as a guide to a group of souls that I was working with through a project that I founded and headed for several years called The Shakti Temple. This group gathered with the purpose of intensive awakening on their own unique soul paths. It was a fertile crucible for awakening and the power that came through the group was fairly potent. Whilst some were actually disturbed by how real the spiritual energy was and the physical experiences they had as a result of it, the majority were grateful, devoted and dedicated to the work we did together, growing considerably as a result.

After receiving guidance to become more focused in my work and to close The Shakti Temple project in early 2013 (soon after which I 'suddenly' had this series of books to write), Merlin popped up again. At the close of The Shakti Temple project, Merlin was unexpectedly present, and I knew that although the physical manifestation of the project was completed, the love that flowed between a number of souls that connected through the work we did would continue, as appropriate, under his care. I noticed that the souls in particular that he held close all had strong Celtic interests, inclinations or backgrounds, which I found interesting, given Merlin's association with Arthurian times and the Celtic magical traditions.

The second encounter I had with Merlin was somewhat more direct. In the midst of a deep meditative healing, this time with me receiving the healing instead of acting as the healer, I encountered a strong masculine presence that identified himself as Merlin. When the healer, who undoubtedly would have accepted this fact given that he seen more spiritual action than even the biggest Hollywood blockbuster could deliver, asked me if that being had a name, I chose to keep it to myself because quite frankly, I questioned its veracity.

Some guidance unfolded from this being about a couple of souls that were involved in The Shakti Temple at the time (the project was continuing at that point) and the nature of our work together at a soul level. To close the discussion the masculine being said, referring to me, "This channel doubts, but I do not only manifest through her, as her, there will be another here to show this" and that was that.

I came out of the healing refreshed, with much positive energy and then proceeded to assist the healer (my dear teacher at the time, Raym) with his next client as I was in the role of his apprentice that day. The next client lay down, went into a deep meditative state and throughout the following 90 minutes began to describe an aspect of his soul as being known as Merlin!

I don't for one minute believe that this experience was for my own personal benefit so much as it was for the understanding that great beings will manifest aspects of themselves through those of us on earth, when the soul is willing and capable. They may choose to do this by being channelled by some, or through a far less visible process of sending spiritual light and their own higher consciousness through our bodies. They may send their energy out through us, via the vibration of words that we didn't know we were going to speak (but mysteriously enough were very helpful to the listener when spoken). They may use us as a vehicle through which we can share their higher vibration through writing or music, or any other plans or projects that simply 'must' be formulated and so forth. This is spirit at work. It might be via our own higher self, or through the Ascended Masters, for example, impressing their energy upon the physical vehicle, via the higher self. The example we contemplated in Chapter 5 on the Christ and the photograph of Sai Baba is an illustration of this receiving of one great being through another being.

The result of this receiving of a specific, high-vibrational spiritual presence is an intense form of spiritual alchemy. If it happens through some channelling or other (conscious or not) over a long time, the transformation stimulated can be profound and life-altering. The influx of spiritual light cranks the fires of transmutation and denser consciousness is mixed with higher vibrational energy, burning bright as fuel for transformation.

The flow of spiritual light is enabled by a fit receiver, the light body. Spiritual energy has its own intelligence and it builds each step as it goes. You could say that the Divine is a master builder. Spiritual energy enters in enough frequency to cause the energy body to adapt and become capable of higher and higher transmissions of light to be received, digested and integrated into the physical vehicle, where divine alchemy or transmutation takes place. Bit by bit, the light body is strengthened and developed, channels cleared and opened and more light flows. Eventually, something of a chrysalis of light is formed, and the golden body that we discussed in Chapter 6 awakens within it.

Merlin helps us stay true to the process. It can be easy to want to run and hide during such a transformation because we are likely going to feel utterly confused, swirling in pain with old issues arising at times. Yet that is happening because we are taking in more divine consciousness to grow, and the old stuff needs to be refined to tolerate us becoming a higher frequency being. Merlin helps us realise that the light and dark dance together inside of us even more so when we are growing. So we think that being upset or uncomfortable can mean something is wrong, but Merlin helps us realise that this is a temporary symptom of something being right – it is our spiritual growth taking place.

As we go through this process, it involves not only emotional suffering but sometimes physical blocks and pain – headaches, stabbing pains, nausea, other random aches and pains in the body itself as it drops density and shifts to holding a higher quotient of light (or in other words, the light body is awakening and growing within us), and even fevers and increased sensitivity (in senses of sight, hearing and smell) can occur as mutational or developmental symptoms with our growing light body.

We need to pay attention to our wellbeing and seek out health care support from an appropriate practitioner, whilst also being aware that sometimes these very physical symptoms are actually energy moving and nothing more. It is like the student who rushed to hospital after her first meditation circle with me, believing that she was having a heart attack and in fact, when the doctor told her there was absolutely nothing happening physically (that he could see) she realised that she was experiencing her heart chakra opening and the release of old pain as it did so.

Sometimes the physicality of the subtle light body awakening can be very powerful indeed. Recently I was singing and playing crystal bowls at a beautiful dance celebration of the Winter Solstice in Sydney. Afterwards a vivacious and vibrant woman came up to me and shared the story of why she had come and how she had been led to connect with me through a number of synchronicities. I was so moved by her story. I could see the divine intelligence operating through the highlights that she shared with me. She asked for a hug so that our hearts could connect, which I willingly gave her for a few moments. After patting her on the back with a gentle blessing, which is usually what happens automatically when I hug someone in that sort of situation, we stepped back from each other and smiled. Suddenly she grabbed my arm, swaying a bit and expressing that she felt incredibly light-headed and dizzy. I knew she had just 'tipped over' the edge of what she could comfortably receive energetically. She had been through a huge healing process even to get to that day and participate as wildly as she did. Her physical body was receptive and intelligent enough to let her know how real the effect of that energy was upon her and that she'd had enough by then.

So understanding that energy is very potent and affects the body directly, all the more so as we awaken our light body, we take care, we take appropriate precautions but also remain open to the possibility that our symptoms are not signs that we are sick, dying, or just getting old and stiff, but are passing symptoms of our light body awakening. Prayer to Merlin who loves us unconditionally can help support and guide us through this process.

Calling on the Masters is enough to get the process happening at a higher level. I mentioned how to go about this in the introduction of this book. For me, writing this book, where I am calling in the consciousness of a Master, sometimes more than one, each day over several weeks of intensive writing, has pushed me into a huge spiritual growth process. It happens every time I write one of these books. The energy flows from genuine higher beings into my body so that I can translate that into words on a page (and I always have the intention to impart the energy behind the words too, which you will feel as you read these books and are affected by them). So I experience the destabilising effect of higher consciousness as my light body is forced to grow and adapt, and also the healing effect of it as it does so, quite immediately in my physical, emotional and soul life. I have more energy, more awareness, more insight and more vitality to put to work in my physical expression of my divine path. It isn't an easy process, but it is effective for my spiritual growth.

What Merlin helps us with in our healing process at the end of this chapter, and through one of the stones that bears his name, Mystic Merlinite (which we'll explore below) is how to manage the effects of the increase of spiritual light leading to the growth of our light body or energetic, 'light-receptive' equipment.

MYSTIC MERLINITE – ACTIVATION

Mystic Merlinite doesn't look like much – dark grey, subdued brown, sometimes muted purple and black tones can make it seem unimpressive and those that aren't particularly attuned to the sort of vibration that it emits would simply walk on by it, hardly noticing it at all. Not unlike its namesake, there is far more going on with this stone that what meets the eye. Sourced from Madagascar, this stone is mysterious and powerful. It is when you pick up Mystic Merlinite that it reveals itself to you. I have held a piece that was given to me as a gift only twice. Once when I received it and one before writing this chapter. I love this stone, but to me it is like holding a live firecracker!

Even just gazing at the stone now, which sits nestled next to my laptop on a bed of tissue paper is causing some interesting experiences. The colour is changing before my eyes into emanations of clear translucent spots on the stone, where previously there was only dark opaqueness. Soft white tones are revealing themselves underneath the now sheer windows on the surface of the stone. What was once a brown tone is now glowing as a deep olive green and the aura emanating off the stone is so strong I can see it physically, not unlike seeing heat emanating off a sidewalk on a really hot day, where it seems to shimmer in front of your eyes. It is barely contained in physical form, the energy of Mystic Merlinite. I wasn't sure what its special gift for this book would be, but I can see now why "activation" came so strongly into my mind this morning. The crystal looks like it is moving and buzzing.

When you experience this stone for yourself, you'll sense how powerful it is and why I work with it so judiciously. When I received it as a gift, my partner and his mother both had turns at holding the stone, curious about my strong visceral response to it, to see if they too could feel something. My partner held it and felt energy flowing about his body. His mother took it outside declaring that she couldn't feel crystals but wanted to try anyway, only to walk back inside about a minute later with a surprised and gleeful expression as she described what she had felt. I wasn't surprised that they had responses as both my partner and his mother are energetically attuned, even though they don't necessarily think of themselves in that way. However Mystic Merlinite works with any who are open to its power. Just proceed with awareness that even smaller pieces are powerful (the piece which is the subject of this discussion is only a large tumbled stone, about three inches in length).

Mystic Merlinite is an activator. It stimulates, awakens and yet also anchors energy flow. It functions as an axis point through which even apparently opposing or polarised energies can flow – masculine and feminine, yin and yang, emotional and mental and so on. It creates a point of awakening that happens when opposing forces are tamed into co-operation. Because of the flow of power that this creates, it is extremely stimulating. Even with it wrapped up in tissue paper and out of sight (I had to wrap it up because its natural movement and shifting colours, defying what I thought I would ever see in person I have to say, were distracting me from continuing my writing!), it is a powerful stimulant. If you are tired, it might be of benefit to you to work with this stone, raising your natural energy levels. If however you are somewhat beyond tired, perhaps in fatigue or in a delicate state, this stone may be too strong for you at certain times on your path. Certainly today my nervous system is delicate and holding the stone is actually a bit much for me, it feels like the ends of my nerves are getting a bit frazzled by the intense energy flow. So the stone is shortly to be placed back in my healing room, for today at least.

Mystic Merlinite has a powerful magnetic field and if you place it on your body wherever you feel depleted or in need of energy, it will pull energy to that place. If you need strengthening, you can place it on your lower belly or solar plexus. If you need to shift a headache or light-headedness, place it near your navel or your feet. If you have an injury that needs more energy for healing, place it below that injury if it is below the heart, or above the site of injury if located above the heart. Make sure that you monitor how your body responds when working with this stone, and if it feels like too much at any time, put it away for a while. If you are not sensitive to energy and find it difficult to know when too much is too much, I would suggest that you limit your physical exposure to the stone, holding it or meditating with it, with a time limit of twenty minutes at any given encounter.

Mystic Merlinite helps activate the light body process and integrate its effects. One of the most helpful things that I have learned over the years about managing mutational symptoms that I mentioned at the end of the discussion on Merlin above, is that grounding is essential. With grounding, we have to choose to do it, wanting or asking isn't enough, and no matter how inept you may feel about being able to effectively ground yourself, if I could learn it, you certainly can too. I used to live in my head so severely that I would get cranky at my body because it needed to eat. That was just one of the indications of my frustration with the very nature of having a physical body. It took years of inner work to heal my consciousness around this and shift from frustration to incredible reverence and awe, but as I said, if I, the queen of flying off into other worlds, could learn to ground, and learn to love the experience of being grounded, then so can anyone.

Grounding doesn't just happen for many of us. If we have learned to live in our heads (which seems to be a hallmark of being raised in modern technology-driven cultures), or naturally are very intellectual, mind-oriented people, or even very emotionally-driven people, we will have to use our will and intention to come back to our bodies in the here and now. Grounding is an active choice that we make.

That can start by bringing yourself into your body to really feel what is going on there. You will feel your feelings, you may suddenly notice that you are tired, hungry, hot or cold, angry, peaceful, frightened or some confusing mixture of feelings. That is all just fine. What matters most is not what you feel, but that you are feeling it. Even if its just how nice it is to feel that you are at home and cosy within yourself in that moment of connecting with your body.

It is when we are grounded that we can be present to what is taking place within us and respond intelligently. It's something of a challenge to formulate an intelligent response to a situation if you have no clue what's going on!

There are a number of common mutational symptoms that tend to manifest as your physical body starts to shift to increasing levels of light. When we are grounded and present in our physical body, we can notice them more readily and respond appropriately.

At times it can be hard to tell if it is a physical problem or a psychic one and supportive medical care that works for you is always recommended. Whether apparently physical or psychic in nature, energetic healing like acupuncture can be a wonderful support because it works right into the subtle body and physical body at the same time.

I briefly outlined some possible side effects of spiritual growth and more specifically, light body growth, above, but I'll mention some common symptoms with a little more explanation now.

First and foremost, tiredness can be a mutational symptom – particularly if you know that there is no physical or obvious emotional or psychological cause of your fatigue. Tiredness can indicate a time where your will is causing internal struggle against the manifestation of divine will (perhaps you are resisting an intuition or a certain action you know you need to take or on the other hand, perhaps you are trying to force things to happen rather than letting them blossom in their own time) and therefore you are exhausting yourself until you get to a place where you are too tired to resist any more and then divinity can manifest through you as it wished to in the first place. It's a clever and effective plan, but not much fun. Sometimes just letting go and resting is more fun and just as clever and effective a way to allow the Divine to have its way.

Apart from this, tiredness (especially upon waking or at unexpected points during the day) can indicate that you are dropping density (the counterbalancing act to building your light body – the more light you contain, the less density). If you drop density fast, which can happen for initiates on the accelerated path of spiritual growth, you can experience light-headedness, tiredness, even queasiness or nausea, feelings of sickness (especially with the release of fear) or just a general feeling of temporary un-wellness. After the release, you will feel great and increasingly alive, but you need to know how to manage the related tiredness too. Rest can work wonders.

I recommend that if these symptoms are occurring at a time when you can meditate, that you do so. Sometimes the call to meditation is so strong, I cannot do anything in that moment but meditate. Fortunately the soul chooses such moments as when I am not driving a car or some other potentially dangerous activity! Recently a client who practices regular meditation and has done for years, and has her own conscious spiritual connection firmly established, mentioned that she felt called to meditate and yet keep falling asleep. Frustrated at herself, she would force herself to wake up and go back into meditation, at which point she would fall asleep again. The brilliant conclusion that we both reached about this experience was that at that time, she would have benefited greatly from a nap!

Sometimes spiritual integration will happen most effectively through sleep. I have had moments like that along my path, especially at times when most of my energy was directed towards inner healing and I didn't have as much energy available for use in my physical world as I would usually have had. If I go with the process, I will wake up feeling different. Something has shifted within. It might be a rebalance of some kind or perhaps I have been gifted with an important dream. I recall a story I heard early on in my spiritual teaching career about a man who would nap during the day and when asked why by his wife, he would respond that he was gaining harmony within himself by doing so. As he understood that who we are is our contribution to the world, he dubbed the practice sleeping for world peace. Sometimes we need to sleep for world peace too, especially during intense phases of spiritual growth where we are integrating at many levels and need more rest.

Your spirit will not try to overload you to excess – just enough to stretch you, but there will be times, particularly in meditation, when you will need to monitor how much energy you take on (especially if connecting with Ascended Masters and other high vibrational beings). Sometimes if you have experience in meditation, you'll be whisked off on some great adventures, for hours at a time even, and return feeling refreshed. It is unlikely that this would be an everyday happening, but each will have their own experience of course.

Higher energies, when genuinely experienced, change us. The Ascended Master Helios, whom we met in Chapter 15 teaches us to sense what works for us and not fall into the error of imagining you can never have too much of a good thing. This is why meditations that work with higher energies are sometimes best kept relatively short – around twenty minutes in duration (are you listening, you people who want my meditations to go on for longer?!). We can build up the length of time that we meditate slowly and surely and avoid overloading of our energy system in that way – which may feel great for the moment, but may well leave us exhausted for the following week as our system tries to repair the 'blow outs' that occurred.

Keep this in mind if you are getting recurring tiredness after spiritual work, or if you just have lots and lots of pain, physical or emotional, when you meditate or afterwards. It is possible that you may be moving too fast. Don't be reluctant to ask your spirit to slow down a little. Take a day off from practice now and then, if you need it. I don't like to do this often, but sometimes it is actually helpful, especially if you aren't feeling well and just need sleep! That being said, if you are working with more grounding meditations that help you feel more body-aware, and you feel supported and well through that practice, then by all means, you may like to do longer sessions. An hour or longer of such a meditation can feel wonderful, especially if you increase the time of your sessions in increments, over a period of months or years.

As your spiritual practice through meditation, yoga, conscious dance, gardening or swimming in the ocean (essentially, through whatever works for you) develops, your light body activation will increase naturally. Then so will other mutational symptoms. Some common ones are also flu-like symptoms without influenza, sometimes tingling in the hands and feet or finding that hands and feet fall asleep. When this is extreme around the hands – particularly tingling – energy channels for hands-on healing may be being laid into your hands, if that is a part of your spiritual plan for this lifetime. As always, please get health checks at the physical level too, so you can rule out blood pressure irregularities and so forth.

Sometimes it is simply a case of energy being moved about and we cannot know much more than that, though I have seen some weird and wonderful processes happening for people in my healing room, and often they are quite unique to each individual.

As mentioned, aches, pains and flu-like symptoms usually indicate a clearing or a dropping of density (such as fear-based approaches to life being upgraded to more trusting approaches to life, for example). If it is joint-related, it often has to do with resistance of divine will – going with the flow is needed and any type of hydrotherapy would be beneficial as would the practice of yin yoga that works with the joints. Any symptoms centring around the solar plexus such as nausea and anxiety can indicate releasing of fear. Panic attacks can also indicate this, as well as clearing on a heart level, which can result in muddled meditation and the mind being constantly busy. As the heart clears, the mind will usually follow.

Headaches, feelings of pressure at the base of the skull, back of the head, around the eyes or even behind the eyes, feeling like your skull is being restructured and short, sharp jabbing pains around the head or brain area can indicate shifts at a subtle level, a bit like building a more effective spiritual receiving dish in your head.

I have a wonderful chiropractor who practices a gentle "activator" technique and works also with kinesiology which has been very restorative of my nervous system over the years and really helps with managing spiritual growth spurts to the psychic organs. Acupuncture has been so helpful at times too, as has yoga, meditation, dance and Chi Gung. Anything nourishing to the body in terms of supportive holistic healthcare is highly recommended for prevention of imbalance. The correction of imbalance at the energy level before it manifests as physical disease is an effective and sensible use of health care.

When you know something is wrong and you need health care, trust that and act on it, even if medical professionals do not yet have the capacity to perceive at the level you are consciously able to perceive. I have had experiences where I have known I have been imbalanced and felt really unwell. After a battery of tests by my local doctor, it was finally declared that I would indeed live forever. Though nice to hear that I was so healthy by conventional standards, it was most unhelpful in solving my problem. I promptly took myself to my acupuncture master who read my pulse and ticked off all the things I could be feeling – a very accurate diagnosis of energetic imbalance if there ever was one. He wasted no time in jabbing needles in various points as I was swept up in waves of exhilarating chi (though sometimes it was quite painful as blocks were unplugged). My energy field was supported in naturally healing itself by coming back to balance and I felt marvellous.

Other mutational symptoms are fever and sweats, which usually indicate an extreme rise in your energy level that will usually stabilise at a higher level within a period of days. Extreme sensations of heat can also indicate energetic burning through blocked energy. Pleasant feelings of warmth and sometimes feeling temporarily overheated can also occur if that is the case. Sometimes this is painful, sometimes pleasurable. We will talk much more about kundalini and its awakening in *Crystal Goddesses 888*. For now, know that such symptoms will usually settle relatively soon, and a feeling of increased clarity, cleanness and power will usually be the result of the clearing. Acupuncture again can be wonderful to balance this process out too.

Vagueness and spacey-ness indicate the absence of grounding and the possibility of being too mentally focused, not allowing integration time to embody your learning and a consequent excess of energy around the head that hasn't been connected with and digested by the body. For those that are spiritually attuned more so than physically connected, and that will include the star-baby souls that have incarnated to bring unique vibrations to our planet (your book in this series is *Crystal Stars 11.11*), then grounding is essential. If you are already pretty grounded, and still experiencing these phenomena, then it may also indicate energy leaks as a result of psychic interference or cords of connection in relationships that really drain you. Focusing on the feet and drawing up energy of the earth, and doing the healing processes of Chapter 9 (St. Germain) and Chapter 14 (the Buddha) will help end that difficulty.

Alterations in your vision or hearing abilities that appear to come and go – strange sights, shimmering, fuzzy sights or strange sounds that are temporary – can indicate awakening of perceptive faculties such as clairaudience (spiritual hearing) and clairvoyance (spiritual seeing). I remember when I was first consciously studying meditation this lifetime and my psychic abilities were opening up. I went through a stage where I felt so like a vampire or a hung-over person (who didn't drink – blood or alcohol!) as I was so incredibly sensitive to sunlight for several months. I have a distinct memory of being in my late teens and sitting at a bus stop on a bright day, feeling like my eyes were being burned away! I had to pop on dark sunglasses over my closed eyes to deal with the intensity of the glare, and normally I don't like wearing sunglasses. Fortunately that particular symptom passed reasonably quickly.

Objects appearing to move are also quite common indications of the onset of multi-dimensional sight. The bizarrely behaving piece of Mystic Merlinite this morning was perceived through multi-dimensional sight, which sounds pretty fancy, but is a normal part of how we see through the inner eye when the light body is awakened to some extent.

If you are unsure about your wellbeing during any of these symptoms, or others that you intuitively feel are connected with your spiritual growth and the opening of chakras or expansion of your auric field as a consequence of that growth, go ahead and get second opinions to rule out any neurological complications or other issues.

If these symptoms belong to the subtle body rather than the physical level, which more often than not they will, they should settle down quite quickly and with minimal interruption to your 'regular' life. Of course these symptoms, especially when hitting your centres of perception, can be quite disorienting at first, challenging your sense of what is tangible and 'real' at a physical level, but it is also very exciting as it is the gateway to piercing illusion and seeing the divine reality standing before us, within us, just waiting to be witnessed! It is a lovely change of consciousness and eventually you will become quite comfortable with the visions that accompany your daily life, even if they take you by surprise at times.

If these things are not quite happening for you as yet, and you never imagine that they will, take heart. I have seen clients naturally have their abilities awaken and they have been absolutely stunned that they could perceive in that new way. But it happens when and how it is meant to, in service of the soul path of each person. It is not an indicator of spirituality; it is an indicator of what will be helpful on the path. So if it isn't happening for you as yet, don't make that mean something more than simply 'this is what works for you best at this time in your life'.

And now for the better news – mutational symptoms will also include greater energy levels once the clearing has taken place, a renewed sense of inspiration, vitality and greater enthusiasm for life, increased levels of trust and abundance, a sense of freedom and empowerment as you realise that you are creating your life and a deep sense of gratitude and joy as your spiritual talents emerge, offering you new ways of being in the world and new ways of helping create our world. Thank the heavens for that!

HEALING WITH MERLIN AND MYSTIC MERLINITE

Have your stone or your mandala with you, near your body, resting at any place on your body that feels good, or simply next to you on either left or right side, above your head or below your feet depending on what feels appropriate for you. If you are tired you may wish to lie down and treat this healing as a rest. If you are feeling energised, you may wish to be seated and treat this healing as a meditation.

Close your eyes and focus on your breathing, allowing your awareness to rest on the breath for a few moments as you centre yourself. Imagine that you can scan your body with your awareness just noticing lightly where there is tension or relaxation, where you feel light and/or heavy, open or blocked. Notice this without judgment.

When you are ready, say the following, "I call upon my own higher self, my soul, the true Ascended Master Merlin who loves me unconditionally and the Angel of Mystic Merlinite. I call upon divine grace, divine kindness and divine mercy. Bless my process of spiritual alchemy and the building of my light body, that I may come to light according to my highest good. Through my own free will, so be it!"

Perceive that all around you there is a swirling vortex of dark light, as though you are in deep space. Far below you, you sense the beautiful green-blue sphere of the earth, glowing radiantly. High above you is the burning star of our sun.

Before you appears a mysterious silver light, glowing bright and vast. It spans the breadth of sun and earth, and you feel yourself gently blessed by this light. Receive that blessing into your heart, or any other part of your body that naturally draws the light to it. Let this happen for several moments, breathing in and out as you receive, for around at least 33 breaths.

You become aware then of a magnetic force. You feel your awareness and energy being pulled with gravity towards a central point deep within the heart chakra of this great silver light being. As you flow with that gravitational field greater than your own, you feel your energy field respond. Energy moves up and down your spine more freely, and blockages within your energy field begin to release. You may feel the effect of this energetic movement now physically or in the days following the process.

Stay with your breath and focus on the magnetic centre of this process so that you don't become dizzy or overwhelmed by the multiple shifts and directions of energy flow. Let the magnetic pull of the centre point of this being's heart be strong, as though your awareness is concentrated, focusing there.

Stay with that awareness for at least 33 breaths.

In your own time, eventually you feel that magnetic pull release itself, feeling lightness, expansion and grace flowing through you as the process is completed for now.

You start to slowly descend, your awareness returning to the earth, to your connection of your feet to the earth, and feeling as though you are breathing through your feet, in and out, as you ground.

Take your time to ground thoroughly. It may take you several minutes or even twenty or thirty minutes. Breathe and let it happen in your own time.

Then a bubble of silver light forms around you, as you continue breathing through your feet.

When ready, place your hands gently in prayer and say thank you.

You may wish to continue with deeper meditation, continuing with the breathing through the feet until your breath gently expands to include breath through your entire body, until even your hair is breathing in and out. Or you may wish to descend into sleep and simply rest.

When you are done, simply open your eyes.

If at any point following this exercise you are feeling mutational symptoms, ask for Merlin who loves you unconditionally to assist with the process and listen to your intuition, which may be to rest, to exercise, to dance, to have a salt bath or go for a swim or take a shower. It might be to put clay on your body or have a massage or healing. Trust what you feel and know that you are being guided.

17.

ASCENDED MASTER BABAJI (Soul Star)
DIAMOND (Dorje)

INITIATION OF SPIRITUAL FRUITION

Pure white light shatters into coloured rainbows, spreading far and wide. Retracting back to a pure core of white light, it bursts into an eternal flame.

The initiation of spiritual fruition is the manifestation of the best possible version of yourself. Let us say that you are something like a dessert. There will be many possible versions of a dessert, but there will be one that is just so fantastic, so perfectly concocted that it deserves the accolade of the best possible fruit cake (talking about myself there) or best possible strawberry flan, or whatever it is that you consider you could be (best possible lemon tart?).

That best possible version of yourself is living up to your divine potential in your own unique way, the fulfilment of all your life lessons on earth to the extent that you have mastered them enough to be able to continue on to the next stage of spiritual evolution. It is like graduation with honours, at the top of your class. We don't have to do this. We can learn a bit and grow more slowly, learning lessons over a course of several lifetimes. Initiates however are enrolled in an accelerated learning process, which doesn't always make for the smoothest life path (evolution can be bumpy at times) but it does make for an interesting life and a very refined vehicle through which divine essence can permeate the world.

If you are graced with the capacity for spiritual growth, then you will be in line to receive the blessing of spiritual fruition. You can imagine it like this – say a bunch of souls were gathered at an athletics carnival. Your soul has been in training as a runner. It has a personal best time for a certain race and a time that it aspires to reach, which would set the next record. Maybe the soul has an unexpectedly good run, after much dedication and training, and it suddenly seems possible and even likely that the soul will be able to set a new record, rather than getting somewhere near it.

In such cases, you will be given more specific training, afforded an opportunity to be treated to additional care and nurturing. That the goal is in sight for you is acknowledged and whilst all are nurtured towards their own goal, your particular aptitude at this particular time is noted and responded to by those that can help you.

This is akin to a spiritual 'time in the sun', a time when you are noticed spiritually as approaching a goal, in this instance, the rather heady goal of fulfilling your soul task of which this physical worldly life is one important facet, and you are supported.

In the guru tradition of ancient India, certain spiritual teachers who are completely at one with divine consciousness are said to be in possession of the power of a divine grace that what has been spoken will manifest, essentially as a word of the Divine, and it is a done deal. It cannot be counteracted by any interference, karma or anything else for that matter. It is a statement of what is now spiritual fact, a blessing or big thumbs up from the Divine that this particular manifestation shall be, without question. This is the blessing and consequent initiation of spiritual fruition, but it can come through the Divine in any number of ways, whether a physical guru or spiritual teacher be present or not. That blessing can be bestowed by the Ascended Master Babaji, for example, as he is a completely surrendered channel to the Divine. Any teacher who claims this ability for themselves is best subjected to much discernment. This is something that happens through a completely surrendered channel acting as one with the Divine, not a power that is held within an individual. Because of that, claiming it as a personal power is nonsensical.

The blessing of spiritual fruition is that you shall fulfil your divine potential and be guided and nurtured spiritually that this may happen, usually within the lifetime in question. It means that things are, spiritually speaking, about to speed up! You might have to drop a lot of emotional baggage to be able to keep up with the pace of your spiritual path.

The initiation is the consequence of the blessing. What this means is that once such a blessing has been given, circumstances to manifest the blessing are set in motion. Whether we are conscious of having received such a blessing because it happened in a way we were able to perceive, or unconscious, because it happened at a soul level and we were not able to be consciously aware of the blessing taking place, we will feel its effect in a groundswell of support from life for our 'cause'. We'll undoubtedly still have challenges, but they will very particularly be evoked in order for our success to happen spiritually. If we received such a blessing before birth, our entire life will be unfailingly geared towards our divinity manifesting according to its highest potential this lifetime. It simply will be that way, markedly so, according to divine grace.

Everything that happens in life serves us, whether we have received a particular blessing of fruition for this lifetime or not. Sometimes that service is through challenge if that is most effective at the time, sometimes through graceful flow. What happens in the life experiences following this type of divine blessing however is that we surge onto our path. Sometimes there are great changes, sometimes they are completely unexpected and yet when you look back over your life, you will see that it makes perfect sense from the bigger scheme of things. It is a bit like instead of progressing at a more moderate pace, all of a sudden the Divine yells, "All systems are go!" and suddenly we are powering through spiritual growth and initiation at a rapid pace. It's not always much fun as sometimes we grow more quickly through a challenge, but there will be a clear sense of the purpose driving our entire life existence as being about us reaching our absolute spiritual fulfilment.

The initiation is the readying of our own consciousness to receive its spiritual birthright and destiny. Even if we are far along on our path, which is what would have to be in order to receive this blessing, we may still have a lot of healing to do to receive the fullness of this blessing. We might be clearing out old emotional patterning of sadness or anger, or coming to resolution with one last issue that we just hadn't as yet got a handle on. We may feel that our personal growth is accelerating and becoming quite bumpy as we feel challenged in many directions. If we are aware at a soul level we may equally have the sense that we are growing and any challenges that are presenting themselves to us are actually calling us further forward on our path. Initiation generally is a time of rapid growth, and initiation following this blessing is a 'take no prisoners' mandate from the Divine. This is why it is granted only when the goal is so near. Otherwise it would make a person utterly miserable because spiritual light evokes growth and the divine mandate of enlightenment for one who is almost ready but not quite would be like asking a child to take on adult responsibilities – just not appropriate, not loving and not wise in the long run.

If you worry that you cannot relate to this chapter, have heart. There is a reason that you have been drawn to this book and that will include messages in its content to you. From Babaji there is this guidance – whatever you are working through on a more personal scale, any issue or problem that you believe is getting in the way of your spiritual growth, ask for his blessing (using the healing process below) and know that a resolution will be sent to you promptly, to the extent that you are willing to let go and receive it. That is an incredible honour in itself and I am so happy that you can partake of it.

ASCENDED MASTER BABAJI – SOUL STAR

The soul star is the vehicle for our higher self, a body in a spiritual sense, through which our soul light can manifest, receiving energy from the pure source and directing its own growing energy into our physical body. The soul star is a natural dwelling place for the soul, in between the nourishing source of pure light from which it has emerged, and the challenging gift of manifesting itself in a physical body, becoming an embodied golden divine being through the illumination and integration of that physical body into complete divine consciousness.

I saw a picture once that pretty much described what the soul star is like. It was a picture of a little girl, leaping in the air with a look of utter glee and delight on her face, arms flung open, legs dangling freely, as she felt completely alive, blissfully free and happy beyond measure. The caption on the picture was, "This is what your soul always feels like." The soul star is that place where the soul emanates its essence – which is that bliss, love and light, in a way, something like a baby gurgling blissfully in it's mother's loving arms. The soul, like that divine child, grows to know itself, to become all it can be. The soul does this through its expansion from the soul star and into the human body. It never loses its soul star chakra in this process, it just grows beyond it. The eternal bliss, light and love of the soul is always there, vibrating at the frequency of the soul star chakra.

It is the light of highly refined beings, such as the Master Babaji that shine in this eternal light and can help our souls if they are struggling to bring that light into the body as they incarnate. That assistance can help prevent the soul from getting stuck in habitual disconnection from the body so that it can stay in the light.

The soul is supported by Masters such as Babaji to learn that there is a more whole experience of the Divine awaiting it. This is possible if the soul is prepared to leave behind the light in order to enter into the darkness of matter and awaken to the light that is hidden, at first, within matter. Babaji can do this because he is a Master that has been able to attain union of body and soul, to experience the Divine that is in this world of forms just as much as it is in the pure light of the source. He is spiritually advanced and empowered enough to support a soul in overcoming the resistance to the new challenge of growth, and to instead continue to embrace it, even when it gets painful or confusing at times, which it undoubtedly will for a while, until the next level is attained.

If you considered Merlin to be mysterious, Babaji is even more so. Babaji simply means 'father' and many teachers are called by this name in India. The Babaji that we are speaking of in this text is the teacher of the teacher of Yogananda (whom we met in Chapter 7). This Babaji is known quite dramatically as the deathless Master for he has reached a level of spiritual consciousness that is beyond death and rebirth.

There are accounts of rather dramatic stories of Babaji sightings. The teacher is said to be of such refined vibration that he appears in physical form now, as a young man with vibrant coloured hair, only when strictly necessary. He is said to reside in high mountains upon the earth with his closest students by his side. Over hundreds of years, without aging, he would appear and disappear, with people accurately and independently describing his appearance, with consistency.

One story in the Babaji legend that stayed with me because it was so shocking and abrupt was of a man desperate for enlightenment who had, amazingly enough, managed to reach the mountain peak through sheer effort, where Babaji and his disciples resided. Declaring to Babaji that he simply must be enlightened, for nothing else mattered to him anymore, the man was met with detachment. Babaji told him to throw himself over the edge of the cliff, to his certain death, because it would be the only way he would reach his desired spiritual state of freedom.

Much to the shock of the disciples witnessing this apparently heartless exchange, the man instantly did so! Babaji bade them to go and collect the man's broken body, and upon bringing the body to the Master, he brought it back to life, perfectly healed and granted the man discipleship.

Before we all contemplate tossing ourselves off cliffs (not the moral of this story!) we should be aware that this is a teaching story. It is meant to teach that the way to the Divine is to have such passion that it becomes what matters most to us. As those of us on the spiritual path know, it gets pretty damn tough the more we progress and it is the passion for the Divine that is the heart-fuel that keeps us going when it's all going to hell in a handbasket!

What Babaji and his teachings offer us, at least in the context of this chapter, is the spiritual fruition of our soul purpose, which serves not only ourselves but all of evolution. This Master, like Merlin, works on a higher plane of existence where individuals are connected with insofar as they can assist others. It is a group consciousness.

That being said, the teachings that he has passed on to his beloved students say that anyone who sincerely speaks Babaji's name with love and respect is given blessing, which is an extraordinary generosity.

I had a special experience of this recently. I was lying in the sun, resting, and flicking through the blog of another spiritual teacher on my mobile phone. As I read of various travels that teacher had taken in India, feeling that tug that India has upon my heart, I spontaneously spoke Babaji's name. It just came out of my heart, out of my mouth, whilst my conscious mind was surprised.

In an instant, I saw a shimmering light before me and this reality of the physical world appeared to open up, somehow cracking open, even whilst I was lying in the sun, completely connected to my body, in my green, leafy backyard in Sydney. Beyond the shimmering vortex of light, and the cracking open of this reality, I could clearly perceive Babaji, though it was as if he was at a great distance. He made a simple declaration which I understood to be a blessing and without thinking the response erupted from me, "By your grace, Master." My heart swelled whilst my mind was curious as I had never consciously connected in a direct fashion with this Master, nor ever imagined I would.

What I learned from my encounter with him is that although he is so far advanced that I couldn't have imagined he would be so aware of individuals unless they were disciples of his from other lifetimes, demonstrating great spiritual promise, he is compassionate and interested in all beings.

To be offered a blessing in response to a simple prayer genuinely requesting it, is an incredible grace. Some may think that the ease of asking for this blessing renders it of less importance, but blessings are powerful. They can ameliorate karma and open up a path of grace, a proverbial path through the wilderness.

The times when we are doing 'okay' are not the times when the energy of grace received through a blessing matters the most. It is when we are in darkness, struggling with the weight of human experience and trying to keep our light burning, but fearing that we cannot, that the grace of a blessing is important. It is the energy of grace that is there for us when we cannot rely on anything else. In those rare moments that we may feel that we cannot even rely upon our own inner spiritual resources, gained through our divine connection, which are vast indeed, to see us through, a blessing will support us. Blessings are given when needed, whether we are in struggle or not. When they 'vest' or come to life is when needed also. The helping hand of the Divine reaching to hold us when we are falling is the action of the blessing in motion. All we need do is ask.

DIAMOND – DORJE

In Tibetan Buddhism there is a commonly found spiritual tool called the Dorje. It is a small staff in a particular shape, and it symbolises the lightning bolt of truth and the indestructible nature of divine truth, in that it prevails no matter what may try to thwart or distort it.

In the spiritual tradition there is a third body that is built through the process of initiation, which is known as the diamond body. We have the golden body that is the fusion of spirit and matter, bringing the body to consciousness. We explored that in Chapter 6. There is the light body, which we explored in Chapter 16, which is the energetic apparatus through which light can enter matter and allow for the golden body, and eventually the diamond body to come to fruition. The diamond body is the body of the Master that has reached spiritual culmination and will no longer be subject to transformational forces, becoming a deathless and indestructible form of consciousness, beyond death and anchored in radiant clarity, just like Babaji.

I wondered about including this topic in the book because although it made sense, I am always questioning myself (and my guides) about my spiritual teachings. I want them to be practical, useful and accessible, relevant to our daily lives. The answer that I promptly received to my questioning on this topic is that whilst we will be in differing stages of approaching the diamond body, the preparation for it is still relevant to those that will be reading this work, so I have included it willingly.

A diamond is formed through intense heat and pressure within the earth, becoming a gem so stunning and hard that it can cut glass. It is this symbology that relates to the diamond body. That a diamond can cut rather than be cut suggests that it is indestructible and that is mirrored by the teaching that the diamond body is the last vehicle of higher consciousness in ascended human form – it is the divine human at the highest level of initiation. Beyond that, there are other initiations in other realms of evolution perhaps, but for our human school, the diamond body is the highest level of service that we can attain – at least that I am aware of at this time through my spiritual teachers on the inner planes.

That a diamond is formed through pressure mirrors the process of spiritual initiation itself, which is like being inside a pressure cooker, integrating and breaking down, emerging in a different state at the end – a divine meal rather than raw uncombined ingredients.

What contributes to the worth of a diamond is its brilliance and clarity. These qualities are developed within us over lifetimes of initiation. The initiation process strips us of attachment, of stories and memories that we have used to identify ourselves, to create a compelling illusion of ego, which 'explains' who we are and how we are in the world.

These stories will often arise in meditation as memories and discursive thought that have no relation to the present moment. The trick is to learn to change our relationship to them. Rather than falling into them, we can observe and let them pass through. Neither indulging nor resisting, there is an open awareness created through which our replaying of past experiences can be released. We can actually allow it to 'play itself out' and lose steam, rather than fuelling it with our energy and contributing to its momentum to keep going.

It isn't an easy habit to develop, this changing relationship to our stories and dramas, but with will power and compassion, patience and a sense of humour, it can happen over time and we can create a deep sense of inner spaciousness and breathing room as a result. In the absence of those stories there is openness and receptivity within us, and much more room for the divine light to shine. We become more brilliant, our light shining brighter. We are being polished into more clarity.

The diamond itself may have come into your life as piece of jewellery or not at all. You can work with the mandala and the Angel of Diamond just as well. Diamonds are expensive, clear when polished, often yellow and opaque when raw. When polished they can be clear, yellow (champagne is very pale or cognac is much darker), pink or even black in colour.

Diamond amplifies energy without discriminating between what we want amplified or not. This can seem merciless and hard at times, as whatever is in the energy field, positive or negative, will be amplified. It may be one of the reasons that a lot of relationship issues 'hit the fan' when a woman starts wearing a diamond engagement ring! The positive view of this is that diamond is a healer without partiality.

What struck me about Babaji was that although there is an unflinching hardness within him, no amount of cajoling or manipulation would have any effect on him whatsoever, his aim is benevolent; it is to uncover the divine truth within, assisting all who call upon him. Diamond is the same. There is no partiality or preference, just genuine assistance and nothing is held back.

In the diamond trade there are diamonds known as war diamonds, conflict gems or blood diamonds. These are sold in situations where proceeds are used towards violent ends, often to promote political insurgency. To avoid fuelling this process, attempts were made to certify where stones were sourced, so that purchasers could be sure that their purchase had not led to warfare and furthered violence. Bribery and corruption has been uncovered and the effectiveness of certification has been questioned. If in doubt, ask your angels to help you, particularly the Angel of Diamonds, so that you acquire a diamond with harm to none.

The pursuit of spiritual wealth, just as material wealth, can come at great cost. The teachings that we can take from the conflict diamond industry are manifold. That in seeking the spiritual goal there can be war and violence and we have to pay special attention not to fuel this process, to find a path of balance (we spoke of the middle way in Chapter 10). That we have a choice where we invest our energy, even in pursuit of something valuable, the end does not necessarily justify the means. And perhaps finally that despite the appearance of great spiritual value, we must trust what we feel – not our emotional reactions or pre-conditioned opinions – but our intuition that shines pure and quiet underneath all psychological anguish and debate. In trusting in that feeling, quiet and pure, shining bright like a diamond, we can be unmoved by that which is not worth building up with our attention and energy, and instead stay lovingly focused on truth.

HEALING WITH BABAJI AND DIAMOND

This quick and simple healing process can be done with the mandala or stone, or on its own at any time. Save it for those moments however when you can be still, connect with your heart, even if just for that moment, and sincerely ask for help. It will be given.

Close your eyes and place your hands in prayer at your heart. Breathe deeply and slowly in and out and bring your attention to your heart centre.

When you are ready, say the following, "Babaji who loves me unconditionally, I offer myself in service to your task and open myself to your blessing (you can ask for a specific blessing if you wish to or just be open to a general blessing knowing that it will be what is needed). Thank you for your grace, merciful father of light. May the diamond light of your truth cut through illusion and allow me to see and know what will best serve now. Through divine grace and mercy, so be it."

If you wish to extend this simple healing practice, say, "I call upon the Angel of Diamond and ask for your healing truth, through mercy and compassion, so be it." Then simply sit with the intention to receive diamond light into whatever part of your body, or whichever chakras, require it.

When you are ready, simply bow your head and say 'thank you' and you have completed your healing session.

Be open to the truths that come to you in the coming days, weeks and months following this healing. They may not always be easy to receive, although sometimes they will bring you great joy, and whether palatable at the time or not, they will always be leading you more deeply into divine grace, towards your absolute spiritual fulfilment.

If this chapter and also the next one, where we explore not only the soul star but also the earth star, hold some personal meaning for you, you may like to explore the popular "Earth Star Soul Star" meditation on the *Mystical Healing* meditation CD released by Blue Angel Publishing.

18.

ASCENDED MASTER MATAJI (Earth Star)
CRIMSON CUPRITE (Divine Feminine)

INITIATION OF FEMININE CONSCIOUSNESS

Gleaming rich red mud sparkles with shimmering flecks of gold. What is of earth, is of heaven.

In India there is a guru called Amma, which means 'mother'. To be distinguished from the better-known 'hugging saint' Amma, this 'other' Amma is a man. He carries this name as his spiritual task is to help others on their spiritual path, as a manifestation of the Divine Mother.

This might seem strange to Westerners, where we tend to associate the feminine and the Divine Mother with women. Those of us that have explored psychology will understand that within each human being, whether man or woman, there are both masculine and feminine energies that we are learning to make conscious and integrate. In India, this concept is more generally understood and the manifestation of divine energy can occur in men or women, with a particular masculine or feminine flavour, without being limited by gender.

It occurred to me as I was receiving the 'download' for this chapter that my closest friends are very balanced in their masculine and feminine sides.

My two closest female friends have well developed inner masculinity. They are feminine, receptive and attractive women, both dancers and healers by profession, and very health-conscious. They both value their relationships and are focused and passionate about their work as well. They have leadership ability and are independent thinkers, they can discern and cut through the appearances to get to the truth of a matter. They are in touch with their masculine side, powerful and effective in the world, whilst remaining in touch with their surrendered feminine state which expresses itself in a number of ways, but perhaps most strongly through their love of dance.

My two closest male friends are healthy, fit and strong. They love physical activity and have a strong connection to nature. They are both musicians and play from a surrendered and spontaneous place, on a number of instruments, and with their voices. They are relationship-oriented and place great worth on their friendships, and in particular, their connections with feminine energy, whether in the form of spiritual consciousness or their daughters. They are strongly masculine and feminine in a balanced way.

All of these precious friends of mine lead balanced lives, experience wellbeing and a living spiritual connection and are also tremendous fun to be around, whilst also being able to travel into the depths of human connection.

I have around me examples of men and women who are awakened and balanced, partaking of the gifts that Mataji promises us, which is the initiation of feminine consciousness. Feminine consciousness is less about how we dress or what we look like, whether men or women, and more about how we are within ourselves. Feminine consciousness creates space for life to happen, it is a receiving energy, a receptive and magnetic energy. It is expressed through the yin power that we spoke of in chapter 10 with the Old Master Lao Tzu. A well-developed feminine energy attracts a well-developed masculine energy that helps us set boundaries, discern and protect that which is important to us and to cut ties with that which no longer serves.

Sometimes it is just as hard for women in the modern Western world, as it is for modern Western men, to take this initiation into feminine consciousness. Particularly in the West we are just learning what it is to hold feminine wisdom and how essential that is to the survival and growth of the human species. Where we seem to get confused is when cultural stereotypes about what it is to be a successful person (woman or man) conflict with feminine wisdom, which is based in an understanding that an individual cannot prosper truly at the expense of another, ever.

Divine Feminine consciousness plays a special role on this planet and its spiritual growth, particularly for those of us in the Western world that have been learning to heal a split between the masculine and feminine consciousness within ourselves and in our culture that has led to many problems in our own relationships and the environment.

I had a short, amusing dream that helped me understand this. Proving that the unconscious mind, which is a vehicle of Divine Feminine consciousness, has a sense of humour and much efficiency, the dream consisted of one scene. A woman with long red curly hair was peacefully lying on her belly, flat on the earth. A tall man stood above her, scratching his head in puzzlement, asking her what she was doing. "I am listening to the earth through my belly," replied the woman, as though it were the most obvious and sensible thing in the world to do, even though the man found it unfathomable.

The dream showed me how different masculine and feminine consciousness were and at that time in my personal path, how they really didn't understand each other's modus operandi! The woman, listening through her belly to feel the communications of the earth, much like a snake, was a symbol of the feminine consciousness. This is the part of us that feels for guidance, for direction, for union with greater spiritual beings (such as the earth, crystals, our angels and master guides), rather than the masculine consciousness that seeks to analyse and understand, to perhaps formulate a plan in advance and proceed to bring it to fruition. It is more dynamic and active in comparison to the receptive state of feminine consciousness. They can ultimately serve each other, working well together. Ideally, as we explored in Chapter 10, we will master balance.

However for that to happen, just as with any team, we have to know more of the players, what their strengths are, how they can be able to blossom to be all that they can be and how their natural tendencies can be best used in service to a group purpose. To that end, there will be times when we need to focus more on the feminine to gain healing and wisdom before integrating it back into relationship with the masculine energy. At other times we will need to focus on the masculine and so on. It is balancing a marriage of energies within that can be opposing or complementary, depending on how we work with them. It is the feminine consciousness itself that enables what was once opposing to become integrated and complementary.

At any time that we are going through a growth spurt, trying to integrate new ideas, new behaviours, new vibrations into our being, feminine consciousness is going to create a holding space through which transformation can happen. So when we want to shift from one level of being to another (perhaps a healthier, more abundant, more open or more confident version of ourselves), focusing on feminine consciousness will help to get us there. Remember in Chapter 15 when we spoke of the grace of spiritual growth, and how it is a divine happening in the sense that we cannot force it, it is conferred as a talent and a gift? Opening up and developing our feminine consciousness increases our capacity to receive that gift – indeed all spiritual gifts and assistance.

In the nature-based pagan tradition of Wicca (also sometimes known as the Craft or the Old Religion), and in the Celtic spiritual traditions of the Arthurian legend, the masculine is symbolised by the sword, which cuts and clarifies, and the feminine by the chalice, that receives and holds. These old traditions realise what we are attempting to remember as modern humanity, which is that these energies are meant to go together, not that one is to be preferred over another.

The cultural shift in modern humanity is towards reclaiming and valuing the feminine role in this process without discounting the significance of the masculine as a partner to the feminine. This can mean finding a way to express one's masculine role as protector, provider, leader and guide to the feminine internally and externally. The internal feminine is essentially one's own values and one's own body and one's relationship to oneself. The feminine externally is essentially our relationships with others – women and men, animals and the environment. Allowing the feminine, that part that genuinely feels and expresses our truths, to be heard and honoured, supported by our actions in the world, builds a happier psychic marriage between these energies within us. We can then be a healthier, more stable and empowered presence in our outer relationships and the world around us.

What that looks like, expressed through a physical body, is profound. It is a different relationship to the environment, to our own bodies and health, to how food is grown and tended, to the sorts of chemicals and medications that we accept or do not accept. It is demonstrated in a healing of the relationship to our own bodies, to exercise, to eating and to our mothers and fathers. It is a surrender of the fear of men or the hatred of women, or vice versa. It is a shift from power plays between masculine and feminine, to relationship that is working towards a common goal, inner team work rather than feeling at odds with yourself, pulled in differing directions. There will still be difference between the masculine and feminine energies, and even tension as we grow and develop at times, but rather than responding to that tension with aggressive attempts to dominate or reject, it can bring energy and excitement to life.

Men have a particular role in this process. Some of the most spiritually aware men that I have met are staunch defenders and protectors of the feminine. They are frequently surrounded by female admirers who are attracted to their masculinity and also feel safe because they know that they are accepted and appreciated for who they are as women, rather than being treated as something to acquire or as a challenge that needs to be conquered and turned into a trophy.

For women, we have a particular ability to help birth this new consciousness on earth. To be able to fulfil our spiritual potential as the co-creatrix or mother of new consciousness and culture on earth, we need to learn to recognise and appreciate innate feminine spirituality.

Part of our soul task in living in a female body is to take this journey. The soul that chooses to incarnate in female form is choosing to have a direct and immediate experience of the feminine wisdom of cycles of life, death and regeneration, and the capacity to gestate and give birth in a way that is unique to our gender.

A man can experience the feminine, and it is important for his own growth that he does, but he will not experience it in exactly the same way that a woman is able to do, although both men and women can learn to live in a way that is respectful of Divine Feminine consciousness, and the Divine Feminine needs to live in both men and women.

How and what we choose to give birth to, how we choose to nourish and mother that creation, and how willing we are to release it into the world, is how we grow spiritually on the Divine Feminine path.

Our spiritual growth may come through how we raise our children if we choose to have them. It can also happen through our art, music, writing or creativity in any form. Or through our vocation, our work, relationships. Perhaps most profoundly, our growth can occur through how we choose to be true to our feminine knowledge in a world that is only just beginning to learn the necessity of such wisdom – even though we need it to move from barely surviving as a species and a planet, to thriving. This is the same for men and women.

Thanks to your soul for the courage to incarnate as a woman this lifetime, or as a man who has the wisdom and sense to recognise and honour, rather than fear or degrade, the feminine principle. May you taste the delights of feminine power and potency, have the strength to experience what it is to be a wise woman or man of wisdom, sharing that with others to cultivate a new human consciousness of loving support and feminine wisdom on this planet.

ASCENDED MASTER MATAJI – EARTH STAR

The Earth Star is how our soul connects to the earth. It is also how the earth connects with our soul. What we experience as our day-to-day consciousness is what manifests energetically through the living flow between the Soul Star and Earth Star.

In the early days of my spiritual training this lifetime, much focus was on reaching the soul star. All I wanted to do was consciously connect with spirit in continually clearer and more expanded ways. I believed it would hold the answers to all my questions and become a divine best friend on my path. I knew it held the energy to awaken the spiritual gifts that I wanted to access too – like clairvoyance and channelling ability.

I would gaze at my first spiritual teacher, an attractive, eccentric blonde Aquarian with a penchant for constantly exploring new topics, and wish with all my heart that I could tap into the spiritual source with the same confidence and certainty that she had attained. In time, my wish came true, and my conscious connection to the spiritual worlds was strengthened, the natural spiritual awareness that I had as a child was expanded into a clearer experience of conscious divine presence. I had access to spiritual worlds and information that I used to help myself, but just as much to help others too. I became a spiritual reader and more tentatively, a spiritual healer too. I worked with many clients, testing my levels of trust in divine guidance to grow more with each session, running workshops, writing articles for spiritual magazines and stepping into my heart-centred vocation of spiritual teacher.

After about seven or so years of this, with my constant urging to go beyond what I had done and explore the 'next level' of divine experience, awakening and manifestation, my prayers were answered, as all prayers always are. I didn't realise it at the time, as it didn't seem like an answer to a prayer but a huge block to my progress. During the lead up to a series of workshops that I taught every year, I felt like I suddenly hit a wall that had never been there before! I couldn't access higher guidance through my crown chakra, as I had done relatively easily my entire life. It was like going to take a breath, with every expectation that I would indeed breathe, only to find that I couldn't. It was something of a shock, as instead I felt as though I was plopped crown-first, like a turnip, into the earth.

I couldn't channel as I normally did and I felt that my spiritual wings had been clipped. I wasn't devastated, because some part of me somehow knew that I was a light being and would always be no matter what else happened, but I was certainly confused and frustrated and uncertain about how to proceed with my work if I couldn't do what I had always done, which was lead, crown-first, through many a spiritual encounter.

I finished up those workshops – which fortunately enough were run with long-term clients who were advanced in their own right and more than happy to roll with the changes that I was experiencing. However soon after this I stopped teaching for some years and began an entirely new level of personal development and spiritual growth work to deal with the changes that I couldn't understand but expected were at least trying to lead me somewhere.

I only realised years later what was actually happening during that time. I was going into the earth star chakra to learn what it was that my soul light wanted to do through this particular 'Alana body' this lifetime. Some ten years later or so, that message is still unfolding in some surprising directions. I had a conversation with a long-term mentoring client the other day about how the most surprising spiritual direction will be withheld until we trust enough to receive it, even whilst part of us (like that tall inner man, scratching his head with puzzlement in my dream) wonders if we are off track somewhat.

Eventually my crown connection opened in luscious fullness again, of its own accord, quite naturally. After many years of deep connection with my own unconscious (my feminine consciousness) through dream work, deep healing work with my body through journaling those dreams, and body-centred meditation (I wasn't able to go flying out of the top of my head around the universe, I was 'spiritually grounded', excuse the pun), my experience of the energy entering the crown chakra was so much more powerful and physical.

My whole body could receive the light in a way that I had not previously been able to, nor ever really considered was important. This then started a process of physical transformation that still continues to this day. I have been on journeys with my body, as an expression of spirit, that I never imagined in my wildest dreams would have happened. For me this has been so special, but unless I was 'spiritually grounded', I never would have 'stayed home' in my body long enough to have such experiences.

I have shared my teaching about the importance of trust in your life experience numerous times in this book. To trust in your life experience is to trust in the Divine Feminine and how it chooses to unfold through you, knowing it will always serve your growth, whether you are initially comfortable with that process or not. Another teaching I have to share with you about this is that it can be wise to court the edge of our discomfort, that is the growth edge rather than the comfort zone, at least as often as we can bear.

As we connect with the Earth Star, which holds the earth-part of the soul plan, our life path opens up, sometimes in unexpected, but always in soul-oriented, ways. We may want to be a healer and be inspired by other healers that we admire, and yet find that our method of healing is to be quite different, and that this suits us perfectly. We are not all meant to be the same colour or the same shape. Nature is an abundance of creative diversity. Our earth-existence is held within the protection and wisdom of nature. As we explore our Earth Star connection, we awaken the promise of our earth-based spiritual path, of why we are here, for what purpose we were born and what task we have to attend to this lifetime. Mataji helps us with this connection, to realise and express our own unique natural spiritual beauty upon the earth, just as she does.

Mataji, an Indian term meaning 'great mother', is said to dwell underground, deep in the body of the earth, in blissful and ecstatic meditation. The fact that she has reached the bliss of divine union, whilst deep in the earth, makes her a guiding light for all of us in earthly form advancing towards the realisation that heaven is not only over our heads, but underneath our feet and in fact in every part of our being. For those advanced spiritual seekers that are learning to honour the feminine path that receives all, including the earth itself and her sacred flesh manifest as our bodies, Mataji is a loving benefactor.

Beings such as Mataji and Babaji that are ascended and therefore no longer subject to the laws of the physical world, such as death, but choose to remain upon the earth, hold a great light for evolving humanity. The great sages choose their moment of departure from the earth very carefully. They understand that their light holds a certain balance and that their departure will have an effect on that balance. Timing is chosen so that the earth can handle the shock of changing light. Often other light beings incarnate so that a change-over can occur and the evolution of humanity, and the earth, will be held, stable and supported. We will explore more about the sages and saints and their wonderful spiritual help for us in *Crystal Saints and Sages 777* later on in this series.

There is a particular story about Mataji that I like. It is said that her spiritual brother, Babaji, was speaking to his disciples and his beloved spiritual sister Mataji was also present, rising up out of the earth in a golden bubble of ecstatic bliss, as she was prone to do from time to time.

Babaji said that he was going to plunge himself back into the cosmic currents, free from his physical form now, because he was so at one with the Divine that his separate existence was of no relevance. Mataji asked him to stay on the earth. Babaji replied, "There is no difference whether I stay or leave, as this physical form is not real, only the divine light is real." Mataji replied, with Divine Feminine wisdom, "If there is no difference whether you stay or leave, then I ask you to stay." Babaji agreed to serve her wish, which in turn served the planet.

Mataji and her feminine wisdom understands that whilst the divine light of which Babaji spoke is reality, the Divine Feminine expressing itself as this world of forms is real too. The physical world is the Divine in form and it is another legitimate face of the Divine. She understands that there needs to be light, and that this light exists for the purpose of serving the enlightenment and spiritual freedom of all beings. She dwells in the darkest recesses of our earthly world, and is luminous. She is the master of demonstrating that even in darkness, our light is alive, and where the light is needed, it must shine.

It is Mataji's wisdom that prompts us to live in a certain area, where our light is needed, or to travel to a certain country, or take a particular job or even go to a particular gym or supermarket. We will be bringing our light there, and as silly or useless as that may seem, it is actually important and helpful. This becomes more so as we progress on the spiritual path and our light becomes more powerful and effective. So there is great value in us learning to honour what our heart intuitions tell us about which places to visit and when, what groups to join or leave, and when, and so forth.

A good prayer to Mataji is, "Beloved mother who loves me unconditionally, may I be guided to shine my light where it can best serve." Then trust in your life experiences and where you are led. It can be the smallest encounters that make a huge difference and simply even having you drive a particular way to work can serve. Don't work yourself into a state of worry. Mataji loves and serves us all. To return that service to her through opening to allow her to guide us to our 'right place' in the physical world is a beautiful devotional gesture. She can then help us to manifest our highest expression of soul light through our Earth Star chakra awakening. Our experience of our physical life then becomes even more spiritually rich, authentic and integrated.

If you are on the other side of this pattern, having awakened a strong connection to the earth, and perhaps also your body, and are now wishing to call to you the awakening light of spirit, then work with the exercise in the previous chapter after you complete the healing process at the end of this chapter. We are all ultimately reaching the same destination, we just may take different routes to get there.

CRIMSON CUPRITE – DIVINE FEMININE

Cuprite grows in crystal formations that are geometric, hinting at its ability to work with the sacred geometry of our body and soul, bringing healing to our innate patterning. Crimson Cuprite is the most red and vibrant form of Cuprite which can otherwise be brown or black. It looks like the red blood of the earth and is drenched in a lush feminine energy. As soon as I saw it for the first time, I was under its spell. As I held it, I knew it to be a tantric stone in the sense that tantra is the healing of relationship between masculine and feminine, spirit and matter, and that this stone would support and stimulate that process with passion.

My first personal encounter with Crimson Cuprite happened when I was at the end of a rather intense teaching tour in a mining town in the north of Australia. The area was very polarised, with a lot of negativity, suffering and pain. A number of very light, luminous souls were drawn to live and work in the area, undoubtedly drawn to the darkness and realising, as Arlo Guthrie put it, "You can't have a light without a dark to stick it in."

With the support of some faithful and powerful students, we did a huge amount of lightwork and healing in the area. The physical work of spiritual healing through music and teaching workshops and offering readings was a small percentage of the work that I did there, spiritually speaking. It felt like a lot of heavy lifting to bring through light and consciousness, integration and peace to such a polarised community, even though the desire for it was very strong, which helped a lot. At times it felt like my students and I were standing in the midst of light and dark, trying to hold them in relationship with each other. Sort of like brokering peace in the Middle East!

At the end of my time there I felt shattered. Soon after I had finished my work there, one of my advanced mentoring clients, a crystal master in her own right, provided me with a piece of Crimson Cuprite, which was my first physical experience of the stone. The energy rebalancing, the healing and the strengthening that this little stone gave me was tremendous. It is a small flat piece of rock but it packs a punch. I am actually sitting on the stone as I write this chapter (it works on the base chakra!) and it is helping the writing flow and my energy levels increase rather than deplete through the work.

It was the sense of being held and regenerated through that holding, that was my visceral experience of Crimson Cuprite. To connect with this stone is to connect with the Divine Feminine in all of her wisdom – her powers of restoration and re-energising, of rebalancing and cleaning of the blood and igniting of the divine light within the form of our cells. We will explore the concept of shakti or Divine Feminine energy in more depth in *Crystal Goddesses 888,* but for now it is enough to know that Crimson Cuprite stimulates our shakti or vital life force and encourages it to rise up through the chakras. This is helpful when we are excessively weighed down by astral gravity. That is the weight of our own habits and the habits of others around us that may create resistance to raising our vibration as we seek to leave fear behind us in favour of trust. It is helpful also if we are unable to easily access the refined vibration of the higher spiritual planes. Crimson Cuprite gives us a boost. It will also pull down higher light into form, so if we tend towards 'flying about' we will be more grounded.

This stone builds our connection to the Earth Mother and goddess energies more generally, helping women in particular to learn how to hold such divinity in conscious awareness in their own bodies. To awaken to the goddess in us is to connect to a transpersonal, eternal truth of the feminine which can nourish and inspire us to let go of issues that would limit us and hold us back, such as guilt, shame, doubt, hate or self-worth and self-esteem issues. You probably can't imagine a goddess saying, "Oh I couldn't do that!" – she would be too busy already doing what she felt in her heart to do! This fearless willingness to live the heart truths is what Crimson Cuprite can help women, and men, to access.

If you are working on issues of healing through the generations of women in your family, Crimson Cuprite will help. In this process we can become aware of what transmissions of spiritual light, biological balance or weakness, or psychological functioning has been handed down through our DNA. We can then work to rebalance this within us, healing the family legacy, which may well be part of our spiritual task this lifetime. Crimson Cuprite helps bring what was hidden in family stories or shame to light so that it can be dealt with and released. That information may come through feminine sources such as inner vision or meditation, or knowing that just arises from within, and through our dreams.

I had an experience of this once as I was grieving for a love that I had lost. Except I hadn't lost a love. As I was letting this grief be expressed and released, it hit me that I was releasing the grief that belonged to my grandmother who had lost her most beloved husband at a young age and had never fully gotten over it. That was in her cells, passed on to my mother and then to me. As my heart expanded and opened through my own path, that old energy had to go. So out it came. Crimson Cuprite helps us have awareness of this process whilst stimulating it to occur for our own growth.

Crimson Cuprite also helps to awaken talents that were never fully developed through the family line so that the soul light seeking to manifest itself through the family group can be expressed. We don't live the unlived lives of our predecessors, but we can sometimes be asked to bring through talents that we are able to handle, which our forebears, for various reasons, may not have been able to express. If this resonates for you, you may like to work with the previous chapter on Babaji to really pull in spiritual light before doing the healing process at the end of this chapter to anchor it in the body.

Crimson Cuprite helps us connect as spirit to the earth, to strengthen the base chakra, where we heal issues of survival and being in a body, and learn to move deeper into the earth being herself, to connect with the spiritual light made manifest in our Earth Star chakra. From that place we can manifest our light through how we choose to live and become capable of holding the container of Divine Feminine wisdom – openness, receptivity, wisdom, patience, willingness and strength – so that this sacred life can occur through us.

HEALING WITH MATAJI AND CRIMSON CUPRITE

Have your stone and/or mandala with you, preferably near the base of your spine.

Sitting comfortably, say the following, "I call upon the true Ascended Master Mataji, dwelling in ecstatic bliss within the earth, and through her unconditional love, I call for her blessing now. I call upon the Angel of Crimson Cuprite and her feminine power. I call upon Divine Feminine wisdom and presence, that the masculine and feminine energies within me may experience healing, reconciliation and sacred marriage, according to the highest good, so be it."

Close your eyes and focus on your breath, becoming aware of the breath deepening and beginning to reach down to your deepest belly. Relax and let the breath flow for at least 33 breaths.

Beneath you, sense an opening up of vast space. There is openness, emptiness and peace. Allow your awareness to descend, moving into that vast space and feeling peace as you do so.

There is great power here, but also deep peace and stillness. Keep breathing and going deeper and deeper, descending with each breath. If you find yourself resisting or coming up out of the space, simply breathe and descend once more. See if you can become still, heavy and focused, with your awareness following your breath and your perception of the space opening up beneath you.

Spend as long as you like in that space, or at least 33 breaths.

When you are ready, perceive a warm vibrant red light glowing and pulsing beneath you, deep in this space. As you observe the light you are drawn to it. You notice that it glows and vibrates with golden light within the red. It crackles and fizzes with life force and expands. You may perceive that it has its own vibration, perhaps a low, slow deep sound or a subtle higher pitched resonance.

Let yourself simply observe this, your Earth Star chakra. If you wish, allow some of your awareness to blend with the chakra, feeling how you come alive with great potency.

When you are ready, perceive energy from that Earth Star chakra beginning to push up towards the base chakra of your body, flowing up through your spine with exactly the right amount of intensity for you at this time. The energy rises and expands out from your spine in all directions. It is reaching for the crown of your head. It may reach up and out of the crown, pouring down over you like a golden fountain of light, or it may stay at a particular part of your body, burning through blockages, bringing healing. Trust. What you need is what will occur.

Stay with the presence of this light for however long feels good or for at least 33 breaths.

Become aware of a source of light above your head, the Soul Star chakra. The light from this chakra is drawn, as if by a magnetic force, towards your Earth Star chakra. The intensity of light that serves your highest good at this time is what will be attracted to your Earth Star chakra now. Trust. Notice the flow of light between the Soul and Earth Star chakras. Stay with your breath and allow this process to happen.

You may notice tingling, warmth, thoughts or feelings arising. Let any such sensations simply come and go. Stay with the process for as long as feels appropriate for you.

When you are ready simply place your hands in prayer and say, "Thank you Mataji, for your blessing which I gratefully receive now, so be it."

Surround yourself with a rich red and golden light, using your intention. Allow this light to form a perfect bubble around you and feel that it is close enough that you feel held in it and spacious enough that you have plenty of room to breathe and move freely within that force field of light.

Bring your attention to your feet and your bottom sitting in the chair, letting your awareness expand to your hands and moving your fingers and toes, gently bringing your awareness fully back into the room and the present moment.

You have completed your healing process.

You may find in the following days (or even weeks if the process has been deep), that there are symptoms of healing. You may notice changes in blood pressure, dizziness, or even nausea followed by feelings of being very grounded and energised. Be kind to yourself, and if in doubt, consult your health practitioner. Exercise to an extent that feels good for your body. Also trust in the physical changes that occur in other ways in your life as the mother's blessing, though it may seem subtle, will have a powerful effect over time.

SPIRITUAL GUIDANCE FROM THE CRYSTAL MASTERS

We, your guiding Ascended Masters, love you without condition
We help you remember and fulfil your divine life mission
We remind you to let go of your doubt and trust yourself completely
We help you remember that you, just like us, are divinity

We reach to you from within your own heart
We are always with you, never apart
We guide you to heal yourself and in doing so, the earth
You are a sacred mid-wife, helping her rebirth

We speak to you through signs, through intuition and dreams
We call you to trust in what you feel, all is not as it seems
We ask you to trust in the divine plan that is at play
Surrender into it now, let the divine have its way

It is your job to be all that you can possibly be
To live, to feel all that you feel, to know you are free
Choose love over fear, we'll help you if you ask
We are always supporting you in your divine life task

PRAYER – AFFIRMATION

To invoke the healing power of all the crystal masters, at any time, you can repeat the
following affirmation quietly in your mind, or aloud:

Crystal Masters, help me through unconditional love
With the power of Earth below and Heaven above.
Of my own free will, so be it.

AND FROM HERE?

I have loved having your energy as a part of the experience of this book – it comes to life through you, dear one. Continue on the journey together if you wish, I would love to have you be a part of it. Your loving respect for the Crystalline kingdom is always returned as respect, support and abundance to you. May your heart open to receive and may all beings benefit from your healing journey.

New Blue Angel Publishing titles in this series by Alana Fairchild are coming soon.

In *Crystal Goddesses 888 – Manifesting with the Divine Power of Heaven and Earth*, Alana guides you into a world of abundance, prosperity and manifesting your soul destiny through the Divine Feminine wisdom.

In *Crystal Lifetimes 999 – Past Life Healing with the Divine Power of Heaven* and Earth, Alana channels guidance for identifying and resolving past life patterns through the portal of crystal healing, bringing new life to your current lifetime!

And Alana will take you on a sublime spiritual journey to the loving wisdom teachers from star systems far and wide, that love the Earth and wish to help human spiritual evolution and ascension in *Crystal Stars 11.11 – Awakening with the Divine Power of Heaven and Earth*.

This series began with *Crystal Angels 444 – Healing with the Divine Power of Heaven and Earth* and more in the series are soon to come.

ABOUT ALANA

When something is natural for you, especially if it has been that way since childhood, you can assume for a long time that it is natural for everyone. It took me some years to realise that my sensitivity, healing ability and natural conscious connection to the higher planes of spiritual guidance was unusual.

It wasn't long after that realisation that I stepped away from a career as a lawyer (spiritual law was always more interesting to me anyway) and I began my vocation as a spiritual healer and teacher.

From the earliest memories I had, I was always in conscious connection with spirit. It has always been as natural as breathing to me and is probably the gift that I am most grateful for this lifetime – though I have gratitude for plenty.

I felt the call to spiritual guidance at age nine, and began offering advice to my fellow classmates in a schoolyard healing centre (under the tree, by the back gate in the playground). I remember at the time thinking, "I need more life experience to be able to do this properly!" which was quite a thought for a nine-year-old. Yet I knew that sitting under that tree in the playground like a wise old sage (instead of a primary-school girl) offering some sort of wisdom was exactly what I was meant to be doing.

Not so many years later, as a young woman in my teens, I realised that my soul was a shaman and a priestess on this earth. The shaman is one who ventures into alternative realities to bring back wisdom, truth and insight for healing in this earthly reality. The priestess is one who honours the bridge between the inner and outer worlds, between heaven and earth, keeping the bridge open and helping others to learn how to walk that bridge, drawing the earth and heaven closer together.

The role of the modern shaman priestess is to keep the sacred intact and awaken it in the world. It is about living with head in the heavens and feet on the earth and pulling the two together into oneness through all parts of her being, in service of love.

My own sense of my ancient spiritual connection has manifested as a full-time vocational dedication to living, walking and talking the path of the soul, with special attention to healing for those seeking to carve out a life of individuality, courageously breaking with mass-opinion in favour of independent thought and personal spiritual integrity (a bit of rebellion can go a long way to finding your own truth, then you don't need to be the rebel quite so much, you can just be).

My work as a shaman and priestess is expressed in soul whispering, being a divine voice channel and a healer, teaching, dancing and singing (and playing!) with an international client base and creating broad product range including DVDs, CDs and the beautiful *Kuan Yin Oracle* and *Isis Oracle*.

To learn more about Alana and her work, visit her online at: **www.alanafairchild.com**

ABOUT THE ARTIST

Jane Marin is an accomplished artist, intuitive healer/coach, past life regressionist, author and Reiki/ Seichim Master/Teacher.

She holds diplomas in Child Psychology, Hatha Yoga Teaching, Bach Flower Essences and Certificates in Past Life Regression, Journal Therapy, Angel Therapy™, Crystal Light Healing Practitioner Level III, and Motivational Kinesiology IV.

Her background in dance prompted her to explore the healing powers of music and dance leading her to the ancient art of bellydance. She has been teaching this form of dance since 2004.

Jane's spiritual art and photography can now be purchased in her online shop as can her beautiful coffee table books.

Jane is the author of *The Me Book – A Journey of Self-discovery*, published in 2011 by Balboa Press to compliment her popular "Me Book" workshops.

To find out more about Jane Marin and her work, please visit her website: **www.inspiredartbyjanemarin.com**

THEMATIC INDEX BY CHAPTER

1. ASCENDED MASTER SERAPIS BEY (Karmic Grace)
CLEAR CALCITE (Detoxification
INITIATION OF DIVINE ALIGNMENT

divine grace
free will
getting published
healing power of loneliness
higher guidance
karma
soul plan
soul purpose
spiritual growing pains
spiritual urgency
spirituality and relationships
staying on your true path

2. ASCENDED MASTER EL MORYA (Higher Will)
BLUE STAR SAPPHIRE (Focus)
INITIATION OF YOUR PATH

constructive and destructive
    energy
death
direction
divine life path
focus
humility
integrating the shadow
positive destruction
psychic awakening
releasing the old for the new
saying no
self-belief
spiritual visions
terrorism
violence

3. ASCENDED MASTER LADY NADA (Sensitivity)
RHODOCHROSITE (Emotional Healing)
INITIATION OF THE CHILD WITHIN

awakening new talents
cats
comfort in the body
emotional healing
family of origin
force
gentleness and power
honouring all your feelings
inner child
parenting
power
sensitivity
sexuality
sharks

4. ASCENDED MASTER HILARION (Higher Mind)
GREEN CHRYSOPRASE (Renewal)
INITIATION OF DISCERNMENT

boundaries
compassion
discernment
higher mind
judgement
mental cleansing
new beginnings
number patterns
numbers
receiving guidance
sacred food ritual
trusting yourself

5. ASCENDED MASTER JESUS (Christ Consciousness)
ROSOPHIA (Love of the Mother)
INITIATION OF SACRIFICIAL LOVE

addictions
alcohol
betrayal and abandonment
Christ and sacrifice
divine mother
drugs
emotional boundaries
martyr
rescuer
sacred marriage of masculine and
    feminine
spiritual addiction
spiritual escape
trusting yourself

6. ASCENDED MASTER MARY MAGDALENE (The Awakened Feminine)
AQUA AURA QUARTZ (Crystal Alchemy)
INITIATION INTO THE BODY AWAKENED

devotion
divine experiences
divine feminine creation
family systems healing
healing the relationship to the body
living more creatively
opening to more energy channels
sacred body and enlightenment
sacred feminine
seeing God in the everyday
spiritual alchemy
staying conscious

7. ASCENDED MASTER YOGANANDA (Loving Service)
RHODONITE (Awakening Talent)
INITIATION OF EMPOWERED SERVICE

building a spiritual business
divine timing
genuine divine power
law of attraction
making it happen or allowing it to
    happen
making the impossible possible
patience and endurance
ready to be a healer
service and contribution
spiritual ability brought down to
    earth
vocation
your time to shine

8. ASCENDED MASTER KUTHUMI (Planetary Consciousness)
MOSS AGATE (Earth Healing)
INITIATION INTO PLANETARY HEALING

advanced healing path
chakra cleansing
chaos
earth healing
earth's spiritual evolution
enlightenment as spiritual
    graduation for humans
keeping calm in chaos
mass panic
spiritual purpose
the living tree

9. ASCENDED MASTER ST. GERMAIN (Violet Flame) AMETHYST (Spiritual Connection) INITIATION OF CONSCIOUS SPIRITUAL COMMUNICATION

alcohol addiction
channelling your own guidance
clearing the crown chakra
connecting with the soul through
    prayer
divine mother
dreams and spiritual schools
drug addiction
free will
gurus and charismatic teachers
healing others through your own
    healing
loving the earth
prayer and surrender
spiritual addiction
spiritual light
talking with the divine
your higher self as a phone line to
    heaven

10. ASCENDED MASTER LAO TZU (Eastern Wisdom) ZINCITE (Power) INITIATION INTO BALANCE

balance and integration
becoming more receptive
growing up spiritually
healing
law of attraction
letting go
power or force?
small can be powerful
spirituality of the lower chakras
star children
trust
trusting in the flow
yin and yang

11. ASCENDED MASTER KUAN YIN (Spiritual Rebel) PEARL (Amrita) INITIATION INTO ENLIGHTENMENT

being the change
blessings
charities
darker energies and interference
darkness serves the light
forgiveness
hate
individual consciousness
light and dark forces
mass consciousness
our own shadow
power of choice
protection
psychic attack
spiritual energies
spiritual rebels
vote with your wallet
we have so much power!

12. ASCENDED MASTER WHITE MATTHEW (Purity) DANBURITE (Innocence) INITIATION OF ORIGINAL SELF

becoming and being
divine co-creation
effects of schooling
healing shame and guilt
hope
innocence and purity of spirit no
    matter what
letting the past be the past
negative self-fulfilling prophecy
reality
spiritual insight
unveiling what already is

13. ASCENDED MASTER MOTHER MARY (Protection)
CELESTITE (Serenity)
INITIATION OF TRUST

abuse of power
dark side of spiritual teachers
divine intervention
getting published
grace and blessings
guiding hand
mini-miracles
power
protection
shadow side of spiritual
    organisations
She is with you even when you
    don't know it

14. BUDDHA (Compassion)
PERIDOT (Increase)
INITIATION OF THE BODHISATTVA VOW

being a healer
Bodhisattva vow
buddhas of past, present and future
childhood issues
compassion
compassionate listening
darkness and demonic energies
integrity and trust
moved by the cries of the world
overcoming negativity
personal agendas in healing
psychic clearing and protection
shadow and inner demons
shadow healers
soul breakthroughs
spiritual liberation
suffering and ego
tough love
truth-tellers

15. ASCENDED MASTER HELIOS (Consciousness)
CITRINE (Radiance)
INITIATION OF SPIRITUAL GROWTH

appearances can be deceiving
caterpillar and chrysalis
control and karma
disease, health and karma
from survival to abundance
generating optimism
healing inflation or feeling 'better
    than'
healing the solar plexus
integration
seeing the spiritual connections in
    relationships
spiral of growth
spiritual growing pains
spiritual teachers and their
    students
sun exposure
the consciousness of the earth
too much too soon
transformation
trusting what you feel
weight loss and eating issues

16. ASCENDED MASTER MERLIN (Alchemy)
MYSTIC MERLINITE (Activation)
INITIATION OF LIGHT BODY

advanced souls with multiple
incarnations
building light body
guilt, shame and environmental
    issues
Kali Yuga
living in your head versus
    grounding
mutational or spiritual growth
    symptoms

physical symptoms of energy flow
spiritual energy
spirituality in business
the dark age
undercover healers
vagueness and feeling spaced out

17. ASCENDED MASTER BABAJI (Soul Star) DIAMOND (Dorje) INITIATION OF SPIRITUAL FRUITION

advanced initiates
amplifying energy
bliss
bringing stuff to the surface
dropping emotional baggage
ego stories
passion for God
receiving a blessing directly
spiritual fulfilment in this lifetime
spiritual path speeding up
true nature of the soul
when a blessing helps us

18. ASCENDED MASTER MATAJI (Earth Star) CRIMSON CUPRITE (Divine Feminine) INITIATION OF FEMININE CONSCIOUSNESS

comfort zone vs. growth zone
Earth mother and goddess energies
feminine spiritual path for men
    and women
generational or family system
    healing
getting 'earthed' for a while
giving up power games
healing the physical body after
    spiritual work
masculine and feminine energies

men with a strong feminine energy
relationships
spiritual light via the body
unique spiritual purpose for men
unique spiritual purpose for
    women
women with a strong masculine
    energy
your light and your location

INDEX

Note to reader: The page numbers listed below refer to the page number on which the chapter dealing with each theme begins.

Crystal Angels 444
Healing with the Divine Power of Heaven & Earth

You have loving guides from the spiritual worlds of Crystals and Angels. They are ready to help you now.

In *Crystal Angels 444*, Alana Fairchild, author of the bestselling *Kuan Yin Oracle*, offers a truly unique approach to crystal healing, combining the natural healing properties of each crystal and its 'crystal angel' or 'spirit' with divine guidance channelled from heavenly angels such as Archangels Raphael, Gabriel, Metatron & Melchizedek. Together they help you bring your spirit and body together as one and live with more peace and prosperity, passion and purpose. Each chapter deals with a powerful precious stone and its heavenly angel and features a range of sacred rituals and processes to help you fully harness the healing potential of that stone, deepen your connection with yourself and the divine guidance supporting you and tap into the many gifts hidden within you.

You will delve deeply into a variety of topics including love, power and protection, eating and body image, self-esteem, addiction, feminine/masculine balance, wealth and prosperity, connecting with divinity, speaking your truth, dealing with your emotions, developing your spiritual talents and much more.

The book is enriched with many personal stories and spiritual experiences from the author which offer practical examples to bring the material to life.

You have important healing work to do on yourself and for the planet. *Crystal Angels 444* is written for you, to help you successfully complete your task, with greater happiness and fulfilment.

Featuring 18 full-colour Crystal Angel Mandalas by artist Jane Marin.

Paperback book, 368 pages.
ISBN: 978-1-922161-13-0

ALSO AVAILABLE IN THIS SERIES BY ALANA FAIRCHILD

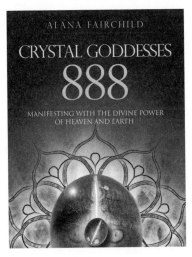

Crystal Goddesses 888
Manifesting with the Divine Power of
Heaven and Earth

*You have wise spiritual guides from the mystical worlds
of Crystals and Goddesses. They are ready to help you
now.*

Manifesting from your soul feels good. It isn't about
forcing the world to bend to your will, it is about
co- creating with the power of life itself. When you
manifest from your soul, you not only bring your visions to life, but you become more alive too. You are
healing yourself through the process of creation whilst your world transforms along with
you. This book is your guide to the many ways you can manifest from your soul. From
exploring the power of sound and light, to embracing darkness and healing through joy,
celebrating being different, honouring being a rebel and expressing your passion as well as
your compassion, you will be offered many ways to heal and manifest your divine destiny.

Crystal Goddesses 888, the next volume in the highly successful Crystal Spirituality
Series, will connect you to the power of heaven in the form of the wild and loving divine
feminine (and her many faces as goddesses from different spiritual traditions), and the
power of the earth in the form of crystals that support each goddess in bringing her gifts
of healing to you. With real life stories from the author to make the material practical
and accessible, this book guides you with humour and love to take the next step on your
path, creating your own version of heaven on earth. Whether you are new to all this, or
have been on your conscious path for years, you'll find a wealth of treasures in here. May
you blossom wildly on your beautiful life journey, held in the grace of the wild feminine
spirit that loves you unconditionally.

Featuring 18 full-colour Crystal Angel Mandalas by artist Jane Marin

Paperback book, 452 pages
ISBN: 978-1-922161-25-3

ALSO AVAILABLE IN THIS SERIES BY ALANA FAIRCHILD

Crystal Stars 11.11
Crystalline Activations with the Stellar Light Codes

The star light within your heart will lead you to sacred fulfilment for the spiritual benefit of all.

This book is for star seeds, old souls, lightworkers, visionaries, healers and hearts who hold a curiosity for the stars. This unique and powerful approach to crystal healing connects you with loving stellar beings and the precious stones that embody and enhance their transformational energy. Alana grounds the teachings with relevant and practical examples and the healing processes help you harness the therapeutic potential of each stone and form a bond with the stars so you can receive their wisdom and blessings.

Aligned with the 11.11 frequency, your celestial guides will help you shift personal paradigms and make rapid spiritual progress. Discover the healing and belonging that only comes from experiencing unity with the stars and the earth. Connect with Sirius, Andromeda, Alcyone in the Pleiades, Vega, Arcturus and others as you delve into treasured spiritual lessons on authenticity, soul passion, dark initiations, the cosmic priestess, supreme spiritual protection and more.

Beloved, you have illuminating sacred work to accomplish for yourself and the planet. Prepare yourself for the next stage of your journey with teachings and tools to help you shine like the star being you truly are.

Featuring 18 full-colour Crystal Angel Mandalas by artist Jane Marin.

Paperback book, 328 pages.
ISBN: 978-1-925538-76-2

ALSO AVAILABLE IN THIS SERIES BY ALANA FAIRCHILD

Crystal Mandala Oracle
Channel the Power of Heaven & Earth

This unique oracle deck is encoded with crystal frequencies, and the high vibrational energy of angels, ascended masters and goddesses, to empower you to channel the divine healing power of Heaven and Earth.

In this stunning, stand-alone deck, you will work with the vibrant crystal mandalas by Jane Marin, as featured in Alana Fairchild's popular books *Crystal Angels 444, Crystal Masters 333* and *Crystal Goddesses 888*. Alana shares loving spiritual guidance from the angels, masters and goddesses to help you integrate the frequencies of the crystals and higher beings that are featured in each of the cards. The Crystal Angels will help you heal your body, mind and soul. The Crystal Masters will support your spiritual growth and help you successfully pass through spiritual tests and initiations. The Crystal Goddesses will empower you to embody your spirit and express your soul purpose in the world.

This powerful deck will enhance your connection to the sacred worlds of higher beings and crystal energy, opening your heart to divine beauty and empowering your soul with loving consciousness.

Artwork by Jane Marin

54 cards and 244-page guidebook, packaged in a hardcover box set.
ISBN: 978-1-922161-89-5

ALSO AVAILABLE BY ALANA FAIRCHILD

BOOKS
The 3 Cs, Crisis, Confusion, Chaos
333 Oracle of Heart Wisdom
55 Keys
Crystal Angels 444
Crystal Goddesses 888
Crystal Stars 11.11
Happiness
The Kuan Yin Transmission™
Love your Inner Goddess
Magic of Isis
Messages in the Numbers
Sleep
Trust
What to do when you don't know what to do
Wisdom of Kuan Yin

DVDs
Kuan Yin: A Visual Meditation

JOURNALS
Goddess Isis Journal
Kuan Yin Oracle Journal
Lightworker Journal
Rumi Journal
Sacred Rebels Journal
Wild Divine Journal
Crystal Mandala Journal
Earth Warriors Journal
Love Your Inner Goddess Journal

ORACLE DECKS
Butterfly Affirmations
Crystal Mandala Oracle
Divine Circus Oracle
Earth Warriors Oracle

Isis Oracle
Isis Oracle: Pocket Edition
Journey of Love
Kuan Yin Oracle
Kuan Yin Oracle: Pocket Edition
The Kuan Yin Transmission™
Lightworker Oracle
Love Your Inner Goddess Oracle
Mother Mary Oracle
Rumi Oracle
Sacred Rebels Oracle
White Light Oracle
Wild Kuan Yin Oracle
Wild Kuan Yin Oracle: Pocket Edition
Wings of Wisdom Affirmation Cards

AUDIO CDS
Black Madonna
Chakra Meditations
Christ Consciousness Meditations
Divine Lotus Mother
For Love & Light on Earth
Ganesha: Meditations for Spiritual Success
Holy Sisters
Inner Power
Isis Power of the Priestess
The Kuan Yin Transmission™
Meditations with God
Meditations with Sekhmet & Narasimha
Mother Mary: Meditations for Grace
Mystical Healing
Past Life Healing
Radiance
Rumi Meditations
Star Child
Voice of the Soul

1.
ASCENDED MASTER SERAPIS BEY (Karmic Grace)
CLEAR CALCITE (Detoxification)
INITIATION OF DIVINE ALIGNMENT

2.
ASCENDED MASTER EL MORYA (Higher Will)
BLUE STAR SAPPHIRE (Focus)
INITIATION OF YOUR PATH

3.
ASCENDED MASTER LADY NADA (Sensitivity)
RHODOCHROSITE (Emotional Healing)
INITIATION OF THE CHILD WITHIN

ASCENDED MASTER HILARION (Higher Mind)
GREEN CHRYSOPRASE (Renewal)
INITIATION OF DISCERNMENT

5.
ASCENDED MASTER JESUS (Christ Consciousness)
ROSOPHIA (Love of the Mother)
INITIATION OF SACRIFICIAL LOVE

ASCENDED MASTER MARY MAGDALENE (The Awakened Feminine)
AQUA AURA QUARTZ (Crystal Alchemy)
INITIATION OF DISCERNMENT

7.
ASCENDED MASTER YOGANANDA (Loving Service)
RHODONITE (Awakening Talent)
INITIATION OF EMPOWERED SERVICE

8.

ASCENDED MASTER KUTHUMI (Planetary Consciousness)
MOSS AGATE (Earth Healing)
INITIATION OF PLANETARY HEALING

9.
ASCENDED MASTER ST. GERMAIN (Violet Flame)
AMETHYST (Spiritual Connection)
INITIATION OF CONSCIOUS SPIRITUAL COMMUNICATION

10.

ASCENDED MASTER LAO TZU (Eastern Wisdom)
ZINCITE (Power)

INITIATION INTO BALANCE

11.
ASCENDED MASTER KUAN YIN (Spiritual Rebel)
PEARL (Amrita)
INITIATION INTO ENLIGHTENMENT

12.

ASCENDED MASTER WHITE MATTHEW (Purity)
DANBURITE (Innocence)
INITIATION OF ORIGINAL SELF

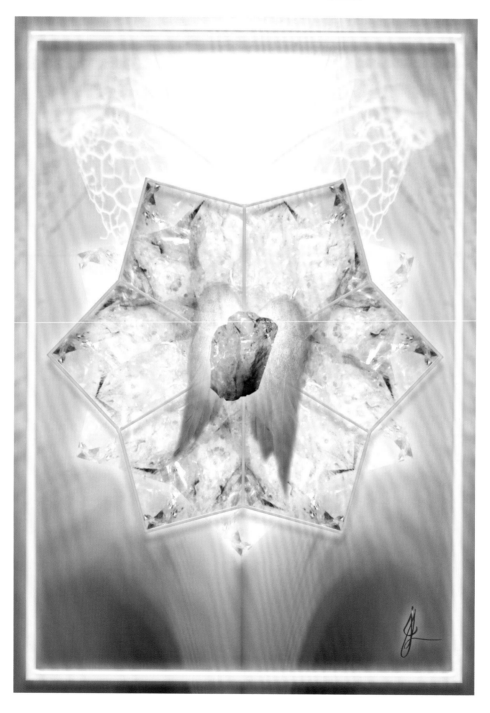

13.
ASCENDED MASTER MOTHER MARY (Protection)
CELESTITE (Serenity)
INITIATION OF TRUST

14.
BUDDHA (Compassion)
PERIDOT (Increase)
INITIATION OF THE BODHISATTVA VOW

15.
ASCENDED MASTER HELIOS (Consciousness)
CITRINE (Radiance)
INITIATION OF SPIRITUAL GROWTH

16.
ASCENDED MASTER MERLIN (Alchemy)
MYSTIC MERLINITE (Activation)
INITIATION OF LIGHT BODY

17.
ASCENDED MASTER BABAJI (Soul Star)
DIAMOND (Dorje)
INITIATION OF SPIRITUAL FRUITION

18.
ASCENDED MASTER MATAJI (Earth Star)
CRIMSON CUPRITE (Divine Feminine)
INITIATION OF FEMININE CONSCIOUSNESS

THE CRYSTALS:

Clear Calcite

Blue Star Sapphire

Rhodochrosite

Green Chrysoprase

Rosophia

Aqua Aura Quartz

Rhodonite

Moss Agate

Amethyst

Zincite

Pearl

Danburite

Celestite

Peridot

Citrine

Mystic Merlinite

Diamond

Crimson Cuprite